The Rhetoric of Conversion in English Puritan Writing from Perkins to Milton

NEW DIRECTIONS IN RELIGION AND LITERATURE

This series aims to showcase new work at the forefront of religion and literature through short studies written by leading and rising scholars in the field. Books will pursue a variety of theoretical approaches as they engage with writing from different religious and literary traditions. Collectively, the series will offer a timely critical intervention to the interdisciplinary crossover between religion and literature, speaking to wider contemporary interests and mapping out new directions for the field in the early twenty-first century.

Series editors: Emma Mason and Mark Knight

ALSO AVAILABLE IN THE SERIES:

The New Atheist Novel, Arthur Bradley and Andrew Tate

Blake. Wordsworth. Religion, Jonathan Roberts

Do the Gods Wear Capes?, Ben Saunders

England's Secular Scripture, Jo Carruthers

Victorian Parables, Susan E. Colón

The Late Walter Benjamin, John Schad

Dante and the Sense of Transgression, William Franke

The Glyph and the Gramophone, Luke Ferretter

John Cage and Buddhist Ecopoetics, Peter Jaeger

Rewriting the Old Testament in Anglo-Saxon Verse, Samantha Zacher

Forgiveness in Victorian Literature, Richard Hughes Gibson

The Gospel According to the Novelist, Magdalena Mączyńska

Jewish Feeling, Richa Dwor

Beyond the Willing Suspension of Disbelief, Michael Tomko

The Gospel According to David Foster Wallace, Adam S. Miller

Pentecostal Modernism, Stephen Shapiro and Philip Barnard

The Bible in the American Short Story, Lesleigh Cushing Stahlberg and Peter S. Hawkins

Faith in Poetry, Michael D. Hurley

Jeanette Winterson and Religion, Emily McAvan

Religion and American Literature since the 1950s, Mark Eaton

Esoteric Islam in Modern French Thought, Ziad Elmarsafy

Djuna Barnes and Theology, Zhao Ng

FORTHCOMING:

Marilynne Robinson's Wordly Gospel, Ryan S. Kemp and Jordan M. Rodgers

Weird Faith in 19th Century Literature, Mark Knight and Emma Mason

The Rhetoric of Conversion in English Puritan Writing from Perkins to Milton

David Parry

BLOOMSBURY ACADEMIC
LONDON • NEW YORK • OXFORD • NEW DELHI • SYDNEY

BLOOMSBURY ACADEMIC
Bloomsbury Publishing Plc
50 Bedford Square, London, WC1B 3DP, UK
1385 Broadway, New York, NY 10018, USA
29 Earlsfort Terrace, Dublin 2, Ireland

BLOOMSBURY, BLOOMSBURY ACADEMIC and the Diana logo
are trademarks of Bloomsbury Publishing Plc

First published in Great Britain 2022
This paperback edition published 2023

Copyright © David Parry, 2022

David Parry has asserted his right under the Copyright, Designs and Patents Act, 1988,
to be identified as Author of this work.

For legal purposes the Acknowledgements on pp. vi–vii constitute
an extension of this copyright page.

Cover design: Eleanor Rose
Cover image © Frontispiece to the first edition of John Bunyan's *The Holy War*, 1682.
Photo © Archivist / Alamy Stock Photo

All rights reserved. No part of this publication may be reproduced or
transmitted in any form or by any means, electronic or mechanical, including
photocopying, recording, or any information storage or retrieval system,
without prior permission in writing from the publishers.

Bloomsbury Publishing Plc does not have any control over, or responsibility for,
any third-party websites referred to or in this book. All internet addresses given
in this book were correct at the time of going to press. The author and publisher
regret any inconvenience caused if addresses have changed or sites have ceased
to exist, but can accept no responsibility for any such changes.

A catalogue record for this book is available from the British Library.

A catalog record for this book is available from the Library of Congress.

ISBN:	HB:	978-1-3501-6514-4
	PB:	978-1-3502-8062-5
	ePDF:	978-1-3501-6515-1
	eBook:	978-1-3501-6516-8

Series: New Directions in Religion and Literature

Typeset by Integra Software Services Pvt. Ltd.

To find out more about our authors and books visit www.bloomsbury.com
and sign up for our newsletters.

Contents

Acknowledgements	vi
Note on references and abbreviations	viii
Introduction: The rhetoric of conversion and the conversion of rhetoric	1
1 A passionate *logos*: The persuasive practical divinity of William Perkins and Richard Sibbes	23
2 Divine excess: The radical *ethos* of prophetic performance	73
3 Light and weight: Richard Baxter's exhortations and meditations	117
4 Serious play: John Bunyan's imaginative persuasion	161
5 To 'make persuasion do the work of fear': The resistible rhetoric of redemption in John Milton	209
Bibliography	249
Index	266

Acknowledgements

This book has had a long gestation. In its original form as a PhD thesis it benefitted from the oversight and guidance of my supervisors Beth Lynch and Jason Scott-Warren, and the insight and critique of my examiners Brian Cummings and Katrin Ettenhuber. In its latter stages it has benefitted from the feedback of expert colleagues, including Bob Owens, Neil Keeble, Niall Allsopp and Nicholas McDowell (whose new Milton biography was published the week I submitted this book to the publisher, so makes less of an appearance than it deserves).

I wish to thank the Levy-Plumb Fund for the Humanities at Christ's College, Cambridge, and the Arts and Humanities Research Council for funding the research giving rise to this book. I would also like to thank my colleagues and students in the Department of English and Film at the University of Exeter for providing a lively and collegial academic home.

I would like to thank Emma Mason and Mark Knight, series editors for New Directions in Religion and Literature, for their enthusiasm for and belief in this project from the time I contacted them, and all the team at Bloomsbury Academic, especially Ben Doyle, Lucy Brown, Laura Cope and Rachel Walker, for shepherding the book to completion. I would also like to thank Suriya Rajasekar and the team at Integra for their hard work in proofreading, copyediting and typesetting the manuscript for production, and Eleanor Rose for her striking cover design (adapted from the frontispiece to John Bunyan's *The Holy War*).

Some material in this book has been published in an earlier form in the following publications, and is reproduced by kind permission of the publishers and editors named below:

"'A Divine Kind of Rhetoric": Rhetorical Strategy and Spirit-Wrought Sincerity in English Puritan Writing', *Christianity and Literature*, 67.1 (December 2017), pp. 113–38.

'As an Angel of Light: Satanic Rhetoric in Early Modern Literature and Theology', in Gregor Thuswalder and Daniel Russ (eds.), *The Hermeneutics of Hell: Devilish Visions and Visions of the Devil* (Palgrave Macmillan, 2017), pp. 47–71.

Acknowledgements vii

The two illustrations in Chapter 3 are reproduced by kind permission of the British Library and of the Burke Library of Union Theological Seminary. Figure 1 from Baxter's *A Call to the Unconverted* is produced by ProQuest as part of Early English Books Online and published with permission of ProQuest.

I would like to thank our family and friends for their interest and enjoyment of the project and for their mandatory sense of humour.

Finally, I would like to thank Jo, my true love, chief collaborator, biggest fan and faithful supporter at all times, without whom this book would not have found a publisher and would not have been finished, who has helped me find confidence and flourish on the pathway, who perseveres, who loves to the end, who holds onto the light that overcomes the darkness, who endures always and in whom I delight.

Note on references and abbreviations

Unless otherwise noted, biblical quotations are taken from the Authorised/King James Version in the generally available standardized text of 1769.

Classical works are cited from the Loeb Classical Library editions, with full citation details available in the bibliography. However, they are cited in my endnotes using the standardized scholarly section numbering rather than by page number to facilitate cross-reference across editions.

Some frequently cited works are referenced using the following abbreviations:

Bunyan, *MW* = John Bunyan, *The Miscellaneous Works of John Bunyan*, 13 vols., gen. ed. Roger Sharrock (Oxford: Clarendon, 1976–94).

Milton, *PL* = John Milton, *Paradise Lost*, ed. Helen Darbishire (Oxford: Oxford University Press, 1963).

Milton, *PR* = John Milton, *Paradise Regain'd*, in *The Complete Works of John Milton*, Vol. 2: *The 1671 Poems: Paradise Regain'd and Samson Agonistes*, ed. Laura Lunger Knoppers (Oxford: Oxford University Press, 2008).

Milton, *CPW* = *Complete Prose Works of John Milton*, gen. ed. Don M. Wolfe, 8 vols. (New Haven: Yale University Press, 1953–82).

Milton, *CWJM* = *The Complete Works of John Milton*, 11 vols. projected, gen. eds. Thomas N. Corns and Gordon Campbell (Oxford: Oxford University Press, 2008–).

ODNB = *Oxford Dictionary of National Biography*, ed. H. C. G. Matthew, Brian Harrison, Lawrence Goldman and David Cannadine (Oxford: Oxford University Press, 2004–present). Online edition accessed at <http://www.oxforddnb.com/>.

OED = *Oxford English Dictionary*, online edition (= 2nd edition, ed. John A. Simpson and Edmund S. C. Weiner (Oxford: Clarendon Press, 1989) plus 3rd edition in progress (2000–present), ed. John A. Simpson and Edmund S. C. Weiner). Online edition accessed at <http://oed.com/>.

Introduction: The rhetoric of conversion and the conversion of rhetoric

Religious conversion can be seen as, among other things, the acquisition of a new language. This conceptualization of conversion is vividly conveyed in cultural anthropologist Susan Harding's ethnographic study of American evangelical Christians. Harding records how, driving home from interviewing a Baptist pastor, she is involved in a near collision:

> Halfway across town, I stopped at a stop sign, then started into the intersection, and was very nearly smashed by a car that seemed to come upon me from nowhere very fast. I slammed on the brakes, sat stunned for a split second, and asked myself 'What is God trying to tell me?'[1]

Harding is startled to find this thought entering her mind:

> It was my voice but not my language. I had been inhabited by the fundamental Baptist tongue I was investigating. As the Reverend Campbell might have put it, the Holy Spirit was dealing with me, speaking to my heart, bringing me under conviction. He was showing me that life is a passing thing, that death could take me in an instant, no matter how much control I fancied I had over my life, and that I should put my life in the Lord's hands before it was too late.[2]

Harding's account then switches from anecdote to analysis, explaining that, by opening herself to listen to the Reverend Campbell, she had unwittingly begun to be converted:

> The process starts when an unsaved listener begins to appropriate in his or her inner speech the saved speaker's language and its attendant view of the world. The speaker's language, now in the listener's voice, converts the listener's mind into a contested terrain, a divided self. At the moment of salvation, which may come quickly and easily, or much later after great inward turmoil, the listener becomes a speaker. The Christian tongue locks into some kind of central, controlling, dominant place; it has gone beyond the point of inhabiting the listener's mind to occupy the listener's identity.[3]

Harding suggests that those undergoing conversion enter into a space halfway between unbelief and belief, a liminal space in which they learn the language of faith that gradually reinscribes their thought worlds. Harding attaches to this liminal state the label 'conviction', borrowing this term from the theological discourse of her Baptist subjects to serve as an analytical tool.

The seventeenth-century Dissenting preacher John Bunyan, best known for his authorship of the allegorical journey narrative *The Pilgrim's Progress*, likewise speaks of 'conviction' as a transitional, liminal state in the process of conversion. In *The Strait Gate* (1676), he exhorts his hearers: 'Be thankful therefore for convictions, conversion begins at conviction, though all conviction doth not end in conversion.'[4] 'Conviction' has a double sense in the early modern period as in our own time – it can refer both to the beliefs of which one is persuaded or convinced (as in the phrase 'a man/woman of conviction') and to a legal sentence of guilt (as in being convicted of a crime).[5] In a theological context such as Bunyan's, 'conviction of sin' also refers to a divinely bestowed feeling of guilt for one's sin, such as is figured in *The Pilgrim's Progress* by the burden on Christian's back when he sets off on his travels. Conviction in this sense is intended to lead to repentance but does not always do so. Conviction is thus a necessary, but not sufficient, stage for full conversion to take place.

Religious conversion and its representation in writing have undergone a resurgence of interest in historical and literary studies of the early modern period – one manifestation of the broader 'religious turn' across the humanities since the late 1990s.[6] This book will add to this body of scholarship with a particular focus on an early modern religious movement that stresses the need for inward conversion, that of English Puritanism, and with a distinctive emphasis, not so much on the recounting of conversion experiences (though conversion narratives will be touched on in passing) as on the rhetoric of conversion that seeks to bring about conversion in its readers. However, my study will not focus exclusively on the initial stages of conversion, moving beyond the initial acquisition of what Puritans would call saving faith to consider other persuasive goals of Puritan writers and preachers as they sought to encourage their readers and hearers to persevere and to grow in godly faith.

Practical divinity as a persuasive project

But what exactly is Puritanism? This is a slippery question – the editors of *The Cambridge Companion to Puritanism* note that 'Defining Puritanism has been a favourite parlour game for early modern historians'.[7] The particular individuals focused on in this study were all, to varying degrees, resistant to confessional labels that identified them as belonging to a particular religious group. One of the most vehement rejections of such labels is found in the mouth of John Bunyan:

> And since you would know by what Name I would be distinguished from others; I tell you, I would be, and hope I am, *a Christian*; and chuse, if God shall count me worthy, *to be called a Christian, a Believer* or other such Name which is approved by the Holy Ghost. And as for those Factious Titles of *Anabaptists, Independents, Presbyterians*, or the like, I conclude, that they came neither from *Jerusalem*, nor *Antioch*, but rather from *Hell* and *Babylon*; for they naturally tend to divisions, *you may know them by their Fruits*.[8]

Surveying the historiographical debates in the scholarly literature around classifying early modern religion confirms Bunyan's observation that such labels 'naturally tend to divisions'. Bunyan wanted to escape the fray with a claim to be a simple Bible Christian, as did Richard Baxter with his insistence that he was 'a CHRISTIAN, a MEER CHRISTIAN, of no other Religion'.[9]

My own working definition of Puritanism is that the Puritans were those English Protestants who thought that the English church and nation were not sufficiently reformed, as measured by an understanding of scriptural teaching and practice that has affinities with the continental Reformed tradition (exemplified, for instance, by Calvin's Geneva). The Puritan desire for further reformation is what gives rise to the Elizabethan pamphleteer Percival Wiburn's comment, popularized in modern scholarship by Patrick Collinson, that 'The hotter sort of Protestants are called Puritans'.[10] This tendency typically entailed a number of characteristics, including an emphasis on the necessity of preaching, strident opposition to the Church of Rome, and a suspicion or rejection of certain ceremonial practices and clerical vesture as extrascriptural and perhaps anti-scriptural. Yet the further reformation the Puritans desired was not only and not primarily an outward reform of ecclesiastical structures, but more crucially a rousing of the spiritual vitality of the nation, bringing individuals to a true saving faith in Christ in accordance with the Gospel of salvation by grace alone through faith alone as understood by the Protestant Reformers.

Thus Puritanism was not only a movement of protest against perceived external corruption in church and nation, but also had a positive agenda focused on the internal spiritual condition of individuals. The term 'the godly' (which has been adopted by historians as a semi-technical label with no implied value judgement) is perhaps better than 'Puritan' as a marker of the self-identity of this group.[11] Though it is hard to demonstrate empirically, I am inclined to agree with Peter Lake's observation that 'the core of the moderate puritan position lay neither in the puritan critique of the liturgy and polity of the church nor in a formal doctrinal consensus' but 'in the capacity, which the godly claimed, of being able to recognize one another in the midst of a corrupt and unregenerate world'.[12] This book takes up Lake's suggestion that the continuous thread that characterizes Puritanism as a distinct movement from the Elizabethan period to the mid-seventeenth-century civil wars and beyond is neither adherence to Calvinist predestinarian doctrine nor agitation for ecclesiastical reform, but rather a shared spirituality and pastoral practice.

More precisely, this book will focus on that strand of English Puritan pastoral practice labelled 'practical divinity', a pastoral methodology which seeks to apply Reformed theology to the experience of ordinary people in order to instruct them in how to be saved, how to know that they are saved and how to live a godly life. English practical divinity has roots especially in the ministry of Richard Greenham, who, from his base as parish minister of Dry Drayton, a small village near Cambridge, established a 'household seminary', making up for the lack of practical vocational training for clergy at that time by having prospective ministers live with him after their university studies to learn what a Reformed pastoral ministry should look like. Since many of these students themselves became prominent ministers, Greenham's methods for the 'physic of the soul' acquired a widespread influence.[13]

The practical divinity of Greenham and those who followed in his train is inherently rhetorical in that it seeks to persuade its readers towards conversion, assurance of salvation and godly living. In attempting to remedy what they perceived as a spiritual darkness over the populace, the hotter sort of Protestants preached for conversion, but the call to conversion was not only an attempt to purge the traces of 'popery' from England but applied even once the majority of the population had become Protestant in self-identification.[14] As Eamon Duffy notes, to the godly, conversion did not connote an external change of affiliation from one religious body to another, but an inward turning from sin to God: 'Conversion, therefore, meant not merely bringing the heathen to knowledge of the gospel, but bringing the tepid to the boil by awakening preaching, creating a godly people out of a nation of conformists.'[15]

Duffy's probing of the meaning of 'conversion' for the godly helpfully reminds us that the word 'conversion' has various meanings even within a broadly religious sphere. Among the more explicitly religious senses of 'conversion' given by the *Oxford English Dictionary* are the following:

8. a. The bringing of any one over to a specified religious faith, profession, or party, esp. to one regarded as true, from what is regarded as falsehood or error. (Without qualification, usually = conversion to Christianity.)
[...]
9. *Theology.* The turning of sinners to God; a spiritual change from sinfulness, ungodliness, or worldliness to love of God and pursuit of holiness.[16]

We should note the difference between these two senses. The first denotes an external change of religious affiliation, while the second refers to an inward change: in a Christian context, the turning from sin to a state of grace. In her study of conversion in early modern poetry, Molly Murray distinguishes these two senses of conversion as 'a change of church' and 'a change of soul'.[17] In the eyes of parties with a vested interest, these two kinds of conversion may coincide, but for clarity of discussion they need to be distinguished.

One of the principal casualties of confusing these two senses of conversion is a recognition that the discourse of conversion can operate within the boundaries of a given religious affiliation. This was often the case with Puritanism, a movement that arose within the established Church of England, and whose ministers were often addressing baptized parishioners of a Protestant established church in their call for inner conversion. Puritan practical divinity sought to persuade its audience to a 'change of soul', whether or not an accompanying 'change of church' was also sought.

The rhetoric of conversion explored in this study, like that experienced by Susan Harding, seeks to use language to reinscribe and reorient the mind, heart and will of its audience, bringing the 'divided self' of the hearer or reader to occupy a new, regenerate identity. In calling the strategies used by these writers rhetorical, I in no way intend to suggest either that their attempts to bring people to conversion are insincere, or that the process of conversion involves solely human agency. The writers to be considered in this study would say that 'God uses means', that is, that acts of human persuasion elicit true and saving faith if and only if divine agency is also involved. Whether or not the readers of this book share that belief, I hope to persuade them that these two levels of agency are at least conceptually compatible.

Converting reason and imagination

Inward conversion, for the Puritans, involves changes in the exercise of all the inner faculties of the soul, notably the reason, the affections and the will. As well as mapping onto the faculty psychology that the early modern period inherited from classical and medieval thought, there are also some instructive parallels with ways of understanding people's beliefs and worldviews found in modern scholarship in the social sciences and intellectual history. Two concepts in particular suggest themselves as being fruitful.

Peter Berger writes of 'plausibility structures' – within a given community or society, Berger argues, certain ideas or patterns of thought feel credible and others do not.[18] The felt plausibility of holding to certain ideas is not solely a product of watertight logical deduction on the part of the individual. Rather, there is a sociology of knowledge, in which one's ideas and beliefs are, to a large extent, formed by the groups to which one belongs.

Nevertheless, for Berger, the views to which an individual adheres are not always those that are most dominant in the larger society that surrounds him or her. The larger society contains within it groups that can be called 'cognitive minorities', whose view of reality in certain respects differs from that of the host society.[19] Being in a cognitive minority exposes individuals to cognitive dissonance, as the group's members are exposed to contrary views on a regular basis and so the plausibility of their beliefs is challenged, but yet minority groups can define themselves over against the wider culture through the use of boundary markers that assert their distinctive identity. It can be argued that Puritans formed a cognitive minority within the wider society of early modern England, though this was a minority with porous boundaries, whose membership cannot be exactly determined and whose distinctness from the wider officially Protestant culture waxed and waned.

Scholarship in several fields has increasingly recognized that people's worldviews through which they navigate their beliefs are not simply a collection of rational or cognitive convictions. Rather, worldviews are lived and expressed through an embodied experience of being in the world shaped by emotion and by imagination rather than by bare reason alone. For instance, Charles Taylor speaks of 'the social imaginary' and 'the cosmic imaginary' to underline the imaginative dimension of people's apprehension of the world.[20] While the social imaginary pertains more to how people perceive that human society should be ordered, the cosmic imaginary (while shaped by social factors) refers to how people perceive the world as a whole and the nature of ultimate reality. For Taylor, in so far as religious beliefs inform the perceptions, emotions and embodied lives of individuals, they form an integral part of those individuals' cosmic imaginary. It is in reshaping people's cosmic imaginaries that their more cognitive plausibility structures are also changed as they undergo the 'paradigm shift' (Thomas Kuhn) of conversion.[21]

Taylor's understanding of cosmic imaginaries can be fruitfully connected to William Dyrness's discussion of the role of the imagination in early modern Protestantism. Dyrness demonstrates that, despite iconoclastic suspicions of images and imagination in many strands of the Protestant Reformation, the Reformers nevertheless fostered a 'mental and narrative structuring of the world and life' that appealed to the imagination and included an 'imaginative picturing and reflection of God' within the minds of believers. Dyrness defines imagination as 'the way people give shape to their world, in particular through the images and practices that express this shape'.[22]

This study will trace how Puritan writers and preachers appeal to both reason and imagination in order to reinscribe their audience's plausibility structures and to reshape their cosmic imaginaries to such an extent as to bring about an inner shift of allegiance and the adoption of a different way of perceiving and interpreting reality.

The importance of appealing to the imagination in the work of godly persuasion will come to the fore when considering allegory as a mode of imaginative persuasion. As with imagination in general, allegory is a concept that attracts suspicion among Protestant Reformers and Puritans but undergoes a partial rehabilitation that enables it to be used in the service of godly ends.

Allegory has a complex relationship with rhetoric in this period. The two terms are curiously conflated at times, including by the German Reformer Martin Luther and by one of the figures considered in this book, the Elizabethan Cambridge minister William Perkins. Luther expresses caution over allegorical readings of Scripture found in some early Christian and medieval interpreters, such as taking Abraham's three visitors to represent the Trinity, characterizing them as rhetorical and useful for expounding scriptural truth in a compelling way but potentially misleading in deriving the intended meaning of a scriptural passage. Luther's *Lectures on Genesis* comment that 'it is one thing to teach and another thing to exhort. Rhetoric, which is useful for exhorting, often plays games and often hands you a piece of wood which you suppose is a sword'.[23]

In the context of Renaissance humanist rhetorical education derived from the classical rhetorical tradition, 'allegory' is used as an English language translation of the term *allegoria* used by Quintilian of a rhetorical figure roughly equivalent to what we might call an extended metaphor.[24] Full-length allegorical narratives such as Bunyan's can be seen as extended metaphors on the level of a whole text. However, from a literary historical perspective it must be admitted that allegory as a genre has a long tradition in English literature going back through the Middle Ages with little direct connection to the classical rhetorical tradition, whose fruits are seen, for instance, in Edmund Spenser's *The Faerie Queene*.[25]

Nevertheless, besides overlap in terminology, allegory and rhetoric have an affinity in their aims. I will argue that narrative allegory as used by writers such as John Bunyan functions as an imaginative mode of rhetoric that bypasses the cognitive defences of readers in order to reinscribe their imaginations from within. This imaginative rhetoric is designed to bring readers within the cosmic imaginaries and plausibility structures of the godly community.

Once entered into, the plausibility structures and cosmic imaginaries of godly faith need to be maintained. For this reason, the persuasive goals of godly rhetoric go beyond the initial conversion of the unregenerate to the subsequent concerns of finding an assured faith in which the believer feels secure, resisting temptations to sin or despair, and dealing with cognitive dissonance in which one's experience of the world or of oneself does not always seem to match what godly faith would predict.

Mark Allen Steiner argues that all rhetoric, whether or not explicitly religious, is a form of 'evangelism' in the sense of attempting to persuade its hearers to adopt a different view of the world: 'Corresponding to my version of rhetoric as evangelism in essence, I offer a definition of rhetoric as *discourse that imposes an invitation/temptation, upon a particular audience, to identify with a partisan perspective*.'[26] Steiner distinguishes agitative rhetoric, which calls on its hearers to change their orientation, and integrative rhetoric, which aims to strengthen an existing perspective.[27] The persuasive project of Puritan practical divinity entails both agitative and integrative rhetoric, seeking both to bring its audience to an inward faith and to strengthen them in it.

Predestination and persuasion

My contention that the work of Puritan divines is a rhetorical project that seeks to persuade its readers and hearers may raise some eyebrows. On the face of it, the adherence of Puritans to the doctrine of predestination might seem to make redundant the persuasive project of practical divinity. On the one hand, one might suppose that it is futile to try to elicit a response of faith or godly living from one's hearers or readers if their response is divinely predetermined rather than freely chosen. On the other hand, it may appear that the readers' or

Introduction 9

hearers' response is irrelevant anyway if their eternal destiny is determined by an apparently arbitrary divine decree. In other words, does predestination make preaching pointless?

While this is a fair question, the way in which it is often asked betrays a common caricature of Calvinism as a deterministic fatalism that denies any role whatsoever for human agency. Both secular and religious critics of Calvinism, as well as many literary scholars and historians, tend to seize upon any appeal to human agency as indicative of a lack of full confidence in or a pragmatic setting aside of predestinarian belief. For instance, in a much quoted aside in his study of sixteenth-century Cambridge, H. C. Porter comments that 'however Calvinist in the study, the preacher must be Arminian in the pulpit',[28] while Kevin Sharpe states that 'the logic of predestination did not square easily with the vocation of a preaching ministry'.[29]

The response given by Reformed Protestants to this accusation of inconsistency from the sixteenth century to the present day is that God uses temporal means to accomplish his eternal purposes. A catechism included with some editions of the Geneva Bible gives this illustration:

> For as waxe is not melted without heate, nor clay hardened but by meanes thereof: so God vseth meanes both to draw those vnto himselfe, whom he hath appointed vnto saluation, and also to bewray the wickednes of them whom he iustly condemneth.[30]

Thus, God does not save his elect irrespective of whether they possess true faith in Christ, but he saves those whom he has chosen by creating in them that faith through which they lay hold of God's saving grace in Christ. This entails the alteration of their will and affections in conversion, which, in turn, leads to changed patterns of behaviour. Hence, Greenham writes, 'It is not as men say, if I am elected I cannot perish, I may liue as I list: but if thou art elected, thou art also elected to the meanes of faith, and the fruites of it, else thou art not elected.'[31]

Furthermore, according to the Reformers and their Puritan heirs, the means (or, at least, the ordinary means) by which God creates this saving faith in those he has elected is the preaching of the word. As Leif Dixon points out, 'puritans were also the chief evangelists of predestinarian Protestantism, and so sought to increase the temporal number of the regenerate.'[32] 'Temporal' here is the operative word – while the eternal number of the elect is divinely decreed and can neither be increased nor diminished, the number of the regenerate increases within earthly historical time as these chosen individuals are persuaded to saving faith and thus manifest their election to salvation from all eternity.

10   *The Rhetoric of Conversion in English Puritan Writing*

A common perception is that Calvinist predestinarianism means that each individual is born either saved or damned and that this is a static state that cannot be altered in any way – all that is left is to discover the category into which one falls. For instance, Karen Bruhn says of belief in double predestination (the doctrine that God has ordained the reprobate to damnation as well as the elect to salvation) that it is apparent that 'such a system must deny categorically the possibility of temporal change in one's spiritual estate' and suggests that, in their self-scrutiny for signs of election, 'The godly injected a note of temporality into a structure that allowed no temporal element'.[33]

However, early modern Reformed Protestantism, on the whole, did not see predestination as a denial of temporality, just as it did not see divine election as a denial of human agency.[34] Rather, election takes place in a prior eternity, but its effects are outworked in time. Conversion is the visible manifestation in time of God's invisible decree in eternity. Thus Calvin, citing Romans 8:30, comments that 'Although in choosing his own the Lord already has adopted them as his children, we see that they do not come into possession of so great a good except when they are called'.[35]

Since election from eternity is manifested through regeneration in time, the elect and the regenerate are thus sets that will ultimately coincide exactly, but at any given point in this present human history they do not entirely coincide, since at a given moment in time not all the elect are yet regenerate. The salvation of the elect is accomplished through the means of the preaching of the word – hence, although the elect cannot fail to be saved, human preaching is the indispensable means by which they are persuaded to saving faith. Thus the persuasive role of the preacher remains vital.

The persuasive project of preaching extends in Puritan thinking to the persuasive mission of edifying writing, although the extent to which preaching was identified with writing varies. In the view of at least some Puritan divines (notably Richard Baxter), the distinction between preaching and writing is elided to the extent that a written text can bring about conversion as effectively as an orally delivered sermon. Baxter writes that 'The Writings of Divines are nothing else but a preaching the Gospel to the eye, as the *voice* preacheth it to the ear'. Although Baxter concedes that 'Vocal preaching hath the preheminence in moving the affections', he notes that 'Books have the advantage in many other respects', particularly their availability when a preacher is physically absent, whether through persecution, lack of local preaching clergy, or a desire to be edified in between sermon times.[36]

Arnold Hunt draws out a contrast between Baxter's comments here and the similar thoughts of Thomas Gataker in the preface to his sermon treatise

Davids Remembrancer (1623), where Gataker states: '*Albeit* Speech *have no small advantage of* Writing; *in that* it hath a greater vivacitie *accompanying it*, [...] *Yet herein hath* writing *the ods of* Speech; *in that by it wee may speake as well to the* absent *as to the* present'.[37] Hunt notes that 'For Gataker, the reading of godly sermons might supplement live preaching but could never wholly replace it. For Baxter, on the other hand, the two were essentially one and the same'.[38]

Puritan writers recognized that there was a certain loss of immediacy and presence in the medium of print, but saw printed sermons as having compensatory advantages. For instance, William Gurnall writes that 'There is as much difference between a Sermon in the Pulpit, and printed in a book, as between milk in the warme breast, and in a sucking bottle, yet what it loseth in the lively taste, is recompenced by the convenience of it'.[39] Baxter says likewise of 'Vocal preaching' that 'This way the Milk cometh warmest from the breast'.[40] Both Baxter and Gurnall assess the relative advantages of speech and writing in terms that echo the association of speech with personal presence in Western philosophy from Plato to Derrida.

The passage from Gurnall is referenced by the editors of one of Richard Sibbes's posthumously published works, who go on to say, alluding to the baskets of bread left over after Christ's feeding of the five thousand, that '*good books are the baskets that preserve excellent lessons that they be not lost.*'[41] Recent historical work on sermons has often focused on recovering the rhetorical occasion of a sermon's first delivery, but the metaphor of baskets for '*good books*' illustrates how, in Puritan print culture, there was more concern to transmit edifying content than to preserve the contingent contexts of the rhetorical occasion that generated that content. From our own distance of centuries, it is necessarily bottled milk that we are drinking. This study, then, focuses not solely on preaching itself but on written practical divinity that seeks to persuade its readers to conversion, assurance and godly living, while acknowledging the roots of many such texts in orally delivered sermons.[42]

Aristotle reconfigured: *Logos, ethos* and *pathos*

The practice of persuasion in early modern England is profoundly shaped by the classical rhetorical tradition deriving from writers such as Aristotle, Cicero and Quintilian and transmitted through the Renaissance humanist education found in grammar schools and universities as well as in vernacular English-language rhetoric textbooks by writers such as Henry Peacham, George Puttenham and

Angel Day.[43] All of the Puritan writers considered in this book, including those such as John Bunyan who adopt the persona of an unlearned artisan, had at least some degree of schooling or formal tutoring that would have exposed them to this rhetorical tradition. In addition, the origin of Puritanism as a movement within the established Church means that later Puritan ministers outside the Church of England are shaped by the preaching and writing of an earlier generation of university-educated clergy. However, this study will argue that the pastoral and theological priorities of Puritan preachers and writers lead them to a radical reworking of classical rhetorical categories.

I agree with Mary Morrissey that the categories of classical rhetoric were not central to the English Reformed model of preaching, but that rather the exposition and application of Scripture as empowered and enlivened by the Spirit was central. However, while Morrissey argues against an over-reading of early modern preaching in terms of classical rhetoric (to which she attributes the simplistic dichotomy between Puritan plain preaching and ornate 'metaphysical' preaching in earlier scholarship), she concedes that English Reformed preachers use the language arts of grammar, logic and rhetoric in a subordinate role.[44] Summarizing Richard Bernard's *The Faithful Shepherd* (1607), Morrissey writes, 'The preacher uses the arts of logic, rhetoric and grammar as best suits his pastoral purpose, just as the theologian uses the liberal arts as handmaids to the "Queen of Sciences" '.[45]

One key conceptual framework of classical rhetoric reconfigured for the pastoral purposes of Puritan persuasion is that of the three modes of persuasion distinguished by Aristotle: *logos* (appeal to reason and rational argument), *pathos* (appeal to emotion or, in early modern parlance, the 'affections' or 'passions') and *ethos* (appeal to the authoritative status of the speaker as perceived by the audience).[46] The godly persuasion of the Puritans entails the strategies of *logos*, *ethos* and *pathos*, but all three modes of persuasion are inflected by theological commitments that generate distinctive versions of *logos*, *ethos* and *pathos*.

R. T. Kendall may be able to help here. While Kendall's 1979 monograph *Calvin and English Calvinism to 1649* continues to be cited, though contested, in studies of early modern religion, the majority of Kendall's over fifty books are written not for the academy but for a popular-level Christian readership. In one of these books, Kendall invokes Aristotle's threefold modes of persuasion for the purpose of encouraging effective preaching, but he adds a twist:

> In my view, experimental preaching will include all three of the elements that Aristotle refers to in his work *Rhetoric*. *Ethos, pathos, logos*. *Ethos* refers to the credibility of the speaker. *Pathos*, the appeal to the senses, so long as this is done with integrity. *Logos*, the reason or logic of the message.[47]

Kendall encourages preachers to balance these three components, but then invokes the agency of the Spirit as necessary for making this preaching fully efficacious:

> But when the Holy Spirit is released to be himself we will not only have the needed balance but the satisfaction that those we address will hear a word from beyond, which defies a natural explanation.[48]

Whether or not we follow Kendall's somewhat controversial scholarly analysis of the doctrinal development of English Calvinism, his own pastoral understanding as a minister of the relationship between rhetorical efficacy and the work of the Spirit resonates with the creative tension characterizing the Puritan practice of persuasion. It is noteworthy that Kendall's emphasis is not so much on what the preacher says but on what the audience hears, 'the satisfaction that those we address will hear a word from beyond'. As in all communication, the effectiveness of preaching in accomplishing its goals depends on what is heard and understood by the receiver, and the hearing and understanding that is needed is, for Kendall, the work of the Spirit. The theological commitments of Puritan ministers, as with Kendall's theological commitments, entail the belief that persuasion to conversion is only efficacious when empowered by the Holy Spirit, thus implying that the human agency of the preacher can accomplish nothing of its own accord, and that rhetorical skill in itself does not suffice for the saving of souls.

Nevertheless, *logos, ethos* and *pathos* remain in play for the Puritans, as they are for Kendall. They are simply reconfigured. In its Aristotelian sense of the persuasive appeal to reason, the *logos* of Reformed Protestant preaching often entails reasoning from scriptural propositions (though reasoning from general human experience or from propositions found in other texts is not entirely absent). Thus the *logos* of Puritan ministers often presumes the authority of the scriptural text as providing a body of data on which we can rely.

Rhetorical *pathos*, the appeal to emotion, or the 'affections', is also retained but reformed and reshaped in godly persuasion. Puritan writers and preachers use verbal techniques, argumentative techniques and visual imagery that the theorists of rhetoric recognize as effective in evoking emotion. However, echoing an emphasis found in Augustine's writings, they attribute the reordering of the affections of the heart to the inward working of the Spirit. Thus the minister can appeal to his hearers' affections, and is expected to do so, but the *pathos* of true conversion is ultimately beyond the control of the human speaker.

As for *ethos*, Puritan ministers of the established Church could rely to a degree on their socially recognized office, which, at least in theory, would confer

14 *The Rhetoric of Conversion in English Puritan Writing*

a degree of respect and provide them with a hearing from their parishioners. In practice, however, ordination did not guarantee clergy immunity from ridicule or indifference on the part of their hearers. Moreover, the godly saw true spiritual authority in preaching as being given not only by outward ordination but also by the inward unction of the Spirit. This emphasis on a Spirit-given *ethos* superior to that conferred by ecclesiastical authorities was to become more crucial in the case of separatist and Dissenting preachers outside the national Church, who claimed a divine calling and empowering that gave their words authority despite an official lack of recognition.

The following two chapters of this book will explore the persuasive practice of individuals and groups whose rhetorical emphasis is on each of these modes of persuasion in turn. Chapter 1 focuses in part on the works of the prolific Elizabethan Cambridge minister William Perkins (1558–1602), a key popularizer of Puritan practical divinity and a key theorist of Puritan preaching in his manual for preachers *The Arte of Prophecying*. Though making use of *pathos* and *ethos*, Perkins's primary mode of persuasion is Aristotle's *logos*, appeal to reason, since he believes that faith is a matter of persuasion and 'there is no perswasion but in the minde'.[49] Perkins thus focuses on the transmission of propositional truth in order to persuade the mind towards faith. Nevertheless, Perkins is not exclusively focused on *logos*, as he believes that the will and affections must also be engaged to bring about full conversion. Perkins expresses significant misgivings about appeal to the imagination and attacks mental as well as physical images as tending towards idolatry and lasciviousness. However, there are moments in which Perkins makes vivid appeals to the imagination despite his strictures elsewhere, and occasionally Perkins takes on literary genres such as didactic dialogues that anticipate more creative literary modes of teaching.

The rehabilitation of the imagination is more apparent in the work of Richard Sibbes (*c.* 1577–1635), a minister in Cambridge and London of the generation following Perkins also discussed in Chapter 1. Although their theological positions were substantially very similar, Sibbes's persuasive practice differs from that of Perkins in its pastoral, psychological and rhetorical priorities. Whereas Perkins's primary mode of persuasion is *logos*, Sibbes's primary mode of persuasion is *pathos*, an appeal to the affections. In contrast to the priority Perkins gives to rational persuasion, Sibbes's understanding of the psychology of conversion sees the affections as the gateway to the will. Yet Sibbes does not neglect *logos* – Sibbes's work *The Soules Conflict* speaks specifically both of 'sanctified reason'[50] and of 'a sanctified *fancie*'.[51] It is the latter that is more distinctive of Sibbes. Although sharing the common Reformed anxiety over the

Introduction 15

tendency of images and imagination to mislead, Sibbes outlines a positive role for the imagination, in which images and imagination can reshape the affections towards repentance from sin and trust in God. The pastoral emphases of Perkins and Sibbes also differed – while Perkins is concerned to stir up the complacent to conversion by urging them not to presume on their final salvation, Sibbes is concerned to console those who are anxious over their spiritual state by persuading them that they indeed have saving faith.

Chapter 2 focuses on the rhetoric of a disparate group of writers on the fringes of the Puritan milieu during the turbulent period of the civil war and Interregnum period of the 1640s and 1650s who are variously labelled 'radical' or 'sectarian'. These include William Dell, a Cambridge college head opposed to university divinity degrees, and the 'Ranter' prophet Abiezer Coppe, who taught that the inspiration of the Spirit exempted him from the typical norms of morality. Taking the trajectory of Sibbes's emphasis on the Spirit beyond what Sibbes would have approved, these radicals adopt *ethos*, appeal to their own authority as Spirit-inspired speakers, as their primary mode of persuasion. These radicals seek to assert their persuasive *ethos* and to express divine transcendence through excessive language and actions that transgress ethical, linguistic and theological norms. This chapter will also discuss the Quakers, who clash with Puritans but emerge out of a broadly Puritan milieu. Early Quakers resort to silence to express the inadequacy of language to convey divine truth, but this is a pregnant silence that gives birth to extravagant speech and provocative prophetic actions.

Chapters 3 and 4 focus on two Dissenting preachers prominent in the later seventeenth century and subject to persecution following the Restoration of the monarchy, Richard Baxter and John Bunyan. Both are intensely focused on conversion, writing treatises dedicated to this end. Both are within the tradition of Puritan practical divinity, but both are largely self-educated and so hard to fit exactly within the intellectual contexts traceable in the works of university-trained ministers such as Perkins and Sibbes. Both Baxter and Bunyan appeal to both reason and imagination, and both write in a wide range of genres, including both sermon treatises and other modes that make a more direct appeal to the imagination.

In Baxter's case, the appeal to the imagination comes largely in the form of his advocacy and exemplifying of meditation – contemplating Scripture, human experience and the afterlife with an imaginative intensity that transcends a merely rational reflection. In Bunyan's case, appeal to the imagination comes most obviously in the form of his full-length allegorical fictions. While Bunyan was not the first author of Puritan allegory, he is the most widely read and the most influential on subsequent generations. Bunyan seeks to persuade his readers not simply through rational argument but through the aesthetic experience of losing themselves in the narrative and so letting down their defences in such a way as to allow their thoughts and feelings to be reinscribed.

Chapter 5 considers how the rhetorical dynamics I have identified in the writing of Puritan ministers are present in the work of John Milton, known principally as the author of *Paradise Lost*, but also the author of didactic and polemical prose as well as of other poetic reworkings of biblical narratives. While it is problematic to generalize across the whole of Milton's varied corpus of writing, Milton, like the ministers considered earlier in the book, appeals to both reason and imagination in order to persuade his readers towards his own somewhat idiosyncratic brand of godly faith and republican politics. However, the Arminian thought of the mature Milton, with its emphasis on the inviolability of the human will, gives a distinctive twist to his understanding of divine rhetoric, which in Milton's eyes is persuasive but never irresistible. '[R]esistless eloquence' for Milton is a satanic fantasy of coercive control through speech that is impossible to exercise in reality, though the slippery nature of satanic rhetoric ultimately leads to Milton's Satan deceiving himself.[52]

It seems fitting to borrow here a phrase used by New Testament scholar Richard Hays: 'the conversion of the imagination.'[53] While Hays uses this phrase to explore the reshaping of motifs from the Hebrew Bible by New Testament writers around the person of Jesus, it seems apt for what takes place in the imaginative literary works of Bunyan and Milton, and, at least incipiently, in appeals to the imagination in sermons and devotional works by Puritan divines such as Richard Sibbes and Richard Baxter. In being put to godly ends, imaginative modes of communication such as fictional narrative are thereby converted and redeemed from their associations with falsehood, in order to serve as instruments for the conversion of their audiences.

Similarly, this book will argue that Puritan writers and preachers radically reconfigured rhetorical practice in pursuit of their persuasive goals of conversion, assurance and godly living. This was in part through what is often known as Puritan plain style, which was not an abandonment of verbal eloquence as often thought but rather a concealing of eloquence – in prioritizing the transparent communication of truth over the ostentatious display of learning and eloquence, Puritan writers display rhetorical skill in the very act of hiding it. It is also the pastoral impulse to persuade their readers into saving truth that leads some Puritan writers to deploy the somewhat undercover modes of persuasion offered by imaginative fiction. For the Puritans, whether with regard to the textbook

Introduction   17

rhetoric of the classical and humanist tradition, or the more imaginative rhetoric of allegorical narrative, the rhetoric of conversion entails the conversion of rhetoric.

Notes

1   Susan Friend Harding, *The Book of Jerry Falwell: Fundamentalist Language and Politics* (Princeton: Princeton University Press, 2000), pp. 33–4.

2   Harding, *The Book of Jerry Falwell*, pp. 33–4.

3   Harding, *The Book of Jerry Falwell*, p. 34.

4   John Bunyan, *The Strait Gate*, ed. Graham Midgley, in *The Miscellaneous Works of John Bunyan* (13 vols.) [henceforth *MW*], gen. ed. Roger Sharrock (Oxford: Clarendon Press, 1976–94), V:121.

5   For the double sense of 'conviction' in Bunyan's writings as meaning both a firmly held belief and a legal judgement, see Beth Lynch, *John Bunyan and the Language of Conviction* (Cambridge: D. S. Brewer, 2004), pp. 11–14, 34–63, and *passim*. Jason Crawford comments similarly, ' "Conviction" can indeed mean both private fixity and legal judgment, and in Bunyan's hands these two senses of the word negotiate and intertwine.' (Jason Crawford, *Allegory and Enchantment: An Early Modern Poetics* (Oxford: Oxford University Press, 2017), p. 179.)

6   Among numerous helpful studies, I recommend the following monographs in particular: D. Bruce Hindmarsh, *The Evangelical Conversion Narrative: Spiritual Autobiography in Early Modern England* (Oxford: Oxford University Press, 2005), Molly Murray, *The Poetics of Conversion in Early Modern English Literature: Verse and Change from Donne to Dryden* (Cambridge: Cambridge University Press, 2009), Craig Harline, *Conversions: Two Family Stories from the Reformation and Modern America* (New Haven: Yale University Press, 2011), and Kathleen Lynch, *Protestant Autobiography in the Seventeenth-Century Anglophone World* (Oxford: Oxford University Press, 2012).

7   John Coffey and Paul C. H. Lim, 'Introduction', in John Coffey and Paul C. H. Lim (eds.), *The Cambridge Companion to Puritanism* (Cambridge: Cambridge University Press, 2008), p. 1. For a sample of the discussion, see, for instance, Basil Hall, 'Puritanism: The Problem of Definition', in G. J. Cuming (ed.), *Studies in Church History*, vol. II (London: Nelson for Ecclesiastical History Society, 1965), pp. 283–96; John Spurr, *English Puritanism, 1603–1689* (Basingstoke: Macmillan, 1988), pp. 1–27; and Peter Lake, 'Defining Puritanism: Again?' in Francis J. Bremer (ed.), *Puritanism: Transatlantic Perspectives on a Seventeenth-Century Anglo-American Faith* (Boston, MA: Massachusetts Historical Society/Northeastern University Press, 1993), pp. 3–29.

8   John Bunyan, *Peaceable Principles and True*, ed. T. L. Underwood, in *MW*, IV:270.

9 Richard Baxter, *Church-History of the Government of Bishops and Their Councils Abbreviated* (London, 1680), sig. (b)1r.

10 Percival Wiburn, *A Checke or Reproofe of M. Howlet's Untimely Schreeching* (1591), fol. 15v, cited in Patrick Collinson, *The Elizabethan Puritan Movement* (1967; repr. Oxford: Oxford University Press, 1990), p. 27.

11 Similarly, Karen Bruhn opts for 'godly' over 'puritan' in order to 'privilege self-appellation over scholarly terminology' (Karen Bruhn, '"Sinne Unfoulded": Time, Election, and Disbelief Among the Godly in Late Sixteenth- and Early Seventeenth-Century England', *Church History*, 77 (2008), 574–95; quotation from p. 575).

12 Peter Lake, *Moderate Puritans and the Elizabethan Church* (Cambridge: Cambridge University Press, 1982), p. 282.

13 William Haller, *The Rise of Puritanism; or, The Way to the New Jerusalem as Set Forth in Pulpit and Press from Thomas Cartwright to John Lilburne and John Milton, 1570–1643* (New York: Columbia University Press, 1938), pp. 25–35.

14 Christopher Hill, 'Puritans and "the Dark Corners of the Land"', in *Change and Continuity in Seventeenth-Century England* (1974; rev. ed. New Haven: Yale University Press, 1991), pp. 3–47.

15 Eamon Duffy, 'The Long Reformation: Catholicism, Protestantism and the Multitude', in Nicholas Tyacke (ed.), *England's Long Reformation, 1500–1800* (London: UCL Press, 1998), p. 42.

16 'conversion, *n*.', senses 8 and 9, *OED*.

17 Murray, *The Poetics of Conversion*, p. 7.

18 Peter L. Berger, *The Sacred Canopy: Elements of a Sociological Theory of Religion* (1967; repr. New York: Anchor, 1969), esp. pp. 45–51, 150–3; Peter L. Berger, *A Rumour of Angels: Modern Society and the Rediscovery of the Supernatural* (1969; repr. London: Allen Lane, 1970), esp. pp. 50–5.

19 Berger, *A Rumour of Angels*, esp. pp. 30–5.

20 Charles Taylor, *A Secular Age* (Cambridge, MA: Belknap/Harvard University Press, 2007), esp. pp. 171–6, 322–51, 361–9, 374–6.

21 Kuhn is a historian and philosopher of science who uses religious conversion as an analogy for the occasional dramatic shifts in scientific understanding he is seeking to understand: Thomas S. Kuhn, *The Structure of Scientific Revolutions* (4th ed. Chicago: University of Chicago, 2012).

22 William A. Dyrness, *Reformed Theology and Visual Culture: The Protestant Imagination from Calvin to Edwards* (Cambridge: Cambridge University Press, 2004), p. 6. Dyrness distinguishes between *Weltbild* ('world picture') and *Weltanschauung* ('world view'), seeing the former as more visual, embodied and pre-cognitive than the latter.

23 Martin Luther, *Lectures on Genesis*, ed. Jaroslav Pelikan, in *Luther's Works*, 55 vols., gen. ed. Jaroslav Pelikan and Helmut T. Lehmann (St. Louis: Concordia/ Philadelphia: Fortress, 1955–86), III:191.

Introduction   19

24 Quintilian, *Institutio Oratoria*, 8.6.44–58; for the use of 'allegory' for Quintilian's *allegoria*, see, for instance, Henry Peacham, *The Garden of Eloquence* (London, 1577), sig. D1r-v.

25 See, for instance, C. S. Lewis, *The Allegory of Love* (London: Oxford University Press, rev. ed. 1938), Chapter 7, 'The Faerie Queene', pp. 297–360. On parallels between Bunyan and Spenser as Protestant allegorists, see especially James F. Forrest, 'Allegory as Sacred Sport: Manipulation of the Reader in Spenser and Bunyan', in Robert G. Collmer (ed.), *Bunyan in Our Time* (Kent, OH: Kent State University Press, 1989), pp. 93–112.

26 Mark Allan Steiner, *The Rhetoric of Operation Rescue: Projecting the Christian Pro-life Message* (New York/London: Continuum, 2006), pp. 24–38 (quotation from p. 31). Italics in original.

27 Steiner, *The Rhetoric of Operation Rescue*, pp. 34–5. Cf. Tuija Virtanen and Helena Halmari's definition of 'persuasion' as 'all linguistic behavior that attempts to either *change* the thinking or behavior of an audience, or to *strengthen* its beliefs, should the audience already agree' (Tuija Virtanen and Helena Halmari, 'Persuasion across Genres: Emerging Perspectives', in Helena Halmari and Tuija Virtanen (eds.), *Persuasion across Genres: A Linguistic Approach* (Amsterdam/Philadelphia: John Benjamins, 2005), p. 3, pp. 3–24.

28 H. C. Porter, *Reformation and Reaction in Tudor Cambridge* (Cambridge: Cambridge University Press, 1958), p. 310.

29 Kevin Sharpe, *The Personal Rule of Charles* I (New Haven: Yale University Press, 1992), pp. 298–9.

30 'Certaine Questions and Answeres Touching the Doctrine of Predestination', in *The Bible and Holy Scriptures Conteyned in the Olde and Newe Testament* (London, 1579), n.p. (inserted at beginning of the New Testament).

31 Richard Greenham, 'Godly Observations, Concerning Divers Arguments and Common Places in Religion', in *The Workes of the Reuerend and Faithfull Seruant of Iesus Christ M. Richard Greenham, Minister and Preacher of the Word of God* (London, 1605), p. 822.

32 Leif Dixon, *Practical Predestinarians in England, c. 1590–1640* (Farnham: Ashgate, 2014), p. 14.

33 Bruhn, 'Sinne Unfoulded', pp. 575, 595.

34 There were some in a broadly Reformed tradition who affirmed the 'eternal justification' of the elect prior to their birth, but this view was rejected by the majority – see Robert J. McKelvey, '"That Error and Pillar of Antinomianism": Eternal Justification', in Michael A. G. Haykin and Mark Jones (eds.), *Drawn into Controversie: Reformed Theological Diversity and Debates within Seventeenth-Century British Puritanism* (Göttingen: Vandenhoeck & Ruprecht, 2011), pp. 223–62.

35 John Calvin, *Institutes of the Christian Religion*, ed. John T. McNeill, trans. Ford Lewis Battles, 2 vols. (London: SCM/Philadelphia: Westminster, 1961), III.xxiv.1 (II:965); see also II.iii.6, III.i.3–4.

36 Richard Baxter, *A Christian Directory* (London, 1673), p. 60.

37 Thomas Gataker, *Davids Remembrancer*, in *Certaine Sermons* (London, 1637), pp. 307–8.

38 Arnold Hunt, *The Art of Hearing: English Preachers and Their Audiences, 1590–1640* (Cambridge: Cambridge University Press, 2010), p. 130.

39 William Gurnall, *The Christian in Compleat Armour* (London, 1655), sig. A4r.

40 Baxter, *Christian Directory*, p. 60.

41 Simeon Ash, James Nalton and Joseph Church, 'To the Reader', in Richard Sibbes, *A Learned Commentary or, Exposition, upon the Fourth Chapter of the Second Epistle of Saint Paul to the Corrinthians* (London, 1656), sig. A2v.

42 Early modern sermon studies has seen a revival of interest since the late 1990s, producing a number of valuable and carefully historicized studies. See especially Peter E. McCullough, *Sermons at Court: Politics and Religion in Elizabethan and Jacobean Preaching* (Cambridge: Cambridge University Press, 1998); Lori Anne Ferrell and Peter McCullough (eds.), *The English Sermon Revised: Religion, Literature and History 1600–1750* (Manchester: Manchester University Press, 2000); Peter McCullough, Hugh Adlington and Emma Rhatigan (eds.), *The Oxford Handbook of the Early Modern Sermon* (Oxford: Oxford University Press, 2011); and Mary Morrissey, *Politics and the Paul's Cross Sermons, 1558–1642* (Oxford: Oxford University Press, 2011). Mary Morrissey provides a helpful brief overview of the English Reformed model of preaching and its decline in the later seventeenth century in 'Scripture, Style and Persuasion in Seventeenth-Century English Theories of Preaching', *Journal of Ecclesiastical History*, 53.4 (October 2002), 686–706.

43 On Renaissance rhetoric, see especially Peter Mack, *Elizabethan Rhetoric: Theory and Practice* (Cambridge: Cambridge University Press, 2002), Peter Mack, *A History of Renaissance Rhetoric, 1380–1620* (Oxford: Oxford University Press, 2011), and Sylvia Adamson, Gavin Alexander and Katrin Ettenhuber (eds.), *Renaissance Figures of Speech* (Cambridge: Cambridge University Press, 2007).

44 Morrissey, 'Scripture, Style and Persuasion', *passim*. Morrissey argues that the precepts of classical rhetoric became more central to post-Restoration conformist preaching due to a reduced emphasis on the role of the Spirit in reaction to perceived claims of direct divine inspiration by Nonconformist 'enthusiasts'.

45 Morrissey, 'Scripture, Style and Persuasion', p. 694.

46 Aristotle, *Rhetoric*, 1356a.

47 R. T. Kendall, 'The Preaching of the Word and Spirit', in Paul Cain and R. T. Kendall, *The Word and the Spirit* (Eastbourne: Kingsway, 1996), p. 72.

48 Kendall, 'The Preaching of the Word and Spirit', p. 72.

49 William Perkins, *An Exposition of the Symbole or Creed of the Apostles*, in *Workes of that Famous and Worthie Minister of Christ in the Vniversitie of Cambridge, M. W. Perkins*, 3 vols. (Cambridge, 1608–9), I:126.

50 Richard Sibbes, *The Soules Conflict with It Selfe, and Victory over It Self by Faith* (London, 1635), pp. 414–15.

51 Sibbes, *Soules Conflict*, p. 200.

52 John Milton, *Paradise Regain'd*, IV:268, ed. Laura Lunger Knoppers (2008), in *The Complete Works of John Milton*, 11 vols. projected, gen. eds. Thomas N. Corns and Gordon Campbell (Oxford: Oxford University Press, 2008–), II:54.

53 Richard B. Hays, *The Conversion of the Imagination: Paul as Interpreter of Israel's Scripture* (Grand Rapids, MI: Eerdmans, 2005).

1

A passionate *logos*: The persuasive practical divinity of William Perkins and Richard Sibbes

'Logicke and Rhetoricke' are 'the practise of the holy ghost'.[1] So says William Perkins (1558–1602), one of the leading 'godly' clergy during the later Elizabethan period in his posthumously published commentary on the book of Revelation.[2] Likewise, Richard Sibbes (*c*. 1577–1635), a luminary of the 'spiritual brotherhood' in the generation following Perkins, writes in the prefatory epistle to his sermon treatise *The Bruised Reede, and Smoaking Flax* that 'the Holy Ghost effectually perswadeth by a divine kinde of rhetoricke'.[3]

When read in context, Perkins and Sibbes are not saying exactly the same thing in these quotations. Whereas Perkins's claim in his sermons on Revelation that logic and rhetoric are 'the practice of the holy ghost' finds these two language arts within the verbal techniques and logical structures of the actual words of Scripture given by the Spirit, Sibbes's reference here to '*a divine kinde of rhetoricke*' has a broader and more metaphorical sense: it refers to the entire divine work of persuasion entailed in conversion, which is analogous to human persuasion through speech but is not limited to the verbal in the means that it uses.

Perkins is a significant figure for our story in two key ways. First, he was one of the chief early popularizers of 'Puritan' practical divinity, especially via his prolific writings, which were bestsellers well into the seventeenth century.[4] Second, Perkins is one of the chief theorists of preaching in an English Reformed tradition, as seen especially in his manual for preachers *The Arte of Prophecying*, and so, more broadly, can be deemed a key theorist of Puritan persuasion. Sibbes, who preached like Perkins in Cambridge as well as in London in the generation following Perkins, is significant for his greater emphasis on appeal to the emotions/affections, his pastoral focus on consoling anxious believers, and the more positive place he gives to the human imagination, helping to open up a space in which the imaginative writing of Bunyan and Milton would flower.

24   *The Rhetoric of Conversion in English Puritan Writing*

Although there are notable differences in the pastoral, psychological and rhetorical emphases of Perkins and Sibbes, these differences should not be unduly exaggerated. Both are non-separatist reformers seeking to inculcate what they would deem a more scriptural piety within the established Church. Both seek an inner conversion of the heart on the part of those who are already notionally members of the Church. Both appeal to the reason and imagination in their godly persuasion, while both express misgivings about the fallen tendencies of human reason and imagination. Both also stress a necessary conjunction of divine and human agency that sees the godly persuader and the potential convert as having real responsibility in the parts that they play, though the persuasive process becomes efficacious only with the agency of the Spirit.

For instance, Sibbes writes:

> Because hee [God] will preserve *Nature,* and the principles thereof, and so he deales with us, working accordingly; the manner of working of the reasonable creature, is to worke freely by a sweet inclination, not by violence. Therefore when he workes the worke of Conversion, hee doth it in a sweet manner, though it bee mightie for the Efficaciousnes of it, he admonisheth us with intreatie, and perswasion, as if we did it our selves. [...] But though the manner be thus sweet, yet with this manner there goeth an almighty power. Therefore hee doth it strongly as comming from himselfe, and sweetly, as the speaking is to us preserving our Nature, so the Action is from him, which hath an almightie power with it.[5]

Sibbes here distinguishes between the human side of the transaction, in which God appeals to the rational and affective faculties with which humans make decisions in a way that is fitting to how humans are designed, and the divine side of the transaction, in which God's word cannot fail to accomplish his sovereign purpose. He gives the telling qualification that it is '*as if* we did it our selves' (emphasis added).[6]

Likewise, Perkins writes that

> in the conversion of a sinner three things are required: the word, God's spirit, and mans will: for mans will is not passive in all and every respect, but hath an action in the first conversion and change of the soule [...] When any man is converted, this worke of God is not done by compulsion, but he is converted willingly: and at the very same time when he is converted, by Gods grace hee wills his conversion.[7]

Conversion is not 'by compulsion' according to Perkins, because at the very moment of regeneration the sinner genuinely wills to be converted, but the sinner is in no way free to will conversion prior to that point because the fallen human will is only able to will conversion when empowered to do so 'by Gods grace'. The human will is thus both active and passive in the process of persuasion to conversion through the preaching of the word, with 'God's spirit' the enabling power joining 'the word' to 'mans will'.[8]

Sibbes explicitly describes this persuasive work of the Spirit in terms of rhetoric:

> No creature can take off wrath from the conscience, but he that set it on, though all the prevailing arguments be used that can bee brought forth, till the Holy Ghost effectually perswadeth by a divine kinde of rhetoricke, which ought to raise up our hearts to him who is the comforter of his people, that he would seale the[m] to our soules.[9]

This divine rhetoric is an experiential (in early modern parlance, 'experimental' or 'affective') revelation of the love of Christ that overcomes the individual's fear of God's wrath, thus conveying an assurance of salvation to the anxious believer. Yet though Sibbes highlights the affective nature of this revelation and the insufficiency of 'prevailing arguments' without it, the divine rhetoric does not move the affections to the exclusion of an appeal to reason. In the terminology of Aristotle's *Rhetoric*, the Spirit makes use of *logos* (appeal to reason) as well as *pathos* (appeal to the emotions/affections).

The mention of '*seal[ing] the[m] to our soules*' echoes Sibbes's distinctive emphasis on the sealing of the Spirit that was taken up by others such as Thomas Goodwin.[10] Sibbes distinguished two aspects of 'sealing': an objective sealing by which the Spirit put the divine stamp of ownership on a true believer, and a subsequent subjective sealing in which the believer became consciously aware of being claimed by the Spirit and so attained to assurance of salvation. Here, though, it is the 'prevailing arguments' that the Spirit seals to the soul of the believer in assurance. Thus the Spirit does not disregard but makes efficacious the persuasive reasoning of human agents such as godly ministers or other true believers in order to accomplish his rhetorical goal of the assurance of salvation.

Sibbes elsewhere speaks of divinely granted assurance as itself having a rhetorical function, that, far from leading to an 'antinomian' carelessness regarding one's behaviour, motivates believers to a holy life:

> there is nothing quickens a soule more to cheerefull obedience, than assurance of Gods love, and that our *labour* should *not be in vaine in the Lord*; this is the Scriptures Logicke and Retoricke to inforce and perswade a holy life from knowledge of our present estate in grace.[11]

Taking Sibbes's references to divine rhetoric together identifies assurance of salvation ('our present estate in grace') as a persuasive goal of the Spirit that itself helps to bring about the persuasive goal of godly living. To say that 'this is the Scriptures Logicke and Retoricke' links the experiential apprehension of assurance to a chain of reasoning deduced from scriptural texts, calling to mind Perkins's *A Golden Chaine* that expounds how each stage in the process of salvation may be logically inferred from the experiential apprehension of any one link in the chain.[12]

While the direct descriptions of the Spirit as rhetorician offered by Perkins and Sibbes have a different focus, each is making a point with which the other would agree: that the Holy Spirit has an inherently rhetorical mission to persuade human beings to conversion, assurance of salvation, and godly living, and that this rhetorical mission can be traced at least in part through rhetorical techniques found in the words of the scriptural text. Both would likewise agree that the divine rhetoric that brings about conversion operates through human rhetorical agents, and through the persuasive work of ministers in particular.

However, for both of these divines, the Holy Spirit is not the only supernatural agent of persuasion. Sibbes speaks of 'Satan (as a cunning Rhetorician),'[13] while Perkins also expresses anxiety over the devil's 'false perswasion'.[14] In the latter part of this chapter, I will explore how satanic rhetoric as described by Perkins and Sibbes can be characterized by means of a particular rhetorical figure, that of paradiastole, the figure that excuses a vice by calling it by the name of the nearest virtue, 'by [which] means even the Devil himself can be transfigured into an Angel of light'.[15]

The rhetoric of the Spirit is seen most concretely, for Perkins and Sibbes, in the words of Scripture. In his manual for preachers, *The Arte of Prophecying*, Perkins makes most explicit use of the terminology of the classical rhetorical tradition in the earlier part of the treatise on scriptural interpretation, since he recognizes the presence of many 'sacred tropes' in Scripture that the exegete needs to recognize in order to understand the text rightly.[16] In some cases this is to explain the proper meaning of certain expressions not to be taken literally. For instance, dealing with scriptural anthropomorphisms for God, Perkins comments, 'An *Anthropo-pathia* is a sacred Metaphor, wherby those things, that are properly spoken of man, are by a similitude attributed vnto God.'[17] For instance:

> His face is put for fauour or anger. [...] His eyes are vsed for grace and prouidence. [...] His eares are put for his accepting of mens prayers. His nostrils for indignation.[18]

In some cases Perkins approaches what we might term literary criticism by paying attention to the literary effect of a trope or figure:

> The Pleonasme of the Verbe doth either make the speech more emphaticall and significant, or els signifieth and sheweth vehemencie, or certentie, or speedines. Gen.2.17. *In dying thou shalt die.* Esay.50.2. *Is mine hand shortened in shortening?* Esay. 56.3. *By separating God hath separated me from his people.*[19]

Here Perkins is noting how the presence of particular rhetorical techniques in Scripture enhances the *pathos* of the scriptural texts in which they are used – as well as underlining emphasis, the use of pleonasm (repetition of meaning in a way that is grammatically unnecessary) can convey the urgent emotion of the text and implicitly cause the reader to feel that emotion.

Sibbes likewise finds rhetorical techniques in the text of Scripture. For instance, in his posthumously published treatise *Bowels Opened*,[20] derived from a series of sermons on the Song of Songs, Sibbes speaks of God's work of persuasion as a wooing of the soul, in keeping with the common Christian allegorization of the Song of Songs as speaking of the love between Christ and his people.[21] Commenting on the words from the biblical text 'My love, my dove' (Song of Songs 5:2), Sibbes sees Christ himself (in the guise of the beloved) as using an affectionate rhetoric:

> There are all words of sweetnesse, he labours to express all the affection hee can, for the conscience is subject to upbraid, and to claimour much, so that there must bee a great deale of perswasion to still the accusing conscience of a sinner, to set it downe, make it quiet, and perswade it of Gods love. Therefore hee useth all heavenly Rhetoricke to perswade and move the affections.[22]

The phrase 'heavenly Rhetoricke' here brings together the actual verbal expression of the scriptural text, the 'words of sweetness', with the 'affection' that they express and the persuasive goal of the divine speaker – that of calming the sinner's conscience and persuading the sinner of 'Gods love'.

'A tongue of the learned': The preacher's preparation

According to Sibbes, Christ's wooing of the soul takes various forms, for instance, through pleasant and painful providential circumstances and through the exemplary lives of the godly, but this persuasive wooing is particularly heard through preachers: 'But besides all this, here is a more neere knocking, that Christ useth to the Church, *His ministeriall knocking*'.[23] Ministers 'are the *paranymphi* the friends of the Bride, that learne of *Christ* what to report to his *Spouse,* and so they wooe for *Christ'* – an analogy later used by William Gouge, Matthias Milward and Thomas Watson.[24]

Thus true ministers are among the principal (though not only) human agents of divine persuasion. In a conjunction of human and divine agency, the preacher persuades on behalf of Christ, but it is the Spirit who makes the persuasion efficacious:

> So Christ by his Spirit cloaths his word in the Ministery, when he speakes to people with a mightie power: as the Minister speakes to the eare, Christ speaks, opens, and unlocks the heart at the same time, and gives it power to open, not from it selfe, but from Christ.[25]

For both Perkins and Sibbes, the authoritative *ethos* of the minister as an agent of divine persuasion (his persuasive authority as perceived by his audience) depends upon due preparation. This preparation is of both educational and spiritual kinds, though Perkins emphasizes the former more strongly than Sibbes, as is intriguingly illuminated by how the two of them use the biblical phrase 'a tongue of the learned'.

Perkins sees the universities as providing ministers with training for the tasks of persuasion that fall to them.[26] This is apparent in Perkins's comments on the biblical gift of 'prophecy', understood by Perkins to mean preaching. In his exposition of the Apostles' Creed, Perkins writes:

> it is manifest, that the gift of prophecie, is the greatest gift that God bestowes on his Church for the building thereof [...] And for this cause also the schooles of learning are to be reuerenced & maintained, & all other meanes vsed for the furthering of them; because they are vnder God the fountains and wel-springs of this gift of prophecie.[27]

In defence of his belief that education is required for the preacher to be effective in his persuasive mission, Perkins cites Isaiah 50:4 – '*The Lord God hath given me a tongue of the learned, that I should know to minister a word in due time to him who is wearie.*' Perkins states that these words of the prophet are to be taken as 'Christ himselfe [...] speaking in his owne person', and argues that

> In this text then, there is set downe one principall dutie of Christs propheticall office, by allusion to the practices of the Prophets in the old Testament, especially those which belonged to the schooles of *Elias* and *Elizeus*, which are here termed *the learned.*[28]

A Passionate Logos

Christ is here identified with Old Testament prophets, at least some of whom appear to have had a measure of formal training in 'the schooles of *Elias* [Elijah] and *Elizeus* [Elisha]'. Perkins is drawing on a familiar Reformed understanding of the threefold office (*munus triplex*) of Christ, who is anointed to act as prophet, priest and king.[29]

While the Nicene Creed (in its commonly received version of 381) expresses belief 'in the Holy Ghost [...] who spake by the prophets', Perkins shares with other Reformed thinkers the understanding that the Old Testament prophets proclaimed God's word as agents of the prophetic ministry of the pre-incarnate Christ:

> For we may not thinke that Christ in his own person, ministred and spake words of comfort to the wearie, in the time of the Prophets, because he was not then exhibited in our nature; and yet he did then speake, but how? in the persons of the Prophets. So likewise, because Christ now in the new Testament, speakes not vnto the afflicted in his owne proper person, it remaineth therefore that he performes this great worke in the Ministerie of Pastors and Teachers upon earth, to whom he hath given knowledge and other gifts for this purpose.[30]

There is thus a parallel between Christ's speaking through prophets before his physical presence on earth and his speaking through the prophetic office of Christian ministers after his ascension to heaven. Through this parallel, Perkins asserts that ministers, like the prophets of old, require learning to carry out their persuasive ministry. The prophetic inspiration of the Spirit, for Perkins, does not preclude the need for study, but works through learning to enable the ministers of the present to participate in the prophetic office of Christ in speaking God's word of consolation to the '*wearie*' (taken to mean those who are anxious about their spiritual condition).

In his commentary on Galatians, Perkins makes a more explicit connection between the ancient schools of the prophets and the contemporary university. Of the cities given to the Levites, Perkins comments, 'One citie among all the rest is called *Cireath sepher, Iosu*.15.15. that is, *the city of bookes*, or as wee say, *the Vniversitie*'. Eliding the distinction between priests, Levites and prophets in the Hebrew Scriptures, Perkins connects the '*city of bookes*' to Samuel's 'Colleges of Prophets' and to the 'schooles of the Prophets' that Elijah and Elisha set up for '*the sonnes of the Prophets*', as well as to Christ's training of the twelve apostles and Paul's encouragement to Timothy to train successors.[31]

Although the English universities of the sixteenth century might not immediately resemble to us the ancient Hebrew schools of the prophets, it was in these terms that Perkins conceived them. In *A Treatise on the Duties and Dignity of the Ministry*, a treatise based on sermons preached in Cambridge's university church of Great St Mary's, Perkins observes that 'The most of vs in this place, are eyther *Prophets*, or the Sonnes of the *Prophets*,'[32] i.e. ministers (college fellows usually being ordained clergy) or ministers in training. The springs of 'prophecie', that is, of godly preaching, are thus found in the undergraduate arts curriculum of Cambridge.

The sources for what this curriculum contained are tantalizingly sketchy.[33] Officially speaking, the university curriculum at Cambridge was laid down in the university statutes of 1570. The 1570 statutes prescribe that the first year of study should be given to dialectic/logic, the second and third year should focus on rhetoric, and philosophy should be added in the fourth year. The entire curriculum presupposes the foundation of 'grammar' (the first of the three language arts of the trivium: grammar, logic and rhetoric), the basic proficiency in reading and writing Latin taught in the grammar schools that often included observing rhetorical figures of speech in classical texts that schoolboys could then use in their own speaking and writing.[34] Perkins can thus presuppose that the ministers in formation that he addresses are well grounded in the kinds of thinking, speaking and writing found in the classical tradition and transmitted in the universities.[35]

In speaking to the assembled company of the prophets in Great St Mary's, Perkins says that 'euery one, who either is or intends to be a Minister, must haue that *tongue of the learned*, whereof is spoken in Esay 50.4.'[36] This tongue of the learned, which all ministers need, is the product both of educational training and of spiritual gifting:

> Now to haue this *tongue of the learned, which Esay* speakes of, what is it but to be this *Interpreter*, which the holy Ghoost here saith a Minister must bee: But to bee able to speake with this tongue is, first *to be furnished with humane learning*. Secondly, *with Divine knowledge*, as farre as it may by outward meanes bee taught from man to man: but besides these, hee that will speake *this tongue* aright, must be *inwardly learned*, and taught by the spirit of God: the two first he must learne from men, but the third from God: a true Minister must be inwardly taught by the spiritual school-maister, the holy Ghost.[37]

In other words, for ministers to speak with power, to attain to the requisite *logos*, *ethos* and *pathos* to convince their audience, they need a liberal arts education, a theological education and the empowering of the Spirit.

Although Sibbes himself clearly possessed the first two of these, he highlights only the third when he uses the phrase 'the tongue of the learned':

A Passionate Logos 31

The wounds of secure sinners will not bee healed with sweet words. The Holy Ghost came as well in *fiery tongues,* as in the likenesse of a *Dove,* and the same holy Spirit will vouchsafe a spirit of prudence and discretion, (which is the salt to season all our words and actions) And such wisedome will teach us *to speake a word in season* both to the weary and likewise to the secure soule. And indeed he had need have *the tongue of the learned* that shall either raise up, or cast downe[.][38]

Sibbes equates Isaiah's '*tongue of the learned*' with a Spirit-bestowed wisdom that enables the minister to distinguish between the 'weary' soul (understood by Puritan divines to mean one anxious about salvation) and the 'secure' (that is, presumptuous) soul and to speak the fitting word to both. The empowering of the Spirit here enables the preacher to adhere to the rhetorical principle of decorum, rightly adapting his speech to the time, place and persons involved. In the context of practical divinity, rhetorical decorum becomes a pastoral decorum that discerns the right application of the Law and the Gospel to the experience of one's readers or hearers.

Perkins's appropriation of the principles of the secular classical rhetorical tradition transmitted through the curricula of early modern English grammar schools and universities for the purposes of sacred persuasion is evident in his manual for preachers, *The Arte of Prophecying,* although the work's more secular sources are somewhat hidden.[39] One can make a plausible case that the structure of *The Arte of Prophecying* broadly follows the pattern of Cicero's five 'canons' of rhetoric, the five stages by which Cicero instructed the orator to construct an effective oration: *inventio* (finding what to say), *dispositio* (arranging one's material into an effective order), *memoria* (remembering one's speech), *elocutio* (expressing oneself in an eloquent style) and *actio/pronuntiatio* (the effective delivery of the speech).[40] Perkins says of preaching that 'The *parts* thereof are two. *Preparation* for the sermon, and the Promulgation or *vttering* of it.'[41] In Cicero's terms, Perkins's '*Preparation*' can be taken as including *inventio* and *dispositio* (finding and structuring what to say) and 'promulgation' as including *elocutio* (style) and *actio* (performance).[42] The 'preparation' section focuses on biblical exegesis as the process for deriving from the biblical text the material to be preached, and it is this section that uses the vocabulary of classical rhetoric rather than the 'promulgation' section. Explicit rhetorical theory, for Perkins, seems to be an exegetical tool for the interpretation of the biblical text more than a homiletical tool for preaching it.

For Perkins, the preacher's *ethos* depends partly on his learning, but also entails the concealment of his learning. I agree here with Mary Morrissey that

Perkins's ideal of a sermon in which the Spirit is demonstrated, or manifest, is not one that is in danger of making the preacher a 'passive medium' for the Spirit. What Perkins is demanding is that the preacher deliver his sermon in an unostentatious way with a primary concern to teach and exhort his hearers, not to demonstrate his learning. If, as he should sincerely wish and pray, the spirit gives him grace to preach 'to edification', then that Spirit will be evident (and so 'demonstrated') in his sermon, making it powerful and effective on all well-disposed hearers.[43]

Morrissey is pushing back here against Debora Shuger's assertion that, in Perkins's model, 'the preacher would fade into a passive medium for a divine "force".'[44] While I agree with Morrissey over Shuger that Perkins's preacher is not passive and that his *ethos* is that of a skilled interpreter of divinely given Scripture rather than a directly inspired divine mouthpiece, I think there is a valid observation underlying Shuger's wording in that Perkins wishes the role of the preacher to fade from prominence in the audience's view while he delivers his sermon.

In the latter sections of *The Arte of Prophecying*, Perkins advocates the concealment of learning in the '*Promulgation*' (performance/delivery) of the sermon (roughly corresponding to the fifth Ciceronian 'canon' of rhetoric, *actio* or *pronuntiatio*): 'In the *Promulgation* two things are required: the hiding of humane wisdome, & the demonstration (or shewing) of the spirit).'[45] The 'demonstration [...] of the spirit' alludes to a phrase in 1 Corinthians 2:4 in which St Paul is speaking about his own preaching and contrasts the 'enticing words of man's wisdom' that he rejects with the 'demonstration of the Spirit and of power'. The Greek word for demonstration used by Paul is *apodeixis*, which is curiously the same word as Aristotle uses for rhetorical demonstration.[46] While the apostle is arguably ambivalent towards the classical rhetorical tradition, Perkins's use of this Pauline contrast links powerful preaching that is able to persuade its hearers with the concealment of human learning.

Yet, as the next paragraph indicates, the concealment of human learning is not the same as its absence, and in fact Perkins considers the intellectual grounding of a liberal arts education to be essential to the minister's task of persuasion:

> If any man thinke that by this means barbarisme should be brought into pulpits; he must vnderstand that the Minister may, yea & must privately vse at his libertie the artes, philosophy, and varietie of reading, whilest he is in framing his sermon: but he ought in publike to conceale all these from the people, and not to make the least ostentation. *Artis etiam est celare artem; it is also a point of Art to conceale Art.*[47]

A Passionate Logos

Perkins holds that the preacher's speech must use correct syntax, intonation and the like, while avoiding 'ostentation'. This is in keeping with the recommendations of Renaissance humanist educators, who would agree that correct style (*elocutio*, in rhetorical terms), comes from absorbing a 'varietie of reading'.[48]

Technical or foreign words will distract the minister's hearers and impede the understanding of the unlearned: 'Wherfore neither the wordes of arts, nor Greeke and Latine phrases and quirks must be intermingled in the sermon.'[49] Yet the minister's laying aside of learning is a conscious step undertaken by a learned individual for persuasive purposes, and is not necessarily a rejection of the precepts of classical rhetoric, some of whose exponents commended an artful plain style in which a learned orator conceals his artfulness for the sake of a simplicity compelling to his audience.[50]

Reason and imagination

Of the three Aristotelian modes of persuasion, one might be tempted to identify Perkins with *logos* (appeal to reason) and Sibbes with *pathos* (appeal to the emotions/affections). Yet while there are passages in each that seem to point to these leanings, both deploy both *logos* and *pathos*, advocating passionate reasoning and reasonable affections. Both also appeal to reason and imagination (or 'fancy'), though both express misgivings about the imagination in particular. Sibbes's work *The Soules Conflict* speaks specifically both of 'sanctified reason'[51] and of 'a sanctified *fancie*'.[52] The qualifier 'sanctified', however, suggests that the kinds of reason and fancy endorsed by Sibbes may differ from their profane or secular equivalents.

An influential study by Janice Knight identifies Perkins and Sibbes as progenitors of two diverging traditions within New England Puritanism, with Perkins (along with William Ames) being identified as one of the founding 'intellectual fathers' who favoured a rational emphasis on doctrinal orthodoxy, and Sibbes being seen as a father of the 'spiritual brethren' whose emphasis was upon mystical affective religious experience.[53] Similarly, recent work by R. N. Frost links Sibbes's emphasis on the affections to an Augustinian psychology recovered by Luther and Philip Melanchthon, over against an Aristotelian intellectualism, which Frost attributes to Perkins.[54] There is some truth in the identification of differing emphases in Perkins and Sibbes made by Knight and Frost, but I would argue that their dichotomies are too tightly drawn, as both Perkins and Sibbes make their pastoral persuasive appeals both to the mind (*logos*) and to the affections (*pathos*). One might say that they are proponents of a passionate *logos*.

Perkins's particular predilection for *logos* can be seen in his argument that faith is to be located in the mind rather than the will:[55]

> The place and seate of faith (as I thinke) is the mind of man, not the will: for it stands in a kind of particular knowledge or perswasion, and there is no perswasion but in the minde. [...] Some doe place faith partly in the mind, and partly in the will, because it hath two parts, knowledge and affiance: but it seemes not greatly to stand with reason, that one particular and single grace should be seated in diuers parts or faculties of the soule.[56]

However, as Paul Schaefer has noted, this observation may have a polemical context countering the medieval Catholic notion of implicit faith:

> The answer could be because Perkins wanted to ground faith in the promise, the sure word of God in Christ. True faith, therefore, had to be knowledge, because an implicit faith, a faith which merely trusted in the word of the Church without knowledge, failed.[57]

Moreover, Perkins elsewhere acknowledges right affections and a rightly inclined will as vital fruits stemming from true faith. In contrast to the superficial receiving of the word by the reprobate, who may, as with the stony ground in Jesus' parable of the sower, receive the word with joy (with understanding and affections), the reception of the word by the elect 'is a deepe and liuely rooting of the word, when the word is receiued into the mind and into the heart by the will and all the affections of the heart'.[58] Thus, though conversion begins in the understanding, understanding the preached word is not enough – the true reception of God's word that brings salvation involves all the faculties of the soul. Schaefer notes that, despite Perkins's adoption of the distinctions of early modern faculty psychology, 'he could also speak of "beleeving with the heart" in a way which transcended such faculty distinctions: "Paul saith indeede, that wee beleeve with the heart, ... but by the heart he understands the soule without limitation to any part."'[59]

Perkins's emphasis on *logos* shapes his reading of the Bible in perhaps unconscious ways. A curious instance of this is found in his reading of the account of the day of Pentecost in the Acts of the Apostles, a key biblical instance of Spirit-empowered speech in which the Spirit was poured out on the apostles, 'And they were all filled with the Holy Ghost, and began to speak with other tongues, as the Spirit gave them utterance' (Acts 2:4). Perkins comments on this passage as follows:

Wisedome in our speech is a goodly ornament. The Apostles when they waited for the holy Ghost in Ierusalem, it descended vpon them in the forme of fierie tongues: and then it is said, that *they spake as the holy Ghost gave them vtterance in Apophthegmes or wise sentences.*[60]

What is odd about the italicized biblical quotation is the addition of '*in Apophthegmes or wise sentences*', a phrase that occurs in none of the English Bible translations available to Perkins, but which is evidently a rendering of a word in the Greek text of Acts 2:4, ἀποφθέγγεσθαι (*apophthengesthai*), a word that appears in the margin of Perkins's paragraph and probably means something closer to 'to speak forth plainly'. However, Perkins's stretching of the meaning of the Greek suggests that apophthegms, concise pithy proverbial statements, are a particularly apt mode of expression for Spirit-inspired speech.

Perkins, more than Sibbes, can come across as a critic of imagination. For instance, in his anti-Catholic polemic *A Warning against the Idolatrie of the Last Times*, Perkins characterizes the visual representation of the Godhead, even by an internal image within the mind, as idolatry: 'So soone as the mind frames vnto it selfe any forme of God (as when he is popishly conceiued to be like an old man, sitting in heauen in a throne with a scepter in his hand) an idol is set vp in the minde'.[61] Passages such as these in Perkins lend support to Raphael Hallett's assertion that, for Perkins, 'A strict internal iconoclasm is provided by this control of imagination, much more profound than the stripping of external images',[62] and Donald McKim likewise dubs Perkins an 'inner iconoclast'.[63] However, Perkins's 'internal iconoclasm', though strongly asserted, is not absolute – elsewhere in the same work, he avers that 'God who allowes internall images rightly conceiued, forbiddes the externall in vse of religion'.[64]

Similarly, Perkins is wary of arousing emotion that is not adequately anchored to doctrine, but he is not as absolute an opponent of appeal to emotion as he might seem. Thus, in his exposition of the Apostle's Creed Perkins denounces 'the manner of Friers and Iesuits in the Church of Rome, to vse the consideration of the passion of Christ, as a meanes to stirre vp compassion in themselues' on the grounds that 'this kinde of vse is meere humane, and may in like manner be made by reading of any human historie.' Instead, Perkins tells us, we should channel our contemplations into doctrinal reflection on 'the horriblenesse of our sinnes', the redeeming love of Christ, and 'our endlesse peace with God and happiness', which is won by Christ's death.[65]

Beyond a general antipathy to Catholic modes of devotion, Perkins seems here to be more specifically attacking the so-called Ignatian method of meditation on the events of Christ's life, developed by Ignatius of Loyola and promoted by the Jesuits, whose literary fruits in English religious poetry Louis Martz has explored.[66] What attracts Perkins's suspicion is what he sees as a misdirection of the devotee's affections into a human sympathy with the figure of Christ that has insufficient or incorrect doctrinal content.

The supremacy of doctrinal statements over idolatrous mental images is put forward in Perkins's catechetical dialogue *The Foundation of Christian Religion*. This work presents the minister catechizing an imagined ideal parishioner, who says that he conceives of God 'Not by framing any image of him in my mind (as ignorant folkes doe, that thinke him to be an old man sitting in heauen) but I conceiue him by his properties and workes'.[67] Thus Perkins's idealized parishioner progresses from the naive ignorance of the masses with folk religious conceptions to a correct Reformed understanding of theology by replacing the mental picture of the old man in the sky with a verbalized list of divine attributes.

Given Perkins's reputation as a rigidly propositional iconoclast and his attacks on popish brooding on the physical suffering of Christ, it is rather startling to come across a vividly physical description of the believer's dependence on the crucified Christ. Drawing an analogy with the Old Testament story of Elisha stretching himself out upon a dead boy to raise him from the dead,[68] Perkins continues:

> So must a man by faith euen spread himselfe vpon the crosse of Christ, applying handes and feete to his peirced hands & feet, and his wretched heart to Christs bleeding heart, & then feele himselfe warmed by the heat of Gods spirit, & sin fro[m] day to day crucified with Christ, and his dead heart quickened & reuiued. And this applying which faith maketh, is done by a kind of reasoning which faith maketh thus.[69]

Although Perkins's exposition of the Apostles' Creed expresses suspicion of an overly emotional engagement with the passion narrative as detracting from a rational apprehension of its doctrinal significance, here the exercise of faith is visualized as a bodily engagement with the crucified Christ, accompanied by a feeling of warmth.

As an opponent of the devotional use of crucifixes,[70] Perkins is not advocating an actual physical embracing of the cross, but a mental imagining. Yet it remains startling for Perkins to invite his readers to imagine themselves physically embracing the wounded and bleeding body of Christ while it is still hanging on the cross, especially given Perkins's critique of Ignatian meditations on the physical suffering of Christ. Nevertheless, the imaginative and emotional engagement presented here by Perkins is not divorced from a cognitive engagement, since it is 'done by a kind of reasoning'. In this way, Perkins suggests that the powerful appeal to *pathos* is not devoid of *logos*.

William Haller tells us that 'We should not take too literally the boast of plainness in the sermons of the spiritual preachers'[71] and that 'Actually it was an immensely imaginative hortatory prose'.[72] Perkins's prose deploys a number of vivid similes and metaphors to convey his message with greater power. For instance, in explaining the tricky idea that God works through the evil intentions and actions of humans and of fallen angels to bring about good, Perkins says:

> As in the mill, the horse blindfolded goes forward, and perceiues nothing but that he is in the ordinary way, whereas the miller himselfe whips him and stirres him forward for an other ende, namely for the grinding of corne. And this is that which we must hold touching Gods prouidence ouer wicked men and angels: & it stands with the tenour of the whole Bible.[73]

Perkins likens the human hand taking hold of an object to 'faith, which is the hand of the soule, receiuing and applying the sauing promise'.[74] Other vivid analogies in his writing include the image of a drowning man getting his head above water and so having a good hope of recovery; likewise, Perkins expounds, Christ our head is risen and therefore we have hope that we as his members will also rise.[75]

Perkins's ambivalence regarding imagination is reflected in his ambivalence towards imaginative modes of writing – although he criticizes popular imaginative genres, Perkins makes use of the genre of didactic dialogue that deploys at least an incipient form of fiction to put across its doctrinal message.

Perkins is often derogatory about the reading of popular literature, such as ballads and chapbooks, which he considers pernicious timewasting when weighty matters of the soul are at stake. One of the errors of the 'ignorant' listed at the beginning of *A Foundation of the Christian Religion* is 'That merry ballads and bookes, as *Scoggin, Beuis of South hampton, &c.* are good to driue away the time, and to remooue heart-qualmes'.[76] Besides the joke book *Scoggin's Jests*, Perkins names the prose romance *Bevis of Southampton*, a favourite whipping boy for English Reformed authors. In Arthur Dent's didactic dialogue *The Plain Man's Pathway to Heaven*, the 'caviller' Antilegon recommends to his friend Asunetus, who is experiencing conviction of sin through the counsel of the godly minister Theologus, that he peruse Antilegon's collection of 'many pleasant and merry books' including *Bevis of Southampton*, as '*excellent and singular books against heart-qua[l]mes*'.[77] For Perkins as well as Dent, the problem with reading *Bevis* and other works of popular fiction is not simply that they take up time that

38 *The Rhetoric of Conversion in English Puritan Writing*

could be better spent elsewhere, but that they occupy their readers' imagination in such a way as to distract their attention away from the 'heart-qualmes' that mark the beginning of true conversion.

But despite this suspicion of imaginative fiction that Perkins perceives to be dulling the conscience by distracting the imagination, Perkins occasionally adopts more imaginative literary genres in his own persuasive practice, through which he seeks to awaken the conscience though at least a limited appeal to the imagination.

In some cases this is in a rudimentary form of dialogue more dominated by didactic exposition than imaginative characterization. This is the case, for instance, in 'The First Epistle of Iohn, in the Forme of a Dialogve', in which the questions of '*Church*' are answered by '*Iohn*' with successive verses of 1 John quoted word for word apart from added glosses by Perkins in square brackets.[78] For instance:

> *Ioh*. My little children, these things I write vnto you, that ye sinne not.
> Ch. *Alas, we fall oft by infirmitie: what shall we then doe?*
> *Ioh*. If any man sinne, we haue an aduocate [*who in his owne name and by his owne merits pleads our cause*] to the Father Iesus Christ the iust [*and therefore fit to make intercession*].[79]

W. B. Patterson observes that 'This dialogue form can be awkward because of such insertions', and I would agree that this dialogue is somewhat lacking as a compelling literary experience if assessed by aesthetic literary criteria.[80] However, by the criteria of didactic effectiveness, the dialogue is helpful as a pedagogical tool. The mode of persuasion still tends more to *logos*, with the focus on the setting forth of propositional doctrinal truth, but the emotional dimension of *pathos* is not entirely lacking. The glosses in square brackets are expository clarifications of the doctrinal logic of the text. However, the dialogic form introduces a modicum of narrative progression in the argument and, as Patterson notes, 'The verses of scripture are thereby made directly relevant to concerns of ordinary Christians'.[81] The Church's response '*Alas, we fall oft by infirmitie*' introduces an element of emotional response to the text ('*Alas*'), to which the following scriptural verse responds. The reader is invited to identify with the figure of 'Church' and thus to take his or her place within the social imaginary of the godly community and to interpret personal experience within a larger framework of redemptive history.

Elsewhere, Perkins shows an incipient talent for dialogues with a literary appeal that lightens the doctrinal exposition with small doses of imaginative fiction, anticipating more fully fledged narrative allegories such as those of John Bunyan and others.[82] This is the case in *A Fruitfull Dialogue concerning the Ende of the World*, in which 'Christian' and 'Worldling' journey together towards Cambridge as they talk:

> *Christian.* Well overtaken honest man: howe farre trauell you this way?
> *Worldling.* As far as Cambridge, God willing.[83]

Although the characters are designated by the names of types rather than personal names, Perkins immediately places these interlocutors into the real geographical and historical context in which he was writing, adding narrative verisimilitude. In her recent study of Bunyan, Nancy Rosenfeld draws on E. M. Forster's distinction between 'flat' characters who represent a single quality or idea and 'rounded' characters who have a more complex individual personality akin to our experience of real people. Rosenfeld argues that Bunyan's characters move along a 'continuum' between the two from strict allegory to the individuated characters of the novel form.[84] While remaining on the flatter end of the continuum, Perkins's Christian and Worldling possess some incipient qualities of individuals in realistic social settings of the time.

The Worldling is carrying a load of corn, and soon outs himself as a hoarder, complaining that, now that grain is plentiful, he cannot sell his grain at the inflated price he extracted in time of scarcity. This elicits a rebuke from the Christian, who calls him 'one of those, that haue brought our countrey into such miserie', along with an apposite denunciation from the prophet Amos of those who oppress the poor through short measures.[85] This work thus dramatizes Perkins's social ethics and his biblically grounded critique of incipient capitalism in the context of real economic concerns surrounding grain hoarding and recurrent food shortages in the 1580s and 1590s.[86]

In a realistic-sounding response from the mouth of a small farmer, the Worlding protests that he is not a bad man, but that he is constrained by market forces:

> *World.* For mine owne part, I could haue been content to haue sold my corne all the yeare through for a lesse price, if other would haue done so: but other men were so hard, that they would sticke for a penny.[87]

Worldling is revealed to be worldly in his reliance on material wealth, but his interests are not entirely secular in the modern sense – he turns out to have a keen interest in prophecies of the end of the world, though Christian is not impressed. Among the prophecies cited by Worldling is the following doggerel:

When after Christs birth there be expired,
of hundreds fiueteene, yeares eightie eight,
Then comes the time of dangers to be feared,
and all mankind with dolors it shall streight,
For if the world that yeare doe not fall,
if sea and land then perish ne decay,
The Empires all, and kingdomes alter shall,
and man to ease himself shall haue no way.[88]

The Christian retorts in a moderately entertaining manner: 'For my part, I make as little accompt of these verses as of Merlins drunken prophesies, or the tales of Robinhood.'[89] He continues with lengthy expositions of how to tell true from false prophecy, the follies of astrology, and the like. One senses that Perkins himself is having a bit of a laugh at the foolish superstitions of the masses. His didactic denunciations of superstition and fortune-telling are leavened by further light lacings of humour that might win over the reader's sympathies. For instance, Christian cites the Marian martyr bishop John Hooper mocking the astrological almanacs: 'The pronogstications (saith he) of these blinde prophets, are good to be borne in a mans bosome, to knowe the day of the moneth. The rest of their practises is not worth an haw[.]'[90]

The two travellers part on relatively good terms, with Worldling inviting Christian in for dinner but Christian declining, bringing to a natural narrative conclusion an exchange that models imaginative characterization, realistic social settings and satirical humour being deployed for didactic purposes. Thus, despite his suspicions of imagination and of imaginative fiction, Perkins provides some precedent for the later use of imaginative fiction as a mode of godly persuasion.

Though in differing proportions, Richard Sibbes likewise appeals both to reason and to imagination in his efforts at godly persuasion. Nigel Smith notes that 'the logical strictures of Perkins remained in the sermons of Richard Sibbes,'[91] and Sibbes commends 'true reason' as a corrective to 'false reason' in his advice on how the godly friend should comfort a dejected fellow believer:

> for oftentimes *grievances* are irrationall, rising from *mistakes;* and *counsell,* bringing into the soule a *fresh light,* dissolves those grosse *fogges,* and setteth the soule at *liberty.* What griefe is contracted by *false* reason, is by *true* reason altered.[92]

Similarly, although Sibbes has a heavy emphasis on the affections, he asserts that the affections should be regulated and shaped by reason:

A *Passionate* Logos   41

Confidence, and love, and other affections of the soule, though they have no reason grafted in them, yet thus farre they are reasonable, as that they are in a wise man raised up, guided, and laid downe with reason, or else men were neither to be blamed nor praised for ordering their affections a right; whereas not only civill vertue, but *grace* it selfe is especially conversant in ruling the affections by sanctified reason.[93]

Thus although the affections are powerful, people still have a responsibility to govern their affections by reason and can be held accountable for doing so. Hence the affections are not in principle irresistible. This is the case even with the 'civill vertue' of outward morality of which the unregenerate are capable, but those who are regenerate recipients of divine grace have the greater power of 'sanctified reason' that rules the affections. Thus appeal to reason (*logos*) on the part of the preacher or the lay Christian has its place in godly persuasion that seeks to guard against the excesses of a misguided imagination.

Sibbes also invokes appeal to both *ethos* and *pathos* in commending the counsel of the wise friend:

Where these graces are in the *speaker,* and apprehended so to bee by the person *distempered,* his heart will soone embrace whatsoever shall bee spoken to rectifie his judgement or affection. A good conceit of the *spirit* of the speaker is of as much force to prevaile as his *words.* Words especially prevaile, when they are uttered more from the *bowels* then the braine, and from our owne *experience,* which made even Christ himselfe a more compassionate *high Priest.*[94]

Here the speaker's character (*ethos*) and 'experience' (*pathos* – 'more from the *bowels* than the braine')[95] lend weight to the words issuing from the reasonings of his 'braine' (*logos*), and the effects of such persuasion reorient the hearer's cognitive and emotional faculties, paired together as 'his judgement or affection'. For the 'graces' of the speaker's character to be persuasive, they must be 'apprehended' by the hearer. This accords with the consensus of the rhetorical tradition that *ethos* is the speaker's character as it appears to the hearer rather than (necessarily) as it is in itself. However, Sibbes also intervenes here in the classical debate over whether the speaker needs actually to be a good person or only to seem so – Sibbes sides with the former position (though with the Christian and particularly Protestant emphasis that virtue is wrought by the Spirit rather than human effort), holding that godly character has to be genuine to be perceived: the graces must be in the speaker first.[96]

Yet the comfort of the friend's words is not in their rational persuasiveness but in the inbreathing of the Holy Spirit conveyed by them: 'it is the office of the

Holy Ghost to be a *Comforter,* not onely immediately, but by *breathing* comfort into our *hearts* together with the comfortable *words* of others'.[97] One could see this as a division of labour between human and divine persuasion, with human reason correcting faulty thinking and thus dispelling grief while the Spirit brings comfort to the heart. However, I would argue that Sibbes is rather asserting a concurrent agency – it is by means of the human persuader's true reasoning in accordance with divine revelation that the Spirit dispels grief and brings comfort. Human and divine agents are inextricably joined in the persuasive work of godly comfort.

Sibbes's treatise *The Soules Conflict* contains his most sustained discussion of the imagination, which U. Milo Kaufmann deems 'probably the first detailed engagement with the subject in seventeenth-century Puritanism'.[98] Kaufmann and others see Sibbes as rehabilitating imagination from the suspicions expressed by the likes of Perkins and preparing the way for more imaginative modes of didactic literature such as Bunyan's allegories. However, Sibbes's advocacy of the imagination remains ambivalent and partial.

Sibbes sees the faculty of imagination as having an immense power over the other mental faculties that determine human behaviour:

> *Imagination* is the *first wheele* of the soule, and if that move amisse, it stirres all the *inferiour wheeles* amisse with it; It stirres it *selfe,* and other powers of the soule are stirred by its motion: and therefore the well ordering of *this* is of the greater consequence; For as the *imagination* conceiveth, so usually the *judgement* concludeth, the *will* chuseth, the *affections* are carried, and the *members* execute.[99]

This description of the role of the imagination within the human psyche is itself expressed through an extended metaphor that appeals to the reader's imagination – that of a set of interlocking wheels operating like clockwork in which the stimulation of the imagination determines the action of a person's judgement, will and affections, culminating in the physical enacting of a certain behaviour by the '*members*' of the body. The clockwork metaphor could give the impression that once the imagination is triggered, the subsequent effects are inevitable. However, the word 'usually' qualifies this sense of inevitability somewhat, implying some room for the judgement to resist the enticements of the imagination.

The reason the imagination has a tendency to mislead is because it derives the raw data from which it constructs its impressions from the perceptions of the senses (which can be mistaken) rather than from the understanding. However, the solution to this for Sibbes is not to suppress the imagination but to re-educate it by presenting it with objects of inward perception that will reorient the affections and the will to what is truly good. Thus, although 'imagination of it selfe, if ungoverned, is a wilde, and a ranging thing',[100] imagination rightly used can be 'serviceable to us in spirituall things'.[101]

It is not the imagination per se but its 'ill government' that is opposed by Sibbes:

> And amongst all the faculties of the soule Most of the disquiet and unnecessary trouble of our lives arises from the vanity and ill government of that power of the soule which we call imagination and opinion, bordering betweene the senses and our understanding; which is nothing else but a shallow apprehension of good or evill taken from the senses[.][102]

The inadequacy of the imagination lies in the fact that it is a superficial reader: it has only 'a shallow apprehension' of surface impressions. Imagination tends to derive its data from sensory experience, which can be deceived, rather than from divine revelation, 'and the judgement it selfe since the fall, untill it hath an higher light and strength, yeeldeth to our imagination'.[103]

The imagination can be of service when it takes its rightful place in the hierarchy of faculties, not above but subject to judgement and reason: 'the office of imagination is to minister matter to our understanding to worke upon, and not to leade it, much lesse misleade it in any thing.'[104] Here imagining comes before reasoning in the temporal sequence but below reasoning in the authority it should have.

While the senses of 'imagination' overlap with those of 'opinion', Sibbes switches to another partial synonym in order to defend the imaginative faculties and their use in godly persuasion. This is the term 'fancy', which is not a uniformly positive term in the writing of early modern divines. William Dyrness notes that 'it more properly meant a surface delight in what is sensible, or in the specters the mind can produce. [...] Like imagination it was associated with the spectral or illusive productions of the mind which often, so it was feared, distracted one from the concrete life of obedience to God's truth.'[105] However, in Sibbes's usage it comes also to carry connotations of the creative imagination more akin to the positive senses of imagination familiar to us the other side of Romanticism.

Sibbes tells us that 'a sanctified fancie will make every creature a ladder to heaven'.[106] Sibbes is advocating what is known as meditation on the creatures, a practice of reflecting on everyday things in the material world or events in

44   *The Rhetoric of Conversion in English Puritan Writing*

one's life in a way that brings to mind spiritual truths.[107] Yet in Sibbes's case, he is exhorting not only that individual believers should inform their imaginations with godly meditations on the creatures, but also that ministers should use such imaginative analogies between the created order and divine realities in order to entice their hearers into a consideration of divine truth that will reorient their inward affections.

Sibbes expresses the caution that 'Fancie' should 'bee kept within its due bounds'.[108] For instance, Sibbes cautions against deriving notions of God from the imagination: 'But yet it ought not to *invent* or *devise* what is good and true in religion, here *fancy* must yeeld to faith, and *faith* to divine revelation.'[109] Imagination is a faculty of perception, and usurps its proper bounds when it seeks to exercise the active function of defining divine realities rather than the passive role of recognizing them. Hence 'Wee should not bring God downe to our owne *imaginations*, but raise our imaginations up to God.'[110] Nevertheless, imagination has a vital role in presenting spiritual truths in a form that is graspable by embodied human beings:

> But after God hath revealed spirituall truthes, and *faith* hath apprehended them, then *imagination* hath use while the soule is joyned with the body, to *colour* divine truthes, and make lightsome what *faith* beleeves[.][111]

Within these due bounds, Sibbes argues, the fancy can be spiritually beneficial: 'We should make our *fancie* serviceable to us in *spirituall* things'.[112] This is an injunction that Sibbes addresses to all his readers, but it is of particular relevance to the preacher:

> The putting of *lively* colours upon *common* truths hath oft a strong working both upon the *fancy,* and our *will* and *affections:* the spirit is *refreshed* with *fresh* things, or old truths *refreshed;* this made the Preacher *seeke* to finde out *pleasing* and *acceptable words;* and our Saviour CHRISTS maner of *teaching* was, by a lively *representation* to mens *fancies,* to teach them heavenly truths in an earthly sensible manner; and indeed what doe wee *see* or *heare* but will yeeld matter to a holy heart to raise it selfe higher?[113]

Here Sibbes is recommending that the preacher takes aesthetic criteria into account in finding effective persuasive strategies. One of these is the principle of variety – while a reader or hearer might be bored by too much sameness in content or delivery, the refreshing of 'the spirit [...] with *fresh* things' creates the aesthetic pleasure that makes 'old truths' more appealing. Truth is made more effective in its appeal when clothed in verbal ornament or in imaginative similes or metaphors.

A Passionate Logos

Besides Sibbes's appeal to the parables of Jesus as a precedent for imaginative persuasion in spiritual matters, his reference to 'the Preacher' refers specifically to the narrator of the biblical book of Ecclesiastes, traditionally identified as King Solomon and whose enigmatic self-designation *Qoheleth* is translated as 'the preacher' in the King James Version and earlier English translations such as the Geneva Bible. The King James rendering of Ecclesiastes 12:10 says that 'The preacher sought to find out acceptable words', but Sibbes appears to be influenced by the alternative translation of the Hebrew 'words of delight' (found in multiple early modern commentators on Ecclesiastes as well as the margin of the Authorised Version),[114] a rendering that influenced Sibbes's defence of the value of aesthetic delight for the transmission of divine truth in an enticing manner.

Sibbes's sermons practise what they preach, in that they include imaginative analogies that appeal to inward versions of the bodily senses in order to shape the affections and understanding of their audiences. Mark Dever observes that 'Sibbes's own sermons are replete with scores of striking illustrations, so much so that one could almost reconstruct life in Stuart England from Sibbes's sermons alone'.[115] There is a sensory vividness to many of Sibbes's sermonic analogies:

> as we need not take the *Sunne* from Heaven to know whether or not it be up, or be day: which may be knowne by the light, heate, & fruitfullnes of the creature, and as in the *Spring,* we need not looke to the Heaven to see whether the *Sunne* be come neere us or not; for looking on the *Earth* we may see all greene, fresh, lively strong and vigorous. So it is with the presence of *Christ*[.][116]

This kind of description mirrors the sensory appeal that Sibbes attributes to the parables of Jesus, teaching 'heavenly truths in an earthly sensible manner',[117] that here includes the feeling of warmth as well as the sight of flourishing nature as signs of the risen sun that parallel 'the presence of *Christ*'.

Sibbes's pastoral appeal to the imagination of his audience does not extend to the writing of extended narrative allegories such as those of John Bunyan, or even proto-narrative didactic dialogues such as are found in the works of William Perkins, but some of Sibbes's illustrations have a narrative dimension:

> As a man that is rowing in a boate, let him neglect his stroake, the neglecting of one may make him tug at it five or six times after to overtake those that are before him. So nothing is gotten by sloath and negligence, wee doe but cast our selves backe the more.[118]

This narrative vignette draws in Sibbes's audience, inviting readers or hearers to imagine a particular possible incident and to put themselves in the position of the slothful rower getting behind and having to work harder to get ahead. It is

46   *The Rhetoric of Conversion in English Puritan Writing*

in part the imaginative empathizing with the rower that hopefully motivates the reader or hearer to strive after godliness, and thus Sibbes's pastoral persuasion is accomplished here by narrative and proto-literary means.

Passionate *logos* in practice

Perkins and Sibbes's appeals to both reason and imagination are evident in two works that provide case studies of their pastoral persuasion. Both of these works, Perkins's *An Exhortation to Repentance* and Sibbes's *Bowels Opened*, derive from orally delivered sermons, though both evidently reach print publication in an expanded form. Both make use of the rhetorical appeals of *logos*, *ethos* and *pathos*, and both adopt the pastoral decorum of applying Law (God's commands) and Gospel (the good news of salvation) in varying proportions to the spiritual condition of their audience.

Perkins's posthumously published *An Exhortation to Repentance* is a record of two sermons he preached at Stourbridge Fair, a long-running trade fair not far from Cambridge, though since it reads as a continuous discourse, we can presume that this is an edited version of what Perkins said and not a direct transcript. Nevertheless, it is a text that contains markers of oral delivery in its writing style. The audience of these sermons would have been mixed in social standing, in levels of education and in their spiritual experience. This work thus forms a useful case study of Perkins applying his preaching to multiple kinds of hearers, the kind of audience he calls *The Arte of Prophesying* 'a mingled people'.[119] It is also a helpful focal point for our purposes as a sermon aimed at persuading its hearers to conversion, as well as to both a personal and a national reformation.

Perkins takes as his opening text the first two verses of Zephaniah chapter 2: '*Search your selues, euen search you ô nation, not worthy to be beloued: before the Decree come forth, and you be as Chaffe that passeth on a day.*'[120] He then begins his address by analysing Zephaniah's persuasive practice in Zephaniah 2 in terms of doctrine followed by exhortation: 'In the three first verses he propoundeth the Doctrine of Repentance, and addeth some speciall reasons to mooue and stirre them vp to the practise of it.'[121] Perkins is reading the text here as if Zephaniah is a 'doctrine and use' preacher much like Perkins himself, who first outlines a doctrine and then applies it to his audience. Perkins's summary of the chapter also identifies Zephaniah's persuasive practice as *logos* (propounding doctrine) followed by *pathos* (moving and stirring the audience's emotions to guide them to action).

A Passionate Logos

47

In this way, Perkins's sermon is implicitly resuming Zephaniah's preaching, and so presenting himself as a prophet akin to Zephaniah. Perkins thereby adopts Zephaniah's *ethos*, his authoritative persona, as well as his *logos*, the content of his arguments.

Perkins then provides a logical breakdown of the text:

1. The dutie to be performed, *Search.*
2. Who must be searched: *your selues.*
3. Who must doe it. The *Iewes* [...]
4. In the second verse: the time limiting them, when to repent, *before the decree come forth.* [...]
5. A forcible reason vrging them to doe it, which lieth hid, and is necessarily implied in the fourth point: namely, that *there is a decree against them.*[122]

This illustrates the method of deriving propositional content from scriptural texts commended in *The Arte of Prophesying*, with Perkins here using both 'notation', with his first four points taking words directly from the text, and 'collection', his fifth point deriving information indirectly from the logical implications of the text.[123]

Thus far, Perkins's opening is a scholarly logical exegesis appealing to reason, which contrasts with Cicero's advice for the exordium (the opening section of a Ciceronian oration), in which one would expect a clearer *captatio benevolentiae*, seeking to win the audience's goodwill. Similarly, the ensuing references to differing opinions on whether 'Search' should be translated 'Gather' or 'fan' would seem to be of scholarly more than of general interest, but Perkins is about to get to work affectively and effectively with his language. This change of gears accords with Perkins's advice in *The Arte of Prophecying* that the preacher's voice be 'moderate' in the doctrine section but more vehement once he gets on to exhortation.[124]

For the next few pages of the octavo edition of the *Exhortation*, Perkins emphasizes the phrase '*Search your selues*', repeating the word 'search' several times, along with synonyms such as 'examine' and 'try'. As part of this repetition he introduces a related text from Lamentations, familiar to Milton scholars as the epigraph to Stanley Fish's *Surprised by Sin*: '*Let vs search and try our waies* [...] *and turne again vnto the Lord.*'[125] Perkins's words are simple, but their arrangement has an artful simplicity:

But no man can see into himselfe, nor know himselfe, but hee that doth diligently search himselfe: so that the beginning of all grace, is for a man to search and try,

48 *The Rhetoric of Conversion in English Puritan Writing*

> and fanne himselfe, that thereby he may know what is in himselfe: that so vpon the search, seeing his fearefull and damnable estate, hee may forsake himselfe & his owne waies, and turne to the Lord.[126]

This extended periodic sentence imprints itself on the hearer's ear through alliteration ('doth diligently'), rhyme ('try [...] thereby') and assonance ('estate [...] forsake [...] waies'). The word 'himselfe' occurs six times, each time at the end of a phrase and before a pause – an instance of epistrophe which emphasizes 'himselfe' as the focus of this vigorous self-examination. There is the hint of a pun in 'no man [...] nor know', perhaps intimating the self-denial of 'nor no himself'. The sibilance of 'see', 'search' and 'so' reinforces the stress on 'himselfe'. This sibilance is finally left aside with the final phrase 'and turne to the Lord', embodying the forsaking of the self in conversion.

Perkins's sermon makes use of the dichotomy between Law (God's moral commandments, identified particularly with the Law of Moses) and Gospel (the good news of salvation) that is central to the theology of the Reformer Martin Luther and to the pastoral method of Puritan practical divinity, as the Lutheran theologian Niels Hemmingsen recommends in his advice to preachers.[127] Perkins's sermon is a call to individual conversion, but it is also a call to national repentance, in keeping with the corporate focus of the Zephaniah text on the nation of Israel. After spending roughly half the work on the need for repentance, searching oneself by the Law of God, Perkins turns to the promises of the Gospel, speaking of God's love for Israel, and by extension for England. In the case of England, this divine favour is evidenced by the presence of the true gospel for the past thirty-five years of Protestant rule and the material prosperity of the nation under Elizabeth. Yet, Perkins laments, this divine love has been poorly requited by the nation's ingratitude, as England has failed to worship and obey God fully, thus incurring judgement. The failure of England rightly to receive the Gospel brings upon the nation the penalties threatened by the Law.

After the initial rational scrutiny of the text and the subsequent passionate appeal to the audience's emotions, Perkins proceeds to appeal to his hearers' imagination with his vivid extended simile of a man who crosses dangerous mountains at midnight and in the morning light is sobered to see the danger he was in.[128] Perkins draws a parallel with the regenerate believer, who only by the light of the grace he has received can see what danger he was in beforehand:

> for now hee seeth the height of the Mountaines; the steepenesse of the Hilles, the cragginesse of the Rockes, the fearful downfall, and the furious violence of the streame vnderneath, & therby seeth the extreame daunger which afore he saw not[.][129]

A Passionate Logos   49

This is a description that conjures up vivid images in the mind of Perkins's hearers, but the kind of images it conjures are not the kinds of images to which Perkins objects – they are not images of biblical narratives or divine personages that might tempt the reader or auditor to idolatry. Rather, this is a narrative vignette that anticipates the symbolic landscape in full-length literary allegories such as those of John Bunyan – there are striking parallels with an episode in *The Pilgrim's Progress* where Mount Sinai, representing the Law of God given through Moses, threatens to fall on Christian's head.[130]

In his peroration (the rousing conclusion of an oration), Perkins returns to the material surroundings of his sermon:

> Beloued, you come hither to this place, purposely to buy and sell, and thereby, to better your estates in this world: how happy then are you, if besides the good markets, you make for your bodies and estates, you learne also how to make your selues abide the triall of Gods iudgements, and how to be made pure corne, fit to replenish the garners of heauen, & how to continue Gods fauour and the Gospell to this nation.[131]

There is a tension here between Perkins's exhortation to action ('how to make your selues') and his exhortation to his audience to subject themselves to a passive process ('how to be made pure corne'). This grammatical and rhetorical tension echoes the doctrinal tension in Reformed theology between an emphasis on the passive reception of grace in conversion and the need for active human cooperation with the Spirit in the process of sanctification and godly living.

The reference to 'pure corne' alludes to the biblical metaphor of the final judgement as a separation of the wheat from the chaff, as well as the trading in grain at Stourbridge Fair. In accordance with Perkins's Augustinian reading of Jesus' parable of the wheat and the tares (Matthew 13:24-30), the 'pure corne' refers to the truly converted people of God within the mixed national Church.[132] Being 'pure corne' will save Perkins's hearers from eternal judgement, and it may also save the nation from the temporal judgements that Perkins fears will come upon it.

Perkins then develops the metaphor of his message as 'the merchandize that I bring and set to sale vnto you', a commodity offered freely to those who will take it: 'and to euery one of you, I pronounce vnto you, from the Lord, that here this blessed doctrine is offered vnto you all, in his name, *freely, and that you may buy it without money*'.[133] This is a particularly striking instance of *kairos*, the rhetorical principle of fitting one's speech to the occasion in terms of one's time, place and hearers.[134]

50   *The Rhetoric of Conversion in English Puritan Writing*

Perkins highlights the offer of salvation by punning on the word 'fair':

> If thou goe away with this lesson, thou hast a Iewel more worth, then if thou
> shouldest goe home possessed of all the huge riches of this Faire: you call this
> and such like times, *Faire times*: but if thou learne this lesson right, then thou
> maist say, that this was the fairest day in deede, that euer shon vpon thee, since
> thou wast borne.[135]

Perkins captures the rhythms of vernacular speech well here, putting conversational-sounding words into the mouth of his hearers. While punning in this context may seem incongruous, punning is a mnemonic device to help audiences remember that is often used in serious settings in the early modern period, including preaching.[136]

In keeping with classical recommendations, this is a passionate peroration:[137] 'pray against thy speciall sinnes, striue to purge them out as the poyson of thy soul'[138] ... 'Search, O search, and try your hearts and liues, renewe and reuiue your faith and repentance'.[139] This passion too is artful in its use of alliteration and repetition. To borrow a metaphor associated with Zeno of Citium, Perkins's sermon has moved from the closed fist of logical exegesis to the open palm of rhetorical exhortation, outstretched and pleading with his hearers.

Both reason and imagination are likewise at play in Sibbes's appeal to his readers in *Bowels Opened*. Sibbes's dual pastoral objective of converting sinners and consoling saints is encapsulated in one of the section headings from the table of contents in *Bowels Opened*: '*Christs transcendent excellencies serve to draw those that are not yet in Christ unto him and to comfort those that are in Christ*'.[140] The goal of preaching, as understood by Sibbes, is to bring his hearers to an assurance of belonging to Christ: '*the end of all our preaching is to assure Christ to the soule*, that we may be able to say without deceiving our owne soules, *I am my Beloveds and my Beloved is mine*.'[141] One should note, however, the qualification 'without deceiving our owne soules': Sibbes does not want his hearers to presume they have true faith when they do not, but to acquire true faith and then be confident that they have it.

Sibbes's persuasive practice in *Bowels Opened* exemplifies his appeal to both groups of hearers, although even with those 'not yet' truly converted Sibbes offers hope as well as warning:

> All professors of the Gospell are either such as are not Christs, or such as are
> his, for such as are not yet, that you may be provoked to draw to fellowship with
> Christ, Do but consider you are as branches cut off, that will wither and dye, and
> be cast into the fire, unless you be grafted into the living stock, Christ, you are

as naked persons in a storme not cloathed with any thing to stand against the storme of Gods wrath, let this force you to get into Christ.[142]

Sibbes's appeal to the 'professors' (those who profess to have faith) who as yet lack a true 'fellowship with Christ' appeals to both reason and imagination. 'Do but consider' is an appeal to the hearer's reasoning faculties, but it introduces two imaginative similes that picture what it means to be outside of Christ – the 'branches cut off' and the 'naked persons in a storm'. Sibbes apparently hopes that dwelling on these imaginative similes will more effectively communicate the plight of his readers/hearers to them. These images induce fear in these readers and appeal to their self-interest, conveying to those in this portion of Sibbes's audience that they are at risk of suffering divine judgement.

Despite Sibbes's predestinarian beliefs, he here assumes his hearers/readers have the agency to be able to choose 'to draw to fellowship with Christ' or not to do so, though there is a possible connotation of compulsion in 'let this force you to get into Christ'. 'Let this force you' is a passive imperative, enjoining Sibbes's auditors to allow something to be done to them rather than simply doing it themselves, a passive imperative that perhaps smacks of a pastoral preparationism seeking to persuade the unregenerate to do something that will make them more prone to the passive reception of unmerited saving grace. It is not entirely clear whether it is the fear of judgement induced by these images or the work of the Spirit that forces the recipient to 'get into Christ' – perhaps these are not mutually exclusive alternatives.

Yet despite this appeal to fear, Sibbes's wording is encouraging to his readers in so far as it indicates that those who 'are not yet' belonging to Christ can change their spiritual state and become united to Christ. Thus it is not the case that the unconverted are necessarily irreparably reprobate. Even in exhorting unconverted sinners, Sibbes very soon switches from metaphors of wrath to promises of forgiveness, which likewise appeal both to rational consideration and to imaginative meditation on the vivid images that Sibbes offers:

Therefore if there be any that have lived in evill courses, in former times, consider that upon repentance all shall bee forgotten, and as a mist scattered away and cast into the bottome of the Sea. Christ offers himselfe to you, these are the times, this is the houre of grace, now the water is stirring for you to enter: doe but entertaine Christ, and desire that hee may bee yours to rule you and guide you, and all will be well for the time to come.[143]

Whilst a page earlier the waters of the storm are a threatening sign of judgement, here the water imagery offers hope: the sea in which sins are buried and forgotten

52   *The Rhetoric of Conversion in English Puritan Writing*

and the pool of Bethesda in which the sick are healed.[144] There is an insistent urgency to the pulse of the deictic indicators 'these [...] this [...] now' that by indicating time and place call for a response here and now.

Sibbes proceeds to bring together the two halves of the Law-Gospel dialectic, in which the Law convicts people of their guilt and then the Gospel offers them forgiveness, placing them into a highly patterned verbal juxtaposition:

> Doe not object I am a loathsome creature full of rebellions.
> *Christ doth not match with you, because you are good, but to make you good,*
> Christ takes you not with any dowry, all that hee requires is to confesse your beggery and to come with emptinesse. He takes us not because we are cleane, but because he wil purge us, he takes us in our bloud when hee first takes us, Let none despaire either for want of worth or of strength, Christ seeth that for strength we are dead, and for worth, we are enemies, but hee gives us both spirituall strength and worth, takes us neare to himselfe and enricheth us. Let none therefore bee discouraged, it is our office, thus to lay open and offer the riches of Christ[.][145]

The figure of anaphora and near-anaphoric phrasing link 'Christ takes you not' ... 'He takes us not' ... 'he takes us'. The verbal parallelism of 'to confesse' and 'to come', 'not because' and 'but because' weigh the guilt of sin condemned by the Law against the promise of grace held out in the Gospel, with the verbal structure enacting the subsuming of guilt by grace. Even to those who are presently unconverted sinners Sibbes's words are 'Let none despaire' and the similarly sounding parallel 'Let none therefore bee discouraged'. It seems that these particular unconverted persons are not obstinate sinners but rather anxious seekers to whom encouragement can be directed. Though threats of damnation are present in Sibbes's preaching as transmitted in *Bowels Opened*, Sibbes prefers the carrot of grace to the stick of judgement.

The paradiastolic dynamic of satanic rhetoric

However, divine persuasion is not the only variety on offer. Perkins and Sibbes, along with the other Puritan ministers considered in this book, see the devil as a cunning persuader, who like God, also seeks to persuade through the words and actions of human agents.

The slipperiness of satanic rhetoric in the work of Perkins and Sibbes can be illuminated by reference to the sixteenth-century German rhetorician Johann (Johannes) Susenbrotus's textbook *Epitome troporum ac schematum*, which speaks of the devil in relation to paradiastole, the figure that excuses a vice

A Passionate Logos

by calling it by the name of the nearest virtue, for instance, calling cowardice prudence or to calling rashness courage.[146] This way of conceptualizing the perverse rhetoric of vice is based on an Aristotelian view of ethics in which virtue is the golden mean between two opposite vices – in Aristotle's understanding, true courage entails having the right degree of boldness rather than its deficiency, cowardice, or its excess, foolhardiness.[147]

Susenbrotus comments: 'we have an example of *paradiastole* when vices show themselves under the guise of virtue, and by this means even the Devil himself can be transfigured into an Angel of light.'[148] Susenbrotus is here alluding to a biblical phrase from 2 Corinthians 11:14, whose context is a polemical attack by St Paul on his doctrinal opponents, whom he sees as agents of Satan seeking to deceive the Corinthian Christians:

> For such are false apostles, deceitful workers, transforming themselves into the apostles of Christ. And no marvel; for Satan himself is transformed into an angel of light. Therefore it is no great thing if his ministers also be transformed as the ministers of righteousness; whose end shall be according to their works.
>
> (2 Corinthians 11:13-15)

Paradiastole is defined in the Elizabethan rhetoric manuals of Henry Peacham, George Puttenham and Angel Day,[149] but it is more vividly conveyed (though not by name) in an early-sixteenth-century poem by Sir Thomas Wyatt:

> With the neryst virtue to cloke always the vise
> And as to pourpose like wise it shall fall
> To press the vertue that it may not rise;
> As dronkenes good felloweshippe to call,
> The frendly ffoo with his dowble face
> Say he is gentill and courtois therewithal;
> And say that Favell hath a goodly grace
> In eloquence, and crueltie to name
> Zele of Justice and chaunge in tyme and place[.][150]

In early modern studies, interest in the paradiastolic dynamic has been revived by historian Quentin Skinner, who observes that the examples of paradiastole used by Tudor rhetoricians were nearly all taken from the classical accounts, with a few exceptions:

> [Thomas] Wilson proposes one new example, which Peacham repeats: that of excusing gluttony and drunkenness as good fellowship. Peacham adds two

54   *The Rhetoric of Conversion in English Puritan Writing*

more, both of which gesture at his puritan sympathies: one is excusing idolatry as 'pure religion', the other excusing pride as 'cleanlynesse'.[151]

The paradiastolic redescription of drunkenness as good fellowship identified by Wyatt's poem and Peacham's manual is found also in Perkins's work. In a varied list of the moral and religious errors that are characteristic of 'ignorant people', Perkins tells us that one of the errors of the ignorant is to believe 'That drinking and bezeling in the ale-house or tauerne, is good fellowship, and shewes a good kind nature, and maintaines neighbourhood'.[152] This drink-lubricated form of sociability is evidently considered a virtue by the masses (as represented by Perkins) and a vice by Perkins himself.

Sibbes similarly characterizes the carnal self-deception of sinners in excusing their vices as paradiastolic:

> Though we desire to know all diseases of the body by their proper names, yet wee will conceive of sinfull passions of the soule under milder termes; as *lust* under *love, rage* under *just anger, murmuring* under *just displeasure, &c.* thus whilest wee flatter our griefe, what hope of cure![153]

The agents of satanic mispersuasion deceive themselves and others through misnaming: they have 'a reprobate judgement of persons and things', which 'commeth under a *woe, to call ill good, and good ill*', and they 'abuse the judgement of others by sophistry and flattery, *deceivers, and being deceived*'.[154]

However, the satanic paradiastole that Perkins and Sibbes are most concerned to counter is not the paradiastole of outward actions, with which the classical ethical tradition was primarily concerned, but a paradiastole of inward spiritual experience leading those deceived into misreading their experience in relation to the Law and the Gospel. It is here that satanic paradiastole is most deadly.

In Perkins's didactic dialogue, *A Dialogue of the State of a Christian Man*, a character named Eusebius tells his friend Timotheus that, prior to his conversion, the devil 'did often perswade my secure conscience that I was the child of God'.[155] This is a false persuasion that counterfeits to the pre-regenerate Eusebius the assurance attainable by the elect before he is entitled to it, designed to make Eusebius complacent and thus keep him from seeking true repentance and saving faith. In *A Golden Chaine*, Perkins tells us that those who are certain of their salvation may be relying either on the 'full perswasion' of the Holy Spirit or on 'their owne carnall presumption'.[156] It is difficult for the observer to distinguish the two.

Conversely, while the devil endeavours to have 'carnall presumption' taken for godly persuasion, he tries to make the Christian doubt his assurance by

A Passionate Logos

55

making it appear to be presumptuous. This is also illustrated by the experience of the fictional Eusebius, when Eusebius takes Timotheus into his confidence as 'a Christian and a faithfull friend' and confesses that the 'dearth' of the previous year led him into the sin of sheep-stealing. Afterwards, although he confessed to his neighbour and made restitution, Eusebius was afflicted with doubt regarding his spiritual status: 'Then the deuill assailed me on euery side, to perswade me that God had cast me away'.[157] Both Eusebius's pre-conversion belief that he was already a child of God and his recent fear that he might be reprobate after all are deceptions of Satan. Though apparently opposite in content, both of these states of mind are doctrinally erroneous and so both are identified as false persuasions that misread the available signs.

In another of Perkins's dialogues, Satan himself appears, telling the Christian who claims to be 'fully perswaded' that 'This thy full perswasion is onely a phantasie, and a strong imagination of thine owne head: it goeth not with thee as thou thinkest'.[158] Conviction of sin (from the Holy Spirit) and despair of salvation (from the devil) are perilously close to one another.

In *A Treatise Tending unto a Declaration*, Perkins warns:

> it may be thought that Satan is ready with some false perwasion to deceiue him. For this is his propertie, that vpon whom God threateneth death, there Satan is bold to pronounce life and saluation: as on the contrarie, to those, to whom God pronounceth love and mercie, to those (I say) he threatneth displeasure and damnation: such malice hath he against Gods children.[159]

Perkins seeks at the same time to console true believers who think that they are devoid of faith when they are not and to warn hypocrites who think that they have faith when in fact they do not. This is a tricky pastoral endeavour, and R. T. Kendall, for one, thinks that Perkins falls off the tightrope by attributing to both true believers and reprobates states of mind that are subjectively indistinguishable from one another.[160]

Conviction can be tipped into despair, and presumption can be passed off as assurance.[161] It would not be quite accurate to describe this spiritual deception in terms of the Aristotelian ethics typically exploited in paradiastole. Presumption does not consist in overmuch confidence but in misplaced confidence, though despair might be considered an excess of spiritual affliction. However, both paradiastole in the ethical sphere and this paradiastole of spiritual affections exploit the resemblance of the desired state and its counterfeit for nefarious ends.

As in Perkins's warnings on satanic rhetoric, Sibbes's Satan also deploys a kind of spiritual paradiastole that attacks true assurance by telling believers that

56   *The Rhetoric of Conversion in English Puritan Writing*

it is presumptuous and excuses the presumptuous complacency of unregenerate sinners by telling them that it is proper confidence. Whereas the Spirit of God and the judicious physicians of the soul labour to bring low those who are presumptuously complacent and to raise up those who are cast down, Satan's strategy is the opposite: to give false security to carnal sinners and ungrounded fears to those who are in a state of grace. The epistle 'To the Christian Reader' that opens *The Soules Conflict* outlines this dynamic.

> *There be two sorts of people alwaies in the visible Church. One that Satan keepes under with false peace, whose life is nothing but a diversion to present contentments, and a running away from God and their owne hearts, which they know can speake no good unto them; these speake peace to themselves, but God speakes none[.]*[162]

This first group is deceived by Satan but is also self-deceived and thus culpable: there is a sense in which they '*know*' that '*God and their owne hearts*' will not give them spiritual comfort, but they persuade themselves otherwise by suppressing their conscience in order to '*speake peace to themselves*'. Sibbes states that these are not the people to whom his predominantly consolatory treatise is primarily addressed, since '*the way for these men to enjoy comfort, is to be soundly troubled*'.[163]

Sibbes's particular concern is for the second group of people:

> *But there is another sort of people, who being drawn out of Satans kingdome, and within the Covenant of grace, whom Satan labours to unsettle and disquiet: being the God of the world, he is vexed to see men in the world, walke above the world. Since he cannot hinder their estate, he will trouble their peace, and dampe their spirits, and cut a sunder the sinewes of all their endeavours.*[164]

These people are true believers but are troubled by Satan, who seeks to persuade them that their confidence of attaining salvation is unfounded. To counter this satanic rhetoric of anxiety, Sibbes engages in a rhetoric of assurance, seeking to persuade anxious believers that they truly possess saving faith.

Sibbes calls Satan a rhetorician in the context of warning against anxieties that keep believers from a settled assurance of their salvation:

> How many imagine their *failings*, to be *fallings*, and their *fallings*, to be *fallings away*? *Infirmities* to be *Presumptions*: every *sinne against Conscience*, to be the sinne against the *Holy Ghost*? unto which misapprehensions, weake and dark spirits are subject. And Satan (as a cunning Rhetorician) here inlargeth the fancy, to apprehend things bigger then they are, Satan abuseth confident spirits another contrary way: to apprehend great sinnes as little; and little as none.[165]

Satan here appeals to 'the fancy', just as the godly preacher should, and exhibits a diabolic decorum, being able to accommodate his temptations to the characteristic weaknesses of individuals. In this case, 'fancy' refers not so much to visual images in the mind as to misguided opinions that are fantasy in the negative sense. Anxious believers are led by satanic misperception to blow their sins and failings out of proportion in such a way as to doubt that they are in a state of grace. Conversely, in tempting those who are complacently unregenerate, Satan exploits the imagination to confer a diminished perception of the culpability of sin and thus of the need for grace. Satanic rhetoric thus abuses the imagination to make the one deceived prone to either despair or presumption. This abuse of the fancy is closely tied to a misuse of the rational faculties to deceive: '*False reasoning*, and errour in our discourse, as that wee have no grace when wee feele none, feeling is not alwayes a fit rule to judge our states by.'[166]

Satan '*labours to breed misperswasions*',[167] twisting both reason and imagination in order to seduce the unwary. Satan's mispersuasion operates especially through appeal to the affections, which are susceptible to easy manipulation in those whose fancy is not properly regulated by doctrinally informed reason: 'Words affect strangely; they have a strange force with men, especially in weake fancies, that are not grounded in their judgement and faith.'[168] Words 'affect', that is, they have power over the affections, while a faith grounded in 'judgement', that is, a rightly informed rational faculty, is seen here as a defence against the overpowering of the fancy through speech.

Sibbes uses as an example of deceptive words that misdirect the affections the 'shrewd oration' of the ten spies who warned the Israelites against entering the promised land:[169] 'It was a speech discomfortable, and it wrought so, that it made them all murmur, and be discouraged. It is not to be thought what mischiefe comes from speech, cunningly handled.'[170] This rhetoric of unbelief, like the rhetoric of faith, is efficacious – the speech 'wrought so', with a suggestion of compulsion in 'made them'.

Just as godly persuasion appeals to reason as well as imagination, so satanic mispersuasion twists reason as well as imagination in order to accomplish its nefarious purposes:

> But sinne is a worke of darknesse, and therefore shunnes not onely the light of grace, but even the light of reason. Yet sinne seldome wants a seeming reason, *Men will not goe to hell without a shew of reason.* But such be sophisticall fallacies, not reasons; and therefore sinners are said to play the sophisters with themselves.[171]

Sophistry is a term used for deceitful and fallacious rhetoric and logic derived from Plato's attack on the sophists, the itinerant paid teachers of the language arts that Plato suspected of being more concerned about eloquence than truth.

As in the work of other writers considered in this book, at times divine and diabolic strategies of persuasion as presented by Sibbes are disturbingly similar. This is the case, for instance, in a passage of *The Bruised Reede* where Sibbes is reassuring his readers that Christ is merciful to the penitent:

> Since CHRIST is thus comfortably set out unto us, let us not beleeve Satans representations of him. When we are troubled in conscience for our sinnes, his manner is then to present him to the afflicted soule as a most severe Iudge armed with Iustice against us. But then let us present him to our soules, as thus offered to our view by GOD himselfe, as holding out a Scepter of mercy, and spreading his armes to receive us.[172]

Satan misleads and mispersuades the believer by misrepresenting Christ, giving a false picture of Christ to the believer's imagination that will misinform that person's affections. There is a quasi-visual quality to 'Satans representations' of Christ here. The theological problem with the picture of Christ 'as a most severe Iudge' is not that it is inaccurate, but that it is misapplied: Christ will be 'a most severe Iudge' to the impenitent, but to those who are truly repentant he will show mercy. Sibbes counteracts the satanic misrepresentation through his own appeal to the imagination through the pictures of Christ's outstretched sceptre and outspread welcoming arms.

However, Sibbes concedes that Christ is sometimes felt to be an enemy because Christ himself is playing such a role:

> CHRIST may act the part of an enemy a little while as *Ioseph* did, but it is to make way for acting his own part of mercy in a more seasonable time; hee cannot hold in his bowells long, he seemeth to wrastle with us, as with *Iacob*, but hee supplyes us with hidden strength, at length to get the better. Faith pulls off the vizard from his face, and sees a loving heart under contrary appearances.[173]

Christ is here seen as a performer, an actor who plays the enemy. Putting on a mask or 'vizard' echoes the etymology of the rhetorical figure prosopopoeia, which alludes to putting on the mask (*prosopon*) of another like an ancient Greek actor. However, Christ's true affections ('bowells') make him unable to play this role indefinitely – his love must break through. As Alec Ryrie notes of this passage, God himself supplies the strength to contend with God, thus authorizing forceful and importunate prayer in the face of adverse circumstances.[174] This

A Passionate Logos 59

analogy creates a contrast between Christ's temporary hiddenness, which gives way to his manifest goodness, and Satan's wilful misrepresentation of Christ. While Satan is an artist who caricatures Christ in order to alienate the believer from him, Christ is an actor who at times disguises himself in order to teach the believer a lesson.

There is a striking parallel here with Luther's *Lectures on Genesis*, in which he speaks of Joseph as ruler of Egypt 'playing a wonderful kind of game' by acting like an enemy to his brothers in order to bring them to repentance, and uses this as an illustration of how God acts towards his 'saints':

> For in trials God conducts Himself towards His saints just as Joseph conducts himself towards his brothers. He does not play with them in this way and show himself so hard out of a desire for revenge or because he hates them, for he weeps, and his heart is stirred. But he pretends and feigns that he is a tyrant who wants them put out of the way and destroyed [...] with no other end in view than to put their patience to the test and thus to drive them to acknowledge their sin and the mercy of God.[175]

These pages in *The Bruised Reede* also closely echo a section of Luther's 1545 commentary on Galatians, one of Luther's most influential works in the English context.[176] Luther cautions:

> Therfore if Christe appeare in the likenes of an angry iudge, or of a lawmaker that requireth a strait accompt of our life past: then let vs assure our selues that it is not Christ but a raging feende.[177]

Luther assures his readers that the voice that condemns believers is not that of Christ in terms that increase the suspicion that Sibbes has been reading Luther:

> Christ speaketh not to poore afflicted consciences after this maner: He addeth not affliction to the afflicted: He breaketh not the brused reede, neither quencheth he the smoking flaxe.[178]

Elsewhere in *The Bruised Reede*, Satan's misrepresentation seeks to undermine Christ's *ethos* as the divine physician: 'A good conceit of the Physitian (we say) is halfe the cure; Let us not suffer Sathan to transforme Christ unto us, to bee otherwise then he is to those that are his.'[179] Christ is thus falsely represented to the imagination as unmerciful by Satan in order to undermine the rhetorical *ethos* of Christ as the good physician that will encourage the believer to partake of his benefits.

For Sibbes, the remedy for the satanic rhetoric of false guilt is a 'divine Rhetorick' of consolation, in which the believer needs actively to participate:

> When therefore *Conscience* joyning with Sathan, sets out thy sinne in its colours, labour thou by faith to set out *God* in his colours, infinite in mercy and loving kindnesse. Here lies the art of a Christian; It is divine Rhetorick thus to perswade and set downe the soule.[180]

In the war of divine rhetoric against satanic rhetoric, the reader has a rhetorical responsibility to persuade himself or herself of the truth and is thus responsible for the self-persuasion of representing God to oneself in his right 'colours'.

The battle of divine rhetoric against satanic rhetoric in Perkins and Sibbes is one in which the preacher, the lay Christian, and the prospective convert or Christian in need of assurance all have a responsibility to engage. This battle involves both divine and diabolical sides deploying reason and imagination, and both reason and imagination are faculties that can lead individuals astray when abused and, when rightly regulated, can lead people towards an existential engagement with truth that gives them access to and assurance of salvation.

Notes

1   William Perkins, *A Godly and Learned Exposition or Commentarie upon the Three First Chapters of the Revelation* (London, 1606), p. 69.

2   For overviews of Perkins's life and thought, see especially W. B. Patterson, *William Perkins and the Making of a Protestant England* (Oxford: Oxford University Press, 2014), Leif Dixon, *Practical Predestinarians in England, c. 1590–1640* (Farnham: Ashgate, 2014), Chapter 2, 'William Perkins and the Search for Certainty' (pp. 61–122), Richard A. Muller, *Grace and Freedom: William Perkins and the Early Modern Reformed Understanding of Free Choice and Divine Grace* (Oxford: Oxford University Press, 2020), and Ian Breward, 'Introduction', in Ian Breward (ed.), *The Work of William Perkins* (Abingdon: Sutton Courtenay Press, 1970), pp. 1–13.

3   Richard Sibbes, *The Bruised Reede, and Smoaking Flax* (London, 1630), sig. a7v. For overviews of Sibbes's life and work, see especially Mark Dever, *Richard Sibbes: Puritanism and Calvinism in Late Elizabethan and Early Stuart England* (Macon, GA: Mercer University Press, 2000), and R. N. Frost, *Richard Sibbes: God's Spreading Goodness* (Vancouver, WA: Cor Deo, 2012).

4   Whether or not Perkins should be labelled a Puritan is a matter of scholarly debate. W. B. Patterson argues that he should not be as he is a defender of the established Church who is relatively silent on matters of church government and ceremony (Patterson, *William Perkins*, esp. pp. 40–63). I agree with Richard Muller's nuanced middle stance – that 'Perkins was not an Elizabethan Puritan' in the sense of agitating for change in ecclesiastical structures, but that 'The specific aspects of his

thought most distinctively "Puritan" or proto-Puritan are his analyses of the inward person in the examinations of the struggles of sin, faith, and assurance' and 'his thought had a major impact, indeed, an archetypal one, on later Puritan piety and doctrine' (Muller, *Grace and Freedom*, p. 14).

5   Richard Sibbes, *Bowels Opened, or, A Discovery of the Neere and Deere Love, Union and Communion Betwixt Christ and the Church, and Consequently Betwixt Him and Every Beleeving Soule* (London, 1639), pp. 148–9.

6   This is in keeping with a thesis that Sibbes defended on taking his Bachelor of Divinity degree in 1610: '*Dei Decretum non tollit libertatem voluntatis*' ('that the decree of God does not take away the freedom of the will') (Dever, *Richard Sibbes*, pp. 38, 100, citing British Library, Harleian MS, f. 88).

7   William Perkins, *A Reformed Catholike* (London, 1597), p. 640, cited in Muller, *Grace and Freedom*, pp. 126–7.

8   For a thorough technical account of the concurrence of human and divine wills in Perkins's thought, see Muller, *Grace and Freedom*. On how this concurrence operates in conversion, see especially Chapter 5, 'Liberty Restored: Grace and the Will in Redemption and Glorification', pp. 125–54.

9   Sibbes, *Bruised Reede*, sig. a7v.

10   On the sealing of the Spirit and its connection with the experience of assurance of salvation, see, for instance, Frost, *Richard Sibbes*, pp. 257–8, and Brett A. Rempel, 'The Trinitarian Pattern of Redemption in Richard Sibbes (1577–1635)', *Journal of Reformed Theology*, 13.1 (June 2019), 22–5.

11   Richard Sibbes, *A Fountain Sealed: or, The Duty of the Sealed to the Spirit, and the Worke of the Spirit in Sealing* (London, 1637), pp. 243–4.

12   See Richard A. Muller, 'Perkins' *A Golden Chaine*: Predestinarian System or Schematized *Ordo salutis?*', *The Sixteenth Century Journal*, 9.1 (April 1978), 68–81.

13   Richard Sibbes, *The Soules Conflict with It Selfe, and Victory over It Self by Faith* (London, 1635), pp. 25–6.

14   William Perkins, *A Treatise Tending unto a Declaration*, in *Workes of That Famous and Worthie Minister of Christ in the Vniversitie of Cambridge, M. W. Perkins*, 3 vols. (Cambridge, 1608–9), I:360.

15   Johann Susenbrotus, *Epitome troporum ac schematum* (1562), p. 46, cited in Quentin Skinner, 'Paradiastole: Redescribing the Vices as Virtues', in Sylvia Adamson, Gavin Alexander and Katrin Ettenhuber (eds.), *Renaissance Figures of Speech* (Cambridge: Cambridge University Press, 2007), p. 160. For a fuller discussion of this topic, see David Parry, 'As an Angel of Light: Satanic Rhetoric in Early Modern Literature and Theology', in Gregor Thuswalder and Daniel Russ (eds.), *The Hermeneutics of Hell: Devilish Visions and Visions of the Devil* (Cham, Switzerland: Palgrave Macmillan, 2017), pp. 47–71.

16   Perkins, *Arte of Prophecying*, in *Workes*, II:742.

17 Perkins, *Arte of Prophecying*, in *Workes*, II:742.

18 Perkins, *Arte of Prophecying*, in *Workes*, II:742.

19 Perkins, *Arte of Prophecying*, in *Workes*, II:745.

20 As Jennifer Clement notes, 'its title presumably would not have raised eyebrows as it would, and does, today', since it uses 'bowels' to denote the inner organs as the seat of emotion, as in phrases such as 'bowels of compassion' (1 John 3:17) and 'bowels of mercies' (Colossians 3:12) in the King James Bible that are widely deployed by early modern preachers and religious writers (Jennifer Clement, 'Bowels, Emotion, and Metaphor in Early Modern English Sermons', *The Seventeenth Century*, 35.4 (2020), p. 435: see especially pp. 435 and 441–2 for instances of other religious writers using the language of 'bowels').

21 On early modern devotional reading and appropriation of the Song of Songs, see, for instance, Erica Longfellow, *Women and Religious Writing in Early Modern England* (Cambridge: Cambridge University Press, 2009), pp. 26–58, Elizabeth Clarke, *Politics, Religion and the Song of Songs in Seventeenth-Century England* (Houndmills, Basingstoke: Palgrave Macmillan, 2011), and Noam Flinker, *The Song of Songs in English Renaissance Literature: Kisses of Their Mouths* (Cambridge: D. S. Brewer, 2000).

22 Sibbes, *Bowels Opened*, p. 204.

23 Sibbes, *Bowels Opened*, pp. 142–3.

24 Sibbes, *Bowels Opened*, p. 48. These later Puritan authors use the word '*paranymphi*' of ministers in the same context: William Gouge, *Of Domesticall Duties* (London, 1622), p. 71; Matthias Milward, *The Souldiers Triumph and the Preachers Glory* (London, 1641), p. 4; and Thomas Watson, *The Saints Delight* (London, 1657), p. 387.

25 Sibbes, *Bowels Opened*, p. 148.

26 On the wide spectrum of Puritan approaches to education and human knowledge, see John Morgan, *Godly Learning: Puritan Attitudes Towards Reason, Learning, and Education, 1560-1640* (Cambridge: Cambridge University Press, 1986).

27 Perkins, *An Exposition of the Symbole or Creed of the Apostles*, in *Workes*, I:204.

28 Perkins, *The Whole Treatise of the Cases of Conscience*, in *Workes*, II:1.

29 Though not originating with Calvin, Calvin's exposition of the threefold office of Christ in *Institutes* II.15 proved particularly influential in the Reformed tradition. See Richard A. Muller, *Christ and the Decree: Christology and Predestination in Reformed Theology from Calvin to Perkins* (Durham, NC: Labyrinth Press, 1986), pp. 31–3, 193 n. 114.

30 Perkins, *The Whole Treatise of the Cases of Conscience*, in *Workes*, II:2.

31 Perkins, *A Commentarie or Exposition vpon the Five First Chapters of the Epistle to the Galatians*, in *Workes*, II:173.

32 Perkins, *A Treatise of the Duties and Dignities of the Ministry*, in *M. Perkins, His Exhortation to Repentance, Out of Zephaniah: Preached in 2. Sermons in Sturbridge*

Faire. Together with Two Treatises of the Duties and Dignitie of the Ministrie: Deliuered Publiquely in the Vniuersitie of Cambridge (London, 1605), p. 5 (second pagination).

33 See, for instance, William T. Costello, *The Scholastic Curriculum at Early Seventeenth-Century Cambridge* (Cambridge, MA: Harvard University Press, 1958); Lisa Jardine, 'Humanism and the Sixteenth Century Cambridge Arts Course', *History of Education*, 4 (1975), 16–31; Mordechai Feingold, *The Mathematician's Apprenticeship* (Cambridge: Cambridge University Press, 1984), Chapter 1, 'The Statutes' (pp. 23–44); Christopher Brooke, 'Learning and Doctrine 1550-1660', in Victor Morgan with Christopher Brooke, *A History of the University of Cambridge*, Vol II. *1546-1750* (Cambridge: Cambridge University Press, 2004), pp. 437–63.

34 On the rhetorical training found in the grammar schools, see, for instance, Peter Mack, *Elizabethan Rhetoric: Theory and Practice* (Cambridge: Cambridge University Press, 2002), Chapter 1, 'Rhetoric in the Grammar School' (pp. 11–47).

35 However, what was actually taught in the colleges and in what order and proportion varied according to the preferences of each tutor. The surviving account books of Joseph Mede, a fellow of Christ's College who matriculated the year after Perkins's death and taught at Christ's during Milton's student days, show that Mede required that his undergraduate students purchase texts by Aristotle and Cicero, whose works include some that form the fountainhead of the classical rhetorical tradition. See Harris Francis Fletcher, *The Intellectual Development of John Milton*, 2 vols (Urbana: University of Illinois Press, 1956–61), II:32, 38–9, 77–84, and Quentin Skinner, *From Humanism to Hobbes: Studies in Rhetoric and Politics* (Cambridge: Cambridge University Press, 2018), Chapter 6, 'The Generation of John Milton at Cambridge', pp. 118–38.

36 Perkins, *A Treatise of the Duties and Dignities of the Ministry*, p. 11.

37 Perkins, *A Treatise of the Duties and Dignities of the Ministry*, p. 12.

38 Sibbes, *Bruised Reede*, pp. 69–70.

39 The work concludes with a list of writers on preaching from whom Perkins is drawing, but it does not contain the names of writers in the liberal arts such as Aristotle, Cicero and Ramus, all of whom arguably influence *The Arte of Prophecying.*

40 Harry S. Stout uses these five canons of rhetoric to structure his book on preaching in the North American colonies: *The New England Soul: Preaching and Religious Culture in Colonial New England* (Oxford: Oxford University Press, 1986, rep. 2012).

41 Perkins, *Arte of Prophecying*, in *Workes*, II:736.

42 The separation of these processes into two distinct parts, however, echoes the reorganization of the language arts associated with the sixteenth-century French Protestant scholar Peter Ramus and the Ramist tradition that followed in his wake,

which assigns *inventio* and *dispositio* to the domain of logic, leaving *elocutio* and *actio* only to rhetoric. This structure is similar to that of Augustine's *De Doctrina Christiana*, in which the Christian orator's *inventio*, where he finds the matter for his speech, is biblical exegesis, which takes up the first three books of Augustine's treatise, while the fourth book deals with style and delivery. For a sampling of recent work that argues that Ramism is a pedagogical reorganization of the classical logical and rhetorical traditions rather than a radical break with them as supposed by earlier scholarship, see Steven J. Reid and Emma Annette Wilson (eds.), *Ramus, Pedagogy and the Liberal Arts: Ramism in Britain and the Wider World* (Farnham: Ashgate, 2011).

43 Mary Morrissey, 'Scripture, Style and Persuasion in Seventeenth-Century English Theories of Preaching', *Journal of Ecclesiastical History*, 53.4 (October 2002), p. 692.

44 Debora K. Shuger, *Sacred Rhetoric: The Christian Grand Style in the English Renaissance* (Princeton, NJ: Princeton University Press, 1988), p. 70.

45 Perkins, *Arte of Prophecying*, in *Workes*, II:759.

46 Aristotle, *Rhetoric*, 1355a.

47 Perkins, *Arte of Prophecying*, in *Workes*, II:759. The Latin tag is variously attributed and does not seem to correspond exactly to any known classical author, though the sentiment is found in several. The New England Puritan Increase Mather tells us that his father Richard 'would often use that saying, *Artis est celare Artem*' (Increase Mather, *The Life and Death of That Reverend Man of God, Mr. Richard Mather, Teacher of the Church in Dorchester in New-England* (Cambridge, MA, 1670), p. 31). William Dyrness suggests that it can be traced to Ovid's *Ars Amatoria*, Book II, l. 313: 'If art is concealed, it succeeds' (William A. Dyrness, *Reformed Theology and Visual Culture: The Protestant Imagination from Calvin to Edwards* (Cambridge: Cambridge University Press, 2004), p. 189 n. 9). W. B. Patterson also references Ovid, though more circumspectly: 'This saying is a classical adage, one version of which is to be found in Ovid's *The Art of Love*' (Patterson, *William Perkins*, p. 89).

48 See, for instance, G. W. Pigman III, 'Versions of Imitation in the Renaissance', *Renaissance Quarterly*, 33.1 (Spring 1980), 1–30.

49 Perkins, *Arte of Prophecying*, in *Workes*, II:759.

50 See Peter Auksi, *Christian Plain Style: The Evolution of a Spiritual Ideal* (Montreal and Kingston: McGill-Queen's University Press, 1995), Chapter 2, 'The Plain Style in Classical Rhetoric', pp. 33–66, esp. 51–2, citing Dionysius on Lysias ('For this artlessness is itself the product of art: the relaxed structure is really under control, and it is in the very illusion of not having been composed with masterly skill that the mastery lies'), and 55–7 (on Cicero's *Orator*).

51 Sibbes, *Soules Conflict*, pp. 414–15.

52 Sibbes, *Soules Conflict*, p. 200.

53 Janice Knight, *Orthodoxies in Massachusetts: Rereading American Puritanism* (Cambridge, MA: Harvard University Press, 1994), pp. 2–4 and *passim*.

54 Frost, *Richard Sibbes*, esp. pp. 71–113.

55 Cf. Leif Dixon's argument that Perkins sees faith as a certain knowledge (Dixon, *Practical Predestinarians*, esp. pp. 91–9).

56 Perkins, *An Exposition of the Symbole or Creed of the Apostles*, in *Workes*, I:126.

57 Paul R. Schaefer, 'Protestant "Scholasticism" at Elizabethan Cambridge: William Perkins and a Reformed Theology of the Heart', in Carl R. Trueman and R. S. Clark (eds.), *Protestant Scholasticism: Essays in Reassessment* (Carlisle: Paternoster, 1999), p. 159.

58 Perkins, *A Treatise Tending unto a Declaration*, in *Workes*, I:360.

59 Schaefer, 'Protestant "Scholasticism"', citing Perkins, *An Exposition of the Symbole or Creed of the Apostles*, in *Workes*, I:124.

60 Perkins, *A Direction for the Governement of the Tongue*, in *Workes*, I:441.

61 William Perkins, *A Warning against the Idolatrie of the Last Times* (Cambridge, 1601), pp. 107–8.

62 Raphael Hallett, 'Pictures of Print: Pierre Ramus, William Perkins and the Reformed Imagination', in Tara Hamling and Richard L. Williams (eds.), *Art Reformed: Re-assessing the Impact of the Reformation on the Visual Arts* (Newcastle: Cambridge Scholars, 2007), p. 206.

63 Donald K. McKim, *Ramism in William Perkins' Theology* (New York: Peter Lang, 1987), p. 58.

64 Perkins, *A Warning against the Idolatrie of the Last Times*, p. 108.

65 Perkins, *An Exposition of the Symbole or Creed of the Apostles*, in *Workes*, I:191.

66 Louis L. Martz, *The Poetry of Meditation; a Study in English Religious Literature of the Seventeenth Century* (New Haven: Yale University Press, 1954).

67 Perkins, *The Foundation of Christian Religion*, in *Workes*, I:3.

68 2 Kings 4:32–5; cf. 1 Kings 17:17–24 for a parallel story featuring Elisha's mentor Elijah.

69 Perkins, *A Direction for the Governement of the Tongue*, in *Workes*, I:439.

70 Perkins, *A Warning against the Idolatrie of the Last Times*, pp. 101–2, attacks the popish inclination 'to make Gods of crucifixes'.

71 William Haller, *The Rise of Puritanism; or, The Way to the New Jerusalem as Set Forth in Pulpit and Press from Thomas Cartwright to John Lilburne and John Milton, 1570–1643* (New York: Columbia University Press, 1938), p. 132.

72 Haller, *Rise of Puritanism*, p. 129.

73 Perkins, *An Exposition of the Symbole or Creed of the Apostles*, in *Workes*, I:159.

74 Perkins, *An Exposition of the Symbole or Creed of the Apostles*, in *Workes*, I:126.

75 Perkins, *An Exposition of the Symbole or Creed of the Apostles*, in *Workes*, I:241.

76 Perkins, *The Foundation of Christian Religion*, in *Workes*, I:A2r.

77 Arthur Dent, *The Plain Mans Path-way to Heaven Wherein Every Man May Clearly See Whether He Shall Be Saved or Damned* (London, 1601), p. 394.

78 Perkins, *A Case of Conscience*, in *Workes*, I:421–8.

79 Perkins, *A Case of Conscience*, in *Workes*, I:421. Square brackets in original.

80 Patterson, *William Perkins*, p. 96.

81 Patterson, *William Perkins*, p. 96.

82 Rosemary Sisson suggests that 'Perkins' work clearly foreshadows Bunyan's in its lively style and in the comedy of its characterization', as well as in the use of the name Christian for a character ('William Perkins, Apologist for the Elizabethan Church of England', *Modern Language Review*, 47.4 (October 1952), 495–502 (p. 497).

83 Perkins, *A Fruitfull Dialogue Concerning the Ende of the World betweene a Christian and a Worldling*, in *Workes*, III:465.

84 Nancy Rosenfeld, *John Bunyan's Imaginary Writings in Context* (New York: Routledge, 2018), esp. pp. 59–67, drawing on E. M. Forster, *Aspects of the Novel* (San Diego, CA: Harcourt, 1955).

85 Perkins, *A Fruitfull Dialogue*, in *Workes*, III:465.

86 See Patterson, *William Perkins*, Chapter 6, 'The Quest for Social Justice' (pp. 135–67).

87 Perkins, *A Fruitfull Dialogue*, in *Workes*, III:466.

88 Perkins, *A Fruitfull Dialogue*, in *Workes*, III:467.

89 Perkins, *A Fruitfull Dialogue*, in *Workes*, III:467.

90 Perkins, *A Fruitfull Dialogue*, in *Workes*, III:476.

91 Nigel Smith, *Perfection Proclaimed: Language and Literature in English Radical Religion, 1640–1660* (Oxford: Clarendon, 1989), p. 27.

92 Sibbes, *Soules Conflict*, pp. 233–4.

93 Sibbes, *Soules Conflict*, pp. 414–15.

94 Sibbes, *Soules Conflict*, pp. 230–1.

95 In *Bowels Opened*, Sibbes attributes the persuasive *pathos* of godly ministers' 'bowels' to Christ's own *pathos* being imparted to them: 'Christ speakes by them, and puts his owne affections into them, that as he is tender, and full of bowells himselfe, so he hath put the same bowells into those that are his true Ministers' (Sibbes, *Bowels Opened*, pp. 143–4). Jennifer Clement comments: 'It was conventionally believed in the period that preaching could work only when God moved the preacher to eloquence on behalf of his Word, forming a chain of cause and effect: here, Sibbes renders this process as one in which Christ puts his own bowels – meaning his affections – into his preachers, who will then, ideally, transmit those affections through their rhetoric to the congregation' (Clement, 'Bowels, Emotion, and Metaphor', p. 442). Not only Christ's appeal to his audience's affections but Christ's 'owne affections' are given to 'true Ministers', so that they might persuade their flock with the tenderness of Christ himself.

96 See Judith Rice Henderson, 'Must a Good Orator Be a Good Man? Ramus in the Ciceronian Controversy', in Peter L. Oesterreich and Thomas O. Sloane (eds.), *Rhetorica Movet: Studies in Historical and Modern Rhetoric in Honor of Heinrich F. Plett* (Leiden: Brill, 1999), pp. 43–56.

97 Sibbes, *Soules Conflict*, pp. 225–6.

98 U. Milo Kaufmann, *The Pilgrim's Progress and Traditions in Puritan Meditation* (New Haven: Yale University Press, 1966), p. 143. See also Dyrness, *Reformed Theology and Visual Culture*, pp. 168–71.

99 Sibbes, *Soules Conflict*, p. 190.

100 Sibbes, *Soules Conflict*, p. 183.

101 Sibbes, *Soules Conflict*, p. 198.

102 Sibbes, *Soules Conflict*, p. 176.

103 Sibbes, *Soules Conflict*, p. 176.

104 Sibbes, *Soules Conflict*, p. 183.

105 Dyrness, *Reformed Theology and Visual Culture*, pp. 7–8.

106 Sibbes, *Soules Conflict*, p. 200.

107 Regarding meditation upon the creatures, see, for instance, Barbara Kiefer Lewalski, *Protestant Poetics and the Seventeenth-Century Religious Lyric* (Princeton, NJ: Princeton University Press, 1979), pp. 162–7, and Keith G. Condie, 'The Theory, Practice, and Reception of Meditation in the Thought of Richard Baxter' (PhD thesis, University of Sydney, 2010), pp. 77–83.

108 Sibbes, *Soules Conflict*, p. 193.

109 Sibbes, *Soules Conflict*, p. 200.

110 Sibbes, *Soules Conflict*, pp. 182–3.

111 Sibbes, *Soules Conflict*, p. 201.

112 Sibbes, *Soules Conflict*, p. 198.

113 Sibbes, *Soules Conflict*, p. 198.

114 For instance, Hugh Broughton, *A Comment vpon Coheleth or Ecclesiastes* (London, 1605), p. 24, and Thomas Brooks, *The Unsearchable Riches of Christ* (London, 1655), p. 308. Brooks uses this phrase to advocate for rhetorical eloquence on the part of the minister in terms reminiscent of Sibbes:

> Ministers words should be Divinely delectable, and desirable, they should Divinely please, and Divinely profit, they should Divinely tickle, and Divinely take both ear and heart. […] Holy Eloquence is a gift of the Holy Ghost, and may (doubtlesse) as well as other gifts of the spirit, be made prudently usefull to the setting forth of Divine truth, and the catching of soules by craft, as the Apostle speaks; surely where it is, it may be made use of as an Aegyptian Jewel to adorne the Tabernacle. (pp. 307–8)

115 Dever, *Richard Sibbes*, p. 141.

116 Sibbes, *Bowels Opened*, p. 40.

117 Sibbes, *Soules Conflict*, p. 198.

118 Sibbes, *Bowels Opened*, p. 240.

119 Perkins, *Arte of Prophecying*, in *Workes*, II:752–6.

120 Perkins, *An Exhortation to Repentance*, p. 1.

121 Perkins, *An Exhortation to Repentance*, pp. 1–2.

122 Perkins, *An Exhortation to Repentance*, pp. 2–3.

123 Perkins, *Arte of Prophecying*, in *Workes*, II:663.

124 Perkins, *Arte of Prophecying*, in *Workes*, II:761.

125 Perkins, *An Exhortation to Repentance*, p. 5, citing Lamentations 3:40; Stanley Fish, *Surprised by Sin: The Reader in Paradise Lost* (1967; 2nd edn. Cambridge, MA: Harvard University Press, 1998).

126 Perkins, *An Exhortation to Repentance*, p. 4.

127 Nicholas Hemminge [Niels Hemmingsen], *The Preacher, or Methode of Preaching*, trans. I. H. [John Horsfall] (London, 1574), fol. 5v–6r, 9–10r (misnumbered 19r).

128 Cf. Quintilian, *Institutio Oratoria*, VIII.vi.44–58; Henry Peacham, *The Garden of Eloquence* (London, 1577), sig. D1r–2r.

129 Perkins, *An Exhortation to Repentance*, p. 6.

130 John Bunyan, *The Pilgrim's Progress from This World to That Which Is to Come*, ed. James Blanton Wharey; rev. edn, ed. Roger Sharrock (Oxford: Clarendon, 1960), pp. 20–4.

131 Perkins, *An Exhortation to Repentance*, p. 95.

132 See Augustine, *Sermons on Selected Lessons of the New Testament*, Sermon XXIII, trans. R. G. MacMullen, in Philip Schaff and Henry Wace (eds.), *A Select Library of Nicene and Post-Nicene Fathers of the Christian Church* (New York: Christian Literature Co./Edinburgh: T & T Clark, 1886–89), series I, vol. VI, pp. 334–5.

133 See Isaiah 55:1: 'Ho, every one that thirsteth, come ye to the waters, and he that hath no money; come ye, buy, and eat; yea, come, buy wine and milk without money and without price.'

134 *Kairos* (καιρός) is a significant term both for classical rhetoric and for the New Testament and subsequent Christian theology, denoting time in the sense of the right time or appointed time, sometimes contrasted with *chronos* (χρόνος), as the ongoing sequence of chronological time. In the New Testament, *kairos* is linked to the coming of Christ at the appointed time and the availability of salvation in the moment in which the gospel is proclaimed. See, for instance, James L. Kinneavy, 'Kairos: A Neglected Concept in Classical Rhetoric', in Jean Dietz Moss (ed.), *Rhetoric and Praxis: The Contribution of Classical Rhetoric to Practical Reasoning* (Washington, DC: Catholic University Press, 1986), pp. 79–105; Eric Charles White, *Kironomia: On the Will to Invent* (Ithaca: Cornell University Press, 1987); and Phillip Sipiora and James S. Baumlin (eds.), *Rhetoric and Kairos: Essays in History, Theory, and Praxis* (Albany, NY: State University of New York Press, 2002).

135 Perkins, *An Exhortation to Repentance*, pp. 95–6.

136 See, for instance, Sophie Read, 'Puns: Serious Wordplay', in Adamson, Alexander and Ettenhuber, *Renaissance Figures of Speech*, pp. 79–94; and Sophie Read, *Eucharist and the Poetic Imagination in Early Modern England* (Cambridge: Cambridge University Press, 2013), Chapter 2, 'Donne and Punning' (pp. 69–97).

137 See, for instance, Quintilian, *Institutio Oratoria*, VI.ii.9f.

A Passionate Logos   69

138 Perkins, *An Exhortation to Repentance*, p. 92.

139 Perkins, *An Exhortation to Repentance*, pp. 98–9.

140 Sibbes, *Bowels Opened*, sig. A7r.

141 Sibbes, *Bowels Opened*, p. 476.

142 Sibbes, *Bowels Opened*, p. 478.

143 Sibbes, *Bowels Opened*, p. 478.

144 See John 5:1-11.

145 Sibbes, *Bowels Opened*, p. 478. Sibbes's analogy of Christ as the bridegroom to an impoverished and defiled bride echoes Luther's description of the union of Christ with the sinner, 'where this rich and louing husband Christ doth take vnto wife this poore and wicked Harlot, redeeming her from all euils, and garnishing her with all his owne Iewels' (Martin Luther, *A Treatise, Touching the Libertie of a Christian*, trans. James Bell (London, 1579), p. 24), and Ezekiel's narrative of Israel as the unfaithful bride of the Lord, whom God chose as an abandoned naked child 'when thou wast in thy blood' (Ezekiel 16:6).

146 On paradiastole, see especially Quentin Skinner, *Reason and Rhetoric in the Philosophy of Hobbes* (Cambridge: Cambridge University Press, 1996), pp. 142–80; and Skinner, 'Paradiastole', pp. 147–63.

147 See Aristotle, *Nicomachean Ethics*, 1106a–b.

148 Susenbrotus, *Epitome troporum ac schematum*, p. 46, cited in Skinner, 'Paradiastole', p. 160.

149 Peacham, *The Garden of Eloquence*, sig. N4v; George Puttenham, *The Arte of English Poesie* (London, 1589), p. 154; Angel Day, *A Declaration of All Such Tropes, Figures or Schemes, as for Excellencie and Ornament in Writing, Are Speciallye Used in This Methode*, in *The English Secretary, or Methode of Writing of Epistles and Letters* (London, 1599), p. 84.

150 Sir Thomas Wyatt, 'Myne owne John Poyntz', in Kenneth Muir and Patricia Thomson (eds.), *Collected Poems of Sir Thomas Wyatt* (Leicester: Leicester University Press, 1969), p. 90.

151 Skinner, 'Paradiastole', p. 155.

152 Perkins, *The Foundation of Christian Religion*, in *Workes*, I:A2r.

153 Sibbes, *Soules Conflict*, p. 77.

154 Sibbes, *Bruised Reede*, pp. 300–1. See Isaiah 5:20: 'Woe unto them that call evil good, and good evil; that put darkness for light, and light for darkness; that put bitter for sweet, and sweet for bitter!' Cf. Paul Stevens on Milton's Satan: 'On Niphates, his challenge is immediately confounded by the Word: when he insists "Evil be thou my good" (110), Scripture echoes his words and interprets his defiance as the solipsism of unaided reason: "Woe unto them that call evil good, and good evil.["]' ('The Pre-Secular Politics of *Paradise Lost*', in Louis Schwartz (ed.), *The Cambridge Companion to* Paradise Lost (Cambridge: Cambridge University Press, 2014), p. 105.)

155 Perkins, *A Dialogue of the State of a Christian Man*, in *Workes*, I:383.

156 Perkins, *A Golden Chaine: or, The Description of Theologie: Containing the Order of the Causes of Saluation and Damnation, According to Gods Word*, in *Workes*, I:114.

157 Perkins, *A Dialogue of the State of a Christian Man*, in *Workes*, I:389.

158 Perkins, *A Dialogue Containing the Conflicts between Sathan and the Christian*, in *Workes*, I:406.

159 Perkins, *A Treatise Tending unto a Declaration*, in *Workes*, I:360.

160 R. T. Kendall, *Calvin and English Calvinism to 1649* (Oxford: Oxford University Press, 1979), pp. 68–9.

161 Erin Sullivan likewise notes the fine line between godly and carnal sorrow in Perkins: 'While the loss of hope in one's *own* abilities to effect salvation was no bad thing, the line between despairing in oneself and despairing in God could be a fine one' (Erin Sullivan, *Beyond Melancholy: Sadness and Selfhood in Renaissance England* (Oxford: Oxford University Press, 2016), p. 168).

162 Sibbes, *Soules Conflict*, sig. A3r.

163 Sibbes, *Soules Conflict*, sig. A3r.

164 Sibbes, *Soules Conflict*, sig. A3r–v.

165 Sibbes, *Soules Conflict*, pp. 25–6.

166 Sibbes, *Soules Conflict*, p. 25.

167 Sibbes, *Bruised Reede*, sig. A4v. Cf. Sibbes, *Bruised Reede*, p. 164: 'breeding misperswasions in us of CHRIST'.

168 Richard Sibbes, 'The Sword of the Wicked', in *Evangelicall Sacrifices* (London, 1640), p. 232.

169 See Numbers 13 and 14.

170 Sibbes, 'The Sword of the Wicked', p. 232.

171 Sibbes, *Soules Conflict*, p. 57.

172 Sibbes, *Bruised Reede*, p. 160.

173 Sibbes, *Bruised Reede*, p. 165.

174 Alec Ryrie, *Being Protestant in Reformation Britain* (Oxford: Oxford University Press, 2013), pp. 250–1. Ryrie links this passage to Luther's theology of the cross: 'Luther's distinction between God's "strange" work and his "proper" work explains that God's denials of us are mere feints or bluffs, made specifically to build our faith and to redouble our prayers [...] like a parent who lets a child win a game, but not without giving some semblance of a match' (p. 250).

175 Martin Luther, *Lectures on Genesis*, ed. Jaroslav Pelikan, in *Luther's Works*, gen. eds. Jaroslav Pelikan, Helmut T. Lehmann and Christopher Brown, 75 vols. projected (St Louis: Concordia/Philadelphia: Muehlenberg and Fortress, 1955–), VII:225.

176 For more on parallels between Sibbes and Luther, see David Parry, '"Lutherus non vidit Omnia": The Ambivalent Reception of Luther in English Puritanism', in Herman J. Selderhuis (ed.), *Luther and Calvinism: Image and Reception of*

Martin Luther in the History and Theology of Calvinism (Göttingen: Vandenhoeck & Ruprecht, 2017), pp. 363–6. For a literary reading of Luther on the masks of God in relation to Shakespeare, see Tibor Fabiny, 'The "Strange Acts of God:" The Hermeneutics of Concealment and Revelation in Luther and Shakespeare', *Dialog: A Journal of Theology,* 45.1 (Spring 2006), 44–54.

177 [Martin Luther,] *A Commentarie of M. Doctor Martin Luther upon the Epistle of S. Paul to the Galathians* (London, 1575), fol. 226r.

178 Luther, *A Commentarie* [...] *upon the Epistle of S. Paul to the Galathians,* fol. 226v. Since the 'bruised reed' and the 'smoking flax' are taken directly from Isaiah 42:3, this is not conclusive evidence that Sibbes is inspired by Luther as opposed to simply being inspired by the same scriptural text, but the wider similarities in the surrounding discussion suggest a more direct influence of Luther on Sibbes.

179 Sibbes, *Bruised Reede,* p. 330.

180 Sibbes, *Soules Conflict,* pp. 356–7.

2

Divine excess: The radical *ethos* of prophetic performance

On Friday 24 October 1656, James Nayler, a leading preacher among the Quakers, rode into Bristol on a donkey, accompanied by a small group of followers casting their garments before him and, according to a hostile account written at the time, singing *'Holy, holy, holy, Lord God of Sabbath, &c'.*[1] According to the clergyman John Deacon, 'one *George Witherley*' testified on oath that 'they sang, but sometimes with such a buzzing *mel-ODIOUS* noyse that he could not understand what it was'.[2] Nayler's entry to Bristol was clearly intended as a re-enactment of Christ's entry into Jerusalem on Palm Sunday. The intended significance of such an action, however, was less clear.[3]

On being apprehended, Deacon reports, Nayler's followers were found in possession of letters 'infinitely filled with profane nonsensicall language'.[4] These letters appeared to corroborate the suspicion that Nayler's actions were intended to identify him with Christ, perhaps even as Christ. For instance, Deacon reproduces a letter to Nayler from Hannah Strange (or Stranger), which opens, 'Oh thou fairest of ten thousand, thou only begotten Son of God', and a postscript from Hannah's husband John reads, *'Thy name is no more to be called James but Jesus.'*[5] Under examination, Nayler himself, however, seems to use 'Son of God' language in a more inclusive fashion, responding to the query *'Art thou the only Son of God?'* with *'I am the Son of God, but I have many Brethren.'*[6] Likewise, Nayler speaks of *'Jesus, the Christ that is in me',*[7] which could be taken to mean simply that he is indwelt spiritually by Christ, a statement much easier to reconcile with orthodoxy than the claim to be Christ himself. The Nayler incident was debated in parliament for six weeks, with many arguing that Nayler should be put to death for blasphemy. In the end, a more lenient punishment was decided upon, and Nayler had his forehand branded and his tongue bored through with a hot iron before being imprisoned.

Nayler's fate shows that his actions were considered a threat to the 'godly' regime in operation under Oliver Cromwell, whose rule as Lord Protector exhibited a greater tolerance towards diverse practice and convictions among English Protestants than hitherto (officially excluding Roman Catholics, non-Trinitarian groups and the Prayer Book worship of episcopalian royalists).[8] However, Quakers and other groups emerging from the more radical end of the Puritan spectrum were in a marginal position. Although Cromwell had some personal sympathy with Quakers, they were theologically beyond the pale for most Puritans, due to their insistence that internal divine revelation through the light within is of greater value than the external word of Scripture.

Nayler's actions confirmed Puritan suspicions of where the trajectory of Quaker belief in an inward divine revelation to the individual might lead: to a deifying of the self that denied the distinction between Creator and creature. Yet this concern was one held not only by opponents of Quakerism but by Quakers themselves. Thus, as well as a threat to the orthodoxy and social stability of the Cromwellian regime, Nayler's ambiguous performance of Christ also proved to be an embarrassment to the Quaker movement itself. Although Nayler was later reportedly contrite and believed himself to have been misled, the Marxist historian Christopher Hill sees the downplaying of Nayler's significance in later Quaker accounts to be akin to the Soviet rewriting of inconvenient history: 'Thus in Fox's *Journal* James Nayler plays a part only slightly greater than that of Trotsky in official Soviet histories of the Russian Revolution.'[9]

The Nayler incident exemplifies two key ways in which radical figures of the turbulent 1640s and 1650s (the period of the civil wars and Interregnum) pushed aspects of the practice of Puritan persuasion beyond the theological and behavioural norms accepted by earlier writers such as Perkins and Sibbes. The first is with regard to rhetorical *ethos*, the first of the three modes of persuasion outlined in Aristotle's *Rhetoric*.[10] *Ethos* is the persuasiveness given to discourse by the authority of the speaker as perceived by an audience, and Nayler's performance ups the ante with regard to rhetorical *ethos*. While the majority of the writers and speakers considered in this book claim some measure of divinely bestowed *ethos* for their discourse, claiming to speak on behalf of God, the suspicion that Nayler fell under was that of claiming by his actions to be himself divine, a suspicion faced by other figures considered in this chapter, notably Abiezer Coppe.

Secondly, Nayler's rhetoric is one that goes beyond speech to physical performance. It is an instance of what Yvonne Sherwood, speaking of the strange actions of the biblical prophets, has dubbed 'prophetic performance art'.[11] It thus gives at the same time a more concrete sense to the fifth and final stage of rhetoric according to Cicero, that of *actio*, or performance, and a more

The Radical Ethos of Prophetic Performance   75

opaque version of *actio* whose meaning is hard to discern. Cicero's discussion of *actio* (or *pronuntiatio*) refers primarily to the performance of speech, the delivery of an oration formulated through the four previous stages of rhetorical practice outlined by Cicero, though Cicero's discussions of *actio* give limited consideration to physical gestures as well as vocal delivery.[12] Nayler's symbolic action is a literalized, physical *actio* and thus more concrete than the version outlined by Cicero, but the absence of speech that clearly interprets his behaviour means that its meaning remains ambiguous.

It is not even clear that the meaning of Nayler's actions was theologically unorthodox in the way that Nayler's critics inside and outside of the Quaker movement supposed.[13] The indwelling of Christ and the Spirit within the believer is solidly within the boundaries of Protestant and Reformed orthodoxy. For instance, John Calvin's *Institutes of the Christian Religion* contains these emphatic comments at the beginning of Book 3, marking Calvin's transition from discussing the external work of Christ in history to the internal work of the Spirit in the believer:

> First, we must understand that as long as Christ remains outside of us, and we are separated from him, all that he has suffered and done for the salvation of the human race remains useless and of no value for us. Therefore, to share with us what he has received from the Father, he had to become ours and to dwell within us.[14]

This emphasis on the Christ dwelling within by the Spirit is at the core of Quaker spirituality, as is the insistence that the external events of salvation history are 'of no value' unless applied internally to the individual believer. The somewhat unfair suspicion that Quakers faced, especially from Puritans (including Richard Baxter and John Bunyan), was that they believed the events of salvation history to be only internal symbolic events with no external historical reference point.

The Quakers are one of many loosely boundaried religious groupings that emerged from amidst the social, political and religious upheavals of the 1640s and 1650s, decades which witnessed a 'world turned upside down' through the events of two civil wars, the trial and execution of a monarch, the establishment of republican government, the abolition of bishops and the explosion of print publication encouraged by the lapse of censorship of the press. Such groups as the Diggers, the Seekers, the Ranters and the Muggletonians, although wildly disparate in their theology and practice, have been collectively labelled 'religious radicals', 'radical Puritans' or 'sectarians' by scholars in the field.[15]

76   *The Rhetoric of Conversion in English Puritan Writing*

Following Geoffrey Nuttall, I would argue that all these groups, whether or not they fall within the sociological or theological boundaries of 'Puritanism', recognizably emerge from a Puritan milieu, and so their practices of persuasion fall within the scope of this study.[16] Although they are often placed outside the theological boundaries of orthodoxy policed by Puritan polemicists such as the presbyterian Thomas Edwards in his catalogue of heresies *Gangraena*, the boundary is less clear in practice. Arguably the radicals emphasize elements present within Puritan orthodoxy (such as the indwelling of the believer by the Spirit) and follow their trajectory beyond the bounds of acceptability by the orthodox. They thus radicalize Puritan discourse rather than leaving it behind entirely. They also radicalize rhetoric in their persuasive practices: the apparent claim to divine *ethos* and the literalization of *actio* through physical action evident in Nayler's triumphal entry into Bristol surface more widely in the rhetorical expression of other radical groups and figures.

Of the three modes of persuasion outlined by Aristotle, as we have seen, Perkins's emphasis on the rational exposition of Scripture lends itself to *logos* as its chief mode of persuasion, whereas Sibbes's more affective piety gives a greater place to the subjective experience of the Spirit and makes greater use of *pathos*, persuasion through appeal to the emotions/affections. The mid-century radicals, as Nuttall observes, claim a more direct experience of and inspiration by the Spirit than does Sibbes.[17] Correspondingly, of the three Aristotelian modes of persuasion, the primary stress of the radicals is on *ethos*, appeal to the authority of the speaker, since they adopt an oracular prophetic voice to mark themselves out as mouthpieces of the divine.

The literary studies of the radicals by Nigel Smith and Nicholas McDowell lay some important groundwork that this more specifically rhetorical study builds upon. Smith writes that 'Radical Puritans and sectarians continued to apply rhetorical patterns which were derived from the mainstream tradition', which is true whether speaking of mainstream Puritanism or the mainstream rhetorical tradition,[18] while McDowell has established that many leading 'radical' figures were more educated than previously thought and not 'illiterate Mechanick Preachers', as the polemicist Thomas Edwards accused them of being.[19] In particular, McDowell demonstrates that some leading radicals had a university education, and that their writing draws upon intellectual resources derived from such an education, even if they use these resources subversively to undermine conventional learning and orthodox doctrine. While the final chapter of Smith's literary study of the radicals is entitled 'From Rhetoric to Style',[20] implying that the discourse of the radicals leaves behind the more formal rhetoric of mainstream

The Radical Ethos of Prophetic Performance 77

Puritanism in favour of a more free-flowing style, this chapter will demonstrate that the radicals never leave rhetoric behind. Neither do they leave behind the practices of godly persuasion developed by earlier Puritans such as Perkins and Sibbes – rather they push trajectories present within writers such as Perkins and Sibbes up to and beyond the limits of orthodox belief and behaviour.

William Dell versus the 'university spirit'

William Dell is a striking exemplar of some of these paradoxes.[21] Dell was educated at Emmanuel College in the University of Cambridge, and became a fellow there, before serving for a period of time as rector of Yelden in Bedfordshire. His invitation to John Bunyan to preach on Christmas Day 1659 attracted opposition from some of his parishioners – it was one of the complaints made against him in a 1660 petition to the restored House of Lords calling for Dell's ejection from his living. Nevertheless, it illustrates some unexpectedly blurred boundaries between the Cromwellian state church and Puritan Independents including both Dell and Bunyan, who operated partially within the parish system during the Interregnum despite their congregational ecclesiology that seems in conflict with a parish-based national Church.[22] Dell then became a chaplain to the New Model Army and eventually to its commander Sir Thomas Fairfax, and presided at the wedding of Cromwell's daughter Bridget to New Model Army general Henry Ireton.

Dell was imposed as Master of Gonville and Caius College, Cambridge, on 7 May 1649, a few months after Charles I's execution, at which he was one of the ministers on hand to console the king, and remained in post until his resignation on 11 May 1660 just before the Restoration. Dell's university connections make it curious that Dell is remembered largely for his denunciations of university education, many of these denunciations originating as Cambridge sermons to both town and gown.[23]

For instance, *The Stumbling-Stone* (1653) is described on its title page as '*A Discourse [...] Wherein the University is reproved by the Word of God. Delivered partly to the University-congregation in Cambridge, partly to another in the same town*'.[24] This treatise thus originates in a sermon given to the university that denounces the university. Unsurprisingly, perhaps, Dell reports in his preface that it 'met with such *notable* Opposition and Contradiction from the *University* of *Cambridge,* to whom it was delivered, and also from such of the *Town* then present, who are *baptized* into the University *spirit*'.[25]

78   *The Rhetoric of Conversion in English Puritan Writing*

Similarly, *The Tryal of Spirits both in Teachers and Hearers* (1653) is advertised on its title page as '*Testified from the Word of God to the university-congregation in Cambridge*' and refutes a previous sermon to the university the same year by the Independent minister Sidrach Simpson, appointed master of Pembroke College by the parliamentary visitors. Dell's '*plain and necessary confutation*' of Simpson proclaims:

> That the universities (according to their present statutes and practices) are not answerable to the schools of the prophets in the time of the law; but to the idolatrous high places. And, that humane learning is not a preparation appointed by Christ, either for the right understanding or right teaching the Gospel.[26]

Dell is not so much anti-intellectual as anti-clerical, rejecting the idea that a preaching ministry should be limited to state-authorized and university-trained clergy. It is for this reason that Dell vehemently objects to the image of the university as the fountain of the ministry: 'it is *one* of the *grossest errors* that ever reigned under *Antichrists* Kingdom, to affirm that *Universities are the fountain of the Ministers of the Gospel*, which do only proceed out of *Christs flock*'.[27] As seen in Chapter 1 of this book, William Perkins was among those who promoted this image, and it seems that Sidrach Simpson followed the line of Perkins in this regard.

Simpson's sermon text, according to Dell, was the passage about the 'schools of the prophets' that Perkins also applied to the English universities:

> He brought in that Scripture 2 Kings 6. v. 1, 2. which was his Text: the words whereof are these, And the Sons of the Prophets said unto Elisha, Behold now the place where we dwel with thee, is too strait for us; let us go we pray thee unto Jordan, and take thence every man a beam and let us make us a place where we may dwel: and he answered Go yee. This Scripture he used to prove the Lawfulness and Religiousness of the present Vniversities, and the usefulness and necessity of humane Learning to the Church and Ministery of the New Testament. And what the Scripture speaks of those Schools, he brought to countenance, encourage and justifie these: adding, that if it were objected, That that was the Old Testament: He did answer, That the old and the new were not distinct Testaments, but Administrations: thereby holding forth, that the Vniversities now, are answerable to the Schools of the Prophets that were then; and that the Vniversities are as agreeable to the New Testament, as the Schools of the Prophets to the Old.[28]

Dell vehemently rejects the comparison of Oxford and Cambridge to the Old Testament 'schools of the prophets', stating that they are rather like the idolatrous 'high places' of ancient Israel: 'I say, *these Universities* in the time of the *Gospel*,

The Radical Ethos of Prophetic Performance   79

are answerable to the *High-Places* in the time of the *Law*'.[29] The analogy has a greater significance than simply a generic biblical allusion to idolatry: Dell notes that the '*High-Places*', where the Israelites sacrificed in disobedience to the Lord's command to offer sacrifices only in the Temple at Jerusalem, involved a mingling together of 'Judaism, *and* Heathenism [...] *into one* mungrel Religion', and Dell asserts that the mingling of pagan learning and Judeo-Christian revelation in the universities of Christendom does likewise.[30]

In even stronger language, Dell identifies the universities with the throne of the beast on which God's wrath is poured in the book of Revelation: 'Now the *Throne of the beast* in these *Nations*, are the *Universities*, as the *fountaine* of the *Ministery*'.[31] Once again, Dell is using biblical typology with some precision – '*the beast*', for Dell, signifies the union of civil and ecclesiastical power instituted by the Roman emperor Constantine that Dell considers to be the mark of Antichrist.

Among the further 'errors' of Simpson that Dell refutes are 'That the knowledge of heavenly things cannot come to us but by things on earth, and that all Divinity is swadled in Humane Learning', that 'Arts and Tongues are the Cups in which God drinks to us' and that 'We shall never keep up Religion, if we do not keep up Learning: but when Learning goes down, Religion goes down too'.[32] Dell objects especially to the notion that education in the liberal arts is necessary to knowledge of divinity and thus a prerequisite to a preaching ministry.

In connection with this critique, Dell gives a historically implausible account of the founding of the University of Cambridge that appears to derive from the spurious history of Crowland Abbey by 'Peter of Blois'.[33] Dell's account is historically dubious, but is noteworthy for stating that the original Cambridge curriculum consisted of the trivium (the three language arts of grammar, logic and rhetoric) plus divinity:

> Thus it is recorded, *That the Study of* Cambridge *was instituted,* Anno 630. *By* Sigisbert *King of the East Angles, who after changed his Purple or Kingly Robes, for a Fryars Cool or Hood.* And the *Lectures* here were begun by *four Monks,* of which Brother *Odo* (as they termed him) read *Grammar,* according to *Priscians* Doctrine: *Terricus* an acute *Sophister* read *Aristotles Logick,* according to the Institutions of *Porphyrius,* and *Averroes;* Brother *William,* read *Tullies Rhetorick,* and *Gislebertus,* read *Divinity* to them on *Sundays,* and *Saints* days.[34]

Dell here identifies iconic writers for each of the branches of the trivium, including 'Tullies [Cicero's] Rhetorick' alongside Priscian's grammar and Aristotle's logic as transmitted through Porphyry (the classical Neoplatonic philosopher whose *Isagoge* became a standard logic textbook in the Middle Ages) and Averroes (the Islamic philosopher Ibn Rushd who influenced the medieval scholastic reception of Aristotle). Incidentally, even had the University of Cambridge been in existence in 630, it would have been unlikely that logic was taught following the system of Averroes, who lived in the twelfth century. Terricus must have been 'an acute *Sophister*' indeed! Ciceronian rhetoric is thus part of the system of learning that Dell repudiates as necessary for ministers to persuade their hearers to conversion and godly living, even if not the part that attracted his ire in particular.

Yet, although Dell attacks the notion of degrees in divinity and the study of the liberal arts as a qualification for the preaching ministry, he sees a legitimate and beneficial place for a secular university education that serves practical vocational ends:[35]

> If the *Universities* will stand upon an *Humane* and *Civil account,* as *Schools* of good *Learning* for the instructing and educating Youth in the knowledge of the *Tongues,* and of the *liberal Arts and* [...] *Sciences,* thereby to make them *usefull* and *serviceable* to the *Commonwealth,* [...] then let them stand, during the *good Pleasure* of God[.][36]

We should not assume that the phrase 'the *liberal Arts*' necessarily corresponds to the traditional seven liberal arts of the trivium (grammar, logic and rhetoric) and the quadrivium (arithmetic, geometry, music and astronomy). Especially when coupled with '*Sciences*', it may simply designate the curriculum of human secular learning in general.

However, Dell's proposals for educational reform also reference the three arts of the trivium in an apparently positive manner:

> It may be *convenient* also, that there may be some *Universities* or *Colledges,* for the instructing *Youth* in the knowledge of the *liberal Arts,* beyond *Grammer* and *Rhetorick;* as in *Logick,* which, as it is in *Divinity* (as one calls it) *gladius Diaboli,* the *Devils sword,* so in *humane things* it may be of *good use,* if *Reason* manage that *Art of Reason.*[37]

Logic here is given a positive role in secular human affairs even while being stigmatized as devilish when used 'in *Divinity*'. Though Dell's focus here is on logic, grammar and rhetoric are implicitly affirmed as the foundation of a liberal arts education that is beneficial for some.

Nevertheless, regardless of Dell's attitude towards the teaching of formal classical rhetoric, Dell inherits from the earlier Puritan tradition the conviction

The Radical Ethos of Prophetic Performance 81

that conversion is brought about through verbal persuasion, and thus through rhetoric in a broad sense. One can see this in Dell's contrast between the coercion to religious conformity exercised by the Antichristian Constantinian church-state and the unforced persuasion of the elect to salvation exercised by Christ and his true church:

> In that *Christ* will have none brought to *his* Church, by *outward violence,* and *compulsion,* though he have *all Power in Heaven and in Earth;* But in the day of his *Power,* (that is, of the *Gospel,*) he only entertains the *willing People,* and compells no body against their *wills;* seeing he seeks not *his* own *profit,* but *ours.*[38]

A section heading printed in the margin by this passage explicitly uses the language of persuasion: 'Because Christ will force none but perswade all.'[39]

The contrast being drawn here is not between a Calvinist predestinarian doctrine (which Dell affirms) and the view that people can come to Christ through their own free will, but rather between the coercive power of the sword and the persuasive power of the word. Those who are persuaded by Christ into the true church through the preaching of the word are those who have already been predestined by God to be so persuaded:

> Our *Lord Jesus Christ* gathers his *true* Church on *Earth,* according to the *Councel* and *Mind* of his Father in *Heaven,* and so will *entertain* none but whom his Father *draws,* because he will have *his* Church not one jot *larger* then the *Election* of *Grace.*[40]

A fairly standard Calvinist understanding of election thus underlies Dell's more radical views, both his gathered church ecclesiology (the church should contain none but truly elect saints) and his advocacy of the separation of the true church from coercive state power (since it is futile to compel outward conformity from those who are not true believers). Dell's spiritual church is therefore one that is created and sustained by the divine rhetoric of Christ himself.

Dell thus certainly believes in the need for persuasion to bring about faith. However, this persuasion to saving faith is primarily the internal persuasion of the Spirit. The Spirit makes use of the words of human speakers, but the power of these words to accomplish their persuasive purposes is, for Dell, in no way determined by their human eloquence or intrinsically persuasive qualities. Preachers nonetheless require a persuasive *ethos,* but this is an *ethos* bestowed by the Spirit rather than by study. In line with this conviction, he reinterprets a biblical text that Perkins used to argue for the usefulness of human learning to a preaching ministry:

82   *The Rhetoric of Conversion in English Puritan Writing*

> The *true Prophets,* who are *sent of God,* take all their *Warrant* and *Authority* from *God*, for what they teach, and doe not at all regard *Men*, or build on *them.* [...] So *Isaiah* 50.4, &c. saith, *The Lord God hath given me the tongue of the learned, that I should know how to speak a word in due season to him that is weary; he wakeneth morning by morning; he wakeneth my ear to hear as the learned.*[41]

Dell uses the words of Isaiah about the 'tongue of the learned' to draw almost the opposite conclusion to that which Perkins draws from this passage. Where Perkins sees this as an indication that God ordains study as a means by which he equips his ministers, as we saw in Chapter 1, Dell sees this as an indication that the unction of the Spirit displaces the need for human learning. This is one place in which Dell is arguably continuing a trajectory found in the work of Richard Sibbes, who does not deny the preacher's need for human learning, but applies Isaiah's phrase 'the tongue of the learned' not primarily to the preacher's education but rather to the wisdom given by the Spirit that enables ministers to speak the words that are fitting to the varied spiritual conditions of their hearers.

Dell's opposition to the education and formal ordination of ministers is one reason he is typically classified as radical, but he arguably shares many of these attitudes with a figure like Bunyan. Dell, like Bunyan, is in many respects an orthodox English Calvinist. In contrast to the other so-called 'radicals' considered in this chapter, Dell ties the ministration of the Spirit closely to the external means of grace, particularly the preaching of the word. He holds that the New Testament gifts of 'tongues and miracles, and other such like gifts are ceased in the Church, but the gift of the Spirit is not ceased, and this the Lord still joynes with the outward Ministerie of the Gospel'.[42] Besides this cessationist stance regarding the miraculous gifts of the Spirit, Dell warns against displacing the external word of Scripture with internal revelations of the Spirit as did others further along the radical spectrum, stating that the Lord seeks to 'preserve us from the ways of those men who seeke for the Spirit without the Word'.[43]

Moreover, for all his anti-clericalism, Dell does in fact see some believers as being appointed in a particular way to the public ministry of the word, but for Dell it is divine unction and not human ordination or ability that marks out these ministers and gives them their divinely ordained *ethos*:

> it is not naturall parts, and abilities, and gifts, and learning, and eloquence, and accomplishments, that make any man sufficient for the Ministery, but only the power of the Holy Ghost coming upon him.[44]

In the dedicatory letter to his earliest published work, *Power from on High*, Dell complains to his patroness Elizabeth Paulet, Countess of Bolingbroke, 'How little is there (among all our plenty) of that preaching, which is not in the plausible words of mens wisdome, but in the demonstration of the Spirit and of power.'[45] This is so, laments Dell, even among 'forward professors', that is, the most committed of the Puritan godly. Dell here is clearly paraphrasing 1 Corinthians 2:4, a favourite biblical text in Puritan discussions of appropriate preaching style. As noted in Chapter 1, the word for 'demonstration' that St Paul uses in the Greek of this verse is *apodeixis*, the same word as Aristotle uses in his *Rhetoric* for rhetorical demonstration or 'proof'.[46]

Dell sees the preaching of the word in the power of the Spirit as evidenced equally in its acceptance by some hearers and its rejection by others:

> And the ministerie that is in the spirit, is alwayes in power. And being in power, it is always effectuall, either to convert men or to inrage them: And the inraging of men, is as evident a sign of the spirit of power in a mans ministerie, as the conversion of men.[47]

Thus the Spirit-empowered discourse of the minister as envisaged by Dell is not necessarily always rhetorically effective in the straightforward sense of successfully persuading its hearers to conversion. Nevertheless, even when rejected by its hearers, the speech of the true minister still manifests a kind of power that exhibits a Spirit-given *ethos*.

This is in contrast to the false authority appropriated by '*Antichrist* and his *false Teachers*', associated with the royalists and the pre–civil war Church of England ('the *Head* of the *Malignant Church* and *People*'), whose satanic *ethos* comes at least in part from their mastery of formal rhetoric in the classical tradition: 'being full of *fleshly Wisdom, Rhetorical Eloquence*, and *Philosophical Learning*'.[48] This conjunction of apparent learning and eloquence (in Cicero's terms *ratio* and *oratio*) enables these false ministers to be 'to *humane* Judgement [...] most *considerable persons* in the Church, and very *Angels* of *Light* in appearance.'[49] The rhetorical skill of these corrupt clergy is thus one of the features that enables them to appear as '*Angels* of *Light*', thus participating in the satanic paradiastole discussed in Chapter 1, the rhetorical procedure of making vice appear to be virtue and virtue appear to be vice.

Abiezer Coppe's performative pranks

If Dell straddles the borderline between mainstream Puritanism and radical subversion, Abiezer Coppe, at least for the short period from which most of his writings date, is wildly over the line, transgressing received boundaries in his theology, his ethics, and his prose style.[50] Yet Coppe likewise has a conventional Puritan background from which he took an increasingly radical trajectory.[51] Coppe was born in 1619 and raised in Warwickshire, and, from the age of thirteen (according to his own later account), displayed a scrupulously devout youth of memorizing chapters of Scripture, 'secret Fasting', and 'keep[ing] a dayly Register of my sins [...] in a Book'.[52] Coppe studied at All Souls and then Merton colleges in the University of Oxford, where his studies concluded without a degree. Coppe, like Dell, served as a chaplain in the parliamentarian army (under Major George Purefoy), and seems to have moved from Presbyterian to baptistic and Independent convictions that led to his imprisonment for around fourteen weeks in 1646.

Coppe's notorious brief career as a radical provocateur erupted from this context of incarceration, triggered by a mystical experience in his twenty-eighth year that he believed to constitute a call to speak and write as a prophet. Coppe's visionary works published from 1649 to 1657 led to his condemnation for blasphemy by the Council of State and a further imprisonment from January 1650 to June 1651, which concluded in Coppe repudiating his radical writings in a retraction whose sincerity or otherwise remains a matter of lively debate.

Coppe aroused scandal especially for his apparently licentious views on sexual morality and his opposition to private property, but Coppe had Scripture to quote in defence of his position:

> I am confounding, plaguing, tormenting nice, demure, barren *Mical*, with *Davids* unseemly carriage, by skipping, leaping, dancing, like one of the fools; vile, base fellowes, shamelessely, basely, and uncovered too before handmaids,—
>
> Which things was *S. Pauls* Tutor, or else it prompted him to write, God hath chosen BASE things, and things that are despised, to confound — the things are [*sic*].— [...]
>
> *What base things?* Why *Mical* took *David* for a base fellow, and thought he had chosen BASE things, in dancing shamelessly uncovered before handmaids.
>
> And barren, demure *Mical* thinks (for I know her heart saith the Lord) that I chose base things when I sate downe, and eat and drank around on the ground with Gypseys, and clip't, hug'd and kiss'd them, putting my hand in their bosomes, loving the she-Gipsies dearly. O base! saith mincing *Mical*, the least spark of modesty would be as red as crimson or scarlet, to hear this.[53]

Coppe is here expounding the story of King David dancing before the Lord in a state of partial undress to the disapproval of his wife Michal,[54] an episode that

The Radical Ethos of Prophetic Performance 85

Richard Sibbes cited to argue that apparently excessive behaviour and speech can be fitting when speaking of divine realities:

> It is further a cleare evidence of a spirit subdued, when wee will discover the truth of our affection towards God and his people, though with censure of others. *David* was content to endure the censure of neglecting the state and Majesty of a King, out of joy for setling the Arke. *Nehemiah* could not dissemble his griefe for the ruines of the Church, though in the Kings presence: It is a comfortable signe of the wasting of selfe-love, when wee can be at a point what becomes of our selves, so it goe well with the cause of God and the Church.[55]

The phrase 'a spirit subdued' suggests the constraints of decorum, yet Sibbes here cites two biblical examples where the expression of '*affection*', in one case of 'joy' and the other of 'grief', seems to breach the bounds of decorum. It does not seem fitting for the king to dance wildly or for a servant to appear downcast in the king's presence. However, these actions are justified by appeal to a higher standard of rhetorical decorum – the success of God's cause on the one hand and its apparent failure on the other hand call for these apparently excessive responses.

However, I have little doubt that Sibbes would have been horrified with Coppe's use of this passage to extend the transgression of decorum into the sphere of ethics and not just of expression. For Coppe, Michal is an emblem of conventional morality and the straitlaced piety of mainstream Puritanism. Coppe asserts that 'I can if it be my will, kisse and hug Ladies, and love my neighbours wife as my selfe, without sin'.[56]

Coppe's unconventional morality is mirrored in his extravagant writing style, which can be read an expression of his prophetic *ethos*. As well as the tale of David dancing before the ark of the covenant, Coppe here cites St Paul's words in 1 Corinthians 1:28: 'And base things of the world, and things which are despised, hath God chosen, yea, and things which are not, to bring to nought things that are.'[57] Coppe thus claims for his own the early chapters of 1 Corinthians that surface throughout this study. Where the university-trained godly ministers such as William Perkins see Paul as advocating the setting aside of human eloquence, and separatist preachers such as Samuel How and Bunyan's pastor John Burton see Paul as advocating the setting aside of human education,[58] Coppe sees Paul as advocating the setting aside of human morality and piety, even that of the supposed godly. This is a radicalizing of prophetic *ethos* that sees *ethos* not as a performance of upright moral standing as conventionally understood, but a performance of transcending human morality itself.

86   *The Rhetoric of Conversion in English Puritan Writing*

Coppe's account of the spiritual crisis that furnished his prophetic call further displays his tendency to draw on motifs present within the discourse of more mainstream English Puritanism but to take them to transgressive extremes. Coppe begins by recalling a time when he was in disgrace, perhaps coinciding with his imprisonment in 1646:

> First, all my strength, my forces were utterly routed, my house I dwelt in fired, my father and mother forsook me: the wife of my bosome loathed me, mine old name was rotted, perished; and I was utterly plagued, consumed, damned, rammed, and sunke into nothing, into the bowels of the still Eternity (my mothers wombe) out of which I came naked, and whetherto I returned again naked. [...]
>
> And so lay trembling, sweating, and smoaking (for the space of half an houre) at length with a loud voyce (I inwardly) cryed out, Lord, what wilt thou do with me; my most excellent majesty and eternall glory (in me) answered & sayd, Fear not, I will take thee up into mine everlasting Kingdom. But thou shalt (first) drink a bitter cup, a bitter cup, a bitter cup; wherupon (being filled with exceeding amazement) I was throwne into the belly of hell (and take what you can of it in these expressions, though the matter is beyond expression) I was among all the Devils in hell, even in their most hideous howl.[59]

From this experience of apparent damnation, Coppe is caught up into a rapture of 'unspeakable glory' in which he sees first three hearts and then 'an innumerable company of hearts[.] [...] And me thoughts there was variety and distinction, as if there had been severall hearts, and yet most strangely and unexpressibly complicated or folded up in unity.'[60] Although it is hard to extract clear doctrinal positions from Coppe that are capable of being stated in propositional form, the connotations of his words here and elsewhere veer towards pantheism, the belief that God is all and thus everything is divine, with the hearts of all creatures as much part of the divine unity as are the three persons of the Trinity. It is from within this experience of heavenly bliss that Coppe hears voices commanding him to write and to prophesy.

Coppe deliberately uses words and concepts in a transgressive way that would appear blasphemous to orthodox Puritans. His *ethos* depends partly on the use of shock tactics, but yet he is doing more with his words than causing gratuitous offence. Coppe plays with the language of damnation in a way that is scandalous to the godly, but yet gives a different meaning to the concept of damnation within his alternate theological system. In Coppe's system, salvation and damnation become synonymous. The rhyming link between 'rammed' and 'damned' suggests that the damning of the old self takes place through a

The Radical Ethos of Prophetic Performance

regenerative ramming into the universal divine self.[61] This is a quasi-pantheistic vision of death and rebirth that constitutes a conversion of the notion of conversion itself as Puritans would understand it, though orthodox Puritans would see this rather as a perversion of the idea of conversion.

In a marginal comment to the preface of *A Fiery Flying Roll*, Coppe says that he has been 'strangely acted [...] though to the utter cracking of my credit, and to the rotting of my old name which is damned, and cast out (as a toad to the dunghill) that I might have a new name, with me, upon me, within me, which is, I am _____.'[62] The 'I am' breaks off into a dash, perhaps signalling a grammatically incomplete utterance (i.e. 'I am [something unspecified]'), or perhaps signalling the finality of the divine 'I am', the name that God gives to himself in Exodus 3:14 that needs no other words to explain. Coppe's version of damnation is a self-abnegation that destroys the limited human self in order to bring about the rebirth of a superhuman prophetic self that participates in the divine identity. It is in becoming 'nothing' that Coppe attains to the divine identity of 'I am'.

In gaining a prophetic *ethos* through self-abnegation, Coppe is once more continuing a trajectory found among mainstream Puritan ministers but taking it to an extreme that they would abominate. Perkins's *The Arte of Prophecying* advocates that the minister should conceal himself and his reputation for learning to make room for the work of the Spirit.[63] Coppe's self-abnegation extends not just to surrendering his reputation for learning but to surrendering his reputation among the Puritan godly for morality, piety and orthodoxy, and being willing to be stigmatized as a blasphemous heretic for the sake of proclaiming what he feels to be his higher truth. For Coppe, it is not only the carnal self that needs to be sacrificed to attain the prophetic voice, but also the apparently godly self.

For Coppe, prophethood is a function of divine speaking that transcends Coppe's particular human identity but in which he participates:

> But sure I am, there are some, that know me, shall live to see this, and say *Amen* to it: And shall know, that there hath been a Prophet amongst them. Which Prophet is not *Abiezer Coppe*; but the Prophet in him, who is among you all, though, as yet, manifested to few.[64]

Coppe may here be identifying his own prophetic role with that of the scriptural prophet 'like unto Moses', a figure prophesied in the Old Testament whom the New Testament identifies with Christ.[65] If this is the case, Coppe may be picking up on the more conventionally Reformed understanding of the threefold office (*munus triplex*) of Christ as prophet, priest and king, and claiming that Christ as 'the Prophet' speaks through him.[66]

88   *The Rhetoric of Conversion in English Puritan Writing*

Coppe, like Dell, takes Isaiah's 'tongue of the learned' to refer to a facility in speech given by direct divine inspiration rather than by means of human learning: 'To the (nominal) Author is given the tongue of the learned, though he knoweth not letters.'[67] It is not true in any literal sense that Coppe 'knoweth not letters', even if we accept Nicholas McDowell's explanation that claims to be unlettered could refer to a lack of literacy in the learned languages rather than the vernacular,[68] since Coppe's prose plays with Hebrew, Greek and Latin as well as English vocabulary.

Coppe, like Dell, is a university man who denounces the university. The third epistle of *Some Sweet Sips, of Spirituall Wine* is addressed 'especially to my Cronies, the Scholars of Oxford'.[69] In this epistle, Coppe reminds us of his Oxford education at the same time as traducing it, especially in the second chapter, headed:

> (*Being a Christmas Caroll, or an Anthem, sung to the Organs in Christ-Church at the famous University of* _____ *the melody wherof was made in the heart, and heard in a corner of* אביעוד *a late converted JEW.*)[70]

Though the name of the university is blanked out, the reference to 'Christ-Church' (both a college and a cathedral) clearly designates it as Oxford. The opening paragraph of this epistle asserts the radical conviction, shared by Dell and Bunyan, that the Spirit does not need human learning and can speak through uneducated 'Mechanick' preachers, while conceding that the Spirit can use learning of the kind found in the university:

> And it is neither Paradox, Hetrodox, Riddle, or ridiculous to good Schollars, who know the *Lord in deed*, (though perhaps they know never a letter in the Book) to affirm that God can speak, & gloriously preach to some through Carols, Anthems, Organs; yea, all things else, &c. Through Fishers, Publicans, Tanners, Tent-Makers, Leathern-aprons, as well as through University men, _____ Long-gowns, Cloakes, or Cassocks; O *Strange!*[71]

The 'University men' still have a place (if a humbler one than before) in Coppe's prophetic vision.

Coppe alludes to a passage from the Acts of the Apostles about the new Christian converts in Ephesus burning their books of sorcery.[72] Like Dell, he takes this to signify the laying aside of human learning in general:

> Well, hie you, learne apace, when you have learned all that your *Pedagogues* can teach you, you shall be (*Sub ferula*) no longer, under the *lash* no longer, but be set to the *University* (of the universall Assembly) and entered into *Christs* Church (the Church of the first born, which are written in heaven,) [...] and then you will fall upon your books (as if ye were *besides* your *selves*) and bring your books

together, and burne them before all men; so mightily will (ο λογὸς-) *the word* grow in you, and prevaile upon you[.][73]

Here the true λογὸς (*logos*), a word whose various connotations in New Testament and classical Greek usage include the word of God and the principle of rationality underlying the universe, as well as the rhetorical appeal to reason, is furthered through the burning of the Oxford textbooks. Coppe equates the heavenly assembly of the epistle to the Hebrews[74] with 'the *University* (of the universall Assembly)', which is '*Christs* Church', punning on and displacing Christ Church, Oxford.[75] This implies that Coppe sees himself as a member of a community, even if this is a charismatic and eschatological community rather than a visible earthly community with institutional boundaries such as the Church of England or even the visible gathered congregations of Dell or Bunyan.

Coppe's epistle continues with an extended play on the vocabulary of grammatical study, as McDowell has explored. McDowell argues plausibly that Coppe is parodying Lily's *Grammar*, the only officially sanctioned Latin grammar textbook in English grammar schools from the reign of Henry VIII to the mid-eighteenth century. Even the layout of the page is that of the Latin grammar primer, with a bracket running down the page pointing to the word '*Moode*', completing the sense of various numbered grammatical moods, six of them italicized standard grammatical terms ('*Indicative*', '*Imparative*' (repeated), '*Optative*', '*Potentiall*', '*Subjunct.*[ive]', and '*Infinitive*'), but the first being Coppe's addition of 'a Lunatick' mood:

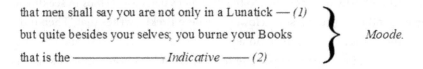

Although McDowell suggests that Coppe draws on his learning only to travesty it and reveal its irrelevance to spiritual revelation, he also notes Coppe's more positive use of the learned languages of Hebrew, Greek and Latin to find meanings of divine significance in a quasi-kabbalistic manner: 'Divine shapes – the *signatura rerum* – are revealed to the saint in the ancient languages as in the entirety of creation, in Latin declensions as in the sun and the moon'.[76] Perhaps the burning of the books is not so much an obliteration of the university-approved grammar rules, but throwing them into the prophetic flame of inspiration to be reconfigured and reconstituted in unexpected ways.

90   *The Rhetoric of Conversion in English Puritan Writing*

Coppe claims a prophetic *ethos* that inheres in his person, not only in his speech. Like the biblical prophets, he says, he is himself 'a signe, and a wonder'.[77] Coppe claims a particular affinity with the prophet Ezekiel, who provides a biblical precedent for the combination of bizarre behaviour with divine prophetic authority that more conventionally pious readers who affirm the inspiration of Scripture cannot deny. Coppe borrows the biblical account of Ezekiel's prophetic call to describe his own:

> And behold I writ, and lo a hand was sent to me, and a roll of a book was therein, which this fleshly hand would have put wings to, before the time. Whereupon it was snatcht out of my hand, & the Roll thrust into my mouth; and I eat it up, and filled my bowels with it, (*Eze.* 2. 8. &c. *cha.* 3. 1, 2, 3.) where it was as bitter as worm-wood; and it lay broiling, and burning in my stomack, till I brought it forth in this forme.[78]

William Perkins alludes to the same biblical metaphor of eating the book, though drawing on a passage from Revelation that alludes to Ezekiel rather than on Ezekiel directly:

> Ministers of the Gospell must learne Christ as *Paul* learned him. […] They that must convert others, it is meet they should bee effectually converted. *Iohn* must first eat the booke, and then prophesie, *Rev.*10.9. And they that would be first Ministers of the Gospell, must first themselves eat the booke of God.[79]

Eating the book, for Perkins, suggests an intimate assimilation of scripture into the being of the preacher, and an experience of what Scripture describes that gives the authority of experience to the preacher's persuasive *ethos* in seeking to persuade others to conversion. However, where Ezekiel writes that 'Then did I eat it; and it was in my mouth as honey for sweetness' (Ezekiel 3:3), and the book that John eats in the parallel passage in Revelation 'was in my mouth sweet as honey' before 'my belly was bitter' (Revelation 10:10), Coppe makes no mention of the roll tasting sweet. His roll, it seems, is unremittingly bitter.

Coppe claims not only to be inspired by the same Spirit who inspired Scripture but to be inspired in the same degree and with the same authority. This is manifest in the way he writes. Coppe's writing style is a pastiche of scripture, as he signals at the beginning of *Some Sweet Sips*: 'Here is Scripture language throughout these lines: yet Book, Chapter, and Verse seldom quoted.'[80] As Noam Flinker observes, 'The biblical sources are not quoted because each reader is expected to provide them.'[81]

This includes the replication of rhetorical figures found in Scripture. For instance, the triple epizeuxis (immediate repetition of words with

The Radical Ethos of Prophetic Performance 91

no intervening words) that opens the first chapter of *A Fiery Flying Roll* – 'Thus saith the Lord, *I inform you, that I overturn, overturn, overturn*'[82] – is a borrowing from Ezekiel 21:27: 'I will overturn, overturn, overturn it'. Coppe's rhetoric is a rhetoric of overturning, of subversive appropriation of the language of the godly to use it against them.

Perhaps most strikingly, Coppe claims scriptural precedent for performing strange acts such as those of the biblical prophets that Yvonne Sherwood has dubbed 'prophetic performance art'.[83] Continuing his identification with the prophet Ezekiel, Coppe describes as 'pranks' Ezekiel's prophetic actions such as shaving his hair, burning some and scattering some to the wind to represent the fate of the people of Jerusalem. Coppe reports his own strange behaviour in London, 'charging so many Coaches' of the rich, 'gnashing with my teeth at some of them', and 'falling down flat upon the ground before rogues, beggars, cripples, maimed[,] blind &c.' Coppe's purportedly prophetic actions also include 'that notorious businesse with the Gypseys and Goalbirds', which Coppe sees as parallel to the prophet Hosea 'playing some of his pranks' by taking 'a whore' as his wife at God's command.[84]

In this way, Coppe's rhetorical performance, like that of James Nayler, involves a literalized rhetorical *actio*: in Ciceronian rhetoric, *actio* is the delivery of a speech that involves gesture as well as voice, though Coppe's *actio* entails a performative persuasion that involves physical actions far beyond the hand gestures described by Cicero. While the invocation of biblical examples of strange prophetic behaviour is intended to lend credibility to actions that seem morally dubious, calling them 'pranks' characterizes them at the same time as light-hearted play, a kind of holy folly.

Coppe accuses the outwardly religious who refuse to accept his antinomian doctrine that 'sinne and transgression is finisht' of the satanic paradiastole of calling darkness light and light darkness:

> But all you that eat of the Tree of Knowledge of Good and Evill, and have not your Evill eye Pickt out, you call Good Evill, and Evill Good; Light Darknesse, and Darknesse Light; Truth Blasphemy, and Blasphemy Truth.[85]

Ironically, Coppe is citing these texts to justify behaviour that is deemed by the godly to be sin, and thus in their eyes calling light darkness and darkness light, thus once again highlighting the inherent reversibility of the paradiastolic dynamic.

This underlines that the meaning of Coppe's excessive experience, behaviour and writing is not incontrovertibly clear to interpreters. Hence the experience

92   *The Rhetoric of Conversion in English Puritan Writing*

that Coppe took as his prophetic call was taken by Richard Baxter as a sign that Coppe 'was in a long trance & hath seene strange Satanicall delusions'.[86] What is taken by Coppe to be a divine excess that overrides convention is understood by Baxter and by the parliamentary authorities as a diabolical excess, dissolving the necessary boundaries of ethical conduct, orthodox doctrine and even basic rationality that are needed to hold out against the forces of psychological, political and spiritual chaos.[87]

Pregnant silence and the rhetoric of Quaker convincement

Where the Ranter rhetoric of Coppe exceeds the boundaries of normal language to signify the inability of human forms to contain the divine, the inadequacies of language are signified by other radicals through silence. This was the case with those dubbed 'Seekers', a loose assemblage of dissenters who considered all existing churches, including the separatist gathered churches of 'visible saints', to be corrupt and lacking the truth.[88] Yet Seekers themselves did not claim to constitute a pure church but rather to be those awaiting a pure church that would be inaugurated through divine agency.

The Seekers' piety of passivity was a form of protest against the claims of existing religious forms to contain the truth of God, but their waiting was not giving up on the possibility of grasping truth. This is apparent in the words of William Erbery, a Welsh minister who followed an increasingly radical trajectory – he underwent a conversion to Puritan spirituality while a minister of the established Church, before becoming a separatist Independent preacher and then army chaplain, and then went further, taking the mantle of a millenarian prophet who denounced all organized churches:

> Another Prophet points at a time, that all the Saints shall be left for many dayes *without a King, and without a Prince, and without a Sacrifice, and without an Image, and without an Ephod, and without a Teraphim:* that is, without all publike Worship or Ministery, true or false […] and they shall sit still in submission and silence, waiting for the Lord himself to come and reveal himself to them[.][89]

We see here that Seeker silence was not an end in itself but rather a pregnant silence into which the future true church of Christ could be born. Many Seekers did not remain in their formless silence. One frequent direction of travel is indicated by Erbery's wife Mary and daughter Dorcas, who shortly after his death joined a new religious movement that shared their rejection of the existing outward forms of religion, that of the Friends (Quakers).[90] Quaker worship likewise featured lengthy periods of silent waiting, but the early Quakers were not entirely silent. In fact, they were often rather noisy, since their silent waiting in worship issued forth in speech, writing and action, often of a radical and provocative kind: Mary and Dorcas Erbery were among the women who followed James Nayler into Bristol singing Hosanna.

The silence of the early Quakers, like that of the Seekers, is a pregnant silence, a silence that incubates speech within the speaker prior to its birth into a public space. This dynamic is illustrated in *The Journal of George Fox*, the posthumously published memoirs of the chief founder of Quakerism:

> I passed on to another *Town*, where there was another great *Meeting*, and the *Old Priest* before-mentioned went along with me; and there came *Professors* of several sorts to it. Now I sate on an *Hay-stack*, and *spake nothing for some Hours*: for I was to famish them from *Words*. And the *Professors* would ever and anon be speaking to the *Old Priest*, and asking him, *When I would begin? and when I would speak?* And he bad them *Wait*; and told them, *That the People waited upon Christ a long while, before he spake*. At last I was moved of the *Lord* to *speak*; and they were struck by the *Lord's Power*, and the *Word* of *Life* reached to them, and there was a *General Convincement* amongst them.[91]

It is from Fox's pregnant silence that 'the *Lord's Power*, and the *Word* of *Life*' emerges, giving Fox an *ethos* of charismatic prophetic authority that brings about 'a *General Convincement*'. The silence is a mystical silence, waiting upon the Lord for inspiration, but it is also a strategic rhetorical silence – Fox's silence disconcerts his opponents so that they refrain from arguing with him, clearing the floor for Fox's prophetic sermon to proceed unopposed. The principle of pregnant silence proceeding prophetic speech is not limited to Fox's own practice – he writes to his followers in 1657, 'you must witness silence before you speak.'[92]

The use of the word 'convincement' here and throughout the writing of Fox and other early Quakers is instructive in considering the rhetorical dimension of Quaker discourse. 'Convincement' and being 'convinced' are the rough equivalent in Quaker vocabulary of 'conversion' in Puritan discourse, implying both an inward spiritual awakening and an identification with the emerging Friends movement – in Molly Murray's helpful formulation, both 'a change of church' (though early Quakers would more typically use the term 'meeting' for their gathered congregations) and 'a change of soul'.[93] The Quaker experience of convincement seems to have been phenomenologically similar to the Puritan experience of conversion, although the doctrinal package through which the experience was interpreted differed. Puritans emphasized the necessity of testing doctrine and experience by the external words of Scripture, while Quakers tended towards elevating the internal revelation of the Spirit above the outward words of Scripture. Most Puritans saw only regenerate true believers as indwelt by the Spirit, while the Friends believed that the light of Christ was within all people (even those who were not professing Christians of any kind), though for the early Quakers this did not imply a universalism in which all people would be saved.

Despite the Quaker emphasis on silence, the 'convincement' of others was often brought about through words. Although the Friends' suspicion of outward church order included the rejection of formal ordination for ministers, they recognized certain Friends as manifesting a more abundant anointing of the Spirit than others to bear public witness to the truth ('public Friends'), and so Quakerism spread through the preaching of a de facto order of charismatic lay preachers. For this reason, although Quakers were distinct from mainstream Puritanism in their doctrine, practice and forms of expression, the rhetorical enterprise of persuasion to conversion that this book explores remains pertinent to early Quaker speaking and writing.

The dynamics of Quaker persuasion of others towards convincement are nuanced and complicated by the Quaker understanding of the 'inward light': 'convincement' is a turning to the Christ within that cannot be manufactured by the persuasions of the human speaker. The human speaker can only encourage potential converts to be open to the ministrations of the light that is already present within them. Yet despite the doctrinal division, this paradox is not dissimilar to the conviction of Puritan divines that true conversion can only be brought about by the Holy Spirit but that the Spirit works through the divinely ordained persuasive entreaties of the human preacher.

The Quaker understanding of the inward light, as well as qualifying the power of the speaker to persuade his or her hearers (Quakers being among the radical sects who deployed female preachers and prophets), also complicates the agency of the hearer, the potential convert whom the Quaker preacher seeks to persuade. Although some later Quakers identify the inward light with a more generalized sense of conscience or spiritual intuition, for the first Quakers, as Michael Graves insists, the inward light was the personal light of Christ.[94] Thus, although the inward light dwells within every person, it is not simply an aspect of that person but rather a manifestation of divine grace given from outside.

Hilary Hinds helpfully describes the effects that this teaching has on early Quaker understandings of the personal agency of the potential convert:

The Radical Ethos of Prophetic Performance 95

This might be understood as a kind of *referred agency*, therefore: the capacity to act and to have effect in and on the world, where that capacity originates elsewhere; it is within and enables but is not of the human subject, a newly animating force which restores to the fallen human a prelapsarian connectedness to the beyond the human.[95]

It is unfortunate that Hinds contrasts her richly nuanced account of human agency in Quaker thinking with a caricature of Calvinism as excluding any place for human agency that I trust other chapters of this book help to dispel. The paradox of the convert's agency in more conventionally Reformed Puritan practical divinity is thus not as dissimilar to the nuances of Quaker conversion as Hinds makes out. The resulting compatibilist model of persuasion is much the same.

To read Quaker persuasion through the lens of the classical rhetorical tradition might appear problematic, however, given that Fox and the early Quakers share the view of other separatists (such as Bunyan) and radicals (such as Coppe) that university education is unnecessary to be a true minister of Christ. This is a view to which Fox attributes divine authority in his account of one of the earliest 'openings' (or inward revelations) that he received. Fox recalls an experience that he had in 1646, aged around 22:

> At another time, as I was walking in a Field on a *First-day* Morning, the Lord opened unto me, '*That being bred at* Oxford *or* Cambridge, *was not enough to fit and qualifie Men to be Ministers of Christ*[']: And I stranged at it, because it was the common Belief of People.[96]

The importance of rhetorical *ethos*, the perceived authority of the speaker, is paramount to the Quakers, but the source of that rhetorical *ethos* is different to the kind of *ethos* presented by Aristotle or Cicero. The *ethos* of the Friends comes from walking in the light (ethical conduct) and speaking in the light (prophetic inspiration). William Penn comments on early Quaker preachers, 'They were *changed* Men themselves before they went about to *change* others,' echoing the principle found in the work of William Perkins and other Puritans that the experience of conversion gives to preachers an authoritative *ethos*, and, like Perkins, echoing the classical principle that the speaker must be moved before moving others. Quakers would thus be in agreement with Perkins's assertion that 'Wood, that is capable of fire, doth not burne, vnles fire be put to it: & he must first bee godly affected himselfe, who would stirre vp godly affections in other men.'[97]

Robert Barclay, in his post-Restoration *Apology* for Quakerism, writes that, in the Friends' meetings for worship:

no man here limits the Spirit of God, nor bringeth forth his own conned and gathered stuff, but every one puts that forth which the Lord puts into their hearts, and it's uttered forth not in man's will and wisdom, but *in the evidence and demonstration of the Spirit and of Power.*[98]

Once again, we encounter St Paul's words on the '*demonstration of the Spirit and of Power*' cited by William Perkins and William Dell among others.[99] For Barclay, all Friends can experience the demonstration/*apodeixis* of the Spirit in their speech. Barclay references the 1 Corinthians text several times in his *Apology*. For instance, he speaks disapprovingly of '*Preaching*, as it's used both among Papists and Protestants', in which the preacher prepares a discourse on a scriptural text 'from his own inventions, or from the writings and observations of others' and is counted as an able preacher by the criteria of 'the excellency of speech and humane eloquence'. Barclay contrasts such human eloquence with the inspired speech of Friends:

To this we oppose, that, when the Saints are met together, and every one gathered to the *Gift* and *Grace of God in themselves*, he, that ministreth, being acted thereunto by the arising of the Grace *in* himself, ought to speak forth what the Spirit of God furnisheth him with, not minding the eloquence and wisdom of words, but the demonstration of the Spirit and of Power[.][100]

This notion goes back to the origins of Quakerism – Fox tells those Friends who want to minister vocally that they must 'be moved of the Lord by the power of the Lord', and that 'when it moves and stirs in you, be obedient; but do not go beyond, nor add to it, nor take from it'.[101] This emphasis on the felt experience of the Spirit moving the speaker to speak both enhances and limits the speaker's authority: when obedient to the inner prompting of the Spirit, the speaker's utterances come with divine authority, but the speaker has no authority to speak beyond that subjectively felt prompting.[102]

Quaker scholarship and divine simplicity

However, as with Dell, this does not mean that Quakers had no place for education. Judith Roads helpfully notes in a recent article that

Some [Quaker] authors were educated and clearly reached for classical Ciceronian-style methods. William Penn, Isaac Penington and Robert Barclay come to mind, for instance. Others, tradesmen and women with some education, or labourers and those in service, relied on native invention, or what they had learnt elsewhere, to get their urgent message out 'from the Lord'.[103]

The Radical Ethos of Prophetic Performance 97

In a posthumously published sermon by leading Friend Stephen Crisp (1628–92), Crisp concedes that being 'Masters of Liberal Arts and Sciences [...] may help to make them men', though 'Men can never attain to the saving Knowledge of God by Study'.[104] Similarly, in his preface to Fox's *Journal*, William Penn, a key second-generation Quaker leader who had a university education at Oxford (unlike Fox), states that 'neither do *Parts* or Learning make Men the better *Christians*, though the better *Orators* and *Disputants*'.[105]

In another prefatory epistle to Fox's *Journal*, several Friends note that Fox 'had the *Tongue* of the *Learned*, and could speak a *Word* in *due Season* to the Conditions and Capacities of most, especially to them, that were *weary*, and wanted *Soul's Rest*; being deep in the *Divine Mysteries* of the *Kingdom* of *God*.'[106] Once again referencing the phrase from Isaiah 50:4 cited by Puritan ministers in similar contexts, Fox's '*Tongue* of the *Learned*', like Dell's and Coppe's,[107] is that of a divinely bestowed learning apart from human learning, enabling Fox to speak with a spiritual rhetorical decorum that addresses 'a *Word* in *due Season* to the Conditions and Capacities of most'; Isaiah's '*weary*' are understood as the spiritually afflicted who 'wanted *Soul's Rest*', just as they are by Perkins.

Though many references to human learning in early Quaker writing dismiss human learning or diminish its importance, early Quakers nevertheless make use of the 'Liberal Arts and Sciences' for their own purposes. One curious instance of this is a work by George Fox and others entitled *A battle-door for teachers & professors to learn singular & plural*.[108] A battledore was a primer for children who were learning to read, but this Quaker battledore is not a straightforwardly educational text. Rather, it is one that makes use of the rules of grammar to make a polemical point, insisting that 'thou' should be used as the second person pronoun for addressing an individual and 'you' as the pronoun for addressing more than one person.

The Quaker insistence on 'thou' over 'you' is presented by Fox and other early Quaker writers as a matter of grammar – surely, they argue, since 'thou' is historically the singular pronoun and 'ye'/'you' the plural, the deferential singular 'you' for social superiors and polite society is grammatically erroneous. For instance, Fox comments as follows in his *Journal*, 'For tho' *Thou* to a *single Person* was according to their own Learning, their *Accidence* and *Grammar* Rules, and according to the *Bible*; yet they could not bear to hear it'.[109] It may seem strange that the theologically radical Quakers are linguistically conservative and grammatically prescriptivist on this point. However, this is arguably a matter of rhetoric more than of grammar – to use 'thou' in addressing every individual

98 *The Rhetoric of Conversion in English Puritan Writing*

regardless of social standing is an assertion of the speaker's *ethos* as equal in status to that of the person addressed.

A Battle-Door engages with the linguistic arts of the trivium at the introductory level of grammar, but the arts of logic and rhetoric come into view in passing:

> But you Teachers, Professors, Schollars and Magistrates, who rages at them that speaks *Singular* to *Sing.* and *Plural* to *Plural,* who pretend that you know Accidence and Grammar, Logick, Rhetorick, and Divinity; yet in practice you must have your BATTLE-DOOR again.[110]

Fox and his collaborators here attack those who claim to be learned in the liberal arts and theology as having erred even in the foundational discipline of grammar, but in doing so they incidentally imply that there could be a trivium reformed according to the dictates of the inward light.

In another educational endeavour, Fox collaborated with the London Friends' secretary Ellis Hookes to write *Instructions for Right Spelling, and Plain Directions for Reading and Writing True English* (1673). This primer, which looks rather more practically useful for schoolchildren than *A Battle-Door*, includes 'The Signification of the seven Arts', a section seemingly validating the traditional seven liberal arts of the trivium and quadrivium:

> The word *Grammer* comes of a word that signifies *to write.*
> *Rhetorick* of a word that signifies *to speak fluently.*
> *Logick,* of a Word that signifies *to speak and Reason.*
> *Astronomy,* signifies *the Law* or *distribution of the Stars.*
> *Geometry,* signifies *measuring of the Earth.*
> *Musick,* signifies *the Muses Art,* or *Authors of Songs,* or *Poetry.*
> *Arithmetick,* comes of a Word that signifies *Number.*[111]

However, the definition of '*Rhetorick*' seems to limit rhetoric to eloquence, or *elocutio*, the third of Cicero's five 'canons' of rhetoric, which in Renaissance humanism came to be conflated with style. The same impression is given in the dictionary section of the primer, headed 'Hard Words used in our *English* Tongue explained', which gives the definition '*Rhetorick,* the Art of Eloquence'.[112] It appears that Fox and Hookes are here replicating standard reference material from the primer tradition. They are arguably thus not presenting a distinctively Quaker perspective on the liberal arts, but this nevertheless indicates that Fox and Hookes have sufficient tolerance for the traditional schema of the liberal arts not to repudiate it.

Some Quakers even had a university education. Among the most notable, though not the most typical,[113] was Samuel Fisher, who, like other figures considered in this chapter, moved in a progressively radical direction in his religious affiliation. After being educated at Trinity College, Oxford, Fisher served as parish lecturer and then vicar of Lydd in Kent, then taking ordination as a Presbyterian minister in 1643 before defecting to the General Baptists and serving as pastor to a congregation at Ashford for a number of years before his Quaker 'convincement' in 1655.[114] Like Dell and Coppe, Fisher is a university man who writes against the university, particularly in his *Rusticus ad Academicos* (1660), whose title he gives in English as 'The *Rustick's* ALARM to the *Rabbies*'. Fisher, like Dell, rejects the identification of the English universities with the schools of the prophets found in the Old Testament, but yet he believes that there is an equivalent to these schools of the prophets in the present day:

> for which work there are now as there were of old (but those are not *Oxford* and *Cambridge* Vniversities as it were *Schools* and *Nurseries* of *young Prophets* at *Iericho* and *Bethel*, [*alias*, by interpretation] the House of God, where Truth, and true Wisdom, and true Religion was, and is learnt, as truly and fully, as it is falsly taught, or rather fully and universally forgotten at our now *Vniversities*, or *Nursing-mothers* of that Wisdom and Religion from beneath, which is but earthly, sensual, or animal and deceitful[.]

While for some Independents opposed to a university-trained ministry the gathered congregation with its spiritually gifted teachers was the 'House of God' and school of the prophets, for Fisher it seems rather to be the experience of communion with the inward light through silent worship that gives access to the knowledge needed for true prophetic ministry. Fisher states that the biblical prophets did not buy the gift of prophecy 'by mens mony at Schools, and Colledges, as our *Accademical Simon Magus's* suppose', but rather that it 'was given in a certain way that ye are so far out of, that ye hate it, of holy waiting on God, and learning of him alone in silence in all subjection in order thereunto'.[115]

Though Fisher engages constantly in efforts to persuade his audience, the actual word 'rhetoric' is generally found in Fisher's writing only in his citations from his opponents.[116] One of the earliest instances of this is in his work *Baby-baptism meer babism* (1653), written prior to his Quaker convincement during Fisher's period as a Baptist preacher, but reissued as *Christianismus redivivus* in 1655, and again in 1669 after Fisher joined the Friends. This is ostensibly a treatise against infant baptism, but frequently gets side-tracked into lengthy diatribes on other matters of dispute raised in previous texts written against 'Anabaptists'.

One of the texts to which Fisher is responding is *Katabaptistai kataptustoi: The Dippers Dipt* (1645) by Daniel Featley (one of the few episcopalians among the divines of the Westminster Assembly), in which Featley claims that 'Anabaptist' preachers are no true ministers since they lack both outward and inward calling. While outward calling refers to lawful ordination, it seems that Featley understands inward calling not as a subjectively felt experience of divine vocation but rather as the possession of the relevant intellectual gifts and training for the ministry, which, Featley asserts, the Baptists lack:

> Though they can vary phrases, and out of broken notes hold out a discourse upon some passages of Scripture for an houre or more; yet they are no wayes furnished with gifts requisite to a faithful Shepherd, and able Minister of the Gospel: for they understand not the Scripture in the Originall Languages, they cannot expound without Grammar, nor perswade without Rhetorick, nor divide without Logick, nor sound the depth of any Controversie without Philosophie, and Schoole Divinity.[117]

Featley thus considers the liberal arts, including the trivium of grammar, logic and rhetoric, the biblical languages, and the kinds of philosophy and theology taught in the universities, to be 'gifts requisite to a faithful Shepherd, and able Minister of the Gospel'. The skills to persuade one's hearers bestowed by the art of rhetoric are, for Featley, necessary to the faithful exercise of the pastoral ministry.

Such human learning has, for Featley, replaced the more direct divine calling that was present in the first generation of the Christian Church, and so the 'Anabaptists' can make no valid claim to derive their ministerial *ethos* from this more immediate kind of calling:

> Neither may they fly to immediate Inspirations of the holy Ghost, and the miraculous gifts of Tongues, and Prophesie, for such have ceased in the Church for these many hundred yeeres.[118]

For Featley, it is not only their perceived departures from Scripture and from longstanding Christian tradition that mark out the 'Anabaptists' as dangerous fanatics, but also their departure from the inherited liberal arts of school and university education.

Against the accusations of Featley and others that 'Anabaptists' are illiterate fanatics, the then-Baptist Fisher states that 'we are also for learning, for tis a good talent, to use for God, and too good for the Devill, a good servant, but a

The Radical Ethos of Prophetic Performance   101

bad master', and even accuses the clergy of the established Church of deficiency in learning:

> we wish that there were more of it then there is among you *CCClergy* [*sic*] (if it may be also well improved, as it seldome is by those of you that have it) [...] no lesse then legions of you are little learned Κατ'ἄνθρωπον, or Κατά χρις[τ]όν either.[119]

Fisher's criticism is double-edged: he is saying that many of the clergy of the established Church are unqualified by their own stated standards of human scholarship ('little learned Κατ'ἄνθρωπον'), but also that they lack the personal knowledge of Christ ('little learned Κατά χρις[τ]όν') that truly qualifies the Christian minister. For Fisher, although human learning is not essential to the minister, it can at least potentially be 'well improved'.

A more intentional Quaker engagement with the liberal arts can be found in Thomas Lawson's *A Mite into the Treasury, Being a Word to ARTISTS, Especially to HEPTATECHNISTS, The Professors of the Seven Liberal Arts, so called, Grammer, Logick, Rhetorick, Musick, Arithmetick, Geometry, Astronomy* (1680), written in the latter years of Charles II's reign. *A Mite into the Treasury* is a polemical work against the need for a formally learned clergy, structured around the seven liberal arts in order to show the insufficiency of each of them in turn. Lawson's assessment of the liberal arts is largely though not entirely negative, 'Shewing what we own herein, being according to God and Godliness, and of God; and what we deny, proceeding from and savouring of those deceitful Lips, which seduced Man from his Primitive Station, a State of Blessedness'.[120]

Lawson studied at Christ's College, Cambridge, the college of Perkins and of Milton, for a year or two from 1650, but left without taking a degree.[121] He was briefly a minister of the established Church in Lancashire before his Quaker convincement. Lawson is thus critiquing the liberal arts as one who has at least some knowledge of them, and he is not opposed to all education, since he became a noted botanist as well as a Quaker preacher, and kept a school of his own.

Lawson's chapter on rhetoric begins with a definition that appears positive or at least neutral towards the art: '*Rhetorick* is defined to be the Art of Speaking Ornately, Finely, Eloquently, with *Rhetorical* Colours and Ornaments.' However, Lawson goes on immediately to contrast the 'Divine Lustre' of the natural eloquence given to Adam in the beginning with the fallen language of the serpent that he identifies with pagan (implicitly classical) rhetoric:

> But the Serpent that deceived Man, and incorporated him into another Power, therein to Think, Speak and Act, brought forth an other Language, out of the

102   *The Rhetoric of Conversion in English Puritan Writing*

simplicity of Truth, savouring of the Womb of its Original; though Plausible, Painted, Eloquent, Garnished with Colours and Ornaments of Pagan Rhetorick, yet 'tis Abomination to the Lord, Stinks in his Nostrils, and in the Nostrils of such as are truly Reborn[.][122]

Lawson thus establishes a dichotomy between a true eloquence that may be plain and simple by worldly standards, and a showy 'Painted' worldly rhetoric with all the classical 'Colours and Ornaments':

This is my Testimony, that that Language which the Lord speaks in and through his People, Sons and Daughters, is the only and heavenly Eloquence and Rhetorick, if I may so call it; though Plain, Simple, and be accounted Rude, Clownish and Babbling by the Worldly Wise.[123]

Lawson's 'heavenly Eloquence and Rhetorick' parallels the 'heavenly Rhetorick' that Richard Sibbes attributed to Christ.[124] Lawson, like Sibbes, sees the Song of Songs in particular as displaying this heavenly rhetoric through which Christ woos his spouse:

And Christ saith to the Church, come and coming out of the Wilderness, leaning upon her Beloved, *Oh my Dove! that art in the Clefts of the Rock, in the secret places of the Stairs, let me see thy Countenance, let me hear thy Voice; for Sweet is thy Voice, and thy Countenance is Comely,* Cant. 2.14. Mark, the Voice of the Church is Sweet, though not Painted with enticing Words of Mans Wisdom, nor Garnished with Pagan Rhetorical Flourishes; 'tis Sweet to Christ, though judged Rude and Babbling by Worldly Sophisters.[125]

The divine drama of the Song of Songs features Christ speaking sweetly and winningly to his Bride the Church, and the Bride responding sweetly in the eyes of the Bridegroom Christ, even though she lacks 'Pagan Rhetorical Flourishes'. Lawson sees the teaching of 'Heathen Rhetorick' to 'Christian Youth' as one of the signs of the Church falling away from its primitive purity into the apostasy of the established churches, but it is somewhat unclear whether Lawson rejects all human attempts at eloquence as 'Pagan' or whether he rejects pagan rhetoric but allows for a human verbal eloquence not measured by the criteria of the pagan classical tradition.[126] The same ambiguity is present in Lawson's praise of the apostle Paul's persuasive speech; once again citing the apparently anti-rhetorical passages from 1 Corinthians that we have considered previously, Lawson affirms that there

was a Divine Excellency in *Paul's* Speech, seasoned with Salt, Heavenly Wisdom, yet he saith plainly to the *Corinthians, That he came not with Excellency of Speech, nor with Enticing Words of Mans Wisdom:* He came not with Frothy Flourishes

The Radical Ethos of Prophetic Performance   103

of Pagan Rhetorick or Oratory, nor with Enchanting Words of fallen Wisdom, which the fallen Mind ascribes Excellency unto, but falsly; but his Preaching was in Demonstration of the Spirit and Power, 1 *Cor*.2.1, 4.[127]

There remains an ambiguity here regarding whether the scriptural authors are discernibly eloquent to a human reader but by different aesthetic criteria to those of classical 'Pagan Rhetorick or Oratory', or whether they are to be deemed eloquent because of their divine inspiration despite their seeming inelegance.

Typological incantation: Quaker *logos* and *pathos*

One has to admit, however, that Quaker preaching and writing, however fluent in expression, is not generally ordered according to the template of a Ciceronian oration or a Perkins-style doctrine and use sermon. In a justly influential article from 1956, Jackson I. Cope argues that the early Quakers have a distinctive '"incantatory" style', involving 'an incredible repetition, a combining and recombining of a cluster of words and phrases from Scripture'.[128] Leo Damrosch, building on Cope, comments that 'The aim, by contrast with Calvinist discursive persuasion, was to interweave scriptural terms and metaphors in order to overwhelm rational resistance by endless variations on a few key words'.[129] A hostile contemporary of the Quakers, the pamphleteer and poet Samuel Austin, characterizes their '*Babylonish Rhetorick*' as overwhelming rational resistance in a similar manner: 'His discourses are nothing but a *Rhapsody* of oft repeated *Non-sense*; and when he hath darkned your understanding with a Cloud of insignificant *Babble*, he cryes, *Ah! friends mind the Light!*'[130]

Damrosch, Cope and Austin are right to highlight how Quaker repetition, circling around particular words and ideas, has an effect on the audience's emotions that somewhat bypasses rational cognitive reflection. However, I think that they overstate the apparent lack of logical argument in Quaker discourse, as the patchwork of scriptural allusions found in Quaker discourse is underwritten by typological and doctrinal logic that makes implicit arguments, even though the connections are not spelled out in the scholastic syllogistic style found in writers such as Perkins.[131]

Fox's incantatory style is not found so much in the narrative portions of his *Journal* as in his numerous 'epistles' that were incorporated into the print edition of the *Journal* published after Fox's death. These epistles adopt an oral, oracular and quasi-scriptural register, and give a sense of how Fox's preaching voice may have sounded. We can see this, for instance, in one of the earlier epistles in the 1694 *Journal*, directed both to confirming Friends in their faith and to winning potential converts to the Quaker understanding of truth: 'to be spread abroad both amongst *Friends*, and other tender People, for the Opening of their Understandings in the *Way* of *Truth*, and directing them to the true *Teacher* in themselves'.[132] Fox's epistle begins with a diagnosis of the human condition that borrows scriptural vocabulary:

> THE *Lord* doth shew unto Man his *Thoughts*, and discovereth all the *secret Workings* in Man. A Man may be brought to see his *evil Thoughts*, and running *Mind*, and vain Imaginations, and may strive to keep them down, and to keep his *Mind* in; but cannot *Overcome* them, nor keep his *Mind* within to the *Lord*.[133]

The vocabulary of 'evil *Thoughts*' and 'vain Imaginations' is borrowed from biblical passages,[134] but Fox arranges such phrases into balanced parallel clauses and triplets that hook the reader into the progression of his thought.

Fox continues by characterizing different kinds of people as being like various kinds of non-human creatures:

> Now some Men have the Nature of *Swine*, wallowing in the *Mire*: And some Men have the Nature of *Dogs*, to bite both the *Sheep* and one another: And some Men have the Nature of *Lions*, to tear, devour and destroy: And some Men have the Nature of *Wolves*, to tear and devour the Lambs and Sheep of Christ: And some Men have the Nature of the *Serpent* (that old Adversary) to sting, envenom and poison: *He that hath an Ear to hear, let him hear*, and learn these things within himself. And some Men have the Natures of other Beasts and Creatures, minding nothing, but earthly and visible things, and feeding without the fear of God.[135]

The anaphoric repetition of 'And some men' has a cumulative rhythmic effect, creating a catalogue of different kinds of vice. Though the repetition of 'some Men' suggests that the bestial varieties of vice differ from one person to another, the exhortation to the hearer to 'learn these things within himself' suggests that there is a devilish serpent nature within all people that they must overcome by means of the light within.

It is this typological account of the divine and demonic principles struggling within each individual that structures much of the imagery in the rest of this epistle, which might otherwise seem like a jumble of vivid but unconnected verbal pictures: the light must overcome the darkness, 'the *Seed* of *Faith*' resist 'the carnal Mind', and Jacob must triumph over Esau.[136] While in mainstream Puritan discourse, Jacob and Esau often signify elect and reprobate individuals (as they do, for instance, in Bunyan's *Grace Abounding*),[137] in Quaker discourse

The Radical Ethos of Prophetic Performance   105

they signify instead elect and reprobate principles within the mind of each individual. In the Quaker scheme of salvation, it is not the case that some individuals are irretrievably reprobate and some are irresistibly elected to receive regenerating grace, but rather that each individual possesses a reprobate carnal self that needs to be repudiated by aligning the conscious self with the divine light within. Thus Fox's epistle concludes:

> But *Esau's Mountain* shall be laid waste, and become a Wilderness, where the *Dragons* lie: But *Jacob,* the *second Birth,* shall be fruitful, and shall arise. For *Esau* is hated, and must not be *Lord:* but *Jacob,* the *second Birth,* which is perfect and plain, shall be *Lord;* for he is beloved of God.[138]

Note here the alliteration of 'waste' and 'Wilderness', 'perfect and plain', and the chiasmus of 'hated […] Lord […] Lord […] beloved'. It is passages such as this that might at first sight read like a concatenation of obscure scriptural phrases working on the emotions more than the reason (as Damrosch suggests), but an understanding of how the biblical typology is being used reveals an underlying logic. Though oracular in style, the content of Quaker rhetoric thus invokes *logos* (appeal to reason) as well as *pathos* (appeal to emotion). However, *ethos* (appeal to the perceived authority of the speaker) is arguably the paramount mode of Quaker rhetoric.

Quaker *actio*: Practice preaching performance

The *ethos* of early Quaker rhetoric is not established only through speech – as Richard Bauman writes, 'the rhetoric of early Quakers was not simply a rhetoric of words, but a unified rhetoric of symbolic action.'[139] The persuasive *actio* of the Quakers goes beyond the restrained gestures accompanying a classical oration or conventional English Reformed sermon into more fully embodied practices. Samuel Fisher writes, '*So our* Practice *will* Preach out *our* Performance *of what we* Promise, *and that* performance *prove* our words.'[140] As Hilary Hinds notes, 'In the alliterative circularity of preaching, practice, performance and promise, Fisher posits a seamless continuity between words and action, promise and fulfilment.'[141]

Although action is seen by Fisher and other Quaker writers as a form of preaching, it is a form of preaching that does not do away with the need for verbal proclamation but rather complements and completes the proclamation of the Quaker testimony in words. In context, Fisher is asserting that the Quaker refusal to swear oaths should not lead people to distrust the Friends, since observation of their honest conduct over time will demonstrate that the word of a Friend can be trusted even without an oath, and so the practice of the Quakers will prove the credibility of their promises.

One might distinguish between two forms of persuasive *actio* on the part of the Quakers, establishing two aspects of Quaker *ethos*, a moral *ethos* and a prophetic *ethos*. On the one hand, Quakers are called to embody their stated values in their everyday mode of living (such as Fisher's example of not swearing oaths). On the other hand, they may feel called to perform more dramatic prophetic actions with a symbolic meaning, such as Nayler's entry into Bristol, or George Fox's divinely prompted visitation of Lichfield, in which, he reports, he entered the city barefoot and cried out, '*Wo unto the bloody City of Lichfield!*' three times, later discovering that Christians were martyred there under the Roman Emperor Vespasian.[142] There is some overlap between ethical and prophetic *actio* – for instance, the routine refusal of Quaker men to doff their hats to supposed social superiors ('hat honour') was a confrontational act of embodied witness to the Quaker belief in the spiritual equality of all humanity.

Another provocative form of prophetic performance by early Quakers was going 'naked for a sign', which has scriptural precedent (e.g. in Isaiah 20), and did not necessarily mean absolute nudity, but could include lesser forms of undress such as wearing only sackcloth and women letting their hair hang loose.[143] Justifying this practice, Richard Farnworth writes of 'Nakednesse a signe or figure':

> for all they that are contrary to the light, are without the cloathing of God, among such doth the Lord send some of his Children, to go naked and put off their cloaths; a figure and signe of their nakednesse, who are naked from God, and cloathed with the filthy garments.[144]

The word 'figure' here probably derives not so much from classical rhetoric as from the widespread early modern mode of biblical interpretation in which Old Testament objects, people and events are seen as 'types and figures' of New Testament realities. Nevertheless, the naked Quaker is an embodied metaphor, a rhetorical agent who speaks not simply through his actions but through his very being. James Nayler was likewise attempting to speak through his triumphal entry into Bristol, though what he was trying to say remains unclear. The embodied rhetorical performance of Quakers such as Nayler and other radicals such as Coppe turns their bodies as well as their words into opaque rhetorical figures, violently disrupting the normal plausibility structures of their audience's experience of reality but not replacing them with a coherent alternative accessible to rational understanding.

Notes

1   John Deacon, *The Grand Impostor Examined: or, The Life, Tryal and Examination of James Nayler, the Seduced and Seducing Quaker* (London, 1656), p. 2. It is striking that, even in this report of oral testimony, Deacon is playing with Witherley's words in a way that is dependent on their written form: in the typographical pun 'mel-ODIOUS', the capitals highlight a word of opposite meaning within the larger word. There is a further play on words in the isolation of 'mel-', Latin for 'honey', juxtaposed with the 'buzzing' of Nayler's Quaker bees.

2   Deacon, *The Grand Impostor*, p. 2.

3   On the ambiguities of Nayler's performative actions and the words with which he and his followers explained them, see Leo Damrosch, *The Sorrows of the Quaker Jesus: James Nayler and the Puritan Crackdown on the Free Spirit* (Cambridge, MA: Harvard University Press, 1996), esp. pp. 146–229; Carole Dale Spencer, 'The Man Who "Set Himself as a Sign": James Nayler's Incarnational Theology', in Stephen W. Angell and Pink Dandelion (eds.), *Early Quakers and Their Theological Thought: 1647–1723* (Cambridge: Cambridge University Press, 2015), pp. 64–82, and Alison Searle, 'Performance, Incarnation, Conversion: Theology and the Future of Imagination', in Trevor Cairney and David Starling (eds.), *Theology and the Future: Evangelical Assertions and Explorations* (London: Bloomsbury T & T Clark, 2014), pp. 197–212.

4   Deacon, *The Grand Impostor*, p. 3.

5   Deacon, *The Grand Impostor*, pp. 10–11.

6   Deacon, *The Grand Impostor*, p. 11.

7   Deacon, *The Grand Impostor*, p. 12.

8   On the qualified embrace of religious toleration by Cromwell and the Cromwellian regime, see John Coffey, *Persecution and Toleration in Protestant England, 1558–1689* (Harlow: Longman, 2000), pp. 147–60, and Blair Worden, 'Toleration and the Cromwellian Protectorate', in W. J. Sheils (ed.), *Persecution and Toleration* (Oxford: Blackwells for Ecclesiastical History Society, 1984) (*Studies in Church History* 21), pp. 199–233.

9   Christopher Hill, *The World Turned Upside Down: Radical Ideas during the English Revolution* (London: Temple Smith, 1972), p. 186.

10   Aristotle, *Rhetoric*, 1.2.3.

11   Yvonne Sherwood, 'Prophetic Performance Art', *The Bible and Critical Theory* 2.1 (2006), pp. 1.1–1.4.

108   *The Rhetoric of Conversion in English Puritan Writing*

12   Cicero, *De Oratore*, III.lvi.213–27.

13   Alison Searle asserts Nayler's orthodoxy more strongly, arguing that 'It is clear from contemporary records of Nayler's examination by Parliament that he did not identify himself as Christ in the blasphemous manner in which he was accused' on the basis of Nayler's response to Parliament that 'I do abhor that any of that honour which is due to God should be given me, as I am a Creature' (Searle, 'Performance, Incarnation, Conversion', pp. 200–1, citing *A True Narrative of the Examination, Tryall and Sufferings of James Nayler* (London, 1657), sig. D3v). However, I think an ambiguity still remains – 'as' could either be read with the sense '[because] I am a Creature' to give the meaning that Nayler is not at all worthy of divine honour because he is human and not divine, or it could be read with the sense '[insofar as] I am a Creature' to mean that Nayler disclaims divine honour being due to his human creaturely nature but leaving open the possibility that Nayler also possesses or participates in a divine nature that is worthy of divine honour.

14   John Calvin, *Institutes of the Christian Religion*, ed. John T. McNeill, trans. Ford Lewis Battles, 2 vols. (London: SCM Press/Philadelphia: Westminster Press, 1961), III.i.1 (p. 537).

15   Classic historical studies include Hill, *The World Turned Upside Down*, and J. F. McGregor and Barry Reay (eds.), *Radical Religion in the English Revolution* (Oxford: Oxford University Press, 1984). Key studies by literary scholars include Nigel Smith, *Perfection Proclaimed: Language and Literature in English Radical Religion, 1640–1660* (Oxford: Clarendon, 1989), and Nicholas McDowell, *The English Radical Imagination: Culture, Religion, and Revolution, 1630–1660* (Oxford: Clarendon, 2003).

16   Geoffrey F. Nuttall, *The Holy Spirit in Puritan Faith and Experience* (1946; repr. with introduction by Peter Lake, Chicago: University of Chicago Press, 1992), esp. pp. 8–15.

17   Nuttall, *Holy Spirit in Puritan Faith and Experience*, pp. 23–4, 38–9, 104.

18   Smith, *Perfection Proclaimed*, p. 309.

19   Thomas Edwards, *Gangraena* (London, 1646), sig. A5v, cited in McDowell, *English Radical Imagination*, p. 1; see McDowell, *English Radical Imagination*, pp. 4–5, 10, and *passim*.

20   Smith, *Perfection Proclaimed*, pp. 308–39.

21   On Dell, see especially Eric C. Walker, *William Dell: Master Puritan* (Cambridge: W. Heffer and Sons, 1970), and Roger Pooley, 'Dell, William, d. 1669', *ODNB*, from which many of the biographical details here are taken.

22   Richard Greaves, *Glimpses of Glory: John Bunyan and English Dissent* (Stanford, CA: Stanford University Press, 2002), pp. 123–6.

23   This paradox is highlighted by Walker, *William Dell*, *passim*, and McDowell, *English Radical Imagination*, pp. 5–6, and Peter Burke, 'William Dell, the Universities and

The Radical Ethos of Prophetic Performance 109

the Radical Tradition', in Geoff Eley and William Hunt (eds.), *Reviving the English Revolution: Reflections and Elaborations on the Work of Christopher Hill* (London: Verso, 1988), pp. 181–9.

24 William Dell, *The Stumbling-Stone* (London, 1653), t.p.

25 Dell, *The Stumbling-Stone*, sig. A2r.

26 William Dell, *The Tryal of Spirits Both in Teachers & Hearers* (London, 1653), t.p.

27 Dell, *The Stumbling-Stone*, p. 27.

28 William Dell, *A Plain and Necessary Confutation of Divers Gross and Antichristian Errors, Delivered to the University Congregation, the Last Commencement, Anno 1653, by Mr. Sydrach Simpson, Master of Pembroke Hall in Cambridge* (London, 1654), pp. 1–2.

29 Dell, *A Plain and Necessary Confutation*, p. 15.

30 Dell, *A Plain and Necessary Confutation*, p. 15.

31 Dell, *The Tryal of Spirits*, p. 43.

32 Dell, *A Plain and Necessary Confutation*, pp. 2–3.

33 Later printed as *Petri Blensensis Continuatio ad Historiam Ingulphi*, in Thomas Gale (ed.), *Rerum Anglicarum Scriptorum Veterum* (Oxford, 1684), 2 vols., I:114–15. This chronicle is probably a fourteenth-century forgery purporting to be an earlier work, but its account of the founding of the university is also followed by Thomas Fuller, *The History of the University of Cambridge since the Conquest*, in *The Church-History of Britain: From the Birth of Jesus Christ, Untill the Year M.DC.XLVIII* (London, 1655), pp. 4–5, as well as by the Quaker Thomas Lawson in a work discussed later in this chapter: Thomas Lawson, *A Mite into the Treasury, Being a Word to Artists, Especially to Heptatechnists, the Professors of the Seven Liberal Arts, So Called, Grammer, Logick, Rhetorick, Musick, Arithmetick, Geometry, Astronomy* (London, 1680), p. 5.

34 Dell, *A Plain and Necessary Confutation*, pp. 44–5.

35 Dell is thus paradoxically remembered as an educational reformer as well as an anti-intellectual antinomian preacher. On Dell as an educational reformer with a vocational emphasis, whose proposals for education reform are comparable to those of Samuel Hartlib, Jan Amos Comenius, and John Milton, see Charles Webster, 'William Dell and the Idea of University', in Mikuláš Teich and Robert Young (eds.), *Changing Perspectives in the History of Science: Essays in Honour of Joseph Needham* (London: Heinemann, 1970), pp. 110–26, and Burke, 'William Dell, the Universities and the Radical Tradition'.

36 Dell, *The Stumbling-Stone*, pp. 27–8.

37 Dell, 'The Right Reformation of Learning, Schooles and Universities according to the State of the Gospel, and the True Light that shines therein', in *The Tryal of Spirits* (third pagination), p. 27.

38 Dell, *The Stumbling-Stone*, p. 22.

39 Dell, *The Stumbling-Stone*, p. 22.

40 Dell, *The Stumbling-Stone*, p. 22.

110   *The Rhetoric of Conversion in English Puritan Writing*

41 Dell, *The Tryal of Spirits*, p. 24.
42 William Dell, *Power from on High* (London, 1645), p. 36. On the spectrum within the Puritan milieu between conservatives who saw the Spirit's work as confined to the exposition of Scripture and radicals who claimed direct inspiration by the Spirit, see Nuttall, *Holy Spirit in Puritan Faith and Experience*.
43 Dell, *Power from on High*, p. 36.
44 Dell, *Power from on High*, p. 18.
45 Dell, *Power from on High*, sig. A2r.
46 Aristotle, *Rhetoric*, 1355a.
47 Dell, *Power from on High*, pp. 19–20.
48 Dell, *The Tryal of Spirits*, p. 66.
49 Dell, *The Tryal of Spirits*, p. 66.
50 On Coppe, see McDowell, *English Radical Imagination*, Chapter 4, ' "In a Lunatick Moode": Humanism, Puritanism, and the Rhetorical Strategies of Ranter Writing', pp. 89–136, and Robert Kenny, '"In These Last Dayes": The Strange Work of Abiezer Coppe', *The Seventeenth Century*, 13.2 (1998), 156–84.
51 In opposition both to Coppe's contemporary opponents who saw him as licentious and heretical from youth and to modern scholarship that doubts the sincerity of his later retractions, Kenny sees Coppe's departure from Reformed orthodoxy as a sincere but brief interlude caused by his sense that the millennial reign of Christ was imminent, followed by a 'return to the fold from which he came' (Kenny, '"In These Last Dayes"', *passim*; p. 172 quoted).
52 Abiezer Coppe, *Copp's Return to the Ways of Truth* [1651], in Nigel Smith (ed.), *A Collection of Ranter Writings from the Seventeenth Century* (London: Junction Books, 1983), pp. 134–5.
53 Abiezer Coppe, *A Second Fiery Flying Roule* [1649], in Smith (ed.), *Ranter Writings*, pp. 106–7.
54 2 Samuel 6:11–23, cf. 1 Chronicles 15:29.
55 Richard Sibbes, *The Soules Conflict with It Selfe, and Victory over It Self by Faith* (London, 1635), p. 147.
56 Coppe, *A Second Fiery Flying Roule*, p. 106.
57 Coppe, *A Second Fiery Flying Roule*, pp. 106–7.
58 Samuel How, *The Sufficiencie of the Spirits Teaching, without Humane-Learning* ([Amsterdam], 1640), sig. C3v–4r; John Burton, 'To the Reader', in John Bunyan, *Some Gospel-Truths Opened According to the Scriptures*, in *The Miscellaneous Works of John Bunyan*, 13 vols., gen. ed. Roger Sharrock (Oxford: Clarendon, 1976–94), I:11.
59 Coppe, *A Fiery Flying Roll*, in Smith (ed.), *Ranter Writings*, p. 82.
60 Coppe, *A Fiery Flying Roll*, in Smith (ed.), *Ranter Writings*, p. 82.
61 Others labelled as Ranters also juxtapose 'ramming' and 'damning', '[Lawrence] Clarkson used the phrase "damm'd and ramm'd into its only Center", while the

Ranters seized at Moor Lane reportedly exclaimed "*Ram me, Dam me*" (ram meant God)' (Ariel Hessayon, 'Abiezer Coppe and the Ranters', in Laura Lunger Knoppers (ed.), *The Oxford Handbook of Literature and the English Revolution* (Oxford: Oxford University Press, 2012), p. 363, citing L. C. [Lawrence Clarkson], *A Single Eye All Light, no Darkness* (London, 1650), p. 12.)

62 Coppe, *A Fiery Flying Roll*, in Smith (ed.), *Ranter Writings*, p. 83.

63 William Perkins, *The Arte of Prophecying*, in *Workes of That Famous and Worthie Minister of Christ in the Vniversitie of Cambridge, M. W. Perkins*, 3 vols. (Cambridge, 1608–9), II:759.

64 Coppe, *An Additional and Preambular Hint*, in Smith (ed.), *Ranter Writings*, p. 77.

65 See Deuteronomy 18:17-19; Deuteronomy 34:10; John 6:14; John 7:40; Acts 3:20-6; Acts 7:37.

66 See especially Calvin, *Institutes*, II.xv.

67 Abiezer Coppe, *Some Sweet Sips, of Some Spirituall Wine* [London, 1649], in Smith (ed.), *Ranter Writings*, p. 74.

68 McDowell, *English Radical Imagination*, esp. Chapter 2, '"Named and Printed Heretics": Literacy, Heterodoxy, and the Cultural Construction of Identity', pp. 22–49.

69 Coppe, *Some Sweet Sips*, in Smith (ed.), *Ranter Writings*, p. 58.

70 Coppe, *Some Sweet Sips*, in Smith (ed.), *Ranter Writings*, p. 60.

71 Coppe, *Some Sweet Sips*, in Smith (ed.), *Ranter Writings*, p. 60.

72 See Acts 19:19.

73 Coppe, *Some Sweet Sips*, in Smith (ed.), *Ranter Writings*, p. 61. Cf. Dell: 'And he so *prevailed* with his *Doctrine*, that *many* which used *curious Arts, brought their books together, and burnt them before all men, and the price of them was counted at fifty thousand pieces of silver*. So that as the *Gospel* prevailed, and the *Name* of *Christ* was magnified; so did people *renounce* Philosophy, and *burn* their books of *curious Arts*: For *which* Books our *Vniversity* would give as much mony (if they could procure it from *good Benefactors*) as *they* were *valued* at: So that as *they*, through the *efficacy* of the *Gospel*, of *Heathens* became *Christians*, and threw away all *other* Learning, and *burnt* their Books of *great value*, least they should *infect* others[.]' (*A Plain and Necessary Confutation*, p. 7.)

74 See Hebrews 12:22-3: 'But ye are come unto mount Sion, and unto the city of the living God, the heavenly Jerusalem, and to an innumerable company of angels, To the general assembly and church of the firstborn, which are written in heaven, and to God the Judge of all, and to the spirits of just men made perfect'.

75 Coppe, *Some Sweet Sips*, in Smith (ed.), *Ranter Writings*, p. 61. Coppe's tutor Ralph Button was a canon of Christ Church, and served as university orator from 1648 to the Restoration.

76 McDowell, *English Radical Imagination*, pp. 111–12.

77 E.g. Coppe, *A Fiery Flying Roll*, in Smith (ed.), *Ranter Writings*, p. 96.

78 Abiezer Coppe, *A Fiery Flying Roll* [London, 1649], in Smith (ed.), *Ranter Writings*, p. 83.

79 Perkins, *A Commentarie or Exposition vpon the Five First Chapters of the Epistle to the Galatians*, in *Workes*, II:179.

80 Coppe, *Some Sweet Sips*, in Smith (ed.), *Ranter Writings*, p. 47.

81 Noam Flinker, 'The Poetics of Biblical Prophecy: Abiezer Coppe's Late Converted Midrash', in Ariel Hessayon and David Finnegan (eds.), *Varieties of Seventeenth- and Early Eighteenth-Century English Radicalism in Context* (Farnham: Ashgate, 2011), p. 121.

82 Coppe, *Fiery Flying Roll*, in Smith (ed.), *Ranter Writings*, p. 86.

83 Sherwood, 'Prophetic Performance Art'.

84 Coppe, *A Second Fiery Flying Roule*, in Smith (ed.), *Ranter Writings*, pp. 104–5.

85 Coppe, *Fiery Flying Roll*, in Smith (ed.), *Ranter Writings*, p. 91.

86 Richard Baxter, DWL Baxter MS, *Treatises*, 3.67, fol. 302r, cited in Ariel Hessayon, 'Coppe, Abiezer (1619–1672?)', *ODNB*.

87 For a more recent theological and rhetorical wrestling with these dynamics, see Stephen H. Webb, *Blessed Excess: Religion and the Hyperbolic Imagination* (Albany, NY: SUNY Press, 1993).

88 On the Seekers, see, for instance, George Arthur Johnson, 'From Seeker to Finder: A Study in Seventeenth-Century English Spiritualism before the Quakers', *Church History*, 17.4 (December 1948), 299–315; J. F. McGregor, 'Seekers and Ranters', in McGregor and Reay (eds.), *Radical Religion in the English Revolution*, pp. 121–40; and Damrosch, *The Sorrows of the Quaker Jesus*, pp. 26–9.

89 William Erbery, *Nor Truth, Nor Error, Nor Day, Nor Night, but in the Evening There Shall Be Light, Zach. 14. 6, 7* (London, 1647), p. 2, citing Hosea 3:4. See Hill, *The World Turned Upside Down*, pp. 192–7.

90 Though Damrosch argues that the volume of this traffic was exaggerated: 'The frequent Quaker assertion that they had recruited large numbers of Seekers was, however, an interpretation through hindsight' (*The Sorrows of the Quaker Jesus*, p. 27).

91 George Fox, *A Journal or Historical Account of the Life, Travels, Sufferings, Christian Experiences and Labour of Love in the Work of the Ministry of That Ancient, Eminent and Faithful Servant of Jesus Christ, George Fox, Who Departed This Life in Great Peace with the Lord, the 13th of the 11th Month, 1690* (London, 1694), p. 63.

92 George Fox, *An Epistle to All People on the Earth*, cited in Michael P. Graves, *Preaching the Inward Light: Early Quaker Rhetoric* (Waco, TX: Baylor University Press, 2009), p. 83. See also Martin L. Warren, 'The Quakers as Parrhesiasts: Frank Speech and Plain Speaking as the Fruits of Silence', *Quaker History*, 98.2 (Fall 2009), 1–25.

93 Molly Murray, *The Poetics of Conversion in Early Modern English Literature: Verse and Change from Donne to Dryden* (Cambridge: Cambridge University Press, 2009), p. 7.

The Radical Ethos of Prophetic Performance   113

94 Graves, *Preaching the Inward Light*, pp. 17, 62–4.

95 Hilary Hinds, *George Fox and Early Quaker Culture* (Manchester: Manchester University Press, 2011), p. 30.

96 Fox, *Journal*, p. 5.

97 William Penn, 'The Preface, Being a Summary Account of the Divers *Dispensations of God* to Men, from the Beginning of the World to That of Our Present Age, by the Ministry and Testimony of His Faithful Servant *George Fox*, as an Introduction to the Ensuing *Iournal*', in Fox, *Journal*, sig. F1r; William Perkins, *Arte of Prophecying*, in *Workes*, II:760. Cf. Cicero, *De Oratore*, II.xlv.189–90. Debora Shuger notes the echo of Cicero in Perkins's words but comments that Perkins highlights 'the spiritual and psychological sources of passionate oratory at the expense of the artistic' (Debora K. Shuger, *Sacred Rhetoric: The Christian Grand Style in the English Renaissance* (Princeton, NJ: Princeton University Press, 1988), p. 70).

98 Robert Barclay, *An Apology for the True Christian Divinity, as the Same Is Held Forth, and Preached by the People, Called, in Scorn, Quakers* (London, 1678), p. 237.

99 1 Corinthians 2:4; Perkins, *Arte of Prophecying*, in *Workes*, II:759; Dell, *Power from on High*, sig. A2r.

100 Barclay, *Apology*, p. 260.

101 Fox, *Journal*, p. 341, and George Fox, 'Epistle CCLXXV', in Samuel Tuke (ed.), *Selections from the Epistles of George Fox* (Cambridge, MA: Riverside Press, 1879), p. 23, cited in Graves, *Preaching the Inward Light*, p. 84.

102 Cf. Graves, *Preaching the Inward Light*, p. 85.

103 Judith Roads, 'Quaker Convincement Language: Using Pathos and Logos in the Seventeenth Century', *Quaker Studies*, 25.2 (2020), p. 190.

104 Stephen Crisp, 'The Divine-Monitor', in *Scripture-Truths Demonstrated* (London, 1707), pp. 11–19; see Graves, *Preaching the Inward Light*, pp. 74–5.

105 Penn, 'Preface', in Fox, *Journal*, sig. E1v.

106 John Rous et al., 'The Testimony of Some of the *Author's Relations*', in Fox, *Journal*, p. x.

107 Dell, *The Tryal of Spirits*, p. 24; Coppe, *Some Sweet Sips, of Some Spirituall Wine*, in Smith (ed.), *Ranter Writings*, p. 74.

108 George Fox, John Stubs and Benjamin Farley, *A Battle-door for Teachers & Professors to Learn Singular & Plural* (London, 1660), title page.

109 Fox, *Journal*, p. 24. The same point is made by Lawson in his discussion of the right teaching of grammar in *A Mite into the Treasury*, pp. 7–9.

110 Fox, Stubs and Farley, *Battle-door*, p. 3.

111 George Fox and Ellis Hookes, *Instructions for Right Spelling, and Plain Directions for Reading and Writing True English* (London, 1673), p. 47.

112 Fox and Hookes, *Instructions for Right Spelling*, pp. 99, 110.

114   *The Rhetoric of Conversion in English Puritan Writing*

113 McDowell comments: 'As a university man, Fisher was an anomaly in the development of early Quakerism' (*English Radical Imagination*, p. 152).

114 On Fisher, see especially McDowell, *English Radical Imagination*, Chapter 5, 'Washing in Cabalinus' Well: Quakerism, Scepticism, and Radical Enlightenment', pp. 137–82.

115 Samuel Fisher, *Rusticus ad Academicos in Exercitationibus Expostulariis, Apologeticiis Quatuor: The Rustick's Alarm to the Rabbies* (London, 1660), 'The Third Apologetical, and Expostulatory Exercitation', pp. 23–4 (separate pagination for each 'exercitation'). Square brackets in original.

116 One instance of this that uses 'Rhetorick' in a generic sense far removed from university-trained eloquence is Fisher's rejection of the accusation that he uses '*Billingsgate Rhetorick*', that is, the vulgar abusive language associated with the Billingsgate fish market, arguing that 'As for *Billingsgate Rhetorick* its more found among the Scribes that are *Scolding, Scuffling*, and *Scrambling* for such petty *Businesses* as *Muscles* and *Cockels-shells*' among the trivialities of 'meer mouldring writings, *Externall Texts, trifling Transcrips, Letters, pedling points, Syllables, Triviall Tittles* and *Iota's*' than among those like Fisher who contend for the '*substantiall* matters, the *faith, that was once delivered to the Saints*, the *Light, Truth* and *Spirit* it self' (Fisher, *Rusticus ad Academicos*, 'The First Apological, and Expostulatory Exercitation', p. 12).

117 Daniel Featley, *Katabaptistai kataptüstoi: The Dippers Dipt* (London, 1645), pp. 133–4.

118 Featley, *Katabaptistai kataptüstoi*, p. 134.

119 Samuel Fisher, *Baby-baptism meer babism* (London, 1653), p. 585. Κατ'ἄνθρωπον (*Kat'anthropon*) = 'according to man', i.e. by human standards, a phrase taken from the Greek text of Galatians 1:12; Κατά χρις[τ]όν (*Kata christon*) = 'according to Christ'.

120 Lawson, *A Mite into the Treasury*, title page.

121 On Lawson, see Richard L. Greaves, 'Lawson, Thomas (bap. 1630, d. 1691)', *ODNB*.

122 Lawson, *A Mite into the Treasury*, p. 17.

123 Lawson, *A Mite into the Treasury*, p. 17.

124 Richard Sibbes, *Bowels Opened, or, A Discovery of the Neere and Deere Love, Union and Communion betwixt Christ and the Church, and Consequently betwixt Him and Every Beleeving Soule* (London, 1639), p. 204.

125 Lawson, *A Mite into the Treasury*, pp. 17–18.

126 Lawson, *A Mite into the Treasury*, p. 18.

127 Lawson, *A Mite into the Treasury*, p. 18.

128 Jackson I. Cope, 'Seventeenth-Century Quaker Style', *PMLA*, 71.4 (September 1956), pp. 736, 733.

129 Damrosch, *Sorrows of the Quaker Jesus*, p. 80.

130 Samuel Austin, *Plus Ultra, or The Second Part of the Character of a Quaker* (London, 1672), p. 8; Samuel Austin, *The Character of a Quaker in His True and Proper Colours, or, The Clownish Hypocrite Anatomized* (London, 1672), p. 3.

131 Judith Roads's recent discourse analysis of early Quaker persuasion notes the prevalence of repetition in Quaker writings as a mode of *pathos* (appeal to emotion), but also argues that there is an increasing presence of Aristotelian *logos* (appeal to reason) in Quaker writing of the later seventeenth century (Roads, 'Quaker Convincement Language', esp. pp. 193–6).

132 Fox, *Journal*, p. 38.

133 Fox, *Journal*, p. 38.

134 For 'evil thoughts', see Matthew 15:19, Mark 7:21, and James 2:4 (cf. Genesis 6:5, Psalm 56:5, Isaiah 59:7, and Matthew 9:4); for 'vain imaginations', see Romans 1:21: 'vain in their imaginations'.

135 Fox, *Journal*, p. 39.

136 Fox, *Journal*, pp. 39–40.

137 John Bunyan, *Grace Abounding to the Chief of Sinners*, ed. Roger Sharrock (Oxford: Clarendon, 1963), pp. 43–4, 48–50, 55, 60–2, 64–72; see Vera J. Camden, '"That of Esau": The Place of Hebrews xii. 16, 17 in *Grace Abounding*', in N. H. Keeble (ed.), *John Bunyan: Reading Dissenting Writing* (Bern: Peter Lang, 2002), pp. 133–64.

138 Fox, *Journal*, p. 40.

139 Richard Bauman, 'Aspects of Seventeenth Century Quaker Rhetoric', *Quarterly Journal of Speech*, 56 (1970), p. 74.

140 Fisher, *Rusticus ad Academicos*, sig. B3r.

141 Hinds, *George Fox and Early Quaker Culture*, p. 31.

142 Fox, *Journal*, pp. 53–4.

143 See, for instance, Kenneth L. Carroll, 'Early Quakers and "Going Naked as a Sign"', *Quaker History*, 67:2 (Autumn 1978), 69–87.

144 Richard Farnworth, *The Pure Language of the Spirit of Truth* (London, 1655), p. 7, cited in Hinds, *George Fox and Early Quaker Culture*, p. 26.

3

Light and weight: Richard Baxter's exhortations and meditations

Richard Baxter (1615–91), known for his devoted parish ministry at Kidderminster, his reluctant Nonconformity following the Restoration, and his astonishingly prolific writing,[1] tells his fellow ministers that 'The work of conversion is the great thing that we must first drive at, and labour with all our might to effect'.[2] William Orme, Baxter's nineteenth-century biographer and editor, concurs that this was Baxter's chief aim, 'While Baxter's talents were adequate to any subject to which they might be directed, the conversion of men was the grand object to which he devoted them, in the fullest extent in which they could be exercised.'[3]

As explored throughout this study, preaching and writing that aims at conversion is inherently rhetorical in its desire to persuade. Baxter speaks of God's grace making use of 'Ministerial perswasions',[4] and, like Perkins and Sibbes, he recognizes both divine and devilish projects of persuasion: 'Both Christ and Satan work *perswasively,* by *moral means,* and neither of them by *constraint* and *force*.'[5] Thus, though John Knott is right to note that 'Baxter was not sufficiently concerned with the workings of language to write anything approaching a formal rhetoric for preachers', Baxter's pastoral persuasion, as with that of the other preacher-writers considered in this book, is inherently rhetorical in purpose and so merits rhetorical analysis, and scattered comments throughout his works provide homiletic guidance to preachers on the persuasive style of their sermons as well as their doctrinal content.[6]

Among the figures considered in this book, Baxter has an unusual degree of emphasis on writing as a form of preaching that can bring about readers' conversion and strengthen them in faith, observing that 'The Writings of Divines are nothing else but a preaching the Gospel to the eye, as the *voice* preacheth it to the ear'.[7] Baxter's acceptance of writing as interchangeable with preaching contrasts with the view of other Puritan ministers such as Thomas Gataker. As Arnold Hunt notes, 'For Gataker, the reading of godly sermons might supplement live preaching but could never wholly replace it. For Baxter, on the other hand, the two were essentially one and the same'.[8] Baxter's emphasis on writing as preaching has possible biographical explanations, related both to his formative youthful experience and to his resort to writing as a means to continue ministry following his ejection from his parish living following the Restoration in 1660.

Baxter was born in Rowton, Shropshire, in 1615.[9] He recounts that he grew up 'in a Country that had but little Preaching at all' and that his father was converted 'by the bare reading of the Scriptures in private'.[10] The adolescent Richard came gradually to a faith of a broadly Puritan character primarily through reading. Among other 'good Books', he recalls providential encounters with 'Dr. *Sibb's bruised Reed*', sold by a 'poor Pedlar' at the door, and 'a little Piece of Mr *Perkins's* Works' in the possession of a family servant.[11] Baxter's youthful religious convictions were thus shaped by the writings of Perkins and Sibbes explored in Chapter 1 of this book, but Baxter's relationship with the tradition of English Reformed practical divinity, put forward by Perkins and Sibbes among others, was not an untroubled one. Baxter records that he was anxious in his youth:

> Because I could not distinctly trace the Workings of the Spirit upon my heart in that method which Mr. *Bolton*, Mr. *Hooker*, Mr. *Rogers*, and other Divines describe! nor knew the Time of my Conversion, being wrought on by the forementioned Degrees.[12]

Yet Baxter emerged from his wrestlings with the conviction that he need not conform to this overly prescriptive script for conversion to be in a state of grace, concluding that, although 'the Change of our Heart from Sin to God, is true Repentance', yet 'God breaketh not all Mens hearts alike'.[13]

Although the young Baxter was intellectually gifted, his schoolmaster persuaded him not to attend university but instead to study with a private tutor, Richard Wickstead, at Ludlow in Wales. Baxter found Wickstead not to be up to the job, 'only he loved me, and allowed me *Books and Time* enough: So that as I had no considerable helps from him in my Studies, so had I no considerable hinderance'.[14] Though Baxter often regretted his lack of a university education, he became an autodidact, and, N. H. Keeble notes, 'through omnivorous reading Baxter became one of the most learned of seventeenth-century divines'.[15]

Richard Baxter's Exhortations and Meditations 119

'The plainest words are the profitablest oratory':
Baxter's rhetorical ambivalence

Keeble's pioneering literary study of Baxter mentions classical rhetoric in passing, primarily as something that Baxter disregards:

> He certainly knew, admired, and often quoted Senecan writers [...] but for the canons of any literary school to have guided him would have been to allow the intrusion of a set of values which had no bearing on the business in hand: for these are of men, and had not God made foolish the wisdom of the world?[16]

Keeble acknowledges that Baxter is not averse to the use of 'imagery in moderation' and elaborates on 'his humanistic love of learning and books', but I think he overstates Baxter's rejection of 'the canons of any literary school', which certainly did not dictate Baxter's manner of communication but may, on occasion, 'have guided him'.[17]

It must be admitted that Baxter rarely uses the term 'rhetoric' or its cognates, and that when he does so the connotations are usually negative – for instance, speaking of preachers more concerned to speak eloquently than to live uprightly:

> O how curiously have I heard some men preach! and how carelesly have I seen them live! They have been so accurate as to the wordy part in their own preparations, that seldom preaching seemed a vertue to them, that their language might be the more polite, and all the Rhetorical jingling writers they could meet with, were prest to serve them for the adorning of their stile, (and gawds were oft their chiefest ornaments.) They were so nice in hearing others, that no man pleased them that spoke as he thought, or that drowned not affections, or dulled not, or distempered not the heart by the predominant strains of a phantastick wit.[18]

Baxter here joins a venerable tradition of anti-rhetorical polemic that associates rhetoric with empty wit and insincere style – the curious and witty preacher is placed in opposition to the preacher 'that spoke as he thought'. Baxter's understanding of 'rhetoric' here reduces rhetoric to the canons of *elocutio* (style) and *actio/pronuntiatio* (delivery), just as the Ramist tradition associated with Peter Ramus did, and also perhaps echoes the frequent reduction of *elocutio* by Renaissance rhetoricians to the use of figures and ornaments.[19]

As is the case with other writers considered in this book, however, Baxter here uses rhetorical techniques and figures of speech in his attack on rhetoric. The parallelism of 'how curiously' and 'how carelesly' uses anaphora, consonance and homoioteleuton (similar word endings) to damn the witty preacher's misplaced

120   *The Rhetoric of Conversion in English Puritan Writing*

efforts, while the sincere preacher to whom the overly 'nice' (meaning picky or fastidious) hearers give no attention is distinguished from the witty preacher by a tricolon of negatives ('drowned not' … 'dulled not' … 'distempered not').

Ironically, Baxter's conception of 'Rhetorical' preaching here is that of an empty wit that 'dull[s]' the heart, 'drown[ing]' the affections in soporific clouds of words that obscure the divine message that should come through preaching. What Baxter calls 'Rhetorical jingling' preaching here is preaching that fails to persuade the heart and is thus rhetorically ineffectual. Furthermore, this 'rhetorical' preaching is deficient in the three modes of persuasion outlined by Aristotle, *logos* (appeal to reason), *ethos* (appeal to the perceived authority of the speaker) and *pathos* (appeal to emotion/the affections), since its rational content is unclear, the persona of the speaker is transparently insincere, and it dulls rather than exciting the affections.

Scholars commenting on Baxter's prose style or preaching frequently cite the epistle to the reader that opens *A Treatise on Conversion*, with its contrast between 'witty' and 'plain' preaching:[20]

> I shall never forget the relish of my soul when God first warmed my heart with these matters, and when I was newly entered into a seriousness in Religion: when I read such a Book as Bishop *Andrews* Sermons, or heard such kind of preaching, I felt no life in it: me thoughts they did but play with holy things. Yea, when I read such as Bishop *Hall*, or *Henshaws* Meditations, or other such Essays, Resolves, and witty things, I tasted little sweetness in them, though now I can find much. But it was the plain and pressing downright Preacher, that onely seemed to me to be in good sadness, and to make somewhat of it, and to speak with life, and light, and weight: And it was such kind of writings that were wonderfully pleasant, and savoury to my soul. And I am apt to think that it is thus now with my Hearers; and that I should measure them by what I was, and not by what I am.[21]

Passages such as these have helped to shape the broader perception of a sharp dichotomy between 'witty' rhetorical preaching (which earlier literary critics dubbed 'metaphysical' or 'Anglican') and plain and powerful 'Puritan' preaching.[22] However, the dichotomy is less sharp if we look more closely at Baxter's words here. To read this passage rightly, we should recognize the layered time frame involved. The mature Baxter is recalling his perceptions as a young man, and while he can now derive sweetness and spiritual benefit from some of these writers, he models his current practice as a preacher and writer on what his younger self would have found beneficial.

Although Baxter may be saying that he can now derive spiritual benefit from all of the writers he lists, there may perhaps be a distinction between Baxter's assessment of the florid preachers, such as Lancelot Andrewes, who 'deal liker to Players than Preachers in the Pulpit' and the 'exactness and brevity' of Joseph Hall and Joseph Henshaw.[23] The style of Andrewes and company reprehensibly 'savoureth of levity, and tendeth to evaporate weighty Truths, and turn them all into very fancies, and keep them from the heart', but Baxter has come to appreciate the scholarly Senecan style of Hall and Henshaw since he 'can better digest exactness and brevity, than I could so long ago'.[24] It is this Senecan style of brief aphorisms that Baxter associates with 'witty things', rather than the more florid 'metaphysical' preaching style designated as 'witty' by twentieth-century studies of the history of preaching. Yet though Baxter now appreciates the 'conciseness, sententiousness, and quickness' of Hall and Henshaw's kind of wit, he states that his treatise will deliberately forgo these qualities.[25] Baxter thus accommodates his style to the needs of his audience, who more closely resemble his younger than his mature self: 'I should measure them by what I was, and not by what I am'.

Baxter's own style is here ornamented by simple verbal techniques, and so is not plain in the sense of being entirely unvarnished. There is an implied opposition of 'play' and 'plain', and a power in the plosives of 'plain [...] pressing [...] Preacher'. Further sound patterning includes 'to me [...] to make', and the sibilance of 'seemed [...] sadness [...] somewhat [...] speak'. The culminating triplet of 'life, and light, and weight' is a phrase that can be taken to encapsulate Baxter's summary of the qualities to which preachers should aspire in their communication.

Keeble notes Baxter's affinity for Seneca, the Roman philosopher and dramatist, and for English 'Senecan' writers such as Joseph Hall and Francis Bacon.[26] In influential histories of English prose developed by Morris Croll and George Williamson, Seneca is generally considered the figurehead for the 'anti-Ciceronian' prose of the seventeenth century that reacted against the florid elaborations of Ciceronian style in the late Elizabethan period, breaking up the long 'periodic' sentences with multiple balancing clauses of the Elizabethan Ciceronians into short aphoristic statements often placed in counterpoint to one another.[27]

Baxter cannot, however, be characterized as straightforwardly anti-Ciceronian, since he cites Cicero on occasion, and even expresses an appreciation for Cicero's rhetoric. Just a page after complaining of preachers 'hiding excellent Truths in a heap of vain Rhetorick',[28] Baxter exhorts young ministers 'that besides your clear unfolding of the Doctrine of the Gospel, you may also be Masters of your peoples Affections, and may be as potent in your divine Rhetorick, as *Cicero* in his Humane'.[29] Baxter cites one of Cicero's rhetorical maxims approvingly when exhorting preachers to a passionate delivery: 'Remember what *Cicero* saith, that if the matter be never so combustible, yet if you put not fire to it, it will not burn'.[30]

In *The Reformed Pastor*, Baxter cites Augustine's *De Doctrina Christiana*, which appropriates Cicero's rhetoric for the Christian preacher. One of these quotations, which Baxter curiously begins in English and continues in Latin, highlights both the necessity of the preacher's human effort and its insufficiency:

> *A Preacher must labour to be heard understandingly, willingly and obediently, & hoc se posse magis pietate orationum, quam oratoris facultate non dubitet: ut orando pro se ac pro aliis, quos est allocuturus, sit prius orator quam doctor; & in ipsa hora accedens, priusquam exeat, proferat linguam ad Deum, levet animam sitientem, &c.*[31]

Perhaps Baxter switches into Latin for the neat parallelism of '*magis pietate orationum, quam oratoris facultate*' ('more by the piety of his prayers than by the skill of an orator'). The preacher needs to exert himself in *oratio* (prayer) as well as *oratoria* (oratory/rhetoric) in order to be persuasive. Hence the preacher is '*prius orator quam doctor*', a speaker (*orator*) to God before he is a teacher (*doctor*) of the people: here the word *orator* does not have the usual meaning of the English 'orator', a speaker with rhetorical eloquence to a human audience, but rather that of one who speaks or prays to God.

Baxter elsewhere provides one of the most eloquent and metaphorical defences of plain style to be found. He follows the straightforward assertion that 'All our teaching must be as Plain and Evident as we can make it. For this doth most suite to a Teachers ends'[32] with a succession of evocative images:

> Truth loves the Light, and is most beautiful when most naked. Its a sign of an envious enemy to hide the truth; and a sign of an Hypocrite to do this under pretence of revealing it: and therefore painted obscure Sermons (like the painted glass in the windows that keeps out the light) are too oft the markes of painted Hypocrites.[33]

Baxter's advocacy of plain style prioritizes edification over erudition, but this does not imply unvarnished literalism with no ornamentation whatsoever. Baxter's attack on the erudite ornate sermons of hypocrites itself makes use of a vivid and memorable simile, 'the painted glass [...] that keeps out the light', to characterize the uselessness of opaque ornament to enable the perception of truth.

Hypocrites are those who perform a role that they do not possess in reality – the word derives from the Greek for a stage actor, and in Puritan usage denoted those who professed godliness and saving faith without truly possessing it. Baxter aligns hypocrisy with rhetoric elsewhere when he relates how the hypocrite criticizes the prayers of the godly poor for violations of social and rhetorical decorum. Baxter does not deny that the godly can be uncouth in their expression, but stresses a different set of priorities for evaluating prayer:

> because the *same spirit* teacheth not *fine words*, and rhetorical language, to all that it teacheth to *pray with unutterable sighs and groans*, Rom. 8. 26, 27. though the *searcher of hearts* (who is not delighted with complements and set speeches) doth well understand the *meaning of the spirit*.[34]

Speech (here, that of prayer) is not to be valued for its polished eloquence but for its Spirit-given sincerity. Here the presence of the Spirit does not confer verbal eloquence but enables spiritual communication between the godly and their God despite their lack of eloquence. Thus, for Baxter, Spirit-given *ethos* can coexist with a lack of verbal skill.

However, Baxter acknowledges that '*ornament and oratory*' are helpful for the preacher's task of persuasion, recommending to ministerial students that they create '*a threefold Common-place-Book*', with

> One part for definitions, distinctions, axioms, and necessary doctrines: Another part for what is useful for ornament and oratory: And another for References as a common Index to all the Books of that Science which you read[.][35]

All three of the verbal arts of the trivium feature here as serving the minister's task: the 'definitions' of grammar, the 'distinctions' of logic and the 'ornament and oratory' of rhetoric.

In Baxter's 1681 Latin treatise *Methodus Theologiae Christianae*, published late in Baxter's life, there is a rather intimidating visual representation of all knowledge in relation to God (reproduced at the end of this chapter).[36] Among many other disciplines swirling around the diagram in tiny handwriting, the arts of speaking are listed:

Artes Organica viz
(a) Loquendi viz
    1. ° Significanter Lexica
    2. ° Pure Grammatica
    3. ° Ornate Rhetorica

124   *The Rhetoric of Conversion in English Puritan Writing*

(b) Dicendi viz
    1. ° Sane, Logica
    2. ° Potenter, Oratoria
    3. ° Suaviter Poetica
[The instrumental arts, viz.
(a) Of speaking, viz:
    1. Clearly – Lexicography.
    2. Purely – Grammar.
    3. Elegantly – Rhetoric.
(b) Of speaking, viz.
    1. Soundly – Logic.
    2. Powerfully – Oratory.
    3. Sweetly – Poetry.]

The *Methodus* is a work intended particularly for ministers, and so this is circumstantial evidence that Baxter would advise ministers to take rhetoric into account in their pastoral labours. This is also implicit in Baxter's comically enormous suggested reading list for 'The *Poor mans Library*' that he provides in *A Christian Directory*, in which John Wilkins's homiletic manual *Ecclesiastes* is included under the heading 'Subordinate Helps for understanding and Preaching'.[37] It is also curious that Baxter identifies 'Rhetorica' and 'Oratoria' as separate arts, as the usage of these terms cannot be neatly separated out in the work of the classical rhetoricians such as Quintilian.[38] Speaking 'Ornate' (elegantly) is not the same as speaking 'Potenter' (powerfully). In Baxter's corpus of writing as a whole, ornamental language is often negatively valued, whereas powerful speech is positively valued.

In *The Saints Everlasting Rest*, Baxter laments two 'extreams in the Ministers of *England*' so far as their style and delivery are concerned. Those who use frothy and 'vain Rhetorick' have a frivolous style not in keeping with the seriousness of their message, and so 'our people are brought to hear Sermons as they do Stageplays, because Ministers behave themselves but as the Actors', yet a disregard for disposition and delivery is no more successful for the purposes of godly persuasion:

> On the other side, how many by their slovenly dressing, and the uncleanness of the dish that it is served up in, do make men loath and nauseate the food of Life, and even despise and cast up that which should nourish them?[39]

Though insisting on care in verbal presentation, Baxter recognizes that the most eloquent style is not always the fittest for purpose:

Richard Baxter's Exhortations and Meditations 125

I know our stile must not be the same with different Auditories; Our language must not only be suited to our matter, but also to our hearers, or else the best Sermon may be worst; we must not read the highest Books to the lowest Form.[40]

Baxter cites Luther in support of this idea: 'Therefore was *Luther* wont to say, That *Qui puerilitèr, popularitèr, trivialitèr, & simplicissimè docent, optimi ad vulgus sunt concionatores*' ('Those who teach in a childish, popular, common and most simple manner are the best preachers to the common people').[41] This is a paradoxical use of the principle of rhetorical decorum, fitting one's speech to the occasion, that suggests that sometimes it is rhetorically fitting to avoid eloquence.

Perhaps surprisingly, Baxter finds Scripture itself wanting in places by conventional rhetorical standards of eloquence, but defends this 'imperfection' as serving Scripture's persuasive purpose:

But an innocent imperfection there is in the Method and Phrase, which if we deny, we must renounce most of our Logick and Rhetorick. [...] Yet was this imperfect way (at that time, all things considered) the fittest way to divulge the Gospel: That is the best Language which is best suited to the Hearers, and not that which is best simply in it self, and supposeth that understanding in the Hearers which they have not.[42]

Baxter here extrapolates a general principle of communication from the particular persuasive strategies of Scripture: given the limitations of one's hearers, to communicate in an 'imperfect way' may be more effective for achieving one's persuasive goals than a more polished eloquence. This is a conflation of the rhetorical doctrine of decorum (fitting one's speech to the audience) with the theological doctrine of accommodation, which states that God communicates with human beings within the limits of their understanding.

Baxter's ambivalence towards rhetoric is typified by his citation of Seneca to excuse the unpolished nature of his writing:

the *Truths of God* do perform their work more by *their Divine Authority*, and *proper Evidence*, and *material Excellency*, than by any *ornaments* of *fleshly wisdom*: and (as *Seneca* saith) though I will not despise an *elegant Physicion*, yet will I not think my self much the happyer, for his adding eloquence to his healing art.[43]

Baxter's thoughts on the relative value of verbal ornamentation in preaching are well summed up in these words:

126 *The Rhetoric of Conversion in English Puritan Writing*

> The plainest words are the profitablest Oratory in the weightiest matters.
> Fineness is for ornament, and delicacy for delight; but they answer not *Necessity*,
> though sometime they may modestly attend that which answers it.[44]

Baxter does not 'reject ornament' and 'delight' wholesale, but they are only to
have an ancillary role. They 'answer not *Necessity*' in matters as weighty as the
salvation or damnation of one's hearers, but, if that chief end is kept in view, 'they
may modestly attend'.

Logos and *pathos*: 'Judgment and affection'

In seeking to persuade individuals to conversion and godly living, Baxter uses
the analytical categories of faculty psychology, the identification of the different
components of the inner self common in early modern analysis, more explicitly
than Perkins and Sibbes, but still in a rather fluid way.[45] In Baxter's psychology,
it is the reason that sways the will,[46] in contrast to the centrality of the affections
for other Puritans such as Richard Sibbes, and so it is the reason that must first
be persuaded: '*The use of the Word, and all ordinances and providences is first
to Rectifie Reason, and thereby the Will, and thereby the Life.*'[47] Similarly, Baxter
states in *A Christian Directory*:

> The *Understanding* (though not the first in the sin) must be first in the cure:
> For all that is done upon the *Lower* faculties must be by the *Governing power* of
> the *will:* And all that is done upon the *will* (according to the order of humane
> nature) must be done by the *Understanding*[.][48]

This prioritization of the understanding as the faculty that needs first to be
persuaded in the work of conversion would appear to suggest that *logos*, appeal
to reason, is the Aristotelian mode of persuasion chiefly adopted by Baxter. But,
as often with Baxter, things are not so simple. For Baxter, the right informing
of the understanding is the necessary precondition of the moral and spiritual
awakening necessary for conversion, but it is not sufficient in itself, since
conversion is a change not only of the mind but also of the heart: 'You are never
truly changed, till your Hearts be changed: And the Heart is not changed till
the *Will* or *Love* be changed. [...] God will not be *your God* against your wills,
while you esteem him as the *Devil*.'[49] Baxter uses 'will', 'love' and 'desire' almost
interchangeably, suggesting that the boundary between will and affections is
blurred for him. For Baxter, one desires what one perceives to be good, and then
acts in accordance with one's desires: thus the intellect determines one's desires,

and the desires sway the will, but yet there is already an element of affection or passion in the intellect's perception of an object as desirable.[50] Keith Condie summarizes Baxter's view of the mutual dependence of reason and passion in persuasion to right action as follows:

> As constituents of the sensitive soul, the passions required the direction of the rational faculties. At the same time, however, the rational soul had need of the passions to catalyse it into action. Baxter held that without the spark of passion, the intellect is slow to receive truth and the will lacks the inclination to choose and to act.[51]

Baxter tells us that Christ 'first revealeth saving *truth* to the *understanding,* and affecteth the *will* by shewing the *Goodness* of the things revealed'.[52] The preacher's persuasive strategy, likewise, should engage each of the mental faculties:

> As we and they have understandings, and wills, and affections, so must the bent of our endeavours be to communicate the fullest Light of Evidence from our understandings unto theirs, and to warm their hearts by kindling in them holy affections, as by a communication from ours.[53]

Similarly, Baxter writes that:

> Every Reasonable soul hath both Judgment and Affection, and every Rational Spiritual Sermon must have both: A Discourse that hath Judgment without Affection, is dead, and uneffectual, and that which hath Affection without Judgment, is mad and transporting[.][54]

Though not using these terms, Baxter is saying that both *logos* (appeal to rational 'Judgment') and *pathos* (appeal to emotion or 'Affection') must be present for preaching to be persuasive. Condie comments on this passage: 'knowledge will not result in faithful Christian practice without the heart and affections being called into play; desire is antecedent to action.'[55]

Baxter stresses the importance not only of the subject matter of a sermon but also of the manner of its delivery:

> A great matter also with the most of our hearers, doth lie in the very pronunciation and tone of speech; The best matter will scarce move them, if it be not movingly delivered.[56]

These concerns about the manner of delivery correspond to the fifth stage or 'canon' of rhetoric in Cicero's schema, that of *actio* or *pronuntiatio*. In this connection, Baxter tells us that God usually makes 'not only the matter that is preacht, but also the manner of preaching to be instrumental to the work'.[57]

128   *The Rhetoric of Conversion in English Puritan Writing*

Yet a persuasive manner of preaching is dependent not only on the preacher's words, but also on the *ethos* of the preacher, his authority (as perceived by his hearers) to preach and to be heard attentively. For Baxter, the *ethos* of the preacher comes from both his inward regenerate state and his visible external status as a minister of the church ordained by lawful authority. These, in Baxter's view, ought to coincide, though, sadly, often do not: 'Verily, it is the common danger and calamity of the Church, to have unregenerate and unexperienced Pastors: and to have so many men become Preachers, before they are Christians.'[58]

Baxter, like Perkins, considers it unfitting but not impossible for listeners to be converted through the preaching of an unconverted minister. Perkins's commentary on Galatians insists that 'Ministers of the Gospell must learne Christ as *Paul* learned him. [...] They that must convert others, it is meet they should bee effectually converted.'[59] Although 'must' seems to suggest an absolute necessity of the preacher being regenerate, 'it is meet' could be read in a weaker sense – it ought to be (but is not always) the case. Perhaps 'must' signals an obligation – what emphatically ought to be the case – rather than an assertion of what is always in fact the case. Baxter recognizes more emphatically than Perkins that conversion can occur through the preaching of unconverted ministers; he writes, 'Many a Taylor goes in raggs that maketh costly cloathes for others: And many a Cook scarce licks his fingers, when he hath dress't for others the most costly dishes.'[60] Hence, early on in *The Reformed Pastor*, Baxter exhorts his ministerial hearers to conversion.

Baxter considers that the godly preacher's *ethos* derives from his own status as a converted sinner, though it is possible (but highly unfitting) for an unconverted preacher to preach awakening sermons. He exclaims: 'O Sirs, all your preaching and perswading of others will be but dreaming and trifling hypocrisie, till the work be throughly done upon your selves.'[61] This *ethos* of the converted sinner is the source of effective and affective *pathos*:

> I tell you, these things are never well known till they are felt, nor well felt till they are possessed: And he that feeleth them not himself, is not so like to speak feelingly to others, nor to help others to the feeling of them.[62]

Though it is possible for one not truly converted to be moved in some measure by spiritual things, they are not 'well felt' except by those who truly possess them. This *ethos* is the basis for authentic *pathos*: 'He is like to be but a heartless Preacher, that hath not the Christ and grace that he preacheth in his heart.'[63]

In his funeral sermon for Baxter, Matthew Sylvester, a fellow ejected minister who prepared Baxter's posthumously published autobiography *Reliquiae*

Baxterianae for the press, praises the verbal eloquence of Baxter's 'Elocution' as flowing out from his inward *ethos* and *pathos*:

> a man of ready, free, and very proper Elocution; and aptly expressive of his own thoughts and sentiments [...] He had a moving πάθος [*pathos*], and useful Acrimony in his words; neither did his Expressions want their emphatical Accent, as the Matter did require. And when he spake of weighty Soul-Concerns, you might find his very Spirit Drench'd therein.[64]

Baxter's pastoral rhetoric embraces Cicero's maxim that a speaker must be moved in order to move others, a principle adopted for the purposes of godly persuasion by William Perkins: 'Wood, that is capable of fire, doth not burne, vnles fire be put to it: & he must first bee godly affected himselfe, who would stirre vp godly affections in other men.'[65] The need for the preacher to be moved himself in order to move others has implications for the mechanics of his verbal delivery such as the tone and volume of his voice:

> When a man hath a Reading or Declaming tone, like a School-boy saying his lesson or an Oration, few are moved with any thing that he saith. Let us therefore rowse up our selves to the work of the Lord, and speak to our people as for their lives, and save them as by violence, pulling them out of the fire[.][66]

It is the responsibility of ministers to 'rowse up our selves to the work of the Lord', transforming a flat delivery into a passionate delivery. The preacher's vehement delivery is a form of verbal violence, which 'lay[s] siege to the souls of sinners' and 'lay[s] the battery of Gods Ordinance' against Satan, beating down the diabolical defences in the sinner's mind.[67]

However, though Baxter considers every part of the sermon to be of urgent and vital importance, he recognizes the need for variety in delivery:

> Though I move you not to a constant lowdness (for that will make your fervency contemptible) yet see that you have a constant seriousness; and when the matter requireth it (as it should do it, the application at least of every Doctrine) then lift up your voice, and spare not your spirits, and speak to them as to men that must be awakened, either here or in Hell.[68]

Baxter's recommendation that the application section of a sermon (which follows the unfolding of the text and the exposition of doctrine) should be delivered in an especially emphatic manner echoes the advice of Perkins's *The Arte of Prophecying* that the preacher's delivery should be 'moderate' in his exposition of doctrine but 'in the exhortation more feruent and vehement'.[69]

It takes 'a great deal of holy skill' for preachers to speak persuasively in 'language and manner as beseems our work, and yet as is most suitable to the capacities of the hearers'.[70] Both adequate technical ability in speaking and a right spiritual disposition are implied in the phrase 'holy skill'. Baxter advises the fitting of one's speech to particular audiences with particular needs. This is a kind of rhetorical decorum, though the sources Baxter draws on are pastoral guides, such as Gregory the Great's sixth-century *Cura Pastoralis*, rather than rhetorical manuals.[71]

Baxter would agree with Perkins's comment that '*Application* is that, wherby the doctrine rightly collected is diuersly fitted according as place, time, and person doe require'.[72] In several works, Baxter produces lists of different kinds of hearers reminiscent of the list in Perkins's *The Arte of Prophecying*. For Baxter, these different audiences are not fixed groups, but rather individuals at different points on the road towards conversion and then through various stages of spiritual maturity. This continuum informs Baxter's ongoing publishing project through his prolific writings that Baxter claims was inspired by a 1654 conversation with James Ussher (Protestant Archbishop of Armagh), in which, according to Baxter, Ussher proposed that they collaborate in the project of writing a comprehensive programme of English practical divinity to guide readers at different stages in the spiritual journey from unregenerate ignorance to mature faith.[73]

Baxter explains that, with the first group (the 'impenitent Unconverted sinners'), 'I thought a wakening Perswasive was a more necessary means then meer Directions'.[74] The 'wakening Perswasive' is an urgent appeal to *pathos* aiming to stir up the affections, rather than the appeal primarily to *logos* of 'meer Directions'. Exhortation is more necessary when speaking to those who are not yet persuaded of the need to be converted – thus the stirring of the affections is a means to turning the will. For those whose will is already set on pursuing the narrow path of faith and godliness, and simply need further instruction on what this is, less passion is necessary; hence, in the introduction to *A Christian Directory*, Baxter writes:

> Expect not here *copious* and *earnest Exhortations;* for that work I have done already, and have now to do with such, as say *they are made willing,* and desire help against their *Ignorance,* that *Skill* and *Will* may concurr to their salvation.[75]

Using the categories of classical rhetoric, the ignorant or obstinate among the unconverted are in need of forceful deliberative rhetoric (the mode of rhetoric seeking to persuade the audience to a particular course of action), whereas, for those who are more receptive, teaching (*docere*) takes precedence over moving (*movere*).

Richard Baxter's Exhortations and Meditations 131

It is not only the minister who is charged with persuading others to saving faith and godly living, but all the godly who have that responsibility. Baxter encourages his readers to observe situational decorum in instructing others, fitting their words to the time, the place and the persons involved. They should be wise

> in choosing the fittest season for your Exhortation [...] when the Earth is soft, the Plow will enter. Take a man when he is under affliction, or in the house of mourning, or newly stirred by some moving Sermon, and then set it home, and you may do him good. Christian Faithfulness doth require us, not onely to do good when it falls in our way, but to watch for opportunities of doing good.[76]

The godly persuader should thus wait until the *kairos*, the opportune time, which twentieth-century rhetorician Eric Charles White calls 'a passing instant when an opening appears which must be driven through with force if success is to be achieved'.[77]

The godly should 'Be wise also in suiting your Exhortation to the quality and temper of the person', accommodating their delivery to both the educational status and the spiritual and emotional state of the hearer. The 'obstinate and secure' should be reproved 'sharply', while those of 'timorous, tender natures [...] must be tenderly dealt with'. With the learned, 'you must deal more by convincing Arguments, and less by passionate perswasions', that is, by appealing to *logos* more than *pathos*, whilst 'If it be one that is both ignorant and stupid, there is need of both'.[78]

Though the divine rhetoric of the Spirit works particularly through the words of the preacher, the Spirit as divine rhetorician can make use of non-verbal as well as verbal means. Baxter asserts that some sinners are brought to repentance only by affliction:

> God will be more regarded when he pleadeth with them, with the rod in his hand: stripes are the best Logick, and Rhetorick for a fool. When sinne hath captivated their Reason to their flesh, the Arguments to convince them must be such, as the flesh is capable of perceiving. [...] The flesh understandeth the language of the rod, better then the language of Reason, or of the Word of God.[79]

While the preacher must reach the will through the reason, God is also able to bend the will through afflicting the body, and thus to overcome the culpable inability of the sinner to understand the logic and rhetoric of the preacher.

'[T]he vizard of Virtue': Satan's apostles and the saints' anxieties

In the works of Baxter, as in the works of the other Puritan writers considered in this book, just as God and the godly seek to persuade, so do the devil and his disciples. 'Wicked men' are persuasive messengers of Satan:

> Also their constant perswasions, allurements, threats, &c. hinder much. God doth scarce ever open the eyes of a poor sinner, to see that all is naught with him, and his way is wrong, but presently there is a multitude of Satans Apostles ready to flatter him, and dawb, and deceive, and settle him again in the quiet possession of his former Master.[80]

'Satans Apostles' may well allude to 2 Corinthians 11:13–15, the biblical passage referred to by Johannes Susenbrotus in his discussion of paradiastole (the figure through which virtue is characterized as vice or vice versa):[81]

> For such are false apostles, deceitful workers, transforming themselves into the apostles of Christ. And no marvel; for Satan himself is transformed into an angel of light. Therefore it is no great thing if his ministers also be transformed as the ministers of righteousness; whose end shall be according to their works.

St Paul here highlights how the 'false apostles' pass themselves off as 'ministers of righteousness', and Baxter similarly dramatizes how the apostles of Satan disguise their advocacy of sinful complacency as an exhortation to trust in God's mercy:

> What, say they, do you make a doubt of your Salvation, who have lived so well, and done no body harm, and been beloved of all? God is merciful: and if such as you shall not be saved, God help a great many: [...] Come, come, if you hearken to these Puritan books or Preachers, they will drive you to despair shortly, or drive you out of your wits.[82]

This is a paradiastolic substitution of unrepentant presumption for true repentant faith in God's mercy to sinners. Note that Satan's apostles denigrate the godly through the pejorative use of the term 'Puritan'; 'books' are here linked with 'Preachers', in keeping with Baxter's conception of godly writing as a mode of preaching.[83]

Baxter more than once refers to Satan as an 'angel of light', echoing the phrase from 2 Corinthians 11:14. At one point, Baxter uses this phrase in connection with the disguising of vice as virtue, conforming more straightforwardly to the classical sense of paradiastole. Speaking of the need for sinners to humble themselves, he says of this self-humbling that:

It unmasketh sinne, which had got the vizard of Virtue, or of a small matter, or harmless thing. It unmasketh Satan, who was transformed into a Friend, or an Angel of light, and sheweth him, as we say, with his cloven feet and horns.[84]

Here, satanic paradiastole is characterized also as a satanic prosopopoeia (the taking on of the persona of another) in which sin puts on a mask or 'vizard', and the sinner's self-humbling removes this mask to show Satan as he is.

Satan, in his adopted persona of the 'angel of light', is proficient in the three Aristotelian modes of persuasion. His transformation into an angel of light is itself an assertion of *ethos*, through which Satan presents himself as a divine messenger who ought to be trusted. In relation to doctrinal controversy, Baxter warns: 'The Devil is a greater Scholar than you, and a nimbler disputant: he can *transform himself into an Angel of light to deceive*.'[85] In Aristotelian terms, this means that the devil can master *logos*, manipulating rational arguments to catch out the unwary. With regard to *pathos*, Baxter warns his readers that a subjective inward spiritual experience is no guarantee of truth: '*If only to inward sense; then how know you but a counterfeit Angel of Light may produce more strange effects in your soul, then these which you take to be such a manifestation?*'[86]

An instance of paradiastole in the more straightforwardly ethical sense of passing off a vice as the nearest virtue is found when Baxter speaks of 'many that affect the Reputation of Orthodox, while they are indeed factious'.[87] Baxter's funeral sermon for Mary Hanmer (whose daughter Margaret Charlton married Baxter shortly afterwards), commends her ability not to be taken in by worldly paradiastole:

She had an honest impatiency of the life which is common among the rich and vain-glorious in the world: Voluptuousness and Sensuality, Excess of Drinking, Cards and Dice, she could not endure, what ever names of good house-keeping or seemly deportment they borrowed for a mask[.][88]

Baxter's characterization of the false 'names' as 'a mask' recalls his earlier description of sin wearing the 'vizard of Virtue'.[89] One might also recall here the example of paradiastole that the Elizabethan rhetorician Henry Peacham adds to the classical lists – the calling of 'glotony and dronkennesse, good fellowship'.[90]

In the sphere of doctrine too, Baxter warns of the possibility of preachers leading their hearers astray with this comment (which has a chiastic mirroring structure): 'The Prince of darkness doth frequently personate the Angels of light, to draw children of light again into his darkness.'[91] This notion of satanic prosopopoeia, masking oneself as another in order to deceive, enables Baxter to attribute the activities of radical Protestant sectarians, especially Quakers, to a popish conspiracy:

The Papists who have found that they could not well play their game here with open face, have masked themselves, and taken the vizards of several sects; and by the advantage of the licence of the times, are busily at work abroad this Land, to bring you back to *Rome*.[92]

For Baxter, the monster of the papacy is a many-headed hydra, taking on multiple guises to bring down English Protestantism from within. Coming from a thinker who emphasizes the importance of reason, this seems oddly paranoid, but it indicates a belief on Baxter's part in the shapeshifting ability of the devil's agents to undermine the preaching of the true gospel.

The satanic paradiastole of counterfeiting true assurance of faith with presumption and counterfeiting true conviction of sin with despair appears in Baxter's writing just as it does in that of Perkins and Sibbes. Baxter warns that most of the ignorant masses

have an ungrounded affiance in Christ, trusting that he will pardon, justifie and save them, while the world hath their hearts, and they live to the flesh: And this affiance they take for a justifying-faith.[93]

This is an instance of paradiastole in spiritual self-examination akin to that explored by Perkins and Sibbes (as discussed in Chapter 1), in which spiritual presumption is falsely construed as true 'justifying-faith'. Since, for Baxter, assurance of salvation is subsequent to saving faith and not essential to it, it is preferable to have an anxious true faith than a presumptuous counterfeit faith:

For as groundless hopes do tend to confusion, and are the greatest cause of most mens damnation; so groundless doubtings do tend to discomforts, and are the great cause of the disquieting of the Saints.[94]

Whereas 'groundless doubtings [...] tend to discomforts' and 'disquieting', 'groundless hopes' lead to 'damnation'. Hence it is more spiritually dangerous for those who are not truly converted to believe that they are than for those who are truly converted to fear that they are not.

'Earnest Baxter': Exhortation and the rhetoric of weight

Describing the work of the sixteenth-century German rhetorician Johannes Sturm, Debora Shuger writes: 'Several times in *De universa ratione elocutionis* he establishes a contrast between what we may call an aesthetic of light and an aesthetic of magnitude or weight, in Sturm's terms *illustratio* and *amplificatio*.'[95]

Sturm's two aesthetics, as understood by Shuger, provide a helpful key for discerning two rhetorical strategies adopted by Richard Baxter. Both light and weight feature in Baxter's call to ministers 'to speak with life, and light, and weight',[96] but Baxter's writings at times lean more towards weight and on other occasions more towards light. Shuger connects the aesthetics of weight and light to two means of moving the passions identified by Renaissance rhetoricians. One is *magnitudo*, the inherent importance of a subject, often conveyed through *amplificatio*, the expansion and repetition of what has been said. The other is *praesentia*, making things vividly present to one's hearers, often through the varied figures of *enargia* (figures that make the subject vivid through lively description).[97] Both are present in Baxter's work. Whereas 'weight' corresponds broadly to *magnitudo*, 'life' and 'light' are more closely connected to *praesentia*.

These two modes of persuasion provide a key to understanding Baxter's contrasting rhetorical strategies in two genres of writing that he adopts. One is the didactic sermon mode, which is characterized primarily by *magnitudo* as a rhetorical strategy, but also contains passages of great passion that seek to persuade through *enargia*. The second genre is that of imaginative meditation, in which Baxter appeals to the reader's affections through the vivid imagery of *enargia*. In the first of these modes, Baxter displays continuities with the English Reformed preaching tradition advocated by Perkins among others. The second provides a bridge between the sermon mode and the adoption of literary genres such as poetry and fictional narrative by later-seventeenth-century Puritan writers, including Milton and Bunyan.

Baxter's writing has an urgent tone, related to his frequent sicknesses and 'expectation of imminent death' and also to the urgent necessity of his hearers attaining salvation.[98] In his autobiographical poem 'Love Breathing Thanks and Praise', he writes:

> Still thinking I had little time to live,
> My fervent heart to win mens Souls did strive.
> I Preach'd, as never sure to Preach again,
> And as a dying man to dying men![99]

In the nineteenth century, the celebrated Baptist preacher Charles Haddon Spurgeon dubbed him 'Earnest Baxter',[100] while Baxter's Congregationalist editor and biographer William Orme noted, 'His eye, his action, his every word, were expressive of deep and impassioned earnestness, that his hearers might be saved.'[101] Though Orme's comments on Baxter's appearance may be stylized hagiography, Baxter's words indeed convey 'deep and impassioned earnestness'

136   *The Rhetoric of Conversion in English Puritan Writing*

befitting his evangelistic agenda. This forms a key part of his *ethos*, his projection of himself as the faithful pastor expending himself to the uttermost to persuade his hearers to repentance and saving faith.

'Weight' and 'life', *magnitudo* and *praesentia*, come together in Baxter's instructions to the minister to stir up his own heart before preaching to the people:

> Go therefore then specially to God for life: and read some rowsing waking book, or meditate on the weight of the subject that you are to speak of, and on the great necessity of your peoples souls, that you may go in the zeal of the Lord into his house.[102]

The content of the preacher's message possesses an intrinsic 'weight', but his hearers will only grasp this weightiness if the preacher displays 'life' and 'zeal'. Though this spiritual vitality is a divine gift for which the preacher must 'Go [...] to God', to obtain this gift of 'life' and 'zeal' requires the active effort of reading or meditation on the part of the preacher.

It is earnest Baxter that we meet in *A Call to the Unconverted* (1658), an evangelistic exhortation that became the most reprinted of Baxter's sermon treatises – within Baxter's lifetime, it reached its twenty-third edition by 1685 and was translated into several languages, including into Algonquian by the 'apostle to the Indians' John Eliot.[103] In this work, the urgency of tone confronts us from the title page onwards.[104] Though the typography of early modern books is generally the work of their printers rather than their authors, the title page of this first edition highlights the salient points of Baxter's rhetorical approach in this work.

'CALL' is in large capitals – this is an urgent plea to readers. The imperatives '*Turn*' and '*Live*' are helpfully italicized, highlighting from the start the response Baxter is seeking. The triple repetition of 'Mercy' has a driving insistence holding it out as the object to which Baxter aims to direct his readers' desire.

The isolation of '*From the Living God*' as a line by itself between two rules is intriguing. Grammatically speaking it completes the title, following on from the colon above, but it is syntactically ambiguous whether the thought it completes is 'Mercy [...] *From the Living God*' or 'A CALL [...] *From the Living God*'. Perhaps both meanings are intended. The implication that the book itself is '*From the Living God*' makes the highest possible claim to authoritative *ethos*, yet this is immediately followed by the self-denigrating 'By his unworthy SERVANT RICHARD BAXTER', though this conspicuous display of humility is also a performance of *ethos*, since it presents Baxter as the humble channel of an imposing divine call.

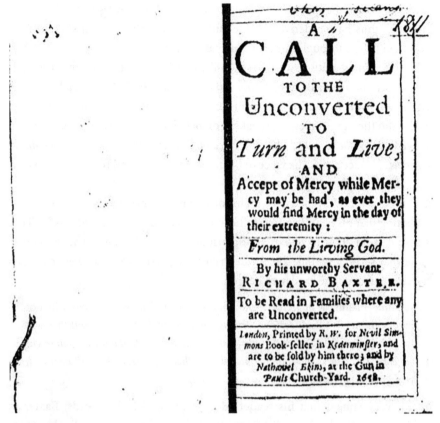

Figure 1 By kind permission of the British Library. Image produced by ProQuest as part of Early English Books Online and published with permission of ProQuest. Further reproduction is prohibited without permission.

Finally, this book is a representation of oral preaching, written down in order to be transformed back into an oral proclamation: 'To be Read in Families where any are Unconverted' seems to refer to reading out loud, as the introduction to the work makes clear that Baxter wants it both to be read out loud by the heads of households and to be read privately by unconverted individuals.[105]

The book has two prefaces preceding the contents pages, of which the second is an address 'To all unsanctified persons that shall read this Book; Especially of my Hearers in the Burrough and Parish of *Kederminster*'.[106] By referring to 'my Hearers in the Burrough and Parish of *Kederminster*', Baxter asserts his authoritative *ethos* as parish minister over them. Baxter informs readers that 'The Eternal God […] hath indited the Gospel and sealed it by his Spirit, and commanded his Ministers to preach it to the world'.[107] Ministers are 'Commissioned

138   *The Rhetoric of Conversion in English Puritan Writing*

by him to preach the same Gospel which Christ and his Apostles first delivered.[108] Ministers thus have a derived divine authority from this commission, and so God's call comes through ministers such as Baxter.

In this printed edition, the divine 'Call' is consistently given an initial capital, whether as a noun or as a verb: '*he hath commanded us to Call after you* [...] *if you would hearken to his Call.*'[109] The ministers' call and God's call are here identified as one and the same. Likewise, speaking on behalf of his fellow ministers, Baxter writes that '*We believe and obey the voice of God*' and so '*lift up our voice like a Trumpet.*'[110] Once again, the voice of the ministers echoes and transmits the voice of God.

Having asserted the authority of his office and his message, Baxter shifts into lamenting that his hearers refuse to hear and respond: '*But, wo and alas!*'[111] This is a shift from *ethos* to *pathos* as the primary mode of appeal. This lament is somewhat self-referential, since it describes the persuasive strategies that have failed to persuade the hardened people:

> *we study* plainness *to make them* understand; *and many of them* will not understand *us. We study serious piercing words, to make them* feel, *but they* will not feel. [...] *[I]f the God that made them, and the Christ that bought them might be heard, the case would soon be altered with them: if* Scripture *might be heard, we should soon prevail*[.]'[112]

In this very lament that his readers do not respond to his words, Baxter is seeking to shame them into listening attentively and acting accordingly: '*Once more in the name of the God of Heaven, I shall do the Message to you which he had commanded us, and leave it in these standing lines to convert your* [sic] *or condemn you*'.[113] This challenge aims to stir readers into hearing Baxter's message with the urgency that Baxter has in delivering it.

This urgency is conveyed in the rest of the preface by the insistent repetition of certain words. The urgency rises to a fever pitch when Baxter warns of impending damnation: '*You sleep; but your damnation slumbereth not: You linger; but your judgment this long time lingreth not*'.[114] The emotional tension that is built up is then unleashed in a cascade of anaphoric 'O's:

> *O that you were wise to understand this* [...] *O careless sinners, that you did but know the Love that you unthankfully neglect* [...] *O that you did but know the Riches of the Gospel! Oh that you did but know, a little know, the certainty, and the glory, and the blessedness of that everlasting life*[.]'[115]

On the other side of this climax we find exclamatory questions about '*how quickly*', '*how quickly*' (repeated), '*How resolutely*' and '*How zealously*' Baxter's hearers would act had they perceived the truth and 'How earnest', 'How diligent', 'How serious', 'How fearful' and 'how careful' they would be.[116] In the midst of these insistent questions is the statement 'He that hath an ear to hear, let him hear the Call of God in this day of his salvation',[117] characterizing these emotionally urgent exhortations as the call of God himself and leading from the preface into the main body of the work.

The biblical text that Baxter expounds in the main sermonic body of the work is Ezekiel 33:11:

> Say unto them, As I live saith the Lord God, I have no pleasure in the death of the wicked, but that the wicked turn from his way and live. Turn ye, turn ye from your evil ways; for why will ye die O house of Israel?[118]

Baxter begins his sermon with the alarming supposition that 'the most will be firebrands of hell for ever'[119] and proceeds to expound his text as a 'Controversie' over who is to blame for the damnation of sinners (with reference to Ezekiel 18 where this theme is addressed at more length).[120] The controversy invokes the questions of forensic rhetoric (the classical mode of rhetoric for the courtroom that argues for blame or innocence), seeking to establish who the guilty party is: 'when we see any hainous thing done, a principle of justice doth provoke us to enquire after him that did it'.[121]

The examples Baxter gives of analogously heinous actions are criminal acts: 'If we saw a man killed and cut in pieces by the way'[122] and 'If the town were wilfully set on fire',[123] reinforcing the sense that this is a legal, forensic enquiry. Baxter tells us that 'we must needs think with our selves, How comes this to pass? and who is it long of? Who is it that is so cruel as to be the cause of such a thing as this?'[124]

Yet the divine rhetoric that Baxter identifies in this verse from Ezekiel is not only forensic. It is also deliberative: 'The direct end of this Exhortation is, That they may Turn and Live'; that is, God's primary goal is to persuade his hearers to adopt a course of action.[125] However, 'The Secundary or reserved ends', in the event of their failure to turn and live, is 'to convince them [...] that it is not long of God if they be miserable' but 'that it is long of themselves': these secondary ends constitute forensic rhetoric, seeking to establish that it is sinners themselves who are guilty of the fact of their damnation and not God.[126]

The weightiness and solemnity of this matter of eternal life or eternal condemnation should, rationally speaking, persuade all those who hear it to be converted: 'If you will but throughly believe this truth, me thinks the weight of it should force you to remember it; and it should follow you, and give you no

140   *The Rhetoric of Conversion in English Puritan Writing*

rest till you are converted.'[127] However, in practice, the 'weight' of truth is often insufficient to persuade sinners, as Baxter laments: 'O what's the matter then that the hearts of sinners be not pierced with such a weighty truth!'[128] '[W]hat's the matter' is that the rational faculties of sinful humans have been disabled by disordered affections and so 'We judge by feeling, which blinds our reason.'[129] For this reason, the preacher must engage his hearers through feeling as well as reason, and Baxter thus frequently appeals to his readers' affections (*pathos* as well as *logos*).

Baxter is seeking to persuade his hearers to turn to God, but he also presents God himself as calling the unconverted to turn in terms that are recognizably rhetorical. Baxter identifies qualities in God's appeal that correspond to the three Aristotelian modes of *logos*, *ethos* and *pathos*. He finds in the text from Ezekiel that he is expounding, 'An express Exhortation to the wicked to Return; wherein God doth not only Command, but perswade, and condescend also to reason the case with them, Why they will die?'[130] God has the right to command humans by asserting his absolute authority over them (in rhetorical terms, his *ethos*), but yet he 'doth not only Command, but perswade' in an 'Exhortation' that Baxter goes on to characterize as passionate pleading (an appeal to *pathos*). God is also willing 'to reason the case' with sinful humanity (an appeal to *logos*).

The expositions of Doctrines 4, 5 and 6 of Baxter's treatise can be read as explorations of these three modes of divine rhetoric. The heading for Doctrine 4 is: '*The Lord hath confirmed it to us by his Oath, that he hath no pleasure in the death of the wicked, but that he Turn and Live: that he may leave man no pretence to question the truth of it.*'[131] This is a forceful statement that the Lord's words should be believed on the basis of his authority, that is, his *ethos*. Baxter comments somewhat threateningly, 'If you dare question his word, I hope you dare not question his oath.'[132] The Lord's *ethos* is not asserted here only by Baxter, but by the Lord himself. Baxter invokes the biblical motif of God's oath, which is God's own testimony to the authority of his words:

> And as the Apostle saith, *Heb.* 6.13, 16, 17, 18. *Because he can swear by no greater then himself,* he saith, *As I live,* &c. *For men verily swear by the greater, and an oath for confirmation is to them an end of strife; wherein God willing more abundantly to shew unto the heirs of Promise the immutability of his counsel, confirmed it by on* [sic] *oath.*[133]

For Baxter, God's oath ought to override the frailties of human reason: the weight of the divine *ethos* means that the truths asserted by Scripture should be believed even if we cannot see how they fit together: 'certain truths must be believed to

Richard Baxter's Exhortations and Meditations 141

agree with it, though our shallow brains do hardly discern the agreeement [*sic*]'.[134] Yet God in his mercy accommodates himself to argue his case in terms accessible to human reason, that is, to appeal to *logos*, as Doctrine 7 makes clear: '*The Lord condescendeth to reason the case with Unconverted sinners, and to ask them why they will die?*'[135] Baxter stresses the incongruity of this divine condescension – it is 'matter of wonder […] That God should stoop so low, as thus to plead the case with man; and that man should be so strangely blind and obstinate, as to need all this in so plain a case'.[136] Yet though incongruous in some ways, in another sense the divine appeal to *logos* is fitting, 'Because that man being a reasonable creature, is accordingly to be dealt with, and by Reason to be perswaded and overcome.'[137] The divine appeal to *logos* is a tribute to the dignity of rationality that God has given to humanity, and the divine conquest that overcomes the sinner does so through rational persuasion.

Doctrine 5 is the most interesting in terms of the implications of divine rhetoric for Baxter's writing style: '*So earnest is God for the Conversion of sinners, that he doubleth his commands and exhortations with vehemency; Turn ye, Turn ye, Why will ye Dye?*'[138] Since Baxter considers the words of Scripture to be Spirit-inspired, the words of Scripture can be analyzed (as we have seen Perkins do in Chapter 1) to find the rhetorical techniques favoured by God himself. Here Baxter identifies the verbal repetition of '*Turn ye, Turn ye*' in the biblical text as demonstrating '*vehemency*'. Since Baxter hears this as a divine 'Exhortation',[139] we might recall here Perkins's advice that the preacher should be 'in the exhortation more feruent and vehement'.[140] It is perhaps in following this divine example of vehement repetition that Baxter repeats '*Turn ye, Turn ye, why will you die?*' five times in the following five pages.[141]

However, Baxter's unrelieved earnestness can at times become wearisome and hence perhaps counterproductive in its efforts to move and awaken the reader. Baxter uses *amplificatio* to convey *magnitudo*, but his works are often excessively amplified. As N. H. Keeble wryly comments, 'in the enlarged *Life of Faith* (1670) he begins a warning to "the ungodly unprepared sinner" on page 597 – few such will have come 600 pages to hear it!'[142] In that same work, the refutation in turn of fifty-eight itemized errors concerning the doctrine of justification may not appear as vital to the reader as it does to Baxter.[143] Keeble writes:

> Baxter's pastoral zeal itself overwhelmed all sense of decorum or proportion. To omit one warning, argument, reason, incentive, or illustration, or to neglect to counter a single error, temptation, or misunderstanding was to run too grave a risk of failing the reader on the very point where he might need guidance.[144]

142   *The Rhetoric of Conversion in English Puritan Writing*

Although Keeble may not be using 'decorum' here in its technical rhetorical sense, I would agree that Baxter's exhaustive earnestness sometimes proves exhausting. Baxter believes that the weightiness of his subject matter should move his readership, but sometimes the weight of his writing becomes suffocating, inhibiting the successful moving of the reader's affections and thus frustrating its intended persuasive purpose.

If we suspect that this is an anachronistic response by today's readers, with a lesser appetite for lengthy godly exhortations than their ancestors, we would do well to remember Thomas Wilson's advice to preachers in *The Arte of Rhetorique* (1553) that congregations need some light relief at times:

> Therefore, euen these auncient preachers, must now and then plaie the fooles in the pulpite, to serue the tickle eares of their fleetyng audience, or els thei are like some tymes to preache to the bare walles, for though the spirite bee apte, and our will prone, yet our fleshe is so heauie, and humours so ouerwhelme vs, that wee cannot without refreshyng, long abide to heare any one thyng.[145]

'As in a glass': Imagination and the rhetoric of light

There is little light relief in Baxter's writings such as Thomas Wilson recommends, but there are places where the heavy rhetoric of weight is alleviated by a rhetoric of light. Baxter at times appeals to the imagination in ways that evoke delight, delighting (*delectare*) being the one out of the three classical tasks of the orator (*officia oratoris*) less often associated with Puritan preaching and writing than teaching (*docere*) and moving (*movere*). In his pursuit of the rhetorical objective of reordering the affections of his readers and hearers into their correct place and proportion (a project outlined influentially in earlier Christian history by St Augustine), Baxter sometimes makes use of the rhetorical technique of *enargia*, appealing to the affections through vivid descriptions that stir the imagination.

It is in this aspect of Baxter's pastoral strategy that many of the more 'literary' aspects of his writing have their roots. U. Milo Kaufmann sees Baxter as a crucial link in the chain between an earlier Puritan suspicion of imagination and the flowering of the imaginative impulse in Bunyan,[146] and Keeble sees the seeds of Romanticism in the tradition of 'meditation upon the creatures' adopted by Baxter.[147] Yet it is an odd kind of *enargia* that Baxter adopts, since he is describing things that cannot be fully visualized or grasped by sensory means. The transcendent nature of Baxter's subject matter means that his descriptions always retain a degree of opacity, and Keeble notes that Baxter, despite his wariness of ornament, 'recognized the inevitability of metaphorical language'.[148]

Building on work by Roger Pooley, Keeble points out that, following the Restoration, there was a change in the understanding of 'plain style'.[149] While Dissenters continued to affirm their adherence to the plain style of the godly, the post-Restoration clergy of the Church of England also adopted an ideal of plain, straightforward communication, and, as well as disowning the floridity of earlier 'witty' preaching, castigated the Dissenters for the extravagance and dense metaphorical character of their style. As Keeble and Pooley point out, however, it was inevitable that the Nonconformists use metaphorical language, since theirs was (in Isabel Rivers's terms) a 'religion of grace' speaking of otherworldly entities, whereas the latitudinarian 'religion of nature' was concerned largely with ethical conduct in this life more readily explicable in literal language.[150]

Baxter sees human knowledge of God as inherently limited and thus unavoidably opaque to some degree, and this enables him to move away somewhat from the typical Reformed suspicion of mental images exemplified by Perkins, among others. Whereas Perkins asserts that an inner mental image of God is 'an idoll [...] set vp in the mind',[151] Baxter points out that mental imaging is unavoidable:

> And if by *an Idol* they mean the *Image* of God in the *mind,* gathered from the appearances of God in *creatures,* man in flesh hath no other knowledge of him: For here we know him but darkly, aenigmatically, and as in a glass, and have no *formal proper* conception of him in his essence.[152]

Baxter, who in his youth found the precision of medieval scholastic theology attractive, is here echoing the scholastic concept of analogical knowledge, in which humans can never know things in the same way as God does, but yet human knowledge has a real though limited correspondence with divine knowledge.[153]

For this reason, although Baxter echoes the iconoclastic aspect of the Reformed tradition in his rejection of the use of physical images of divine realities, he allows space for mental images that fulfil a similar function:[154]

> I would not have thee, as the Papists, draw them in Pictures, nor use mysterious, significant Ceremonies to represent them. This, as it is a course forbidden by God, so it would but seduce and draw down thy heart: But get the liveliest Picture of them in thy minde that possibly thou canst; meditate of them, as if thou were all the while beholding them, and as if thou were even hearing the *Hallelujahs,* while thou art thinking of them[.][155]

144   *The Rhetoric of Conversion in English Puritan Writing*

However, although Baxter rehabilitates the use of the imagination for edifying purposes, he, like Perkins, takes a dim view of imaginative fiction:[156]

> Another dangerous *Time-wasting sin,* is the *Reading of vain-Books, Play-books, Romances and feigned Histories; and also unprofitable studies, undertaken but for vain-glory, or the pleasing of a carnal or curious mind.*[157]

Likewise, Baxter confesses of his youth that 'I was extreamly bewitched with a Love of Romances, Fables and old Tales, which corrupted my Affections and lost my Time'.[158]

Yet despite this denigration of popular fiction as pernicious and time-wasting, Baxter writes some didactic dialogues that take a fictional narrative form, though the fact that the didactic purpose takes priority over aesthetic enjoyment for Baxter means that these dialogues are often deficient when assessed by aesthetic standards. Keeble comments, 'Baxter did set several works in dialogue form, but with disappointing results from a literary point of view',[159] since Baxter's dialogues often lack convincing characterization and plot. Keeble partially excepts from this judgement *The Poor Man's Family Book*, presented in the form of nine days 'conference' between '*Paul*, A Pastor' and '*Saul*, An Ignorant Sinner'.[160] Yet although there is a degree of literary characterization in *The Poor Man's Family Book*, didactic utility still takes precedence over narrative realism: it seems to me that Saul, from his starting point as 'An Ignorant Sinner', is persuaded of what Paul wishes him to believe a little more rapidly than is plausible. Though he interjects occasional objections, Saul more often responds to lengthy exhortations from Paul with a bald and unelaborated acquiescence, such as 'I cannot deny but what you say is the plain truth'.[161] Likewise, a two-page exposition of repentance by Paul is elicited by Saul's convenient request, 'There is a great deal in this: I pray you open it to me more fully, in the particulars'.[162]

Though Paul's speeches are largely didactic expositions of doctrine, he uses some narrative analogies that appeal to the imagination – for instance, the analogy of 'a man rising post towards *York*, and thinketh verily he is in the way to *London*', who must turn around (that is, repent) if he is to reach his hoped for destination.[163] Another analogy asks the reader to imagine that 'you were a beggar or a slave in *England*, and the King should promise you a Kingdom in the *Indies*, if you will but *Trust* your self in the ship with his own Son, who undertaketh to bring you thither'.[164] This thought experiment is an *allegoria* in Quintilian's sense of an extended metaphor and is moving towards allegory in the more fully developed sense of a full-length symbolic narrative text.[165] Although Baxter does not develop the narrative further, this could potentially be the

Richard Baxter's Exhortations and Meditations   145

beginning of an allegorical journey narrative with a cast of multiple characters akin to Bunyan's *The Pilgrim's Progress*.

Though didactic dialogues such as *The Poor Mans Family Book* are fictional in terms of formal genre, the work of Baxter's that has appealed most to the imagination of readers is a work not intended as fiction. Of all Baxter's works, literary critics have been most drawn to *The Saints Everlasting Rest*,[166] which seeks to persuade readers to live in expectation of heaven not so much through weighty earnest exhortation as through making heavenly things present to them by meditation: 'For Faith hath wings, and Meditation is its chariot, Its office is to make absent things, as present.'[167] Helen White calls this work a 'treatise of persuasion to the life of devotion' and finds 'a peculiar satisfaction' in 'so much radiance of conviction, with so affectionate a charity of persuasiveness.'[168]

The Saints Everlasting Rest was Baxter's second published work (after his controversial *Aphorismes of Justification* (1649)), and his first to meet with widespread success. Large sections of *The Saints Everlasting Rest* are in the mode of densely argued doctrinal apologetic that appeals to *logos* rather than *pathos*, and it contains plenty of earnest exhortations that appeal to the affections through the techniques considered above. It is once we reach the final part, Book IV, that there is a noticeable change, an appeal to the affections through *enargia* rather than *magnitudo*. Despite the length of time it takes to get there, it is this advocacy of heavenly meditation that Baxter sees as the heart of the book: in the first edition, Baxter tells us on page 686, 'All that I have said, is but for the preparation to this.'[169]

In the map of the disciplines of learning found in his *Methodus Theologiae Christianae*, Baxter associates speaking powerfully with 'Oratoria' but speaking sweetly with 'Poetica'.[170] Thus it is fitting that it is Baxter's exploration of the delights of heaven that has most attracted 'literary' readers. Yet although delighting (*delectare*) is one of the Ciceronian tasks of the orator (*officia oratoris*), Baxter seems to see delight as the responsibility of the individual Christian to experience through meditation, not the responsibility of the preacher to evoke through verbal ornament.[171]

Baxter states that he 'would fain perswade' his readers to practise meditation,[172] but in advocating this practice of meditation he calls upon his readers to persuade themselves by directing their attention to the right object:

> if you do but see some Jewel, or Treasure, you need not long exhortations to stir up your desires, the very sight of it is motive enough; if you see the fire when you are cold, or see a house in a stormy day, or see a safe harbor from the tempestuous seas, you need not be told what use to make of it[.][173]

Once again, it is perception that arouses desire, and desire that turns the will.

This might, at first glance, appear to be in tension with Baxter's usual rhetorical practice of seeking to stir the affections through convincing the understanding. However, Baxter considers meditation to be an aid to reason: 'Meditation putteth reason in its Authority and preheminence. It helpeth to deliver it from its captivity to the senses, and setteth it again upon the throne of the soul.'[174] Meditation furnishes objects of spiritual perception, overcoming the tendency of the inner faculties to be too closely tied to the outward objects perceived through the physical senses. Kaufmann, noting that Baxter cites Sibbes's *The Soules Conflict*, argues that Baxter 'in all probability' derived from Sibbes the insight that to 'see and feel' something inwardly moves the affections more than a bare verbal affirmation.[175]

Baxter recommends that his readers engage in 'Soliloquy', a self-address that aims at self-persuasion.[176] In doing so, he continues in the tradition of Richard Sibbes, whose *Soules Conflict* commends the use of '*Soliloquies* or *speeches to our own hearts*' 'to awake the *soule,* and to stirre up *reason* cast asleepe by Sathans *charmes*'.[177] The effectiveness of 'holy soliloquies' in stirring up one's affections is also outlined by Paul Baynes, Perkins's successor as lecturer at Great St Andrew's Church in Cambridge, to whose preaching Sibbes attributed his conversion:

> Now there is no one branch of deuout exercise more fruitfull then that of soliloquie, wherein wee commune with our owne soules, and excite them towards God. Words serue not onely to make knowne the conceptions of our minds, but to giue glory to God, who vnderstandeth our thoughts afarre off; and to blow vp deuotion, and kindle our cooling affections towards him.[178]

Baxter sees such a soliloquy on divine matters aiming to stir up one's affections as a kind of sermon to oneself: 'Soliloquy is a Preaching to ones self. Therefore the very same Method which a Minister should use in his Preaching to others, should a Christian use in speaking to himself.'[179] Baxter goes on to outline the parts of a soliloquy in ways that sound very like a Puritan doctrine and use sermon: explication of doctrine is followed by application to oneself 'by strong and effectual perswasion with thy heart', though such preaching to oneself need not exhibit the 'decent Ornaments of Language' and 'good pronunciation' required in public preaching.[180]

This self-persuasion through meditation utilizes *logos, ethos* and *pathos*:

> Why thus must thou do in thy Meditation to quicken thy own heart: Enter into a serious debate with it: Plead with it in the most moving and affecting language: Urge it with the most weighty and powerful Arguments.[181]

Even *ethos*, the assertion of the speaker's authority, can be used in persuading oneself: 'Take up the authority again which God hath given thee; command thy heart; if it rebel, use violence with it.'[182]

However, although Baxter characterizes the soliloquy as like a sermon, the kind of persuasion that comes from heavenly meditation is not something that a preacher can bring about in others; rather, readers need to attain it within themselves, since it is a persuasion that comes from an inward perception and that bypasses persuasion in the rational sense:

> O see what beauty presents it self: Is it not exceeding lovely? is not all the beauty in the world contracted here? is not all other beauty deformity to it? Dost thou need to be perswaded now to love?[183]

For Baxter, this imaginative self-persuasion of meditation can only be undertaken by those who have already been converted: 'It must be a soul that is qualified for the work, by the supernatural renewing grace of the spirit, which must be able to perform this Heavenly exercise. Its the work of the Living, and not of the dead.'[184] This may help to explain why *delectare* is missing from Baxter's descriptions of the aims of his regular preaching: since spiritual delight is the work of regenerate saints, it cannot be evoked by a preacher in a mixed congregation of both regenerate and unregenerate individuals.

The German Reformed rhetorician Johannes Sturm thought that *magnitudo*, with its accompanying technique of *amplificatio*, was to be used particularly in the context of forensic rhetoric, convincing one's hearers of their guilt: 'amplification is directed against the errors of men, when they do not think a thing to be as great or necessary as it is.'[185] Baxter seems to agree, hence perhaps why the dominant tone of Baxter's addresses to the unconverted is an amply insistent earnestness. However, Sturm continues: 'Vividness (evidentia) is directed not only toward showing the magnitude of things but also their splendor, dignity and light.'[186] The incitement to delight in *The Saints Everlasting Rest* is intended to evoke 'splendor, dignity, and light', but the delight Baxter advocates is an imaginative delight accessible only to those who are already regenerate.

In the final chapter of *The Saints Everlasting Rest*, Baxter offers a model meditation, 'An Example of this Heavenly Contemplation, for the help of the unskilful'.[187] Baxter's meditation starts with his scriptural text 'There remaineth a Rest to the people of God' (Hebrews 4:9), and the words of this text call forth an affective response:[188]

> Rest! How sweet a word is this to mine ears? Methinks the sound doth turn to substance, and having entred at the ear, doth possess my brain, and thence descendeth down to my very heart[.][189]

148   *The Rhetoric of Conversion in English Puritan Writing*

Although Baxter is here modelling meditation through the private reading of Scripture, he still presents engagement with the text as aural, entering by the ear. The alliteration of 'sound' and 'substance' enacts the turning of the one into the other in a quasi-sacramental fashion. When scriptural words are carefully heard and dwelt upon, the meditating believer starts to feel the substantive presence of the things considered. The rational apprehension of the truth of the text takes place in the 'brain' (corresponding to *logos*), but to captivate the reader, it must descend to the 'heart' (corresponding to *pathos*).

The meditation continues with a sensory anticipation of the Second Coming of Christ and the Last Judgment:

> Methinks I even hear the voyce of his foregoers! Methinks I see him coming in the clouds, with the attendants of his Angels in Majesty, and in Glory! O poor secure sinners, what will you now do? where will you hide your selves? or what shall cover you?[190]

The vivid visualization (*praesentia*) of this future event, imagining the accompanying sights and sounds, makes it seem already present to the meditating believer. This enables the one meditating to address both sinners and saints as if that day had already come.

Yet, although Baxter is seeking to model an affective engagement with heavenly joys through the imagination, the meditation as written contains less description of future joys than enumeration of present miseries that shall then be done away with:

> Then shall not my life be such a medley or mixture of hope and fear, of joy and sorrow, as now it is; nor shall Flesh and Spirit be combating within me, nor my soul be still as a pitched Field, or a Stage of contention, where Faith and Unbelief, Affiance and Distrust, Humility and Pride, do maintain a continual distracting conflict: then shall I not live a dying life for fear of dying, nor my life be made uncomfortable with the fears of losing it.[191]

This is a rhetoric of presence, but of presence evoked through absence and negation. By making the reader feel the absence of heavenly perfection, a desire for heaven is aroused that stimulates the reader's imagination to reach for heaven and thus make it more present. The one meditating reminds herself or himself: 'There is love in Desire, as well as in Delight; and if I be not empty of Love, I know I shall not long be empty of Delight.'[192]

Nevertheless, there are some instances of the positive use of imagery that approximate more conventional *enargia*, appealing to the senses of sight, sound, taste, touch and smell:

Richard Baxter's Exhortations and Meditations 149

even the silly Flies will leave their holes when the Winter is over, and the Sun draws neer them; the Ants will stir, the Fishes rise, the Birds will sing, the earth look green, and all with joyful note will tell thee the Spring is come[.][193]

However, Baxter clarifies that these are not sensory descriptions of heaven itself but of earthly pleasures that image very imperfectly the joys of heaven:[194]

Can meat and drink delight me when I hunger and thirst? Can I finde pleasure in walks and gardens and convenient dwellings? Can beauteous sights delight mine eyes? and odors my smell? and melody mine ears? And shall not the forethought of the Celestial bliss delight me?[195]

The power of these questions is that they bring into the mind of the questioner tangible sensory pleasures, but then challenge the mind and imagination to stretch beyond known pleasures towards the unknown. Knott suggests that 'To fix them by excessive detail, as by the strokes of a brush, would be to "draw down" the heart and prevent the kind of soaring that he sought to encourage'.[196]

When Baxter seeks to describe the heavenly realm more directly, his descriptions break down:

See what a Sea of love is here before thee; cast thy self in, and swim with the arms of thy love in this Ocean of his love: Fear not least thou shouldst be drowned, or consumed in it; Though it seem as the scalding* furnace of lead, yet thou will finde it but mollifying oyle; Though it seeme a furnace of fire, and the hottest that ever was kindled upon earth, yet is it the fire of love and not of wrath; a fire most effectual to extinguish fire; never intended to consume, but to glorifie thee: venture into it then in thy believing meditations, and walk in these flames with the Son of God; when thou art once in, thou wilt be sorry to come forth again.[197]

The heavenly reality is frighteningly beyond normal human experience, hence the mixture of metaphors. The water and fire imagery merge into each other: from a sea one can swim in we move to a mass of liquid fire in the form of lead or oil, and from there to a furnace that one can walk in, rather than swim in. There are multiple allusions conflated together here – in the book of Revelation, the visionary John reports that 'I saw as it were a sea of glass mingled with fire' (Revelation 15:2), the 'as it were' signalling the difficulty of description; a marginal note pointed to by the asterisk here references an extracanonical tradition that John was cast into a lead furnace 'and came out anointed only'; and, in Daniel chapter 3, three men cast into a furnace are protected from harm and are joined by one 'like the Son of God' (Daniel 3:25).

150   *The Rhetoric of Conversion in English Puritan Writing*

Though the words and images are vivid, the language is paradoxical, and one cannot visualize a single fixed image; this is a fluid and unstable *enargia*. But although Baxter is describing something that he cannot adequately describe in normal terms, the heavenly 'Sea of love' is not so other that it cannot be experienced in this life. The believer can even now 'venture into it then in thy believing meditations, and walk in these flames with the Son of God'. This divine encounter is accessed through the active-passive behaviour of entrusting oneself to the divine love, and it is this active-passive encounter to which *The Saints Everlasting Rest* seeks to persuade readers. It is the activity of meditating on Scripture that brings the devotee to this point, but then divine agency takes over.

The *enargia* of meditation makes heavenly things present in a way that cannot be fully replicated in public preaching for those who have not themselves experienced this heavenly encounter. Nevertheless, for the preacher to have experienced the presence of such things will enhance his *ethos*, bringing a transcendent power and persuasiveness to his public preaching:

> Surely, if we can get into the Holy of Holies, and bring thence the Name and Image of God, and get it closed up in our hearts: this would enable us to work wonders; every duty we performed would be a wonder, and they that heard, would be ready to say, Never man spake as this man speaketh. The Spirit would possess us, as those flaming tongues, and make us every one to speak, (not in the variety of the confounded Languagues, but) in the primitive pure Language of *Canaan*, the wonderful Works of God.[198]

Recalling Baxter's sermons in the last year of his life, his fellow ejected minister Edmund Calamy identified Baxter as having such an authority coming from such an experience:

> He talked in the pulpit with great freedom about another world, like one that had been there, and was come as a sort of an express from thence to make a report concerning it.[199]

Such freedom could not be limited to cool expository prose.

In the diagram of the fields of human learning in Baxter's *Methodus* discussed above, Baxter assigns speaking powerfully to 'Oratoria', but speaking sweetly is assigned by Baxter not to 'Oratoria' but to 'Poetica'. This removes one of the three Ciceronian *officia oratoris* (tasks of the orator), that of delighting (*delectare*), from oratory/rhetoric and assigns it instead to a more imaginative mode of language, that of poetry. Baxter here implicitly opens up a space for imaginative literature as a mode of godly persuasion, a space that is more fully developed in the literary works of John Bunyan and John Milton.

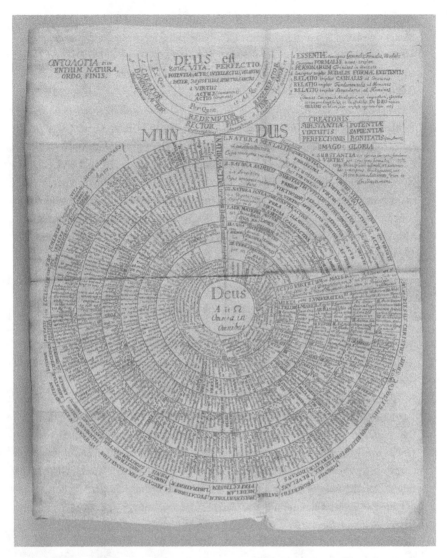

Figure 2 Richard Baxter, *Methodus Theologiae Christianæ* (London, 1681). (Diagram inserted between prefatory material and Part 1.) Reproduced by kind permission of the Burke Library, Union Theological Seminary, New York.

Notes

1   N. H. Keeble notes: 'He was a quite exceptionally prolific writer, the author of more than 130 books (the exact figure depends upon how works published in a variety of forms are counted), several of them folios over 1 million words in length, as well as of hundreds of letters and unpublished papers and treatises' (N. H. Keeble,

'Baxter, Richard (1615–1691)', *ODNB*). The fullest annotated bibliography to date of Baxter's writings is found in Volume 5 of Richard Baxter, *Reliquiæ Baxterianæ: Or, Mr Richard Baxter's Narrative of the Most Memorable Passages of His Life and Times*, ed. N. H. Keeble, John Coffey, Tim Cooper and Tom Charlton, 5 vols. (Oxford: Oxford University Press, 2020), pp. 203–367.

2   Richard Baxter, *Gildas Salvianus; The Reformed Pastor* (London, 1656), p. 68.

3   William Orme, *The Life and Times of Richard Baxter*, in William Orme (ed.), *The Practical Works of the Rev. Richard Baxter: With a Life of the Author, and a Critical Examination of His Writings*, 23 vols (London: James Duncan, 1830), I:435. Cf. N. H. Keeble's similar point: 'Baxter's multifarious activities, the involvement in so many schemes, projects and negotiations and the composition of so many books, were but a means to a pastoral end.' (N. H. Keeble, 'Richard Baxter's Preaching Ministry: Its History and Texts', *Journal of Ecclesiastical History*, 35.4 (October 1984), p. 540).

4   Richard Baxter, *The Saints Everlasting Rest* (London, 1650), p. 277.

5   Richard Baxter, *A Christian Directory* (London, 1673), p. 105.

6   John R. Knott, Jr, *The Sword of the Spirit: Puritan Responses to the Bible* (Chicago: University of Chicago Press, 1980), p. 74.

7   Baxter, *Christian Directory*, Part I, p. 60.

8   Arnold Hunt, *The Art of Hearing: English Preachers and Their Audiences, 1590–1640* (Cambridge: Cambridge University Press, 2010), p. 130.

9   For Baxter's biography, see Orme, *The Life and Times of Richard Baxter*; Frederick J. Powicke, *A Life of the Reverend Richard Baxter 1615–1691* (London: Jonathan Cape, 1924); Frederick J. Powicke, *The Reverend Richard Baxter under the Cross (1662–1691)* (London: Jonathan Cape, 1927); Geoffrey F. Nuttall, *Richard Baxter* (London: Thomas Nelson, 1965); Keeble, 'Baxter, Richard (1615–1691)', *ODNB*. The fullest literary study of Baxter remains N. H. Keeble, *Richard Baxter: Puritan Man of Letters* (Oxford: Clarendon Press, 1982).

10   Baxter, *Reliquiæ Baxterianæ*, I:209.

11   Baxter, *Reliquiæ Baxterianæ*, I:214.

12   Baxter, *Reliquiæ Baxterianæ*, I:220.

13   Baxter, *Reliquiæ Baxterianæ*, I:221. For more on Baxter's struggles with the overly rigid codification of the experience of conversion in the context of early modern conversion narrative, see David Parry '"God breaketh not all men's hearts alike": Early Modern Conversion Narratives in Contemporary Perspective', *The Glass*, 25 (Spring 2013), 3–17 (esp. pp. 14–17).

14   Baxter, *Reliquiæ Baxterianæ*, I:215

15   Keeble, 'Baxter, Richard', *ODNB*.

16   Keeble, *Richard Baxter*, p. 48.

17   Keeble, *Richard Baxter*, pp. 47–8.

18   Baxter, *Gildas Salvianus*, pp. 23–4.

19 Thomas M. Conley, *Rhetoric in the European Tradition* (Chicago: University of Chicago Press, 1994), pp. 130–1. Simon Burton argues that Baxter has an affinity for Ramist logic, but modifies Ramist dichotomies into trichotomies that mirror the three persons of the Trinity (Simon J. G. Burton, *The Hallowing of Logic: The Trinitarian Method of Richard Baxter's Methodus Theologiae* (Leiden: Brill, 2012), esp. pp. 47–55 and 68–72).

20 For instance, Nuttall, *Richard Baxter*, p. 48; Keeble, *Richard Baxter*, p. 51.

21 Richard Baxter, *A Treatise of Conversion Preached, and Now Published for the Use of Those That Are Strangers to a True Conversion, Especially the Grosly Ignorant and Ungodly* (London, 1657), sig. (a)3r.

22 See, for instance, W. Fraser Mitchell, *English Pulpit Oratory from Andrewes to Tillotson* (London: SPCK/New York and Toronto: Macmillan, 1932), esp. pp. 6–7, 148–94, 351–65, and Horton Davies, *Like Angels from a Cloud: The English Metaphysical Preachers, 1588–1645* (San Marino, CA: Huntington Library, 1986). Davies objects to Mitchell's characterization of the metaphysical preachers as 'Anglo-Catholic' on the grounds that this label is anachronistic when applied to the early modern period, and that Calvinists are among the 'witty' or 'metaphysical' preachers, but he still sees 'Puritan preaching' as opposite to 'metaphysical preaching' (Davies, *Like Angels from a Cloud*, Chapter 2, 'The Characteristics of Metaphysical Sermon Styles', pp. 45–98).

23 On Baxter's admiration of Hall, see Keeble, *Richard Baxter*, p. 48.

24 Baxter, *Treatise of Conversion*, sig. (a)3r.

25 Baxter, *Treatise of Conversion*, sig. (a)2r.

26 Keeble, *Richard Baxter*, p. 48.

27 Morris W. Croll, *Style, Rhetoric, and Rhythm: Essays by Morris W. Croll*, ed. J. Max Patrick and Robert O. Evans (Princeton, NJ: Princeton University Press, 1966), and George Williamson, *The Senecan Amble: A Study in Prose Form from Bacon to Collier* (Chicago: University of Chicago Press, 1966).

28 Baxter, *Saints Everlasting Rest*, p. 511.

29 Baxter, *Saints Everlasting Rest*, p. 512.

30 Baxter, *Saints Everlasting Rest*, p. 509.

31 Baxter, *Gildas Salvianus*, p. 125. Baxter's citation diverges slightly from the wording found in R. P. H. Green's edition of Augustine's *De Doctrina Christiana*, including Baxter's substitution of 'doctor' (teacher) for 'dictor' (speaker/orator):

> Et haec se posse, si potuerit et in quantum potuerit, pietate magis orationum quam oratorum facultate non dubitet, ut orando pro se ac pro illis quos est allocuturus sit orator antequam dictor. Ipsa hora iam ut dicat accedens, priusquam exserat proferentem linguam, ad deum levet animam sitientem, ut ructet quod biberit, vel quod impleverit fundat.
>
> [He should be in no doubt that any ability he has and however much he has derives more from his devotion to prayer than his dedication to oratory; and

so, by praying for himself and for those he is about to address, he must become a man of prayer before becoming a man of words. As the hour of his address approaches, before he stretches out his thrusting tongue he should lift his thirsting soul to God so that he may utter what he has drunk in and pour out what has filled him.]

(Augustine, *De Doctrina Christiana*, trans. and ed. R. P. H. Green (Oxford: Clarendon, 1995), XV.32.87 (p. 235). Translation modified.)

32 Baxter, *Gildas Salvianus*, p. 123.

33 Baxter, *Gildas Salvianus*, p. 123. Referenced by Keeble, *Richard Baxter*, p. 49.

34 Richard Baxter, *The Vain Religion of the Formal Hypocrite, and the Mischief of an Unbridled Tongue (as against Religion, Rulers, or Dissenters) Described* (London, 1660), p. 16.

35 Baxter, *Christian Directory*, Part I, p. 321.

36 Richard Baxter, *Methodus Theologiae Christianæ* (London, 1681). Diagram inserted between errata and page 1. On the *Methodus*, see especially Burton, *The Hallowing of Logic*.

37 Baxter, *A Christian Directory*, pp. 922, 928.

38 See Erik Gunderson, 'Introduction', in Erik Gunderson (ed.), *The Cambridge Companion to Ancient Rhetoric* (Cambridge: Cambridge University Press, 2009), p. 3.

39 Baxter, *Saints Everlasting Rest,* p. 511.

40 Baxter, *Saints Everlasting Rest,* p. 511.

41 Baxter, *Saints Everlasting Rest,* p. 511.

42 Baxter, *Saints Everlasting Rest,* p. 188.

43 Richard Baxter, *A Saint or a Brute* (London, 1662), sig. A3r.

44 Baxter, *Treatise of Conversion*, sig. (a)2v.

45 For more thorough accounts of Baxter's faculty psychology, see Keith Condie, '"Light Accompanied with Vital Heat": Affection and Intellect in the Thought of Richard Baxter', in Alec Ryrie and Tom Schwanda (eds.), *Puritanism and Emotion in the Early Modern World* (Houndmills, Basingstoke: Palgrave Macmillan, 2016), pp. 13–45; and Burton, *The Hallowing of Logic*, chapter 4, 'The Soul as the *Imago Trinitatis*', pp. 147–200.

46 Although Baxter elsewhere suggests that a desire to behave in a certain way can shape one's beliefs: '*And this* prophaneness *and* sensuality *tendeth to* greater Infidelity. *They that will not* live *as they* profess *to* Believe, *may most easily be drawn to* Believe *and* profess, *as they are willing to* live' (Richard Baxter, *The Reasons of the Christian Religion* (London, 1667), sig. A3v).

47 Baxter, *Saints Everlasting Rest*, 4th edn. (London, 1653), p. 207.

48 Baxter, *Christian Directory*, Part I, p. 95.

49 Baxter, *Christian Directory*, Part I, p. 23.

50 For a more nuanced and technical account of Baxter's understanding of the will as an appetite for the perceived good, see Burton, *The Hallowing of Logic*, pp. 176–84, and Condie, "'Light Accompanied with Vital Heat'", esp. pp. 18–25, 28–30.

51 Condie, "'Light Accompanied with Vital Heat'", p. 20.

52 Baxter, *Christian Directory*, Part I, p. 110.

53 Baxter, *Saints Everlasting Rest*, p. 278.

54 Baxter, *Saints Everlasting Rest*, p. 511.

55 Condie, "'Light Accompanied with Vital Heat'", p. 33.

56 Baxter, *Gildas Salvianus*, p. 277.

57 Baxter, *Gildas Salvianus*, p. 277.

58 Baxter, *Gildas Salvianus*, p. 264.

59 William Perkins, *A Commentarie or Exposition vpon the Five First Chapters of the Epistle to the Galatians*, in *Workes of That Famous and Worthie Minister of Christ in the Vniversitie of Cambridge, M. W. Perkins*, 3 vols. (Cambridge, 1608–9), II:179.

60 Baxter, *Gildas Salvianus*, p. 15.

61 Baxter, *Gildas Salvianus*, p. 40.

62 Baxter, *Gildas Salvianus*, p. 40.

63 Baxter, *Gildas Salvianus*, p. 264.

64 Matthew Sylvester, *Elisha's Cry after Elijah's God Consider'd and Apply'd, with Reference to the Decease of the Late Reverend Mr. Richard Baxter* (London, 1696), p. 14.

65 Perkins, *Arte of Prophecying*, in *Workes*, II:760; Cicero, *De Oratore*, II.xlv.189–90.

66 Baxter, *Gildas Salvianus*, p. 277.

67 Baxter, *Gildas Salvianus*, p. 277.

68 Baxter, *Gildas Salvianus*, p. 276.

69 Perkins, *Arte of Prophecying*, in *Workes*, II:761.

70 Baxter, *Gildas Salvianus*, p. 19.

71 Baxter, *Gildas Salvianus*, p. 78.

72 Perkins, *Arte of Prophecying*, in *Workes*, II:752.

73 On the impact of Baxter's talk with Ussher, see the preface to Richard Baxter, *A Call to the Unconverted* (London, 1658), sig. A2r–A4v; Keeble, *Richard Baxter*, pp. 73–5.

74 Baxter, *Call*, sig. A3r.

75 Baxter, *Christian Directory*, Part I, p. 2.

76 Baxter, *Saints Everlasting Rest*, p. 472.

77 Eric Charles White, *Kaironomia: On the Will to Invent* (Ithaca: Cornell University Press, 1987), p. 13.

78 Baxter, *Saints Everlasting Rest*, p. 472.

79 Richard Baxter, *Directions and Perswasions to a Sound Conversion* (London, 1658), pp. 140–1.

80 Baxter, *Saints Everlasting Rest*, p. 397.

81 Johannes Susenbrotus, *Epitome troporum ac schematum et Grammaticorum & Rhetorume arte rhetorica libri tres* (Zurich, 1540?), p. 46.

82 Baxter, *Saints Everlasting Rest*, pp. 397–8.

83 Keeble, *Richard Baxter*, pp. 6–7.

84 Baxter, *Directions and Perswasions to a Sound Conversion*, p. 133.

85 Baxter, *Gildas Salvianus*, p. 31.

86 Baxter, *Saints Everlasting Rest*, 4th edn, Part I, p. 207.

87 Baxter, *Gildas Salvianus*, p. 230.

88 Richard Baxter, *The Last Work of a Believer His Passing Prayer Recommending His Departing Spirit to Christ to Be Received by Him* (London, 1682), p. 63.

89 Baxter, *Directions and Perswasions to a Sound Conversion*, p. 133.

90 Henry Peacham, *The Garden of Eloquence* (London, 1577), sig. N4v.

91 Baxter, *Gildas Salvianus*, p. 275.

92 Baxter, *Gildas Salvianus*, sig. (c6)r–v.

93 Baxter, *Gildas Salvianus*, pp. 356–7. Here Baxter appears to use 'affiance' to designate a kind of belief that falls short of saving faith, in contrast to his use of 'affiance' elsewhere, which Simon Burton summarizes as meaning 'that act of the will which serves to distinguish salvific, heartfelt faith from merely intellectual faith' (Burton, *The Hallowing of Logic*, p. 373, referencing Richard Baxter, *Of Saving Faith* (London, 1658), pp. 73–7).

94 Baxter, *Saints Everlasting Rest*, p. 671.

95 Debora K. Shuger, *Sacred Rhetoric: The Christian Grand Style in the English Renaissance* (Princeton, NJ: Princeton University Press, 1988), p. 186.

96 Baxter, *Treatise of Conversion*, sig. (a)3r.

97 Shuger, *Sacred Rhetoric*, p. 193.

98 Nuttall, *Richard Baxter*, p. 44. See also Keeble, *Richard Baxter*, pp. 8–12.

99 Richard Baxter, 'Love Breathing Thanks and Praise', in *Poetical Fragments* (London, 1681), p. 40.

100 C. H. Spurgeon, 'Turn or Burn', in *The New Park Street Pulpit*, 6 vols. (London: Passmore & Alabaster, 1855–60), II:421.

101 Orme, *The Life and Times of Richard Baxter*, I:131.

102 Baxter, *Gildas Salvianus*, p. 275.

103 Keeble, *Richard Baxter*, p. 8.

104 Baxter, *Call*, sig. A1r.

105 Baxter, *Call*, sig. A4r.

106 Baxter, *Call*, sig. A5r–C9.

107 Baxter, *Call*, sig. A5r.

108 Baxter, *Call*, sig. A5v.

109 Baxter, *Call*, sig. A6v.

110 Baxter, *Call*, sig. A6v.

111 Baxter, *Call*, sig. A6v.

112 Baxter, *Call*, sig. A7r–v.

113 Baxter, *Call*, sig. A8r.

114 Baxter, *Call*, sig. A11v.

115 Baxter, *Call*, sig. A11v–12r.

116 Baxter, *Call*, sig. A12r–v.

117 Baxter, *Call*, sig. A11v.

118 Baxter, *Call*, p. 1

119 Baxter, *Call*, p. 3.

120 Baxter, *Call*, p. 4.

121 Baxter, *Call*, p. 2.

122 Baxter, *Call*, p. 3.

123 Baxter, *Call*, pp. 3–4.

124 Baxter, *Call*, p. 3.

125 Baxter, *Call*, p. 6.

126 Baxter, *Call*, pp. 6–7.

127 Baxter, *Call*, pp. 23–4.

128 Baxter, *Call*, p. 25.

129 Baxter, *Call*, p. 19.

130 Baxter, *Call*, p. 6.

131 Baxter, *Call*, p. 101.

132 Baxter, *Call*, p. 101.

133 Baxter, *Call*, p. 101.

134 Baxter, *Call*, p. 103.

135 Baxter, *Call*, p. 149.

136 Baxter, *Call*, pp. 156–7.

137 Baxter, *Call*, p. 158.

138 Baxter, *Call*, p. 117.

139 Baxter, *Call*, p. 117.

140 Perkins, *Arte of Prophecying*, in *Workes*, II:672.

141 Baxter, *Call*, pp. 118, 119, 120 (twice), 121; p. 119 gives the singular form '*Turn, Turn, for why wilt thou die?*'

142 Keeble, *Richard Baxter*, p. 67.

143 Richard Baxter, *The Life of Faith in Three Parts* (London, 1671), pp. 321–61.

144 Keeble, *Richard Baxter*, p. 65.

145 Thomas Wilson, *The Arte of Rhetorique* (London, 1553), fol. 2v.

146 U. Milo Kaufmann, *The Pilgrim's Progress and Traditions in Puritan Meditation* (New Haven: Yale University Press, 1966), pp. 133–50.

147 Keeble, *Richard Baxter*, pp. 111–13. For more on meditation upon the creatures, see Keith G. Condie, 'The Theory, Practice, and Reception of Meditation in the Thought of Richard Baxter' (PhD diss., University of Sydney, 2010), pp. 77–83, and Condie, '"Light Accompanied with Vital Heat"', p. 35.

148 Keeble, *Richard Baxter*, p. 54.

149 N. H. Keeble, *The Literary Culture of Nonconformity* (Leicester: Leicester University Press, 1987), Chapter 8, '"Answerable Style": The Linguistic Dissent of Nonconformity' (pp. 240–62); Roger Pooley, 'Language and Loyalty: Plain Style at the Restoration', *Literature & History*, 6.1 (Spring 1980), 2–18.

150 Isabel Rivers, *Reason, Grace, and Sentiment: A Study of the Language of Religion and Ethics in England, 1660–1780*, 2 vols. (Cambridge: Cambridge University Press, 1991–2000).

151 William Perkins, *A Warning against the Idolatrie of the Last Times*, in *Workes*, I:671.

152 Baxter, *Christian Directory*, Part I, pp. 141–2.

153 See Burton, *The Hallowing of Logic*, pp. 210–20.

154 Keeble, *Richard Baxter*, pp. 100–3.

155 Baxter, *Saints Everlasting Rest*, p. 760.

156 See Chapter 1 for Perkins's disapproving view of *Bevis of Southampton*.

157 Baxter, *Christian Directory*, Part I, p. 292.

158 Baxter, *Reliquiæ Baxterianæ*, I:210.

159 Keeble, *Richard Baxter*, p. 89.

160 Richard Baxter, *The Poor Man's Family Book* (London, 1674), p. 1. Given that Saul is the pre-conversion name of St Paul, the paradigmatic convert-turned-preacher of the New Testament, these characters could be seen as pre-regenerate and regenerate versions of the same person.

161 Baxter, *Poor Man's Family Book*, p. 30.

162 Baxter, *Poor Man's Family Book*, p. 32.

163 Baxter, *Poor Man's Family Book*, p. 24.

164 Baxter, *Poor Man's Family Book*, p. 29.

165 Quintilian, *Institutio Oratoria*, 8.6.44–58.

166 For instance, Helen C. White, *English Devotional Literature (Prose), 1600–1640* (Madison: University of Wisconsin, 1931), pp. 257–62; Louis L. Martz, *The Poetry of Meditation: A Study in English Religious Literature of the Seventeenth Century* (1956; rev. edn. New Haven: Yale University Press, 1962), pp. 153–75; Kaufmann, *Pilgrim's Progress and Traditions in Puritan Meditation*, pp. 133–50, 157–8, 171–4; Knott, *The Sword of the Spirit*, Chapter 3, 'Richard Baxter and the Saint's Rest' (pp. 62–84); Keeble, *Richard Baxter*, pp. 13–17 and Chapter 5, 'Earth and Heaven' (pp. 94–113). Keeble gives further references to literary studies of *The Saints Everlasting Rest* in *Richard Baxter*, p. 200, n. 13.

167 Baxter, *Saints Everlasting Rest*, p. 621. On Baxter's understanding of meditation, see especially Condie, 'The Theory, Practice, and Reception of Meditation in the Thought of Richard Baxter', briefly summarized in Condie, '"Light Accompanied with Vital Heat"', pp. 34–5.

168 White, *English Devotional Literature*, pp. 257, 260.

Richard Baxter's Exhortations and Meditations

159

169 Baxter, *Saints Everlasting Rest*, p. 686. Knott notes that critics 'have tended to consider the fourth part by itself, as a treatise on formal meditation' (*The Sword of the Spirit*, p. 64).

170 Baxter, *Methodus Theologiae Christianæ*. Diagram inserted between errata and page 1.

171 Debora Shuger notes that whereas, in Roman rhetoric, 'delight' signified an aesthetic response to graceful language, the Lutheran divine Matthias Flacius Illyricus 'defines delectare as to rest in God with trust and love' (*Sacred Rhetoric*, p. 178, citing Matthias Flacius Illyricus, *Clavis Scripturae Sacrae, seu de sermone sacrarum literarum, in duas partes divisae* [1652] (Leipzig, 1695), I:206).

172 Baxter, *Saints Everlasting Rest*, p. 601.

173 Baxter, *Saints Everlasting Rest*, p. 603.

174 Baxter, *Saints Everlasting Rest*, p. 722.

175 Kaufmann, *Pilgrim's Progress and Traditions in Puritan Meditation*, p. 146. Baxter quotes Sibbes in *Saints Everlasting Rest*, pp. 406, 412, 413, and names him as one of the blessed in heaven in several places.

176 On Baxter's use of soliloquy, see Knott, *The Sword of the Spirit*, pp. 68, 71–2.

177 Richard Sibbes, *The Soules Conflict with It Selfe, and Victory over It Self by Faith* (London, 1635), 251, 220.

178 Paul Baynes, *Holy Soliloquies: or, a Holy Helper in Gods Building* (London, 1618), sig. A7r.

179 Baxter, *Saints Everlasting Rest*, p. 750.

180 Baxter, *Saints Everlasting Rest*, p. 752.

181 Baxter, *Saints Everlasting Rest*, pp. 749–50.

182 Baxter, *Saints Everlasting Rest*, p. 783.

183 Baxter, *Saints Everlasting Rest*, p. 795. For a discussion of Baxter's celebration of bodily senses fostering spiritual desire in relation to that of other Puritan writers, see Belden C. Lane, *Ravished by Beauty: The Surprising Legacy of Reformed Spirituality* (Oxford: Oxford University Press, 2011), Chapter 3, 'Nature and Desire in Seventeenth-Century Puritanism', pp. 97–123, esp. pp. 105–9.

184 Baxter, *Saints Everlasting Rest*, p. 690.

185 Johannes Sturm, *De universa ratione elocutionis rhetoricae, libri IV* (Strasbourg 1575, 1576), cited in Shuger, *Sacred Rhetoric*, p. 186.

186 Sturm, *De universa ratione elocutionis rhetoricae*, cited in Shuger, *Sacred Rhetoric*, pp. 186–7.

187 Baxter, *Saints Everlasting Rest*, p. 790.

188 Baxter, *Saints Everlasting Rest*, p. 790.

189 Baxter, *Saints Everlasting Rest*, p. 790.

190 Baxter, *Saints Everlasting Rest*, p. 791.

191 Baxter, *Saints Everlasting Rest*, p. 817.

192 Baxter, *Saints Everlasting Rest*, p. 817.

160   *The Rhetoric of Conversion in English Puritan Writing*

193 Baxter, *Saints Everlasting Rest,* p. 804.

194 As Kaufmann observes of meditation upon the creatures: 'In this tradition, then, the gaze of the meditator was assiduously turned to the real world' (*Pilgrim's Progress and Traditions in Puritan Meditation*, p. 174). Keeble comments similarly on Baxter's encouragement of a new attention to the ordinary (*Richard Baxter*, pp. 108–13).

195 Baxter, *Saints Everlasting Rest,* p. 807.

196 Knott, *The Sword of the Spirit,* p. 79.

197 Baxter, *Saints Everlasting Rest,* pp. 797–8.

198 Baxter, *Saints Everlasting Rest,* pp. 621–2. See Noam Reisner, *Milton and the Ineffable* (Oxford: Oxford University Press, 2009), pp. 101–2 on the multiple biblical allusions in this passage. Reisner writes that the 'Language of *Canaan*' is a 'sacred, or pure, meta-language' that 'liberates fallen man from the rhetorical and ideological snares of elaborate rhetoric'.

199 Edmund Calamy, *An Historical Account of My Own Life: With Some Reflections on the Times I Have Lived in (1671–1731)*, 2 vols., 2nd edn (London: Henry Colburn and Richard Bentley, 1830), I:220–1.

4

Serious play: John Bunyan's imaginative persuasion

In *The Second Part of the Pilgrim's Progress* (1684) by John Bunyan, the pilgrims' guide Mr Great-heart has a run-in with a giant, Giant Maull. Apart from his name, the first thing we learn of Giant Maull is that 'This *Maull* did use to spoyl young Pilgrims with Sophistry'.[1] Sophistry refers to a specious kind of reasoning, seemingly clever but in fact deceptive, such as Plato, perhaps unfairly, attributed to the Sophists, the itinerant paid teachers of rhetoric and logic whom he deemed not true philosophers.[2]

Giant Maull displays his sophistry in accusing Great-heart of theft and kidnapping:

> You rob the Countrey, and rob it with the worst of Thefts [...] thou practises the craft of a *Kidnapper*, thou gatherest up Women and Children, and carriest them into a strange Countrey, to the weakning of my Masters Kingdom.[3]

Maull here cleverly characterizes Great-heart's pastoral endeavours as criminal, since they destabilize the prevailing diabolical order by taking people out of Satan's kingdom.

Great-heart answers Giant Maull's charges by identifying himself as a divinely appointed agent of persuasion, thus making him a practitioner of rhetoric in the broad sense of the term:

> But now *Great-heart* replied, I am a Servant of the God of Heaven, my business is to perswade sinners to Repentance, I am commanded to do my endeavour to turn Men, Women and Children, from darkness to light, and from the power of Satan to God, and if this indeed be the ground of thy quarrel, let us fall to it as soon as thou wilt.[4]

With that laying down of the gauntlet, the two begin to fight. After an hour, despite Great-heart courteously allowing the Giant to get up when he is knocked down, Great-heart eventually cuts off Giant Maull's head. This could be read emblematically, suggesting that, although satanic sophistry may put up a tough fight, redemptive rhetoric will ultimately prevail.

Great-heart's reply to Maull could serve as a mission statement for John Bunyan, who likewise saw his business as 'to perswade sinners to Repentance' and 'to turn Men, Women and Children, from darkness to light, and from the power of Satan to God'. Bunyan saw his vocation as a preacher to be primary and his writing to be an expression of this.

Bunyan was born in 1628 in Elstow near Bedford to a family that he describes as 'of that rank that is meanest, and most despised of all the families in the Land', though his more recent biographers suggest that Bunyan exaggerates the poverty of his family background, which was 'Of old and once substantial yeoman farming stock, albeit slipping down the social scale'.[5] After a period as a teenage soldier in the parliamentarian army from 1644 to 1646 during the first civil war, and a return to civilian life and the trade of a tinker, Bunyan underwent an extended spiritual crisis that led to his profession of conversion and joining the Independent congregation in Bedford then led by John Gifford. With the endorsement of his church, Bunyan soon discovered a gift of preaching that would lead both to his writing career and to his imprisonment for gathering unlawful conventicles in 1660 following the Restoration of Charles II. Following his 1672 release, Bunyan was elected pastor of the Bedford congregation, and continued a ministry of preaching and writing that acquired national prominence (aided by the bestseller status of *The Pilgrim's Progress*) until his death in 1688.[6]

Bunyan's goal is emphatically didactic, and he shares the persuasive goals of the Puritan ministers considered earlier in this book: persuasion of his audience to conversion, a rightly grounded assurance of salvation, and upright living in keeping with true faith. Yet, in *The Pilgrim's Progress* and his other allegorical narratives, Bunyan's didactic persuasive goals are worked out through literary means that make an extended appeal to the imagination through stories that have found their way into the literary canon, and appeal to readers who do not share Bunyan's religious convictions.

Bunyan's persuasion to conversion through appeal to the imagination as well as to reason resonates with Charles Taylor's notion of 'cosmic imaginaries', which characterizes people's belief systems and perceptions of reality as a matter of an imaginative engagement with their experience of the world, and not simply a set of cognitively held convictions.[7] Yet the cosmic imaginary into which Bunyan's prospective converts are invited is not that of the culture at large (as in some of Taylor's historical case studies) – rather it is the cosmic imaginary of a godly 'cognitive minority' (Peter Berger's term) that gives access to what Bunyan believes to be true reality.[8]

In terms of sheer volume, the majority of Bunyan's works are non-fictional didactic works in a variety of genres (predominantly prose with a few volumes of verse) – his roughly sixty books include works of systematic theology (e.g. *The Doctrine of the Law and Grace Unfolded*), catechism (*Instruction for the Ignorant*), children's verse (*A Book for Boys and Girls*), and doctrinal controversies with Quakers, latitudinarian Anglicans, and closed communion Baptists.[9] Bunyan's non-fictional prose and poetic works make up the contents of the thirteen-volume Oxford *Miscellaneous Works of John Bunyan*, but they are often neglected by scholars besides brief cherry-picked quotations and almost entirely neglected by general readers. It is arguably in his non-fictional didactic prose that Bunyan's writing most closely resembles the writing of the preachers on whom earlier chapters of this book have focused, and this chapter will accordingly give more attention to such works than is common in scholarly discussion of Bunyan.

Nevertheless, it is for his imaginative narrative works that Bunyan is best known. It is these works that distinguish Bunyan from the ministers considered earlier in this book, although Bunyan was not the first author of Puritan allegory nor of didactic dialogues with a narrative aspect.[10] Along with his viscerally vivid spiritual autobiography *Grace Abounding to the Chief of Sinners* (not a work of fiction but a narrative work with imaginative appeal), such works include Bunyan's allegorical fictions *The Holy War* and the two parts of *The Pilgrim's Progress*, and the somewhat more realistic proto-novel *The Life and Death of Mr. Badman*. This chapter will particularly explore how Bunyan's extended imaginative fiction functions as a vehicle of Puritan pastoral persuasion. Yet the distinction between Bunyan's didactic expository mode and his more allusive imaginative mode of persuasion does not correspond neatly to the generic distinction between his fiction and non-fiction writing or his narrative and non-narrative works. Even Bunyan's 'non-fiction' works contain imaginative similes and narrative vignettes (not unlike those found in the writers considered in earlier chapters), and his allegorical works contain multiple expository monologues and dialogues that often border on the sermonic.

Liminal space and the language of Canaan

Bunyan's appeal for conversion is directed especially to those in a liminal transitional state between the world of the ungodly and the world of the

164   *The Rhetoric of Conversion in English Puritan Writing*

redeemed. In his sermon treatise, *The Strait Gate* (1676), for instance, Bunyan focuses his appeal particularly 'to them that are upon the potters wheel, concerning whom, we know not, as yet, whether their convictions, and awaknings will end in conversion or no'.[11] Conviction of sin is a liminal state between complacent ungodliness and true conversion, though it is not guaranteed to result in full conversion to saving faith: 'Be thankful therefore for convictions, conversion begins at conviction, though all conviction doth not end in conversion.'[12] It is this state in which Bunyan's protagonist Christian begins *The Pilgrim's Progress*, with a burden on his back, crying '*what shall I do?*'[13]

This liminal state is also vividly figured in Bunyan's account of his own spiritual progress in *Grace Abounding*. Although it is notoriously difficult to pinpoint a single moment of conversion for Bunyan in *Grace Abounding*,[14] one major turning point is an encounter in which Bunyan's work as a tinker brings him to Bedford, 'where there was three or four poor women sitting at a door in the Sun, and talking about the things of God'. Though 'now a brisk talker also my self in the matters of Religion', Bunyan finds that

> *I heard, but I understood not;* for they were far above out of my reach, for their talk was about a new birth, the work of God on their hearts, also how they were convinced of their miserable state by nature. [...]
>
> And me thought they spake as if joy did make them speak: they spake with such pleasantness of Scripture language, and with such appearance of grace in all they said, that they were to me as if they had found a new world, as if they were people that dwelt alone, and were not to be reckoned among their Neighbours, Num. 23. 9.[15]

The doorway in which the women are sitting has a symbolic as well as a literal function – it marks the liminal transition point into the world of grace from which Bunyan is at that point excluded. This symbolic significance is confirmed by the young Bunyan's subsequent vision of the women 'as if they were set on the Sunny side of some high Mountain, there refreshing themselves with the pleasant beams of the Sun, while I was shivering and shrinking in the cold, afflicted with frost, snow, and dark clouds'. In Bunyan's vision he has a long struggle to find the doorway through the wall that separates him from these women, though eventually 'with great striving, me thought I at first did get in my head, and after that, by a side-ling striving, my shoulders, and my whole body'.[16]

In recent decades, this episode has been frequently read in psychoanalytic terms, with the biblical metaphor of the 'new birth' for conversion correlating with Bunyan's visionary self (perhaps analogous to the dreamer-narrator of *The Pilgrim's Progress*) struggling to pass through the birth canal into the light of the sun enjoyed by the poor but elect women.[17] The poor women are the privileged inhabitants of 'a new world' from which the young Bunyan under conviction is excluded but that he strives to enter. This is a plausible reading of the symbolism, but needs to be supplemented by attention to the role of language development in the child's acclimatization to the world after birth.

In light of this, and of the literary nature of Bunyan's pastoral endeavours, it is significant that the women's spiritual otherness from the young Bunyan is figured as linguistic as well as spatial difference – they 'spake with such pleasantness of Scripture language', a language that marks them out as distinctive from the wider culture. It is new language that gives access to the new world of the redeemed, as Graham Ward notes:

> It is the appropriation of their language that preoccupies him in the autobiography that follows, for when he looks 'into the Bible with new eyes and read[s] as I never did read before' God begins to 'create still within me such suppositions' (*GA* p. 17) as would form the basis for his own 'new world'; a world revealed through and described in terms of the language of Scripture.[18]

The reference to the women as 'people that dwelt alone, and were not to be reckoned among their Neighbours', along with the scriptural reference given (Numbers 23:9), alludes to the prophecy of Balaam, a pagan prophet who was divinely compelled to bless the Israelites as a chosen nation on their way to taking possession of the promised land of Canaan. Their use of 'Scripture language' marks out these godly women as inhabitants of the promised land of grace. This concept is given striking expression in *The Pilgrim's Progress* when Christian and Faithful arrive at the town of Vanity Fair:

> And as they wondred at their Apparel, so did they likewise at their Speech, for few could understand what they said; they naturally spoke the Language of *Canaan*; but they that kept the *fair*, were the men of this World: So that from one end of the *fair* to the other, they seemed *Barbarians* each to the other.[19]

The 'Language of *Canaan*' marks out Christian and Faithful as like Old Testament Israelites to whom the promised land of Canaan was given, just as *Grace Abounding*'s poor women in the sun are figured as citizens of the promised land. More specifically, it is a phrase with a biblical origin in Isaiah 19:18: 'In that day shall five cities in the land of Egypt speak the language of Canaan, and swear to the LORD of hosts; one shall be called, The city of destruction.' This verse foretells a coming conversion of Egypt, Israel's ancient enemy, to the worship of Israel's God, signified by the Egyptians adopting the same language. 'The city of destruction' is also a familiar location to readers of *The Pilgrim's Progress*, since it is the place from which Christian flees at the beginning of the narrative. Given that 'the language of Canaan', in its original biblical context, signifies the conversion of those previously outsiders to the people of God, it is ironic that it is unintelligible to the inhabitants of Vanity Fair.

In the Puritan tradition 'the language of Canaan' becomes a figurative expression, referring not to a literal language but to the renewed speech of the regenerate.[20] For instance, the Presbyterian Thomas Watson comments that 'our words must be solid and weighty, not feathery; Gods children must speak *the language of Canaan*; many pretend to be Gods children, but *their speech bewrayeth them*'.[21] However, the term became implicitly associated with the literally distinctive lexicon and speech patterns of Puritan and Dissenting communities that marked them out from wider society. To adopt such speech patterns was to assert an identity as one of the godly. While Bunyan probably intends to say that the pilgrims' conversation was unintelligible to the townsfolk for spiritual reasons, the speech of Puritans and Dissenters also attracted mockery and incomprehension from their critics due to its strange-sounding jargon.[22]

Christian's wife Christiana also undergoes a change of speech upon conversion. She, like the godly women of the Bedford congregation, has begun to speak 'Scripture language':

> But while they were thus about to be gon, two of the Women that were *Christiana's* Neighbours, came up to her House and knocked at her Dore. To whom she said as before. *If you come in Gods Name, come in.* At this the Women were stun'd, for this kind of Language they used not to hear, or to perceive to drop from the Lips of *Christiana*.[23]

Christiana's conversion, or at least the initial stage of conversion manifested in conviction of sin, is apparent even to her firmly unregenerate neighbours because her pattern of speech has suddenly changed. As the marginal note comments, '*Christiana's new language stunds her old Neighbours.*'[24]

Conversion is, for Bunyan, at least in part, a linguistic matter, a matter of changing one's language to speak the tongue of the redeemed. But if we read the Vanity Fair episode more closely, there is something problematic about the language of Canaan. Though speaking the godly jargon of scripture language is a sign of having been converted, it seems unlikely to lead to the conversion of those who fail to understand it: 'they seemed *Barbarians* each to the other'. This phrase alludes, as N. H. Keeble notes in his edition of *The Pilgrim's Progress*, to 1 Corinthians 14:11: 'Therefore if I know not the meaning of the voice, I shall be

John Bunyan's Imaginative Persuasion 167

unto him that speaketh a barbarian, and he that speaketh shall be a barbarian unto me.' In context, St Paul is arguing against the use of uninterpreted glossolalia in the gathering of a church congregation, since, for believers, an unintelligible utterance is unable to edify them, and, for outsiders to the believing community who may be present, it will be taken as a sign not of divine inspiration but of insanity. The 'language of Canaan' spoken by seventeenth-century Puritans was not glossolalic but a form of the English language, but there appear to have been similar barriers to its accessibility for those outside the godly community.

Bunyan's pilgrims remain marginal to the world of the fair, refusing to buy anything: 'The men told them, that they were Pilgrims and Strangers in the world, and that they were going to their own Countrey, which was the Heavenly *Jerusalem*'.[25] Bunyan's margin directs us to the biblical source in Hebrews 11:13-16, where the Greek word used for 'strangers' is *xenoi* (singular *xenos*), which can denote people or things that are strange, alien or foreign in literal or figurative senses.

Besides its literal sense, *xenos* is used figuratively in the New Testament both to denote Gentile unbelievers, foreigners in relation to the Jewish nation and strangers to the covenant promises of salvation (Ephesians 2:12, 19), and to denote Christian believers, who are strangers to the present world system and citizens of the heavenly city which is to come (Hebrews 11:13). In *The Pilgrim's Progress*, also, the pilgrims and the townsfolk are strangers to one another, aliens to one another's conceptions of the cosmos 'So that from one end of the *fair* to the other, they seemed *Barbarians* each to the other'.[26]

Xenos is a word that occurs also in Aristotle's *Rhetoric*. According to Aristotle, for the orator's words to be effective, they should be *xenos* but not too *xenos*, that is, there should be sufficient unfamiliarity to draw the audience's attention and sufficient familiarity in language to be able to communicate.[27] One might wonder whether Bunyan's pilgrims are too *xenos* to persuade their interlocutors, although we read that the pilgrims' patient suffering 'won to their side (though but few in comparison of the rest) several of the men in the *fair*',[28] and there is at least one conversion at Vanity Fair, that of Hopeful, who is moved by the sufferings of the martyred Faithful to take his place on the pilgrimage.

The potential unintelligibility of the language of Canaan renders it a problematic vehicle for discourse aiming at conversion. However, I will suggest that the narrative form of *The Pilgrim's Progress* and other imaginative works by Bunyan provides a vehicle for the gradual teaching of the language of Canaan to those who do not as yet speak it. Bunyan adopts the creative language of the prose romance, folktale and other forms of storytelling with which his

168   *The Rhetoric of Conversion in English Puritan Writing*

unregenerate readers have an affinity, and infuses it with the language of Canaan and its associated scriptural thought forms. In this way, he gradually entices his readers from within their current thought world to accept elements of the regenerate thought world of the godly and to have their thinking and feeling gradually influenced towards godly faith. The literary appeal to the imagination thus fosters the liminal space of conviction that, along with the work of the Spirit, offers room to manoeuvre in the gradual transition from complacent godlessness to assured faith.

God's instrument: The *ethos* of the divine messenger

The paradox of believing both in divine predestination and in pastoral persuasion that has been considered in earlier chapters of this book also surfaces in the work of Bunyan. When he writes explicitly about his doctrine in a systematic manner, notably in his early treatise *The Doctrine of the Law and Grace Unfolded* (1659), it is clear that Bunyan is a Calvinist, but in his pastoral practice, as Michael Davies rightly notes, Bunyan downplays questions of election and reprobation, rather emphasizing the call to all to repent and believe.[29] Michael Mullett likewise comments that 'the content of Bunyan's preaching was finding a place for a voluntarism that may seem at odds with the absolute decree of predestination'.[30]

For instance, in his sermon treatise *Good News for the Vilest of Men* (1688), Bunyan addresses his reader/hearer as follows:

> lay the thoughts of thy Election by, and ask thy self these questions; Do I see my lost condition? Do I see salvation is no where but in Christ? Would I share in this salvation by Faith of him? And would I, as was said afore, be throughly saved, to wit, from the filth, as from the guilt? Do I love Christ, his Father, his Saints, his Word and Ways? This is the way to prove we are Elect.[31]

Bunyan here directs attention away from God's inscrutable decree to his reader's faculties of thinking, willing and loving, through a series of first-person questions that he places in the mouth of his readers, inviting them to interrogate their inward apprehension and understanding ('Do I see[?] [...] Do I see[?]'), their desire for salvation ('Would I share in this salvation[?] [...] would I [...] be throughly saved[?]'), and the direction of their affections ('Do I love[?]').

This is a version of the 'practical syllogism' recommended by Puritan divines such as William Perkins and others as a means of discerning whether or not one is among the elect, but, whereas Perkins's practical syllogism is framed as an introspective self-examination to confirm that one already holds to godly faith,[32] Bunyan's version reframes it subtly towards a more evangelistic call for decision – the conditional mood of 'Would I' moves from a present tense perception to more of an invitation to addressees to desire salvation.

Bunyan describes the role that his preaching plays in the salvation of his hearers using the language of instrumentality: 'they would also bless God for me (unworthy Wretch that I am!) and count me Gods Instrument that shewed to them the Way of Salvation.'[33] Nevertheless, divine intervention is essential, as a marginal note in *The Pilgrim's Progress* informs us when Bunyan's protagonist Christian fails to persuade Simple, Sloth and Presumption to awake from their roadside slumbers to escape danger: '*There is no perswasion will do, if God openeth not the eyes.*'[34] The attempts of the godly to persuade sinners can thus be frustrated, and indeed will be frustrated if not accompanied by an effectual divine persuasion, although Christian's attempt to persuade the sleeping trio is evidence that he is a practitioner of pastoral rhetoric seeking to win converts for their own good.

Davies comments, 'Bunyan thus exhorts and pleads with the sinner to turn to Christ [...] However, Bunyan can also maintain that grace is still wholly unconditional by making coming and believing gifts of God's spirit.'[35] Isabel Rivers comments similarly:

> In his writing he habitually combines an emphasis on free grace and faith as a gift to the elect from which holiness inevitably springs with urgent exhortation to his readers to pray, repent, will, strive, and do. This does not seem to have struck him as a contradiction[.][36]

Bunyan's preaching and writing is addressed both to prospective converts who are as yet unregenerate and to the professing members of the godly community. Recounting the beginnings of his preaching ministry in *Grace Abounding*, Bunyan characterizes his work principally as that of an evangelist to the unconverted, telling us that 'my spirit leaned most after awakening and converting Work'[37] and that his work was 'even to carry an awakening Word.'[38] Bunyan hopes his hearers are 'awakened' to a sense of their own guilt for sin and of the mercy of God available to them in Christ, that is, to an experiential engagement with the Law-Gospel dialectic particularly associated with Luther's theology, in which the Law of God shows Christians their sin deserving of divine punishment but the Gospel offers them forgiveness for the guilt shown by the Law.

Bunyan shares the rhetorical goals of the ministers considered earlier in this book, seeking to persuade his readers and hearers to conversion, assurance and

170 *The Rhetoric of Conversion in English Puritan Writing*

godly living, but he lacks direct access to the classical rhetorical tradition that informed Perkins, Sibbes and Baxter. Although Bunyan exaggerates his lack of learning,[39] he lacks the university education of Perkins and Sibbes, and also Baxter's knowledge of the classical languages that made him such an impressive autodidact.

Bunyan once clashed with a representative of university rhetoric in the person of Thomas Smith, Professor of Arabic and university librarian at Cambridge and praelector of rhetoric at Christ's College, the college of Perkins and Milton.[40] Smith heard Bunyan preaching in a barn near the village of Toft, and not only disagreed with Bunyan's exegesis but queried his right to preach at all without proper ecclesiastical authorization. According to Smith, Bunyan's response was: 'Away [...] to *Oxford* with your hell bred Logick.'[41] The editor of the posthumous Bunyan folio, Charles Doe, remembers Bunyan's reply a little differently and more piously: '*Horrid Blasphemy, away with your hellish Logick, and speak Scripture*.'[42]

Bunyan claims an authority to preach from his commissioning by the Bedford Independent congregation, an ecclesiastical authorization not recognized by Smith or the post-Restoration authorities of church and state,[43] but more than this his primary claim is to a rhetorical *ethos* that comes from 'experiential authenticity and divine inspiration'.[44] When on trial, Bunyan asserts this gifting by the Spirit as giving him authority to preach, since, he protests, 'the holy Ghost never intended that men who have Gifts and Abilities should bury them in the earth, but rather did commend and stir up such to the exercise of their gift'.[45]

This gift that confers on Bunyan the authoritative *ethos* of an inspired preacher arises out of Bunyan's traumatic spiritual crises described in his memoir *Grace Abounding*, which he construes as a providential preparation for preaching ministry. Famously, Bunyan writes that 'I preached what I felt, what I smartingly did feel'.[46] Bunyan began preaching his experiential knowledge of the guilt of sin and the terrors of God's Law before he had sufficient sense of the consolation of God's forgiveness in the Gospel to be able to preach this with conviction. Bunyan tells the readers of *Grace Abounding*, 'I went my self in chains to preach to them in chains, and carried that fire in my own conscience that I perswaded them to beware of'.[47] Following some more consolatory experiences of God's grace towards him, Bunyan reports, 'I altered in my preaching (for still I preached what I saw and felt)'.[48]

The positioning of Bunyan's account of his call to preaching at the end of *Grace Abounding* implicitly characterizes the *ethos* of his public persuasive endeavours as the outward overflow of his inward experience. Bunyan claims that his *pathos*, the emotional/affective aspect of his persuasive persona, is also

John Bunyan's Imaginative Persuasion   171

divinely bestowed. Using the same vocabulary as Richard Sibbes, he writes: 'I thank God he gave unto me some measure of bowels and pity for their Souls'.[49]

The preface to *Grace Abounding* contains one of the most passionate and frequently cited defences of 'Puritan plain style', in which Bunyan renounces literary adornment not only on the grounds that it gets in the way of the accessibility of his message to his audience but also because such ornamentation is not fitting to the experience that underlies his message:[50]

> *I could also have stepped into a stile much higher then this in which I have here discoursed, and could have adorned all things more then here I have seemed to do: but I dare not:* God *did not play in convincing of me; the* Devil *did not play in tempting of me; neither did I play when I sunk as into a bottomless pit, when the* pangs of hell caught hold upon me: *wherefore I may not play in my relating of them, but be plain and simple, and lay down the thing as it was*[.][51]

Bunyan here justifies a 'plain and simple' style, which disavows ornamentation, as the most appropriate medium to transcribe his raw spiritual experience, '*the thing as it was*'. Yet, as with the writers considered in previous chapters, Bunyan's defence of plainness is not artless, using the tricolonic 'God *did not play* [...] *the* Devil *did not play* [...] *neither did I play*'. Even the opposition between 'play' and 'plain' plays on the sound between the words. This playful disclaiming of play foreshadows a tension that runs throughout Bunyan's works between the seriousness of Bunyan's didactic intent and his adoption of aesthetic pleasure as a means of effective persuasion.

Bunyan's relatively unlearned status is made a badge of honour by Bunyan's pastor John Burton in Burton's letter to the reader commending Bunyan's first book, the anti-Quaker tract *Some Gospel-Truths Opened* (1656). Burton is aware that Bunyan's lack of formal education is a potential liability, as it means that Bunyan may be lacking in rhetorical *ethos* for his readers:

> be not offended because Christ holds forth the glorious treasure of the gospel to thee in a poor earthen vessell, by one, who hath neither the greatness nor the wisdome of this world to commend him to thee; for as the Scripture saith, Christ (who was low and contemptible in the world himself) ordinarily chuseth such for himself, and for the doing of his work, 1 *Cor.* 1. 26, 27, 28. Not many wise men after the flesh, not many mighty, not many noble are called: but God hath chosen the foolish things of the world, &c. this man is not chosen out of an earthly, but out of the heavenly University, the Church of Christ[.][52]

Burton seeks to turn this liability into an asset highlighting Bunyan's divinely given *ethos* – Burton tells us that Christ 'ordinarily' chooses the unlearned, not only to be saved but also to proclaim the message of salvation. This is a message reminiscent of the Baptist cobbler Samuel How's notorious 1640 pamphlet *The Sufficiencie of the Spirits Teaching, without Humane-Learning*, which likewise comments that God '*chooseth* not onely for *salvation* but for *ministration* the *foolish* in Mans account'.[53]

Burton tells readers that Bunyan has

> the learning of the spirit of Christ, which is the thing that makes a man both a Christian and a Minister of the Gospell, as *Isa.* 50. 4. The Lord God hath given me the tongue of the learned, &c. compared with *Luke* 2. 18. where Christ, as man, saith, the spirit of the Lord is upon me, because he hath anointed me to preach the gospel to the poor, &c.[54]

The verse Burton cites from Isaiah is the same verse that Perkins cites to say that ministers need both human learning and the inward teaching of the Spirit,[55] but Burton's application of this verse is almost opposite to the sense Perkins derives from it. Where Perkins supposes that a minister needs to be educated in order to have 'a tongue of the learned', Burton takes the same phrase to mean that the Spirit can bestow the necessary learning and speech upon a preacher without formal education or ordination.[56]

Nevertheless, Bunyan and Burton, in opposition to the Quakers and other radical sectarians, affirm the need for divine knowledge to be (in Perkins's words) 'by outward meanes [...] taught from man to man': the teaching of the Spirit occurs not solely through private individual experience but also through human teachers in 'the heavenly University, the Church of Christ'. This acknowledgement of the human mediation of spiritual truth reminds us that Bunyan's spiritual vision is not that of a solitary self. There are other pilgrims on the road whose thinking shapes Bunyan's, whether through personal contact or through their writing and preaching. Some of these pilgrims have been formed in an earthly university as well as the heavenly university of the godly community (including William Perkins, Arthur Dent, John Dod, and John Owen), and so, in both content and style, Bunyan's writing may not be as immune from the influence of classical and secular learning as he suggests.

Awakening words: Bunyan's sermon treatises

Much of Bunyan's written corpus is made up of sermon treatises, written versions of orally delivered sermons or written works imitating the oral qualities of a sermon. These treatises appeal to the reason (*logos*) and the affections (*pathos*) using language and techniques similar to those adopted by the Puritan ministers considered earlier in this book.

Bunyan's early biographer, the comb-maker Charles Doe, recalls how Bunyan's preaching captivated both his affections and his understanding, thus implicitly appealing to both *logos* and *pathos*, as well as making use both of reason and of imagination:

> Mr. *Bunyan* went on and Preached so *New Testament*-like, that he made me admire and weep for Joy, and give him my Affections.
>
> And he was the first Man that ever I heard Preach to my new enlightened Understanding and Experience, for me thought all his Sermons were adapted to my Condition, and had apt Similitudes, being full of the Love of God, and the manner of its secret working upon the Soul, and of the Soul under the sense of it, that I could weep for Joy most part of his Sermons[.][57]

Bunyan's sermons, according to Doe, possess the rhetorical and pastoral decorum of being 'adapted to my Condition'. Even while preaching 'to my new enlightened Understanding', Bunyan's persuasion uses the imaginative technique of 'apt Similitudes'. Bunyan's preaching also elevates the necessity of divine agency in spiritual persuasion, through 'the Love of God, and the manner of its secret working upon the Soul', while manifesting divine power through Bunyan's human instrumentality – it is Bunyan, according to Doe, who 'made me admire and weep for Joy, and give him my Affections'.

Most of Bunyan's sermon treatises follow the 'doctrine and use' structure, beginning with explication of a biblical text and then applying it to his hearers.[58] However, though there are often identifiable 'doctrine' and 'use' sections of Bunyan's discourses, these are not sharply distinct, but intermingle. Likewise, Bunyan mingles methodical exposition and passionate exhortation, *logos* and *pathos*, throughout. Teaching and moving go hand in hand for Bunyan.

Bunyan heightens the rhetorical polarities of Puritan practical divinity in its mission to apply the Law and the Gospel to the right people at the right time, affirming the possibility of the most notorious sinners repenting and attaining salvation, and of those who appear most devout proving to be hypocrites devoid of saving faith. The profane should not despair, and 'professors' of godly faith should not presume. This is apparent from comparing two of Bunyan's more specifically conversionist sermon treatises: *The Strait Gate*, which warns that 'great professors' (those who profess saving faith) may fall short of heaven,[59] and *Good News for the Vilest of Men*, which offers salvation to the worst of sinners.

The Strait Gate (1676) begins with an opening epistle to the reader describing the book as 'This awakning work (if God will make it so)', acknowledging both the instrumental agency of Bunyan's writing in the awakening work of conversion and the necessity of divine intervention to make Bunyan's persuasive work efficacious.[60] The sermon text with which The Strait Gate begins is Luke 13:24: 'Strive to enter in at the strait gate, for many, I say unto you, seek to enter in, and shall not be able.'[61]

Bunyan begins by noting that these are the words of Christ in response to the question 'Lord, are there few that be saved?'[62] Bunyan breaks Christ's reply into two parts:

1. An answer, and that in the affirmative, the gate is strait many that seek will not be able, therefore but few shall be saved.
2. The answer, is an instruction also, strive to enter in, &c.[63]

Curiously, this reverses the order of the biblical text, in which Jesus' exhortation precedes his explanation. This suggests that Bunyan is reading the preaching of Jesus through the lens of the English Reformed 'doctrine and use' sermon, in which the exposition of doctrine comes before its application to the hearers. The application is an imperative – 'strive to enter in', meaning that Bunyan's hearers are being called to do something (as are Jesus' hearers in the original context). This is thus an instance of what the classical rhetorical tradition calls deliberative rhetoric, rhetoric that seeks to persuade its audience to action, though there is a paradox here, since the 'strait gate' at which one must strive to enter gives access to an unmerited salvation not achieved by human effort. Thus both Jesus' and Bunyan's hearers are exhorted to do something to access a benefit not won by their own doing.

The doctrine and use paradigm certainly seems to be evident in Bunyan's outline of his discourse on the text, starting with exposition before moving into exhortation:

> But to come to the particular phrases in the words, and to handle them orderly in the words I finde four things.
> 1. An intimation of the kingdom of heaven.
> 2. A description of the entrance into it.
> 3. An Exhortation to enter into it; and,
> 4. A motive to inforce that exhortation.[64]

However, in the body of the treatise, Bunyan moves almost immediately from analysis to exclamation, and from logos to pathos. Bunyan states that 'The general *scope* of the text is to be considered, and that is that great thing *Salvation*; for these words do immediatly look at, point to, and give directions about *salvation*.[65] This appears to be a calm logical exegetical observation, but his mention of salvation launches him into this passionate enquiry:

> To be saved! what is like being saved? to be saved from sin, from hell, from the wrath of God, from eternal damnation, what is like it? To be made an heir of God! of his grace! of his kingdome and eternal glory! what is like it?[66]

Though the exclamatory tone might suggest spontaneous excitement, there is a clear speech rhythm, with a near rhyme between 'to be saved' and 'To be made' and a structural parallel between the four things one is 'saved from' and the four things one is 'made an heir of', in both cases culminating in the exclamatory question 'what is like it?'

Bunyan goes on to pun on the word 'save': 'indeed this word, *saved*, is but of little use in the world, *save* to them that are heartily afraid of *damning*. This word lies in the Bible, as excellent salves lie in some mens houses'.[67] These different senses of save/saved/salve are not entirely distinct but overlapping meanings. This is clearly verbal play, despite Bunyan's disclaiming of play in the preface to *Grace Abounding* referenced above, but it is serious play.

As Bunyan proceeds with his discourse, he continues to intermingle the cool prose of logical exposition and more fervent expostulation. Bunyan makes fine distinctions between different meanings of particular words:

> men enter into heaven then, by him, not as he is the gate or door, or entrance into the celestial mansion-house, but as he is the giver and disposer of that kingdom to them who he shall count worthy, because he hath obtained it for them.[68]

The verbal register is one of precision, with 'not as' and 'but as' signalling differing modes of logical relation that could be intended by the preposition 'by'. For Bunyan, every word of Scripture must be carefully scrutinized, even such a seemingly inconsequential word as 'in', since 'we may easily pass over without any great regard, such a word as may have a glorious kingdom and eternal salvation in the bowels of it'.[69] (Midgley's complaint that 'the bowels of each word are carefully searched, often producing [...] constipated crumbling' displays a dry scholarly wit but gives an anachronistic sense to Bunyan's 'bowels', whether deliberately or otherwise.[70])

In contrast to this close logical scrutiny of the words of his text, Bunyan goes on to pile up words in a way that stirs the affections (the rhetorical mode of *pathos*). For example:

176 *The Rhetoric of Conversion in English Puritan Writing*

> there is the glory, the fulness of joy, and the everlasting pleasures; there is God
> and Christ to be enjoyed by open vision, and more; there are the Angels, and the
> Saints; further, there is no death, nor sickness, no sorrow, nor sighing, for ever:
> there is no pain, nor persecutor, nor darkness to eclipse our glory. O this *Mount
> Sion!* O this *heavenly Jerusalem!*[71]

The prose rhythm here expands and accelerates, with the listing of heavenly joys following each occurrence of 'there' culminating in the climactic exclamations of 'O'. This is an instance of epideictic oratory (the rhetoric of praise and blame), celebrating the glories of heaven, yet building up to the climax is a series of negations ('no [...] nor [...] no [...] nor [...] no [...] nor [...] nor'), signalling the inexpressibility of heavenly glory in much the same way as Richard Baxter does.[72]

Striving for heaven is expounded in terms of several energetic activities commanded in scripture: 'Therefore when he saith, *strive,* it is as much as to say, *run* for heaven, *fight* for heaven, *labour* for heaven, *wrestle* for heaven, or you are like to go without it.'[73] The repetition of 'for heaven' gives an insistence to this injunction, as does the frequent italicized repetition of '*Strive to enter in*'. This emphasis on striving underlines Bunyan's volitional emphasis and his rhetorical goal of moving the will of his hearers, emphasizing his hearers' responsibility to make a decision rather than their prior election by God. This emphasis is on the face of it difficult to reconcile with the Reformed Protestant insistence that heaven and salvation cannot be worked for, but are obtained only by the freely given gift of divine grace, but Puritan practical divinity allows a place for strenuous effort as a sign of seeking grace or as evidence of having received grace.

Bunyan recognizes that many of his hearers may be discouraged by the alarming stringency of his message, but insists that 'I intend not discouragements but awaknings'.[74] As noted earlier, Bunyan focuses his appeal in *The Strait Gate* particularly to those in the liminal state of conviction of sin, 'to them that are upon the potters wheel, concerning whom, we know not, as yet, whether their convictions, and awaknings will end in conversion or no'.[75]

Towards the end of *The Strait Gate*, Bunyan adopts the voice of a troubled reader under conviction. This is an instance of the rhetorical figure of prosopopoeia, in which the speaker adopts the voice of another person, and in this instance it allows space for the rhetorical functions of two of the sections of a classical oration, *refutatio* (acknowledging and dealing with arguments that oppose the speaker's point of view) and *confirmatio* (positive arguments in favour of the speaker's message):

John Bunyan's Imaginative Persuasion

Object. But you have said, few shall be saved, and some that go a great way, yet are not saved; at this therefore, I am even discouraged, and awakned: I think I had as good go no further, I am indeed under conviction, but I may perish, & if I go on in my sins I can but perish, and 'tis ten, twenty, a hundred to one, if I be saved should I be never so earnest for heaven.[76]

As he does elsewhere, Bunyan gives a strikingly everyday vernacular voice to his imagined interlocutor, who seems to speak out of exhausted resignation with 'I think I had as good go no further'.[77] This persona is both 'discouraged, and awakned', in the perilous liminal state of conviction but responding to it in a way that risks giving up hope.

The objector's logic of despair slips into a fatalistic determinism that conforms to a common caricature of Calvinist soteriology. The objection begins with the doctrinal point Bunyan has been seeking to establish – that few shall be saved, even among the apparently godly. However, the response of the persona that Bunyan conjures up is a misapplication of this doctrine: 'I think I had as good go no further'. From the existentially agonizing but in fact hopeful state of being 'under conviction', the voice turns away from hope with 'but I may perish', then suggests circumstances in which it would indeed be the case that he perishes ('if I go on in my sins'). The speaker significantly changes the sense of the word 'but' by changing its position from 'but I may perish' to 'I can but perish', hardening the grammatical modality from the possibility of damnation to its inevitability.[78] Finally, this despondent reader concludes that the odds are against being saved 'should I be never so earnest for heaven'.

Bunyan's answer to this interlocutor reaffirms the doctrine 'That few will be saved' but then challenges the objector's misreading of the import of the text: 'but what then? why then I had as good never seek: who told thee so? must no body seek, because few are saved, this is just contrary to the text, that bids us, *therefore* strive'.[79] The sharp staccato questioning of 'what then', 'why then' and 'who' breaks up the chain of despairing reasoning and brings it to a halt. Bunyan seeks to defuse and circumvent the logic of despair: 'why go back again, seeing that is the next way to hell, never go over hedge and ditch to hell, if I must needs go thither, I will go the fardest way about'.[80]

There is a colloquial ingenuity to this answer that would be almost humorous were the terror not so real. Rather than starting with the possibility of salvation and then tumbling into despair, Bunyan's reply concedes the possibility of damnation but then turns the gaze of the convicted sinner the other way. He seeks to reassure the reader that those whose will and desires are truly oriented

178 *The Rhetoric of Conversion in English Puritan Writing*

towards God will not perish, since only those who do not truly desire salvation will miss it:

> They that miss of life perish because they will not let go their sins [...] They perish I say, because they are content with such things as will not prove graces of a saving nature, when they come to be tryed in the fire, otherwise the promise is free and full, and everlasting.[81]

One might query how rhetorically efficacious this reassurance is, coming after an 'otherwise' at the end of a treatise the majority of which has sought to persuade readers that apparent faith and godliness may not be efficacious for salvation, but it is a pastoral attempt to assert a balance. Though hypocrites dangerously delude themselves and others, 'the promise is free and full, and everlasting' to all those who rightly read and apply to themselves that promise.

The particular promise cited here is one to which Bunyan often returns:

> *Him that cometh to me,* says Christ, *I will in no wise cast out for God so loved the world, that he gave his only begotten son, that whosoever believeth in him might not perish but have everlasting life. Ioh.* 6. 37. wherefore let not this thought, *few shall be saved,* weaken thy heart, but let it cause thee to mend thy pace, to mend thy crys, to look well to thy grounds for heaven; let it make thee fly faster from sin, to Christ, let it keep thee awake and out of carnal security, and thou maist be saved.[82]

The words of John 6:37 (here supplemented unannounced by those of John 3:16), which emphatically exclude the possibility of rejection ('*in no wise*') for those who come to Christ, consoled Bunyan himself, according to *Grace Abounding,* and he often returns to them in his own preaching.[83] One could plausibly identify this verse as lying at the heart of Bunyan's conversionist appeal – in particular, this is the sermon text expounded in his 1678 work *Come and Welcome to Jesus Christ.*

To counsel his readers on how to be among those who rightly receive God's promises, Bunyan concludes *The Strait Gate* with 'a little advice'. The exhortations that he gives place his readers into a position at once active and passive:

> Doest thou love thine own soul, then pray to Jesus Christ for an awakned heart, for an heart so awakned, with all the things of another world, that thou maiest be allured to Jesus Christ.[84]

Bunyan's readers here are exhorted to pray, an action that they can choose, but he instructs them to pray to 'be allured', that is, to be acted upon. The next piece of 'advice' given is to 'beg again for more awaknings'.[85] For professors to be truly converted requires the desires of their hearts to be changed, and, although this is beyond their unaided power to accomplish, Bunyan exhorts them to desire that change in their desires. This is, once more, an instance of how Reformed practical divinity modifies deliberative rhetoric (which in its classical form seeks to persuade people to act in a certain way). Given that people cannot do anything to save themselves, they need to be persuaded not to act but to be acted upon.[86]

However, *The Strait Gate* does not quite end with this rousing reassuring climax. Bunyan's methodical structure means he cannot always end on a rhetorical high point – his applications must run their course. Thus he concludes with a warning to professors, that, if they fall into unrepented sin,

> an hundred to one if at last, it doth not drive all the grace in thee into so dark a corner of thy heart, that thou shalt not be able, for a time, by all the torches that are burning in the Gospel to finde it out to thine own comfort and consolation.[87]

The final words of *The Strait Gate* are thus 'comfort and consolation', but the paragraph that they conclude is one that brings discomfort and an ambivalent consolation. The paragraph discourages the believing reader from indulging unrepented sin by threatening the excruciating consequence of doubt over one's salvific status, though with the implicit reassurance that consolation will be withheld only 'for a time'.

Bunyan's works often end, as here, on a note of warning – in *The Strait Gate* this is the warning of a temporary loss of spiritual consolation, but it is often the starker warning of damnation with which Bunyan concludes, as is the case in *The Pilgrim's Progress*, whose final image is of Ignorance being cast into hell from the gates of heaven.[88]

Contrasting in tone with *The Strait Gate* is *Good News for the Vilest of Men* (1688), another sermon-based book published and probably composed in the last year of Bunyan's life. Whereas *The Strait Gate* is a warning to the apparently godly, the conversion appeal of *Good News for the Vilest of Men* is targeted towards those who are apparently the worst sinners:

> One reason which moved me to Write and Print this Little Book, was, because, though there are many Excellent Heart-affecting Discourses in the World that tends to Convert the Sinner; yet I had a desire to try this simple Method of mine: Wherefore I Make bold *thus* to Invite and Encourage the *Worst* to come to *Christ* for Life.[89]

Bunyan's pastoral decorum adopts a different tone for this differing audience. Whilst one might imagine that a preacher would address visibly worse sinners

180   *The Rhetoric of Conversion in English Puritan Writing*

with greater condemnation, the opposite is the case. Where *The Strait Gate* seeks to warn hypocrites who falsely think themselves to be under the covenant of grace, *Good News for the Vilest of Men* is predominantly consolatory in tone, since it aims to assure those manifestly under the curse of the Law of God that grace is still available for them.

In this work Bunyan appropriates for his own preaching voice the preaching of Peter in Acts 2 and of Jesus in Luke 15. Peter's preaching is an 'Exhortation',[90] and Bunyan likewise adopts an exhortatory style. The first part of *Good News for the Vilest of Men* recounts Peter's preaching in Jerusalem on the day of Pentecost, arguing that those in Jerusalem were the greatest sinners because of their killing of Christ, and so their repentance and salvation provide an example of grace being available to the most notorious sinners on the condition of their repentance. Bunyan's exposition of Peter's sermon mingles logical exposition (appealing to *logos*) with passionate exclamation (appealing to *pathos*) much as he does in his other preaching, although there is an element of dramatization of the narrative when Bunyan takes on the voice of the penitent Jerusalem sinners and Peter's response to them:

> Object. *But I was one of them that plotted to take away his Life. May I be saved by him?*
> Peter. Every one of you.
> Object. *But I was one of them that bare false Witness against him. Is there Grace for me?*
> Peter. For every one of you.[91]

However, while Peter's Pentecost sermon is reported by Bunyan in terms of emphatic exhortation, Jesus' preaching to notorious sinners in Luke 15 makes use of imaginative narrative, as does Bunyan's recounting of it. Bunyan does this by borrowing 'a Story that I have read of *Martha* and *Mary*; the Name of the Book I have forgot'.[92] The story of Mary and Martha, the sisters of Lazarus often visited by Jesus in the village of Bethany, is given an imaginative reconstruction by Bunyan and his anonymous source and is, perhaps unconsciously, transposed into the terms of early modern English religious culture.

Martha is characterized as being like the Puritan 'sermon-gadders' who went in search of sermons beyond the boundaries of their own parish – she 'did seldom miss good Sermons, and Lectures, when she could come at them in *Jerusalem*', making Jerusalem sound much like seventeenth-century London with its networks of the godly. Mary, on the other hand, frequents 'the company of the vilest of Men for lust' and despises Martha's 'Zeal and Preciseness in

Religion', adopting the language used to attack Puritan Dissenters in Restoration England.[93] (Bunyan here adopts the common though unbiblical conflation of Mary of Bethany and Mary Magdalene, thought by tradition to have been converted out of prostitution.) One day Martha cunningly lures Mary to the Temple to hear Jesus by telling her sister that the preacher is a handsome man, but when

> *Jesus* Preached about the *lost Sheep*, the *lost Groat*, and the *prodigal Child* [...] she began to be taken *by the Ears*, and forgot what she came about, musing what the Preacher would make on't: But when he came to the Application, and shewed that by the lost Sheep was meant a great Sinner; by the Shepherds care was meant God's love for great Sinners; and that by the joy of the Neighbours, was shewed what joy there was among the Angels in Heaven over one great Sinner that repenteth; She began to be taken *by the Heart*.[94]

Mary's redemptive engagement with the sermon moves from her eyes to her ears to her heart. Jesus is seen as a doctrine and use preacher, whose 'Application' is a clearly demarcated second part of his sermon. However, Jesus' doctrine section is taken up by the imaginative narratives of the parables, anticipating Bunyan's own use of fictional narrative to communicate doctrine. In this instance, the narrative bypasses Mary's carnal mindset and opens her heart to persuasion by an appeal to *pathos* that brings her to repentance. Arguably, this is the persuasive strategy that Bunyan himself adopts in his extended imaginative fictional works, and it is this distinctive strategy of persuasion through imaginative narrative that will be considered in the remainder of this chapter.

To lose oneself and catch no harm: Bunyan's imaginative preparationism

Bunyan's imaginative persuasion can be read as providing an imaginative variant of Puritan 'preparationism', a tendency that emerged within some strands of Puritan piety and pastoral guidance that exhorted those who were as yet unregenerate (or who feared that they were unregenerate) to prepare themselves for the reception of saving grace through attendance on the ordinances of prayer, scripture reading and meditation, public preaching and the like.[95] Preparationism treads a tricky theological tightrope – while Reformation convictions insist that the grace that brings salvation is always unmerited and can never be earned by human actions, some Puritans argued that these spiritual exercises expose the

182   *The Rhetoric of Conversion in English Puritan Writing*

unconverted to the means of grace and can thus be encouraged as increasing their likelihood of being converted (though never their deservingness of conversion). Rather than these more typical spiritual exercises that Puritan divines commended to those seeking salvation, Bunyan's narrative works and didactic verse invite the reader into a spiritual exercise of the imagination designed to incline the inner faculties of the reader to receive the unmerited divine grace offered through Bunyan's message.

Yet, although Bunyan's use of imaginative fiction is a somewhat indirect means of persuasion towards conversion, his methodology is not so subtle that his message is not apparent. We are rarely allowed to forget for long that Bunyan is a preacher with a didactic message. Writing in the 1920s, Hoyt Hudson hailed Bunyan as 'The supreme example of a rhetorician who became a poet'.[96] Hudson is here using both 'rhetorician' and 'poet' in expansive senses, designating Bunyan as a figure with an agenda to persuade his audiences of a particular viewpoint who succeeded in becoming a creative literary artist. We cannot do Bunyan's body of writing justice without taking both aspects of his writing seriously. I would argue that Bunyan's 'poetic' imagination serves his rhetorical agenda rather than departing from it.

There is some irony in the fact that literary and scholarly readers after Bunyan's time have often found Bunyan's allegorical narratives too preachy and didactic (too dominated by *logos*), whereas for Bunyan and his godly contemporaries the anxiety was rather that they might be too indirect and allusive. One famous example of the former criticism of Bunyan is found in the Romantic poet Samuel Taylor Coleridge's reflections on the tension between Bunyan as Dissenting preacher and Bunyan as creative artist:

> in that admirable Allegory, the first Part of Pilgrim's Progress, which delights every one, the interest is so great that spite of all the writer's attempts to force the allegoric purpose on the Reader's mind by his strange names – Old Stupidity of the Tower of Honesty, &c &c – his piety was baffled by his Genius, and the Bunyan of Parnassus had the better of the Bunyan of the conventicle – and with the same illusion as we read any tale known to be fictitious, as a Novel – we go on with his characters as real persons, who had been nicknamed by their neighbours.[97]

Coleridge here praises Bunyan as a creative literary artist in spite of himself – the story brings aesthetic delight to its readers 'spite of all the writer's attempts to force the allegoric purpose'.

Yet, in a less frequently cited remark, Coleridge praises Bunyan precisely for his effective encapsulation of evangelical doctrine:

John Bunyan's Imaginative Persuasion

183

I know of no book, the Bible excepted, as above all comparison, which I, according to my judgment and experience, could so safely recommend as teaching and enforcing the whole saving truth according to the mind that was in Christ Jesus, as the Pilgrim's Progress. It is, in my conviction, incomparably the best *Summa Theologiae Evangelicae* ever produced by a writer not miraculously inspired.[98]

The Pilgrim's Progress is here celebrated not for its imaginative diversion but for its didactic function and success in 'teaching and enforcing the whole saving truth', though 'enforcing' suggests that the kind of teaching found in Bunyan's allegory has a rhetorical power to compel his audience.

The tension between Bunyan's didactic aims and his creative method is apparent in Bunyan's own defence of his approach in 'The Author's Apology for his Book', a verse prologue to the first part of *The Pilgrim's Progress* (1678), and again in 'The Authors Way of Sending Forth his Second Part of the Pilgrim', which opens his 1684 sequel. These verse apologies wrestle with anxieties around whether fiction is a fit vehicle for truth and lay out an agenda for persuasion through the imagination.

Bunyan, as a literary evangelist, compares himself to '*the Fisher-man*' who tries multiple ways '*To catch the Fish*', and observes that some fish resist capture by conventional means:

> *Yet Fish there be, that neither Hook, nor Line,*
> *Nor Snare, nor Net, nor Engin can make thine;*
> *They must be grop'd for, and be tickled too,*
> *Or they will not be catcht, what e're you do.*[99]

Bunyan implies that, as a 'fisher of men', he may need to go beyond the usual hooks of passionate preaching in order to reel in prospective converts. Those who are particularly resistant to godly exhortations may succumb to subversive modes of persuasion that bring them pleasure like the fish being tickled, but yet draw them into the gospel net, perhaps without their being conscious that this is taking place. These are fish that succumb to serious play.

Whereas Perkins's *The Arte of Prophecying* recognizes that scriptural communication is sometimes veiled in obscurity but insists that the preacher's communication should be characterized by clarity, Bunyan's 'Apology' appeals to oblique communication in Scripture as a model for his own somewhat oblique mode of writing. He defends his '*dark and cloudy words*' by pointing out that '*holy Writ [...] Is every where so full of all these things, / (Dark Figures, Allegories,)*'.[100] The epigraph to *The Pilgrim's Progress* also aligns Bunyan's allegorical method with scriptural precedent: '*I have used Similitudes, Hos. 12. 10*'.[101]

184   *The Rhetoric of Conversion in English Puritan Writing*

Even under fictional disguise, Bunyan explains, the truth works on the various inward faculties of the mind:

Come, Truth, although in Swadling-clouts, I find
Informs the Judgement, rectifies the Mind,
Pleases the Understanding, makes the Will
Submit; the Memory too it doth fill
With what doth our Imagination please;
Likewise, it tends our troubles to appease.[102]

Bunyan implicitly adopts all three of the Ciceronian tasks of the orator (*officia oratoris*): while his ministerial goals entail teaching (*docere*) and moving (*movere*) his audience, Bunyan justifies delighting (*delectare*) as an effective pedagogical mode for teaching and moving:

This Book is writ in such a Dialect,
As may the minds of listless men affect:
It seems a Novelty, and yet contains
Nothing but sound and honest Gospel-strains.[103]

The narrative mode of *The Pilgrim's Progress*, which adapts and reconfigures the prose romances of popular print culture at the time, entices those not prone to perusing doctrinal tomes to lose themselves in an imaginative world where their affections come to be reoriented. Despite Bunyan's scathing comments about romances and folk tales elsewhere that resemble those of Perkins and Baxter noted in previous chapters,[104] the romance '*Dialect*' provides Bunyan with familiar imagery that intersects with the thought world of the unregenerate reader but then reinscribes it with new and godly meanings. Bunyan's allegory is thus an imaginative rhetoric that seeks to persuade the reader to conversion through reinscribing the reader's perception of reality.[105]

Nick Davis writes of romance as offering a kind of 'cognitive dislocation', in which things happen that would seem improbable within the everyday experience of waking reality, such as St George being born with the likeness of a dragon on his skin, and states that romance 'casts its materials – virtual people, places, objects, situations – by expeditious means into a state of transformation, including openness to transformation'.[106] By inviting his readers into a dream landscape reminiscent of romance, Bunyan invites them into a liminal mental space that induces a cognitive dislocation in his readers' experience, causing them to be open to the transformation of the cosmos as they experience it and thus to the transformation of their own selves.

John Bunyan's Imaginative Persuasion 185

Bunyan asks:

Wouldest thou loose thy self and catch no harm?
And find thy self again without a charm?[107]

The idiom of 'losing oneself' in a good book may not have been current in Bunyan's time, but the idea seems to be present here – Bunyan is inviting his readers to an aesthetic absorption in his narrative that enables them to detach themselves temporarily from their ordinary cognitive preoccupations. However, to lose one's self also has theological resonances with the words of Jesus: 'If any man will come after me, let him deny himself, and take up his cross, and follow me. For whosoever will save his life shall lose it: and whosoever will lose his life for my sake shall find it' (Matthew 16:24–5). The world of imaginative leisure that provides an escape from everyday labour becomes analogous to and porous to the world of faith that transcends the mundane realities of earthly life.

Yet the dynamic of losing one's self to find one's self suggests that Bunyan does not want the reader's loss of self to be total. Bunyan wants his readers to lose themselves in the story, but not entirely to lose themselves in the sense of dissociating from their rational cognitive faculties. After the imaginative narrative provides a liminal space in which the unregenerate reader can dissociate from former patterns of thinking and feeling, the ultimate goal is a reintegration of thought and feeling around a scriptural and godly faith.

Given the non-standardized nature of early modern spelling, I suspect that the typical reading 'lose thy self' in modern spelling editions of Bunyan's work is correct so far as Bunyan's primary meaning is concerned. However, the sense of 'loose' (release) may not be entirely absent. In losing himself or herself in aesthetic enjoyment of the narrative, the reader also loses his or her self in the sense of becoming detached from the preconditioned thought forms and affective dispositions of their unregenerate persona, and thereby comes to loose the self from the bonds of sin and its corruptions of thinking and feeling in a way that facilitates the reader's redemption.

Bunyan continues:

Would'st read thy self, and read thou know'st not what
And yet know whether thou art blest or not,
By reading the same lines?[108]

The reading of Bunyan's text is a reading of the reader's own self that reveals the reader's spiritual state. Roger Pooley comments wryly, 'Bunyan's book may work like other fictions in which readers might lose themselves; but knowing whether their eternal life is or isn't secure is a more unusual feature.'[109]

186   *The Rhetoric of Conversion in English Puritan Writing*

U. Milo Kaufmann comments:

In his query, 'Would'st read thy self, and read thou know'st not what?' Bunyan implies a conception of his narrative as one which speaks on the intuitive levels of communication, the fictive life evoking those subtle responses in the reader which enable him to discern that the narrative is faithful to the mysteries of the heart.[110]

Intuition is a mode of perception that bypasses the conscious processing of cognitive reasoning, though things that are intuitively perceived can be brought to conscious cognitive awareness. I would caution, however, against equating intuition too directly with the voice of the Spirit for Bunyan, as Bunyan would not have accepted everything that his contemporaries intuitively felt in the realm of spiritual experience to be divine revelation (as indicated especially by Bunyan's attacks on Ranters and Quakers).[111] Intuitive feeling was, for Bunyan, susceptible to deception, just as cognitive reasoning was capable of being led astray.

Bunyan's imaginative writing is a subversive apologetic for a vital Christian faith seeking to habituate the imagination of the hearer or reader to the realm of grace in order to incline the reader/hearer's mind to be a passive recipient of the divine grace that brings salvation. Using the categories of Charles Taylor and Peter Berger, the aesthetic experience of enjoying Bunyan's storytelling is intended to reshape the inner imaginary world of readers in order to bring them closer to a believing cosmic imaginary that in turn reshapes readers' plausibility structures towards the convictions of godly faith.[112]

The 'Apology' states:

This Book will make a Traveller of thee,
If by its Counsel thou wilt ruled be.[113]

A variant reading renders 'Traveller' as 'Travailer'.[114] As with 'lose'/'loose', both senses could be intended. The book makes readers travellers, who engage in the pilgrim journey along with Christian and his companions (and with Christiana and her companions in the Second Part), but it also causes them to travail, to work actively to understand and to process the book's message. 'Travail' could also have connotations of the labour pains of childbirth, suggesting the spiritual struggle of the new birth of which Bunyan learned from the poor women in the sun. The active-passive dynamic called for by Reformed practical divinity is once again apparent here. The reader is made (passively) a travailer/traveller, but to travail and to travel are actions to which the reader is called.

Bunyan provides similar justifications for teaching doctrinal truth through aesthetic delight in the small handful of volumes of didactic verse that he wrote.

John Bunyan's Imaginative Persuasion

187

For instance, Bunyan writes in *Profitable Meditations* (1661) that *''Tis not the Method, but the Truth alone / Should please a Saint, and mollifie his heart'*.[115] Truth should be delightful to the truly godly in whatever literary mode it is presented. However, Bunyan recognizes that '*Man's heart is apt in Meeter to delight*', and so uses metre to win a hearing for the truth.[116]

The delight of literary genre is treated by Bunyan as a concession to human weakness, with a functional purpose: '*When Doctors give their Physick to the Sick, / They make it pleasing with some other thing'*.[117] The honey of poetry sweetens the pill of truth – Bunyan agrees with Mary Poppins that 'A spoonful of sugar helps the medicine go down [...] In a most delightful way'. But yet there is a danger in appealing to aesthetic delight, as those who engage with such medicinal texts only on the level of aesthetic appreciation will fail to receive their due benefit:

> *You also that content your selves to see*
> *Man's Wit in verses, and no further look:*
> *You will not by them edified be;*
> *You see only the back-side of the Book.*[118]

However the '*Truth*' taught in the poems is enlivened and made '*quick*' by aesthetic delight '*When men by Faith it in their hearts do sing'*.[119] Thus, for Bunyan, delighting is not a sufficient end in itself but can be a means to effective teaching and moving when combined with faith by readers.

The verse address to the reader that opens *The Second Part of The Pilgrim's Progress* is much less apologetic in the more common modern sense than the 'Apology' to Part I. Bunyan, emboldened by the international commercial success of *The Pilgrim's Progress*, has become much more confident regarding his method and its propriety. In response to the accusation that 'his Head is in a Cloud', Bunyan gives this defence of obscure modes of writing as fitting vehicles for godly persuasion:

> *Things that seem to be hid in words obscure,*
> *Do but the Godly mind the more alure;*
> *To study what those Sayings should contain,*
> *That speak to us in such a Cloudy strain.*
> *I also know, a dark Similitude*
> *Will on the Fancie more it self intrude,*
> *And will stick faster in the Heart and Head,*
> *Then things from Similies not borrowed.*[120]

188 *The Rhetoric of Conversion in English Puritan Writing*

In an apparent reversal of the typical Puritan valuation of plainness as a stylistic ideal, Bunyan here holds up obscurity as a virtue, because it ensures the deeper rooting in the psyche of truths that have taken more effort to dig out. The metaphor of speaking with one's head in the clouds is one that Richard Sibbes uses as a negative image to tell divines what not to do: Sibbes says that ministers should 'take heed [...] that they hide not their meaning in darke speeches, speaking in the clouds'.[121] The process of extracting truth from apparently obscure modes of communication is what the godly routinely had to do in biblical exegesis – hence Perkins's recommendation in *The Arte of Prophecying* that the minister should know rhetorical figures in order rightly to read Scripture.[122] What is distinctive and potentially problematic for Puritan readers about Bunyan's narratives is that he affirms the legitimacy not only of decoding indirect literary modes of communication found in Scripture, but also of encoding truth in a similarly allusive way.

Similarly, Bunyan opens his collection of verse for children, *A Book for Boys and Girls* (1686), with a verse address 'To the Reader' in which he justifies his choice of genre by noting that his verse may be beneficial not only to children but also to grown men and women whose judgement in spiritual things remains childish:

> Our Bearded *men, do act like* Beardless *Boys;*
> Our Women please themselves with childish Toys.
> Our Ministers, long time by Word and Pen,
> Dealt with them, counting them, not Boys but Men:
> Thunder-bolts they shot at them, and their Toys:
> But hit them not, 'cause they were Girls and Boys.
> The better Charge, the wider still they shot,
> Or else so high, those Dwarfs they touched not.
> Instead of Men, they found them Girls and Boys,
> Addict to nothing as to childish Toys.[123]

Bunyan suggests that the conventional persuasive strategies adopted by grave ministers hurling thunderbolts from the pulpit are inefficacious when it comes to these childish adults, and that imaginative verse ostensibly written for children may be more effective in persuading them. Just as the 'Apology' for *The Pilgrim's Progress* cites scriptural precedent for its persuasive strategy, so does *A Book for Boys and Girls*:

> Paul *seem'd to play the Fool, that he might gain*
> Those that were Fools indeed, if not in Grain.[124]

John Bunyan's Imaginative Persuasion   189

Bunyan is here alluding to the words of St Paul, who tells the rhetorically sophisticated Corinthians that 'I speak as a fool' (2 Corinthians 11:23), and adopts the modes of speaking of his doctrinal opponents in order to show them up as ridiculous. This Pauline paradox of taking on the persona of the fool in order to subvert the foolishness of one's audience is picked up in the early modern period, for instance, by Erasmus's *Praise of Folly*.[125] Similarly, Bunyan is adopting the seemingly foolish genre of children's verse in order to speak in a way that is accessible to those who are fools in a spiritual sense.

In Chapter 1, I noted how Richard Sibbes cites the example of Solomon (in the guise of the 'Preacher' of Ecclesiastes who sought out 'words of delight') as a model for the Christian minister to follow.[126] Bunyan's opening address in *A Book for Boys and Girls* similarly appeals to Solomon as the author of the book of Proverbs as a model for using analogies from nature and human observation to appeal to 'fools' who ignore divine revelation.

> *Wise* Solomon *did Fools to Piss-ants send,*
> *To learn true Wisdom, and their Lives to mend.*
> *Yea, God by Swallows, Cuckows, and the Ass,*
> *Shews they are Fools who let that season pass,*
> *Which he put in their hand,* that *to obtain*
> *Which is both present, and Eternal Gain.*[127]

Solomon's example in Proverbs thus provides a precedent for Bunyan's edifying poems on frogs, eggs and candles that will follow later in the volume. Bunyan's *A Book for Boys and Girls* largely consists of poems that comment on an everyday object or experience before drawing a religious message from them in the manner of the emblem book genre. Typical emblem books feature symbolic images that would be accompanied by text drawing a moral – English examples include books by George Withers and Francis Quarles. Although Bunyan's *Book for Boys and Girls* originally lacked pictures, its verbal descriptions are vividly visual, and woodcut emblems were added to the book in its 1710 edition after Bunyan's death. The poems in this work typically sketch out a description of an object or experience in the everyday life of the child before following it with an explanatory moral. To take an entertaining example, 'Upon the Frog':

> The Frog by Nature is both damp and cold,
> Her Mouth is large, her Belly much will hold:
> She sits somewhat ascending, loves to be
> Croaking in Gardens, tho unpleasantly.

Comparison
> The Hyppocrite is like unto this Frog;
> As like as is the Puppy to the Dog.
> He is of nature cold, his Mouth is wide,
> To prate, and at true Goodness to deride.
> He mounts his Head, as if he was above
> The World, when yet 'tis that which has his Love.
> And though he seeks in Churches for to croak,
> He neither loveth Jesus, nor his Yoak.

Here the brief imaginative emblem is clearly separated from the longer doctrinal explanation. The amusing picture of the frog here is expounded by the rather sombre comparison with the hypocrite, the one who professes true saving faith but lacks it, as evidenced by his loving the world above Jesus. The 'morals' drawn by Bunyan, however, focus not primarily on encouraging ethical good behaviour on the part of children, but rather on teaching them the right reading of Law and Gospel. The priority is not to teach children to try to be good but to teach them to renounce their sins through an inward change of heart wrought by the unmerited grace of God.

As has been noted by Roger Sharrock and David Alpaugh, the Interpreter's House, which is visited by the pilgrims in both parts of *The Pilgrim's Progress*, is a kind of emblem palace, in which the Interpreter shows the pilgrims still pictures and living tableaux.[128] As with *A Book for Boys and Girls*, the living emblems of the Interpreter's House teach Bunyan's characters and his readers to discern between Law and Gospel, learning to seek salvation through free grace before seeking to live a godly life that evidences the presence of grace.

For instance, the Interpreter shows Christian a parlour 'full of dust', and calls for a man to sweep it, stirring up the dust and making Christian choke, and then asks 'a *Damsel* that stood by' to sprinkle water on the dust before cleaning it away. Christian's question '*What means this?*' is followed immediately by the explanation that the dust is the 'Original Sin, and inward Corruptions' in the human heart, and that 'He that began to sweep at first is the Law; but She that brought water, and did sprinkle it, is the Gospel'.[129]

Christian and Christiana's sojourns in the Interpreter's House, coming as they do towards the beginning of both the first and second parts of *The Pilgrim's Progress*, provide both Bunyan's characters and his readers a kind of training in allegorical reading. Bunyan's imaginative mode of teaching is found in a concentrated and controlled form in the scenes shown to Christian and Christiana in the Interpreter's House.[130] Like dramatized emblems, the episodes in the Interpreter's House harness the imagination in a limited and controlled way to communicate clearly identified didactic points.

Such self-contained emblematic episodes train the pilgrims, and also Bunyan's readers, to read the larger scale symbols in the narrative, such as Christian's burden, Doubting Castle or Vanity Fair. In reading these larger narrative symbols, not every detail is given an explicit didactic gloss. This allows a greater space for the image to work on the reader's imagination, on the level of *pathos*, without being subordinated too quickly to *logos*.

For instance, when Christian takes the path up the hill of Difficulty while Formalist and Hypocrisy take what they expect to be shortcuts, Bunyan writes:

> So the one took the way which is called *Danger,* which led him into a great Wood; and the other took directly up the way to *Destruction,* which led him into a wide field full of dark Mountains, where he stumbled and fell, and rose no more.
>
> I looked then after *Christian,* to see him go up the Hill, where I perceived he fell from running to going, and from going to clambering upon his hands and his knees, because of the steepness of the place.[131]

Although the alliterative labels Danger, Destruction and Difficulty are fairly clear in intent (with a didactic gloss clarifying somewhat redundantly that they signify '*The danger of turning out of the way*'), the destinations of Formalist and Hypocrisy are conveyed through evocative visual images. The 'wide field full of dark Mountains' in particular is hard to logically conceptualize, yet carries a sense of foreboding that warns the reader off straying from the path. Similarly, the need to persevere in faith through difficult circumstances is impressed on the reader through inviting an embodied empathy for Christian as he becomes progressively more tired but keeps going.

Kaufmann characterizes Bunyan's adoption of allegory as a shift from *logos* (didactic, propositional communication) to *mythos* (allusive, indirect communication).[132] Kaufmann develops these terms from their usage in Aristotle's *Poetics,* and so is using *logos* in a different sense to its meaning in Aristotle's *Rhetoric,* though *logos* in Kaufmann's sense of propositional discourse is a mode of communication that appeals to *logos* in the rhetorical sense of persuasion by rational proof. Arguably, the more allusive and imagistic discourse that Kaufmann calls *mythos* persuades by appealing to the reader's affections (rhetorical *pathos*). Kaufmann's sympathies are apparently with *mythos*, perhaps because narrative symbolism that is not tied down by explicit explanations and allows for a pluriformity of responses on the part of the reader is more congenial to a literary scholar.

My analysis is informed by Kaufmann's, but I would argue that, for Bunyan, *logos* always remains key: the didactic is not displaced by the imaginative and creative but interwoven with it. *Mythos* is constrained by *logos*. As Maxine Hancock has explored, Bunyan's printed marginal notes also provide a controlling restraint on the reader's interpretation of the text.[133] Besides 'the Interpreter', other characters (such as Evangelist and Great-heart) offer authorized interpretations that channel the reader's response in the right direction.

Literary scholarship has long noted the indebtedness of *The Pilgrim's Progress* to the written traditions of the prose romance, a form of popular literature telling tales of chivalric adventure, courtly love and supernatural beings, and to the oral traditions of folktale and the like that underlie romance. One episode that has attracted particular attention is the sequence in which Christian and Hopeful stray from the way and are captured and imprisoned by Giant Despair for three days in Doubting Castle until they finally escape.

The search for specific identifiable literary or folktale sources for particular episodes in Bunyan's allegory is a fraught and perhaps futile one, but finding one identifiable source for a given episode or character may be missing the point. Writing in the early twentieth century, Harold Golder notes of the Giant Despair episode that its details do not exactly fit any known written source:

> This source may have been a single tale combining, with the fluidity characteristic of folk-narrative, details which are not to be found together in any one tale today. Or, quite as probably, remembrances of this tale and that may have joined themselves in the texture of Bunyan's story.[134]

This dynamic of eclectic borrowing from a range of sources is apparent across *The Pilgrim's Progress* and Bunyan's other allegorical narratives. The mental furniture of Bunyan's target readership was not provided by only one story but by many in combination with one another, and so it is not so much specific romances or folktales but the idioms and symbolic landscape of romance and folktale in general into which Bunyan transfuses his godly message. It is this appropriation of the romance idiom that appropriates and rearranges the mental furniture of readers to bring about the conversion of the unregenerate and the edification of those professing godly faith.

For instance, in Emanuel Ford's multipart tale *Parismus*, the knight Pollipus is imprisoned in the 'Castle of the mightie Gyant *Brandamor*' after a fight with Brandamor's brother in defence of a damsel in distress, leaving Pollipus 'for that

John Bunyan's Imaginative Persuasion 193

night put into a close prison, hauing an olde woman to dresse his wounds'.[135] The narrative is not identical to that of Bunyan's Giant Despair episode, but it has imaginative elements in common. When we read in *The Pilgrim's Progress* that 'The *Giant* therefore drove them before him, and put them into his Castle, into a very dark Dungeon, nasty and stinking to the spirit of these two men',[136] we are placed into a folktale world with details evocative to the reader's senses – 'nasty and stinking' appeals to the sense of smell as well as sight. Ford's 'Brandamor, who had Maiestically seated himselfe in a chaire, with his firie redde eyes swolne with rage, vttering these speeches' finds an echo in Bunyan's trembling Giant Despair, and Ford's detailing of the 'goodly Hall, hung with ancient clothes of Tapistrie' is paralleled by Bunyan's attention to the physical details of Doubting Castle,[137] but the narrative context differs. Brandamor is in quest of a lady, not the Celestial City, and Brandamor is a lone knight whereas Christian has a brotherly companion in Hopeful.

Bunyan's episode contains details whose primary function is to have an aesthetic appeal to the reader rather than to make a specific doctrinal point. These elements conjure up the atmosphere of the scene, such as the sights, sounds and smells of the dungeon, 'without one bit of bread, or drop of drink, or any light'. These elements of the narrative co-exist with interventions whose primary purpose is doctrinal and that at times strain narrative credibility.[138] It is after three days that Christian suddenly recalls 'I have a *Key* in my bosom, called *Promise*, that will, (I am perswaded) open any Lock in *Doubting-Castle*.'[139] In due course, the key does so, though not without a Hollywood-worthy chase sequence to escape the giant. While an implausible *deus ex machina* in plot terms, Christian's key is a prop that underlines the edifying point that the promises of God will deliver believers from despair. The dialect of romance is here being infused with the language of Canaan.

I would argue that *logos* and *mythos*, didactic direction and aesthetic indirection, Conventicle and Parnassus (in Coleridge's terms) remain in creative tension with one another throughout Bunyan's narrative works. Both those who commend and those who lament the tying down of imaginative engagement to doctrinal statement in Bunyan's writings give an insufficient account of them; so do those who celebrate and those who criticize the transcendence of doctrine by art. Bunyan's allegorical fictions will thus frustrate both readers seeking literal propositional statements of doctrine with no ambiguity and those who prefer a free play of signifiers devoid of dogma and open to endless reinterpretation.

'Satanical Rhetorick': The paradiastolic dynamic of diabolical persuasion

Yet the slippage between perception and reality in human apprehension of both physical and spiritual realities also opens the door for sinister diversions and mispersuasions on the part of the devil and of satanic agents. In Bunyan's writings, diabolical rhetoric is contrasted with, but also sometimes confusingly intermingled with, divine rhetoric.

This is the case in *The Barren Fig-tree* (1688), a sermon treatise warning those who are 'professors' of godly faith but lack the fruit of godly living that gives credible authentication to their faith. These hypocritical professing believers are compared, using a parable of Jesus, to a fig-tree that bears no fruit. Following the outline of the parable, Bunyan recounts God's patience with this fruitless tree, but warns that this patience will eventually run out. Just before God brings down his axe, 'he will try one more way at the last [...] Now this last way is *to tug, and strive with this Professor by his Spirit*.'[140] This gracious divine exertion on the professing believer involves the divine rhetoric of the Spirit: 'he will also present perswasive Arguments, encouraging Promises, dreadful Judgments, the shortness of time to repent in; and that there is hope if he come.'[141] It is possible here at least in principle for the barren professor to repent and to live an appropriately upright life evidencing godly faith and thus being among the elect.

In the case of the permanently fruitless (and thus demonstrably unregenerate) professor, however, the Son's appeal to spare the tree and the Spirit's efforts to persuade the sinner ultimately fail to accomplish their ostensible object.[142] At face value, this passage seems to suggest that divine rhetoric is not invariably efficacious. There is a paradox here arising from Bunyan's doctrinal commitments to a Calvinist understanding of predestination and reprobation. Divine rhetoric seeks to persuade barren professors to true repentance and faith, and those who respond accordingly evidence their prior election to salvation from eternity, while those whom divine rhetoric fails to persuade demonstrate that, although appearing previously to be part of the elect community, they are in fact reprobates who have never been truly elect.

Bunyan warns that professors who remain persistently barren will be cut off. It is this process of cutting off that disturbingly intermingles divine with diabolical rhetoric. The cutting off of these fake believers is ultimately by death, but often involves a prior removal from the godly community through their falling into '*Strong Delusions*' (doctrinal error) or '*Open Prophaneness*' (scandalous behaviour).[143] Though these professors are culpable for their error

John Bunyan's Imaginative Persuasion

and sin, their falling away is a divine judgement by which God hands them over to Satan and brings to light their previously hidden status as hypocrites. Divine rhetoric comes disturbingly close to diabolic rhetoric here, or, rather, diabolic rhetoric serves the divine purpose of judgement.

Bunyan invokes two alarming biblical passages in defence of this idea. One concerns Ahab, the wicked king of Israel:

> *And the Lord said, Who shall perswade* Ahab, *that he may go up, and fall at* Ramoth-Gilead? *And one said on this manner, and another said on that manner: And there came forth a Spirit, and stood before the Lord, and said, I will perswade him. And the Lord said unto him, wherewith? And he said, I will go forth, and be a lying Spirit in the mouth of all his Prophets. And he said, Thou shalt perswade him, and prevail also, go forth, and do so.* Thou shalt perswade him *and prevail,* do thy will, I leave him in thy hand, *Go forth, and do so.*[144]

In this narrative, although the deceitful persuasion of Ahab to his death is not directly attributed to divine agency but to the lying spirit, the lying spirit nevertheless accomplishes the divine purpose. In the early modern context, preachers and expositors of Scripture are often identified as 'prophets' (as is the case in Perkins's *Arte of Prophecying*), and so this could be warning that preachers of false doctrine are a means through which the divine sentence of damnation is put into effect.

Hence, while the Holy Spirit and the true gospel preachers who function as his agents are engaged in the work of persuasion, so are the devil and his agents. Disturbingly, one of the chief rhetorical tactics of these diabolic persuaders is to disguise themselves as godly voices. Hence Bunyan's Satan cites Scripture, exploiting the knife edge between assurance and presumption, on the one hand, and conviction and despair, on the other: this is the case in the young Bunyan's experience recounted in *Grace Abounding* and also in Bunyan's poem 'A Discourse between Satan and the tempted Soul' (found in *Profitable Meditations*).[145] In causing the religiously deluded to remain in error 'the Devill is wonderful cunning', even to the point of representing the preaching of truth itself as satanic temptation: 'And now he begins first to cry, avoyd Satan'.[146]

In *Good News for the Vilest of Men*, Bunyan gives presumption the suggestive name of 'wild faith', that is, an apparent faith not rightly cultivated:

> I have observed, that as there are Herbs and Flowers in our Gardens, so there are their Counterfeits in the Field; only they are distinguished from the other by the Name of *Wild Ones*. Why, there is Faith, and *Wild Faith*; and *Wild Faith* is this Presumption.[147]

196   *The Rhetoric of Conversion in English Puritan Writing*

For Bunyan, as for the practitioners of Puritan practical divinity considered earlier in this book, satanic rhetoric not only seeks to persuade sinners to mistake presumption for true faith, but also to persuade saints to mistake true faith for presumption: 'The design of Satan is to tell the Presumptuous, that their presuming on Mercy *is good*; but to perswade the Believer, that his believing is impudent bold dealing with God.'[148]

In *The Strait Gate*, Bunyan outlines the presumption of hypocritical professors, who exercise an apparent repentance and faith that is not true repentance or faith but comes alarmingly close to it:

> There is a repentance that will not save, a repentance to be repented of, and a repentance to salvation, not to be repented of, 2 *Cor.* 7. 10. yet so great a similitude, and likeness there is betwixt the one and the other, that most times the wrong is taken for the right, and through this mistake professors perish.[149]

The reader might be disoriented here by 'a repentance to be repented of', a kind of double negative, and, given Bunyan's use of 'similitudes' in his allegorical works, it is disconcerting here to see that satanic 'similitude' can lure to destruction even those who believe themselves to be truly converted.

In Bunyan's world, words and things are not inevitably conjoined: 'partly also because some men have the art to give right names to wrong things.'[150] This is the case in Bunyan's battle allegory *The Holy War*, which tells the story of the capturing of the city of Mansoul by Diabolus (Latin for 'devil') and its recapturing by the Christ figure Emanuel on behalf of his father Shaddai (a Hebrew name for God Almighty). The persuasive lies of Diabolus, persuading the Mansoulians to disregard the warnings of the conscience/preacher figure Mr Recorder, are labelled '*Satanical Rhetorick*' by Bunyan in a marginal note.[151] When the Diabolonians (the followers of Diabolus who represent various vices) are put on trial, their defence strategies include the rhetorical ploy of paradiastole, passing off vices as the virtues they resemble, as their prosecutor Mr Knowledge recognizes:

> But these *Diabolonians* love to counterfeit their names: Mr. *Covetousness* covers himself with the name of *good Husbandry*, or the like; Mr. *Pride* can, when need is, call himself Mr. *Neat*, Mr. *Handsome*, or the like; and so of all the rest of them.[152]

Christopher Hill notes that there are 'examples of vices disguising themselves as virtues', including covetousness masquerading as '*good Husbandry*' and gluttony as hospitality, in religious books that Bunyan read by Arthur Dent, Lewis Bayly, and Richard Bernard.[153] However, Hill does not observe that these are textbook examples of paradiastole, as listed by the rhetorician Henry Peacham, among others.[154] Even if Bunyan did not know the word paradiastole, he appears to be drawing on a rhetorical analysis of vice mediated through vernacular godly works that recognize the paradiastolic dynamic of the deceitfulness of sin.

The paradiastolic dynamic is also deployed by the figure of Shame in the first part of *The Pilgrim's Progress*. Faithful remarks that 'of all the Men that I met with in my Pilgrimage, he, I think, bears the wrong name', being 'bold faced' in his approach. This is because Shame is not himself ashamed; rather, he seeks to induce shame in the pilgrims by inducing social embarrassment over being associated with the godly – 'he said it was a pitiful, low, sneaking business for a man to mind Religion' and 'that it was a *shame* to sit whining and mourning under a Sermon, and a *shame* to come sighing and groaning home'. Shame objects to the often poor and poorly educated social demographic with whom these overly serious believers align themselves, and 'He said also that Religion made a man grow strange to the great, because of a few vices (which he called by finer names) and made him own and respect the base, because of the same Religious fraternity'. In calling the 'vices' of the great 'by finer names', Shame is a practitioner of paradiastole, who seeks to make godliness and scrupulous living contemptible, and socially congenial sins praiseworthy.[155]

A more subtle form of satanic rhetoric dramatized in *The Holy War* involves Diabolus confusing the boundaries between the Law and the Gospel. In negotiating over the contested city of Mansoul, Diabolus offers to make a deal with Prince Emanuel to '*perswade* Mansoul *to receive thee for their Lord*', with Diabolus as Emanuel's deputy. Diabolus even offers to establish and fund a preaching ministry in Mansoul. The fatal deception, coming in the middle of Diabolus's proposals, is '*I will press upon them the necessity of a reformation according to thy Law*'.[156] It is implied that Diabolus's ministers will persuade the people to seek salvation through the good works of God's moral law, like the young Bunyan of *Grace Abounding* in what he calls 'my great Conversion, from prodigious profaneness, to something like a moral life', and like Christian going astray to Mount Sinai at the behest of Worldly-Wiseman.[157] Emanuel identifies this advocacy of legal reformation as just as satanic as the openly profane lives that Diabolus has previously encouraged in Mansoul:

> Often hast thou made thy Proposals already, nor is this last a whit better than they. *And failing to deceive when thou shewed thy self in thy black; thou hast now transformed thy self into an Angel of light, and wouldest to deceive, be now as a minister of righteousness.*[158]

198   *The Rhetoric of Conversion in English Puritan Writing*

A marginal note ensures that we recognize the citation of 2 Corinthians 11:14, which German rhetorician Johannes Susenbrotus cites in his discussion of paradiastole.[159] Presumably the '*sufficient Ministry, besides Lecturers*' that Diabolus offers to establish would comprise preachers who deceive their hearers with the same kind of satanic legalism as Diabolus advocates.[160] Such a diabolical ministry might be identified with the latitudinarian clergy who dominated the post-Restoration Church of England, whose preaching, from the perspective of Bunyan and other Dissenters, focused on moral injunctions rather than on divine grace.

From Bunyan's standpoint, not only latitudinarians but also Quakers are victims and perpetrators of such satanic paradiastole. In his early pamphlet controversy with Edward Burrough, the young Bunyan identifies the Quaker confidence in the light within with the ability of Satan to appear as an angel of light:

> Again, that the Devil might be sure to carry on his design, he now begins to counterfeit the work of grace: Here he is very subtil, and doth transforme himselfe into an Angel of light 2 *Cor.* 11. 14. Now he makes the soul beleeve that he is its friend, and that he is a Gospel-Minister; and if the soule will but be led by what shall be made known unto it by the light (or conscience) within, it shall not need to fear, but it shall do well.[161]

Even the moral uprightness of the Quakers becomes part of a satanic strategy to distract them from faith in Christ. Bunyan uses the same imagery that he will use later in *The Holy War*:

> And if he will deceive a professing generation, he must come in this manner; first, under the name of Christ; secondly, with a fair shew in the flesh of outward holiness, Gal. 6. 12. Thirdly, he must come with good words and fair speeches, *Rom.* 16. 18. Now though he come to drunkards, swearers, whoremongers, thieves, liars, murderers, and covetous persons, in his black colours; yet if he will come to deceive a professing party, he must appear like an angel of light.[162]

Coming 'under the name of Christ' suggests that satanic paradiastole is here accompanied by satanic prosopopoeia, taking on the persona of another (as is also the case in Richard Baxter's account of satanic rhetoric),[163] while talk of 'good words and fair speeches' suggests that Satan and his representatives can adopt eloquent rhetoric.

Sometimes the true and the false path appear indistinguishable from one another. At one point in *The Pilgrim's Progress*, the pilgrims 'saw a *way* put it self into their *way*, and seemed withal, to lie as straight as the way which they should

John Bunyan's Imaginative Persuasion   199

go; and here they knew not which of the two to take, for both seemed straight before them'.[164] The reader might also be justifiably puzzled by how there can be two paths that appear equally straight and in the same direction to the characters but yet are discernibly distinct to the narrator, perhaps a reflection of the literary limits of allegory.[165] In their confusion, Christian and Hopeful take directions from 'a man black of flesh, but covered with a very light Robe', but as they follow him, their path turns 'by degrees'.[166]

The pilgrims follow their companion into a net, at which point '*the white robe fell off the black mans back*'.[167] They are rescued, rebuked and whipped by 'a shining One', who informs them, alluding once again to 2 Corinthians 11:14, that their advisor was '*Flatterer*, a false Apostle, that hath transformed himself into an Angel of Light'.[168] The pilgrims lament to the Shining One that, though the shepherds warned them about the Flatterer, 'we did not imagine […] that this fine-spoken man had been he'.[169] The marginal note generalizes the observation – '*Deceivers fine spoken*' – and directs us to Romans 16:8, which warns of those who 'by good words and fair speeches deceive the hearts of the simple'. This echoes classical anxieties about rhetoric as a tool of deception, such as are found in Plato's *Gorgias*.[170]

The Shining One reminds them of their meeting with the shepherds of the Delectable Mountains:

> He asked them then, if they had not of them Shepherds *a note of direction for the way*? They answered; Yes. But did you, said he, when you was at a stand, pluck out and read your note? They answered, No.[171]

Reading the note of direction would have kept them from dangerous diversion.

The Pilgrim's Progress itself is a written '*note of direction for the way*' provided by a spiritual shepherd. Whilst Bunyan's narrative is presented by the 'Apology' as a means to '*divert thy self*', Bunyan also promises: '*It will direct thee to the Holy Land / If thou wilt its Directions understand*'.[172] In relation to its oblique narrative mode of communication, the 'Apology' speaks of '*the ways the Fisher-man doth take / To catch the Fish*'.[173] Bunyan is a both a shepherd of his flock, who gives propositional instruction to keep them on the straight path, and a fisherman, who offers imaginative bait to lure sinners into the gospel net.

While Bunyan's sermon treatises intermingle *logos* and *pathos*, teaching and moving, methodical exposition with passionate exhortation, Bunyan's allegories exhibit a novel rhetorical strategy of godly persuasion through fictive narrative. It has been suggested that Bunyan's fictions are not only novel but also novelistic (or proto-novelistic), pointing towards and contributing to the 'rise of the novel' in the eighteenth century.[174] Yet regardless of their place in this literary lineage, Bunyan's narratives have a redemptive rhetorical power of their own. In keeping with the active-passive dynamic of Puritan conversion, Bunyan's allegorical fictions persuade us into an imaginative space in which our thought patterns are reinscribed by the language of Canaan: they are diversions in which we find direction.

Notes

1 John Bunyan, *The Pilgrim's Progress from This World to That Which Is to Come*, ed. James Blanton Wharey; rev. edn, ed. Roger Sharrock (Oxford: Clarendon, 1960), p. 244.

2 Especially in *Gorgias*; see Brian Vickers, *In Defence of Rhetoric* (Oxford: Clarendon, 1988), Chapter 2, 'Plato's Attack on Rhetoric', pp. 83–147.

3 Bunyan, *The Pilgrim's Progress*, p. 244.

4 Bunyan, *The Pilgrim's Progress*, p. 244.

5 John Bunyan, *Grace Abounding to the Chief of Sinners* [1666], ed. Roger Sharrock (Oxford: Clarendon, 1962), p. 5; Michael A. Mullett, 'Bunyan's Life, Bunyan's Lives', in Michael Davies and W. R. Owens (eds.), *The Oxford Handbook of John Bunyan* (Oxford: Oxford University Press, 2018), p. 22.

6 Among numerous biographies, the most comprehensive current scholarly account of Bunyan's life and works in relation to his historical contexts is Richard Greaves, *Glimpses of Glory: John Bunyan and English Dissent* (Stanford, CA: Stanford University Press, 2002). A brief introduction can be found in Tamsin Spargo, *John Bunyan* (Tavistock: Northcote House, 2016), and key multi-author reference works include Anne Dunan-Page (ed.), *The Cambridge Companion to Bunyan* (Cambridge: Cambridge University Press, 2010), and Davies and Owens (eds.), *The Oxford Handbook of John Bunyan*. All the above provide judicious suggestions for selected further reading, while the International John Bunyan Society hosts an online bibliography of publications on Bunyan since 1988 that aspires to comprehensiveness, and the journal *Bunyan Studies* provides a regular home for scholarship on Bunyan and his Dissenting milieu.

7 Charles Taylor, *A Secular Age* (Cambridge, MA: Belknap/Harvard University Press, 2007), esp. pp. 322–51, 361–9, 374–6.

8 On cognitive minorities, see Peter L. Berger, *A Rumour of Angels: Modern Society and the Rediscovery of the Supernatural* (1969; repr. London: Allen Lane, 1970), esp. pp. 30–5.

9 See the Appendix to Greaves, *Glimpses of Glory*, pp. 637–41, for a comprehensive list including dates of publication and provisional dates of composition.

John Bunyan's Imaginative Persuasion

10 One of the two books Bunyan's first wife brought as a dowry was Arthur Dent's *The Plain Man's Pathway to Heaven*, a work in dialogue form in which the minister Theologus interacts with the godly Philagathus, the enquirer Asunetus ('ignorant'), and the sceptic Antilegon ('against the word'). Previous allegories that may have influenced Bunyan include Richard Bernard's *The Isle of Man* (1627): Bernard's character Sir Worldly Wise has a clear parallel in Bunyan's Mr Worldly Wiseman.

11 John Bunyan, *The Strait Gate, in The Miscellaneous Works of John Bunyan* [henceforth *MW*], 13 vols., gen. ed. Roger Sharrock (Oxford: Clarendon, 1976–94), V:121.

12 Bunyan, *Strait Gate*, in *MW*, V:121. For the double sense of 'conviction' in Bunyan's writings as meaning both a firmly held belief and a legal judgement, see Beth Lynch, *John Bunyan and the Language of Conviction* (Cambridge: D. S. Brewer, 2004), pp. 11–14, 34–63, and *passim*. Jason Crawford comments similarly, '"Conviction" can indeed mean both private fixity and legal judgment, and in Bunyan's hands these two senses of the word negotiate and intertwine.' (Jason Crawford, *Allegory and Enchantment: An Early Modern Poetics* (Oxford: Oxford University Press, 2017), p. 179.)

13 Bunyan, *The Pilgrim's Progress*, p. 8.

14 See, for instance, Anne Hawkins, 'The Double-Conversion in Bunyan's *Grace Abounding*', *Philological Quarterly*, 61.3 (Summer 1982), 259–76, which speaks of Bunyan's conversion as 'a kind of conversion which is by definition diffuse, repetitive, and cumulative' (p. 259).

15 Bunyan, *Grace Abounding*, pp. 14–15.

16 Bunyan, *Grace Abounding*, pp. 19–20.

17 Psychoanalytic readings of this episode and its imagery can be found, for instance, in Vera J. Camden, 'John Bunyan and the Goodwives of Bedford: A Psychoanalytic Approach', in Dunan-Page (ed.), *Cambridge Companion to Bunyan*, pp. 51–64, and Thomas H. Luxon, '"Other Mens Words" and "New Birth": Bunyan's Antihermeneutics of Experience"', *Texas Studies in Literature and Language*, 36.3 (Fall 1994), pp. 276–83. Cf. Greaves, *Glimpses of Glory*, pp. 41–3.

18 Graham Ward, 'To Be a Reader: John Bunyan's Struggle with the Language of Scripture in *Grace Abounding to the Chief of Sinners*', *Literature and Theology*, 4.1 (March 1990), p. 37.

19 Bunyan, *The Pilgrim's Progress*, p. 212.

20 See Mason I. Lowance, Jr., *The Language of Canaan: Metaphor and Symbol in New England from the Puritans to the Transcendentalists* (Cambridge, MA: Harvard University Press, 1980).

21 Thomas Watson, *The Beatitudes: or A Discourse upon Part of Christs Famous Sermon on the Mount* (London, 1660), p. 344.

22 See, for instance, the dialogue given to Zeal-of-the-land Busy in Ben Jonson's play *Bartholomew Fair*, which parodies Puritan speech habits.

23 Bunyan, *The Pilgrim's Progress*, p. 181.

202   *The Rhetoric of Conversion in English Puritan Writing*

24   Bunyan, *The Pilgrim's Progress*, p. 181.

25   Bunyan, *The Pilgrim's Progress*, p. 212.

26   Bunyan, *The Pilgrim's Progress*, p. 212.

27   Aristotle, *The Art of Rhetoric*, III.ii.

28   Bunyan, *The Pilgrim's Progress*, p. 213.

29   Michael Davies, *Graceful Reading: Theology and Narrative in the Works of John Bunyan* (Oxford: Oxford University Press, 2002), esp. pp. 45–52. Richard Greaves equates Bunyan's 'evangelical concern to convert unbelievers' with a 'pastoral Arminianism' (*Glimpses of Glory*, pp. 110–11, 149, 171–2, 331, 583), but I agree with Dewey Wallace that this is theologically questionable given that 'works of Calvinist piety are filled with pleading requests for sinners to come to Christ' (Dewey D. Wallace, Jr., 'Bunyan's Theology and Religious Context', in Davies and Owens (eds.), *Oxford Handbook*, p. 78.

30   Mullett, 'Bunyan's Life, Bunyan's Lives', in Davies and Owens (eds.), *Oxford Handbook*, p. 31.

31   John Bunyan, *Good News for the Vilest of Men*, ed. Richard L. Greaves, in *MW*, XI:88.

32   For instance:

> The second action of faith in the case of our reconciliation with God, is to certifie and assure vs in conscience thereof: and that is done by a practicall syllogisme, which faith frames in the minde on this manner:
>
> > *He that beleeues the gospel, shall haue all the benefits and blessing of God promised therein;*
> >
> > *But I beleeue the Gospell, and I beleeue in Christ:*
> >
> > *Therefore the benefits promised therein, are mine.*

(William Perkins, *How to liue, and that well in all estates and times, specially when helps and comforts faile* (Cambridge, 1601), pp. 25–6).

33   Bunyan, *Grace Abounding*, p. 85.

34   Bunyan, *The Pilgrim's Progress*, p. 39.

35   Davies, *Graceful Reading*, p. 50.

36   Isabel Rivers, *Reason, Grace and Sentiment: A Study of the Language of Religion and Ethics in England, 1660–1780*, 2 vols. (Cambridge: Cambridge University Press, 1991–2000), I:135.

37   Bunyan, *Grace Abounding*, p. 89.

38   Bunyan, *Grace Abounding*, p. 87.

39   See Roger Pooley, 'Bunyan's Reading', in Davies and Owens (eds.), *Oxford Handbook*, pp. 101–16.

40   Thomas Smith, 'A Letter Sent to Mr. E. of Taft Four Miles from Cambridge a Year since, to which no Answer Hath Been Returned', in *The Quaker Disarm'd* (London,

John Bunyan's Imaginative Persuasion   203

1659), sig. B4r–C4v; Paul Hammond, 'Smith, Thomas (1624–1661)', *ODNB*; Greaves, *Glimpses of Glory*, pp. 121–3.

41   Smith, 'A Letter Sent to Mr E. of Taft', sig. C1v.

42   Charles Doe, 'The Struggler', in *MW*, XII:457.

43   Smith, 'A Letter Sent to Mr E. of Taft', sig. C3r; Bunyan, *Grace Abounding*, p. 83.

44   N. H. Keeble, 'John Bunyan's Literary Life', in Dunan-Page (ed.), *Cambridge Companion to Bunyan*, p. 19.

45   Bunyan, *Grace Abounding*, p. 84.

46   Bunyan, *Grace Abounding*, p. 85.

47   Bunyan, *Grace Abounding*, p. 85.

48   Bunyan, *Grace Abounding*, p. 86.

49   Bunyan, *Grace Abounding*, p. 86. Cf. Richard Sibbes, *Bowels Opened, or, A Discovery of the Neere and Deere Love, Union and Communion betwixt Christ and the Church, and Consequently betwixt Him and Every Beleeving Soule* (London, 1639).

50   See, for instance, Keeble, 'John Bunyan's Literary Life', pp. 20–1; Roger Pooley, 'Plain and Simple: Bunyan and Style', in N. H. Keeble (ed.), *John Bunyan: Conventicle and Parnassus: Tercentenary Essays* (Oxford: Clarendon, 1988), p. 91.

51   Bunyan, *Grace Abounding*, pp. 3–4.

52   John Burton, 'To the Reader', in Bunyan, *Some Gospel-Truths Opened According to the Scriptures*, ed. T. L. Underwood, in *MW*, I:11.

53   Samuel How, *The Sufficiencie of the Spirits Teaching, without Humane-Learning* ([Amsterdam], 1640), sig. C3v. On the wider 'learned ministry controversy' of this period, see Howard Schultz, *Milton and Forbidden Knowledge* (New York: Modern Language Association of America, 1955), pp. 184–218, and Barbara Kiefer Lewalski, 'Milton on Learning and the Learned-Ministry Controversy', *Huntington Library Quarterly*, 24.4 (August 1961), 267–81.

54   Bunyan, *Some Gospel-Truths Opened*, in *MW*, I:11.

55   William Perkins, *The Whole Treatise of the Cases of Conscience*, in *Workes of That Famous and Worthie Minister of Christ in the Vniversitie of Cambridge, M. W. Perkins*, 3 vols. (Cambridge, 1608–9), II:1; William Perkins, *A Treatise of the Duties and Dignities of the Ministry*, in *M. Perkins, his Exhortation to Repentance, out of Zephaniah: Preached in 2. Sermons in Sturbridge Faire. Together with Two Treatises of the Duties and Dignitie of the Ministrie: Deliuered Publiquely in the Vniuersitie of Cambridge* (London, 1605), p. 12.

56   Samuel How similarly understands 'the tongue of the learned' to be 'the *Spirit of God*' and emphatically not human learning (*Sufficiencie of the Spirits Teaching*, sig. C2r).

57   Charles Doe, *A Collection of Experience of the Work of Grace* (London, 1700), p. 52.

58 On Bunyan's preaching style, see Graham Midgley, 'Introduction', in *MW*, V:xiii–li; E. Beatrice Batson, *John Bunyan: Allegory and Imagination* (London: Croom Helm, 1984), Chapter 7, 'The Sermon-Treatise', pp. 102–47; Henri Talon, *John Bunyan: The Man and His Works*, trans. Barbara Wall (London: Rockliff, 1951), pp. 106–30.

59 Bunyan, *Strait Gate*, in *MW*, V:66 (title page).

60 Bunyan, *Strait Gate*, in *MW*, V:69.

61 Bunyan, *Strait Gate*, in *MW*, V:71.

62 Bunyan, *Strait Gate*, in *MW*, V:71.

63 Bunyan, *Strait Gate*, in *MW*, V:71.

64 Bunyan, *Strait Gate*, in *MW*, V:72–3.

65 Bunyan, *Strait Gate*, in *MW*, V:71–2.

66 Bunyan, *Strait Gate*, in *MW*, V:72.

67 Bunyan, *Strait Gate*, in *MW*, V:72.

68 Bunyan, *Strait Gate*, in *MW*, V:75.

69 Bunyan, *Strait Gate*, in *MW*, V:74.

70 Graham Midgley, 'Introduction', in *MW*, V:xliii.

71 Bunyan, *Strait Gate*, in *MW*, V:73.

72 See the concluding section of Chapter 3 of this book.

73 Bunyan, *Strait Gate*, in *MW*, V:81.

74 Bunyan, *Strait Gate*, in *MW*, V:127.

75 Bunyan, *Strait Gate*, in *MW*, V:121.

76 Bunyan, *Strait Gate*, in *MW*, V:123.

77 Cf. the similar temptation of his own that Bunyan recounts in *Grace Abounding*: 'Why then, said Satan, you had as good leave off, and strive no further; for if indeed you should not be Elected and chosen of God, there is no talke of your being saved' (*Grace Abounding*, p. 21).

78 On the potentially crucial theological differences made by different forms of modal verbs, see Brian Cummings, *The Literary Culture of the Reformation: Grammar and Grace* (Oxford: Oxford University Press, 2002), pp. 213–21.

79 Bunyan, *Strait Gate*, in *MW*, V:123.

80 Bunyan, *Strait Gate*, in *MW*, V:123.

81 Bunyan, *Strait Gate*, in *MW*, V:124.

82 Bunyan, *Strait Gate*, in *MW*, V:124.

83 Bunyan, *Grace Abounding*, pp. 67–8, 77–8.

84 Bunyan, *Strait Gate*, in *MW*, V:129.

85 Bunyan, *Strait Gate*, in *MW*, V:129.

86 See Thomas Hyatt Luxon, 'The Pilgrim's Passive Progress: Luther and Bunyan on Talking and Doing, Word and Way', *ELH*, 53 (1986), 73–98.

87 Bunyan, *Strait Gate*, in *MW*, V:129–30.

88 Bunyan, *The Pilgrim's Progress*, p. 163.

89　Bunyan, 'To the Reader', in *Good News*, in *MW*, XI:7.

90　Bunyan, *Good News*, in *MW*, XI:19.

91　Bunyan, *Good News*, in *MW*, XI:20.

92　Bunyan, *Good News*, in *MW*, XI:42.

93　Bunyan, *Good News*, in *MW*, XI:42.

94　Bunyan, *Good News*, in *MW*, XI:43.

95　See especially Norman Pettit, *The Heart Prepared: Grace and Conversion in Puritan Spiritual Life* (1966; 2nd ed. Middletown, Conn., Wesleyan University Press, 1989). For a recent study from a confessionally Reformed standpoint, see Joel R. Beeke and Paul M. Smalley, *Prepared by Grace, for Grace: The Puritans on God's Ordinary Way of Leading Sinners to Christ* (Grand Rapids, MI: Reformation Heritage Books, 2013).

96　Hoyt H. Hudson, 'Rhetoric and Poetry', *Quarterly Journal of Speech*, 10.2 (1924), p. 153.

97　*The Collected Works of Samuel Taylor Coleridge*, vol. 5: *Lectures 1808–1819: On Literature*, Part 2, ed. R. A. Foakes (London: Routledge & Kegan Paul, 1987), 103.

98　*The Literary Remains of Samuel Taylor Coleridge*, ed. Henry Nelson Coleridge, 4 vols (London, 1836–39), III:391–2, excerpted in *Coleridge on the Seventeenth-Century*, ed. Roberta Florence Brinkley (Durham, NC: Duke University Press, 1955), p. 476.

99　Bunyan, 'The Author's Apology for His Book', *The Pilgrim's Progress*, p. 3.

100　Bunyan, 'Apology', *The Pilgrim's Progress*, p. 4.

101　Bunyan, *The Pilgrim's Progress*, p. xxxvi (original title page).

102　Bunyan, 'Apology', *The Pilgrim's Progress*, p. 5.

103　Bunyan, 'Apology', *The Pilgrim's Progress*, p. 7.

104　In *A Few Sighs from Hell* (1658) Bunyan recalls his pre-regenerate thoughts thus: 'Alas, what is the Scripture, give me a Ballad, a Newsbook, *George* on horseback, or *Bevis* of *Southhampton*; give me some book that teaches curious arts, that tells of old fables; but for the holy Scriptures I cared not' (ed. T. L. Underwood, *MW*, I:333).

105　For a comparison of Bunyan's imaginative persuasion with similar techniques in the work of another English Protestant allegorist, the Elizabethan poet Edmund Spenser, see James F. Forrest, 'Allegory as Sacred Sport: Manipulation of the Reader in Spenser and Bunyan', in Robert G. Collmer (ed.), *Bunyan in Our Time* (Kent, OH: Kent State University Press, 1989), pp. 93–112.

106　Nick Davis, 'Bunyan and Romance', in Davies and Owens (eds.), *Oxford Handbook of John Bunyan*, pp. 385–7.

107　Bunyan, *Pilgrim's Progress*, p. 7.

108　Bunyan, *Pilgrim's Progress*, p. 7.

109　Roger Pooley, 'The *Pilgrim's Progress* and the Line of Allegory', in Dunan-Page (ed.), *Cambridge Companion*, p. 91.

110 U. Milo Kaufmann, *The Pilgrim's Progress and Traditions in Puritan Meditation* (New Haven: Yale University Press, 1966), p. 14.

111 See, for instance: 'the *Ranters* will owne Christ no other waies, then only within: and, this is also the principle of the *Quakers,* they will not owne Christ without them. 2. the *Ranters,* they crie down all teaching, but the teaching within; and so do the *Quakers*' (Bunyan, *Some Gospel-Truths Opened*, in *MW*, I:138).

112 See notes 7 and 8 above.

113 Bunyan, *The Pilgrim's Progress*, p. 6.

114 Bunyan, *The Pilgrim's Progress* (1678), sig. A6v. There is a similarly resonant textual variant in Milton's *Areopagitica*, which speaks either of the 'true warfaring Christian' (as in the Yale *Complete Prose Works*, II:514–15), or of the 'true wayfaring Christian' (in the first edition of 1644, p. 12).

115 John Bunyan, *Profitable Meditations* [1661], ed. Graham Midgley, in *MW*, VI:4.

116 Bunyan, *Profitable Meditations*, in *MW*, VI:4.

117 Bunyan, *Profitable Meditations*, in *MW*, VI:4.

118 Bunyan, *Profitable Meditations*, in *MW*, VI:4.

119 Bunyan, *Profitable Meditations*, in *MW*, VI:4.

120 Bunyan, *The Pilgrim's Progress*, p. 171.

121 Richard Sibbes, *The Bruised Reede, and Smoaking Flax* (London, 1630), pp. 63–4 (repeated page numbers).

122 William Perkins, *The Arte of Prophecying*, in *Workes of That Famous and Worthie Minister of Christ in the Vniversitie of Cambridge, M. W. Perkins*, 3 vols. (Cambridge, 1608–9), II:742.

123 John Bunyan, 'To the Reader', in *A Book for Boys and Girls* [1686], in *MW*, VI:190.

124 Bunyan, 'To the Reader', in *A Book for Boys and Girls*, in *MW*, VI:191.

125 See M. A. Screech, *Laughter at the Foot of the Cross* (Harmondsworth: Penguin/ Allen Lane, 1997).

126 See Ecclesiastes 1:1-2; 12:8-10.

127 Bunyan, 'To the Reader', in *A Book for Boys and Girls*, in *MW*, VI:192. Cf. Proverbs 6:6: 'Go to the ant, thou sluggard; consider her ways, and be wise.' For an exploration of Bunyan's imitation of Solomon in dialogue with current educational thought, see Robin Barfield, 'John Bunyan's Solomonic Pedagogy', *Christian Education Journal*, forthcoming.

128 See Roger Sharrock, 'Bunyan and the English Emblem Writers', *Review of English Studies*, 21.82 (April 1945), 105–16; David J. Alpaugh, 'Emblem and Interpretation in *The Pilgrim's Progress*', *ELH*, 33.3 (September 1966), 299–314.

129 Bunyan, *The Pilgrim's Progress*, pp. 29–30.

130 On Interpreter's House, see Thomas Luxon, 'Calvin and Bunyan on Word and Image: Is There a Text in Interpreter's House?', *English Literary Renaissance*, 18.3 (Autumn 1988), 438–59; Davies, *Graceful Reading*, pp. 252–62.

131 Bunyan, *The Pilgrim's Progress*, p. 42.

132 Kaufmann, *The Pilgrim's Progress and Traditions in Puritan Meditation*, pp. 8–21, 151–74.

133 Maxine Hancock, *The Key in the Window: Marginal Notes in Bunyan's Narratives* (Vancouver: Regent College Publishing, 2000).

134 Harold Golder, 'Bunyan's Giant Despair', *Journal of English and Germanic Philology*, 30.3 (July 1931), p. 378.

135 Emanuel Ford, *Parismenos: The Second Part of the Most Famous, Delectable, and Pleasant Historie of Parismus, the Renowned Prince of Bohemia* (London, 1599), sig. F2r, F3v.

136 Bunyan, *Pilgrim's Progress*, p. 114.

137 Ford, *Parismenos*, sig. F3v–4r.

138 Bunyan, *Pilgrim's Progress*, p. 114.

139 Bunyan, *Pilgrim's Progress*, p. 118.

140 John Bunyan, *The Barren Fig-tree*, ed. Graham Midgley, in *MW*, V:54.

141 Bunyan, *Barren Fig-tree*, in *MW*, V:54.

142 This seems to suggest that divine rhetoric is not invariably efficacious, though, theologically, this is not the case for Bunyan, since Christ only pleads as an advocate, and thus efficaciously, for those who are truly his people, and this does not include the hypocritical barren professors who are only apparently elect.

143 Bunyan, *Barren Fig-tree*, in *MW*, V:35.

144 Bunyan, *Barren Fig-tree*, in *MW*, V:60. The margin gives the biblical reference as 1 Kings 22:20–22.

145 Bunyan, 'A Discourse between Satan and the Tempted Soul', in *Profitable Meditations, MW*, VI:11–21.

146 John Bunyan, *A Vindication of Some Gospel-Truths Opened*, ed. T. L. Underwood, in *MW*, I:216.

147 Bunyan, *Good News*, in *MW*, V:67.

148 Bunyan, *Good News*, in *MW*, V:69.

149 Bunyan, *Strait Gate*, in *MW*, V:115.

150 Bunyan, *Strait Gate*, in *MW*, V:119.

151 John Bunyan, *The Holy War*, ed. Roger Sharrock and James F. Forrest (Oxford: Oxford University Press, 1980), p. 20.

152 Bunyan, *Holy War*, p. 130.

153 Christopher Hill, *A Turbulent, Seditious, and Factious People: John Bunyan and His Church 1628-1688* (Oxford: Clarendon Press, 1988), pp. 161–6 (p. 164); Arthur Dent, *The Plaine Mans Path-way to Heauen* (London, 1601), p. 102; Lewis Bayly, *The Practise of Pietie Directing a Christian How to Walke That He May Please God*, 3rd edn (London, 1613), pp. 253–4; Richard Bernard, *The Isle of Man: or, the Legall Proceeding in Man-shire against Sinne*, 4th edn (London, 1627), p. 27.

154 Henry Peacham, *The Garden of Eloquence* (London, 1577), sig. N4v.

155 Bunyan, *The Pilgrim's Progress*, pp. 72–3.

156 Bunyan, *Holy War*, p. 84.

157 Bunyan, *Grace Abounding*, p. 13.

158 Bunyan, *Holy War*, p. 84.

159 Johannes Susenbrotus, *Epitome troporum ac schematum et Grammaticorum & Rhetorume arte rhetorica libri tres* (Zurich, 1540?), p. 46.

160 Bunyan, *Holy War*, p. 84.

161 Bunyan, *Some Gospel-Truths Opened*, in *MW*, I:59.

162 Bunyan, *Some Gospel-Truths Opened*, in *MW*, I:101.

163 Richard Baxter, *Directions and Perswasions to a Sound Conversion* (London, 1658), p. 133, discussed in Chapter 3 of this book.

164 Bunyan, *The Pilgrim's Progress*, p. 132.

165 Cf. Stanley Fish, *Self-Consuming Artifacts: The Experience of Seventeenth-Century Literature* (Berkeley and Los Angeles: University of California Press, 1972), pp. 224–64 on the disjunction between spatial and spiritual senses of 'way' in *The Pilgrim's Progress*.

166 Bunyan, *The Pilgrim's Progress*, p. 133. On the question of the racial implications of the Flatterer's blackness, see Margaret Sönser Breen, 'Race, Dissent, and Literary Imagination in John Bunyan and James Baldwin', *Bunyan Studies*, 21 (2017), pp. 9–16.

167 Bunyan, *The Pilgrim's Progress*, p. 133.

168 Bunyan, *The Pilgrim's Progress*, p. 134.

169 Bunyan, *The Pilgrim's Progress*, p. 134.

170 Plato, *Gorgias*; Vickers, *In Defence of Rhetoric*, pp. 83–147.

171 Bunyan, *The Pilgrim's Progress*, p. 134.

172 Bunyan, 'Apology', *The Pilgrim's Progress*, pp. 6–7.

173 Bunyan, 'Apology', *The Pilgrim's Progress*, p. 3.

174 See, for instance, Wolfgang Iser, *The Implied Reader: Patterns of Communication in Prose Fiction from Bunyan to Beckett* (Baltimore: Johns Hopkins University Press, 1974), Chapter 1, 'Bunyan's *Pilgrim's Progress*: The Doctrine of Predestination and the Shaping of the Novel' (pp. 1–28), and Nancy Rosenfeld, *John Bunyan's Imaginary Writings in Context* (New York: Routledge, 2018).

5

To 'make persuasion do the work of fear': The resistible rhetoric of redemption in John Milton

The most prominent 'Puritan' writer in the canon of English literature is John Milton (1608–74), best known for *Paradise Lost*, his transposition of the Genesis accounts of humanity's creation and fall into a lengthy epic poem. This is so despite various theological idiosyncrasies and biographical complications that might call into question Milton's identification as a Puritan. This chapter will argue that, despite these problems of definition, Milton's writing participates in the rhetorical project of Puritan practical divinity in that he seeks to persuade his readers to conversion and to strengthen them in his own idiosyncratic brand of godly faith.

Milton seeks to achieve these persuasive goals both through polemical prose works that argue for controversial political and religious ideas and through his imaginative verse, in which, like Bunyan, he entices his readers into a space in which their thought worlds are reinscribed. However, Milton's Arminian theology radically modifies the relationship between the human and divine aspects of conversion typical of the Puritan practical divinity we have encountered in earlier chapters – for Milton, the inviolability of human free will means that divine rhetoric can entice but never compel. This chapter will also explore how Milton's imaginative divine rhetoric is versatile enough to make use of the diabolical rhetoric of Satan to accomplish its good purposes, and will offer a fresh rhetorical reading of Milton's Satan in *Paradise Lost*, in which the rhetorical figure of paradiastole helps us to understand how Milton's Satan is self-deceived by his own rhetoric.

While N. H. Keeble writes that 'To read Milton is to know what it was to be a Puritan',[1] biographical scholarship in recent decades has called into question how Puritan Milton was or even whether he was a Puritan at all. In sharp contrast with Keeble's identification of Milton as a paradigmatic embodiment of Puritanism, Catherine Gimelli Martin argues that 'while Milton certainly

210   *The Rhetoric of Conversion in English Puritan Writing*

sustained a career *among* the Puritans, [...] he was probably never *of* them.[2] While earlier biographies of Milton read his earlier life (at least from his time at university) through the lens of his later religiously and politically radical commitments, biographical accounts since Milton's quartercentenary in 2008 in particular have suggested that Milton was radicalized after his student days, in which he was a religious conformist and perhaps, as Gordon Campbell and Thomas Corns suggest, even a Laudian, aligned with the more sacramental and ceremonialist tendencies of Archbishop William Laud's vision for the national Church that Puritans opposed.[3] While Martin's view that Milton was never a Puritan remains a minority one, the view that Milton became a Puritan in adulthood rather than always having been one has gained considerable ground among Milton scholars in recent years.

Yet, though Milton is debatably a Puritan, he is indisputably a rhetorician, having received a classical education including the key texts of classical rhetoric at St Paul's School in London, at Christ's College, Cambridge (the college at which William Perkins had previously studied and taught), and through his several years of private reading following his university studies at his parents' homes in Hammersmith and Horton, through which Milton sought to remedy what he saw as gaps in his knowledge.[4]

For the purposes of this study, however, what is most pertinent is not whether Milton conforms to a precise definition of 'Puritan', but whether Milton's work engages in a rhetorical enterprise akin to that of Puritan practical divinity. That is, does Milton's writing seek to persuade its readers to conversion, assurance of salvation, and godly living, as with the writers considered earlier in this book? I would argue that it does, though with some qualifications with regard to assurance of salvation given the Arminianism of Milton's mature thought in which salvation is available to those who choose it and persevere in faith rather than those who are irresistibly predestined to salvation. In his theological treatise *De Doctrina Christiana*, left in manuscript in Milton's lifetime and unpublished until its rediscovery in the nineteenth century, Milton defines '*the assurance of salvation*' as 'a kind of stage of faith whereby – with the spirit testifying – a person has been persuaded and firmly believes that if he believes and persists in faith and charity [...] he will most surely obtain everlasting life and consummate glory.'[5]

This differs from Calvinist accounts of assurance in its conditionality – for Milton, the believer can be assured that (s)he will 'most surely obtain everlasting life' only 'if he believes and persists in faith and charity', rather than being persuaded that (s)he is irrevocably destined for glory. Nevertheless, Milton's account of assurance has in common with more standard Puritan understandings that it is an experiential state that is available to true believers but not felt by all true believers instantly (it is a 'stage of faith'), and that is the result of persuasion by the Spirit. Thus although Milton's doctrine of assurance differs from that of Perkins, Sibbes or Bunyan, it remains a rhetorical doctrine of assurance it that it relies on persuasion. There is for Milton an additional rhetorical dimension in that final salvation is only assured to those who persevere in faith and charity, making more emphatic their need to be persuaded to persevere, and so the rhetorical objectives in Puritan practical divinity of persuasion to assurance and persuasion to godly living converge for Milton.

Stephen Fallon and Catherine Gimelli Martin both observe that Milton does not report a clear conversion experience readily assimilable to the expected pattern of Puritan practical divinity.[6] Yet the same is true of Richard Baxter, who concluded of his own experience that 'God breaketh not all Mens hearts alike', and retained a strong emphasis on the centrality and necessity of conversion, however varied its experiential manifestations might be.[7]

Conversion is likewise central to the resolution of *Paradise Lost*, whose final books dramatize Adam and Eve's repentance after their fall in terms that are in significant continuity with Puritan understandings of conversion and regeneration. Benjamin Myers notes that, while critics from E. M. W. Tillyard to the present have sought to highlight the narrative importance of this episode, 'The theological significance of the conversion scene, however, remains often overlooked'.[8]

Prevenient persuasion: Conversion and rhetoric in *Paradise Lost*

The opening of Book 11 of *Paradise Lost* makes clear that Adam and Eve's repentance is enabled by 'Prevenient Grace':

> Thus they in lowliest plight repentant stood
> Praying, for from the Mercie-seat above
> Prevenient Grace descending had remov'd
> The stonie from thir hearts, and made new flesh
> Regenerat grow instead, that sighs now breath'd
> Unutterable, which the Spirit of prayer
> Inspir'd, and wingd for Heav'n with speedier flight
> Then loudest Oratorie:
>
> (*PL*, XI:1–8)[9]

212 *The Rhetoric of Conversion in English Puritan Writing*

'Prevenient Grace' is a technical theological term meaning grace that comes before, referring to divine grace that is bestowed upon humans prior to any human response such as repentance, faith or good works. Although the reader of this passage encounters the repentant Adam and Eve praying before we reach the description of divine grace regenerating them, the chronological sequence is the opposite, as is shown by the sequence of tenses: while Adam and Eve 'stood / Praying', they can do so only because grace 'had remov'd [pluperfect tense] / The stonie from thir hearts' already. These two contrasting orders represent the epistemological order of human knowledge, in which humans experience repentance before they come to understand the divine grace that has inspired it, and the logical and theological order in which human initiative towards repentance and faith is possible only due to the prior bestowal of divine grace.

The 'sighs [...] Unutterable' here inspired by the 'Spirit of prayer' allude to St Paul's assertion that 'the Spirit itself maketh intercession for us with groanings which cannot be uttered' (Romans 8:26), a text cited by Richard Baxter to affirm the divine approval of prayer that may not appear eloquent by human standards: 'the *same spirit* teacheth not *fine words*, and rhetorical language, to all that it teacheth to *pray with unutterable sighs and groans*, Rom. 8. 26, 27'.[10] Milton's narrator, like Baxter, sees human sighs inspired by the Spirit as superior to human 'Oratorie', but yet these Spirit-inspired sighs have a divinely rhetorical purpose, in that they persuade God to offer forgiveness and to regenerate human hearts. Though the identity of the divine persons is complicated by Milton's heterodox Trinitarian theology, it remains the case that divine persons are both the instigators and the objects of this act of persuasion.

As well as the divine agency of the Spirit preceding and inspiring Adam and Eve's prayer, their prayers are followed by the divine agency of the Son persuading the Father to accept them. Adam and Eve's repentance is followed by a change of scene to heaven, where the Son pleads with the Father:

> Now therefore bend thine eare
> To supplication, heare his [man's] sighs though mute;
> Unskilful with what words to pray, let mee
> Interpret for him, mee his Advocate.

(PL, XI:30–3)

It is the Son who translates the unutterable sighs of Adam and Eve and who persuades the Father to accept them. This acceptance and granting of mercy to humanity is, in turn, felt by Adam in terms of 'perswasion':

Methought I saw him placable and mild,
Bending his eare; perswasion in me grew
That I was heard with favour.

(*PL*, XI:151–3)

The first humans need not only to be persuaded to seek forgiveness but also to be persuaded that forgiveness has been granted. Milton's verse narrative is here in keeping with the persuasive project of Puritan practical divinity, in which individuals are taught to read their own experience for signs that grace has been bestowed upon them. Adam's 'perswasion' that his repentance has been accepted approximates the experience of assurance of salvation that Puritan divines deem desirable for the elect even if sometimes hard to find. Yet, as Myers rightly observes, Adam and Eve are unaware of the degree of divine agency that makes their persuasion of God efficacious. Adam perceives the Father 'Bending his eare' but not the Son asking the Father to bend his ear:

> Thus a richly ironic interplay of verbal echoes and allusions illustrates the two sides of regeneration: the divine initiative, and the free human response. Adam is aware only of the human role in initiating conversion through freely willed prayer and repentance; but the reader is privy to the initiative of grace that has liberated Adam and Eve and enabled them freely to turn towards the God who has already turned towards them. All that Adam says, then, is true, but all that he says is qualified and deepened by the reality of the primacy of prevenient grace.[11]

The human rhetoric that pleads for grace participates in an enfolding divine rhetoric within the community of the Godhead in a way that has parallels with Richard Sibbes's account of divine-human communication, also conveyed through intricate verbal echoes: 'God communicates himselfe to us by his Spirit, and we communicate with God by his Spirit. God doth all in us by his Spirit, and we doe all backe againe to God by the Spirit'.[12] The two parts of this movement in each sentence are made to seem equivalent by the parallel wording either side of the caesura (pause) signalled by the comma. The reciprocity follows the mirroring figure of chiasmus: 'God communicates [...] to us [...] and we communicate with God [...] God doth all in us [...] and we doe all backe againe to God'. The action performed from God to us and from us to God is in both sentences the same. The caesura is the pivot in which the speaking and doing proceeding from God turn back again towards him from humanity.

What prevents the structures of these sentences being entirely chiastic is the repetition of 'by his Spirit' after each action of either God or believers. This gives the divine agency of the Spirit a presence outweighing human agency on

214   *The Rhetoric of Conversion in English Puritan Writing*

both sides of the equation. While Sibbes's underlying theology here includes an orthodox Trinitarianism and a Calvinist compatibilism foreign to the Milton of *De Doctrina*, the dynamics of Sibbes's description and of Milton's dramatization of this moment in *Paradise Lost* are remarkably similar.

While the human event of conversion takes place in historical time following the Fall in Book 11, a theological account of what takes place in conversion is given much earlier in the poem in God the Father's address to his Son in Book 3 that anticipates humanity's fall from obedience and God's remedy for it before it takes place. In outlining his plan to redeem humanity from the Fall, the Father states:

> Man shall not quite be lost, but sav'd who will,
> Yet not of will in him, but Grace in mee
> Freely voutsaf't; once more I will renew
> His lapsed powers, though forfeit and enthralld
> By sin to foul exorbitant desires;
> Upheld by mee, yet once more he shall stand
> On even ground against his mortal foe[.]

(*PL*, III: 173–9)

The emphasis of the Father's discourse is on salvation being owed wholly to God and not to human initiative, articulating the Reformation emphasis on salvation being *sola gratia* (by grace alone). Taken in isolation, this passage is also open to reading in light of the Calvinist compatibilism in which the human 'will' that chooses salvation is itself determined by an irresistible 'Grace'. However, in light of Milton's non-deterministic theology outlined in *De Doctrina*, Myers plausibly reads the renewal of man's 'lapsed powers' by grace here not as God choosing redemption on man's behalf but as God restoring the undetermined human power to choose. Myers argues that Milton's God here agrees with Arminius, who

> regards prevenient grace as bringing about a restoration of the liberty of indifference, in which the individual becomes capable both of 'freely assent[ing]' to grace and of freely 'withholding his assent.' So too in *Paradise Lost*, prevenient grace places the human will's power of choice back on the balanced scales, so that the alternative decision between good and evil becomes an authentic possibility.[13]

Milton's 'prevenient grace' removes the effects of original sin sufficiently to allow humans to repent when they would otherwise lack the power to do so, but leaves it up to the exercise of their free will to choose whether or not to take advantage of the opportunity to repent. Myers summarizes helpfully: 'In short, for Arminianism the initial influence of prevenient grace is only a *necessary* condition for conversion, while for Reformed orthodoxy the initial influence of grace is a *sufficient* condition for conversion.'[14]

Adam and Eve thus owe their conversion to a hidden divine persuasion that operates beyond the limits of their perception, but it is a persuasion that entices rather than compels. This resistible divine persuasion of the Spirit is consistent with Milton's framing of divine rhetoric throughout his writing career.

Resistible rhetoric and the Miltonic elect

While Milton's self-representations are slippery and his ideological convictions may have shifted across the course of his life, there are certain convictions that are consistent across Milton's writing with regard to the rhetorical project of persuading his readers towards truth and godliness. Among these is the conviction that moral and religious truths should be advanced through reasoning and persuasive means rather than through physical violence.

In the epistle to the readers that opens *De Doctrina Christiana*, Milton asserts the necessity of rational persuasion to true faith, and continues, 'Without that liberty, there is no religion, no Gospel; violence alone prevails; but it is disgraceful and shameful that the Christian religion should stand upon violence.'[15] This conviction is not unique to Milton, but underlies the emerging case for religious toleration put forward by early modern writers such as Roger Williams and John Locke.[16] However, Milton goes further, insisting that verbal persuasion likewise must be non-coercive – it must not seek to and in the ultimate analysis is not capable of overpowering the free will of the hearer without the hearer's consent. For Milton this limitation applies not only to human verbal persuasion, but even to the divine and diabolical rhetoric with which God and Satan seek to persuade the human race.

The radical distinctiveness of Milton's rejection of coercion can be found in a comparison with the radical Puritan minister William Dell, considered in Chapter 2 of this study. Like Dell, Milton opposes the Constantinian marriage of church and state that allows religious orthodoxy to be maintained by coercive state power. For both Milton and Dell, the truth of Christ is advanced by the word and not the sword. Dell states that

> *Christ* will have none brought to *his* Church, by *outward violence*, and *compulsion*, though he have *all Power in Heaven and in Earth*; But in the day of his *Power*, (that is, of the *Gospel*,) he only entertains the *willing People*, and compells no body against their *wills*.[17]

216   *The Rhetoric of Conversion in English Puritan Writing*

Yet for Milton, unlike for Dell, those persuaded by the word to embrace saving truth are not part of an unchangeable predestined elect that cannot do otherwise. Dell's Christ 'will *entertain* none but whom his Father *draws,* because he will have *his* Church not one jot *larger* then the *Election of Grace*'.[18] Although, for Dell, Christ 'compels no body' to conversion 'against their *wills*', Dell's Calvinist compatibilism asserts that the wills of the elect are already drawn to receive grace by the Father's prior election, and thus the divine rhetoric of Christ is ultimately irresistible by the elect.[19] This is not the case with Milton's Christ in *Paradise Regained*, who explicitly rejects the prospect of irresistible rhetoric.

Paradise Regained is an imaginative retelling of the gospel narrative of Christ's temptation in the wilderness by Satan, which, although much shorter than *Paradise Lost*, is like *Paradise Lost* in greatly elaborating on its source material. The gospels describe three temptations – in Luke's account, whose order is followed by Milton, the first is to turn stones into bread to prove that he is the Son of God and, presumably, to satisfy his hunger. The second is the temptation to worship the devil in exchange for 'all the kingdoms of the world' (Luke 4:5). In the third temptation, Satan brings Jesus to Jerusalem and places him on a pinnacle of the temple, urging him to jump off to demonstrate his divine identity, trusting that the angels will carry him to safety.

Milton's narrative, however, stretches out and elaborates these temptations into several temptations falling under these three headings, rather than three discrete temptations. The first temptation, to turn stones into bread, appears first in Book 1 with the literal temptation to turn stones into bread. However, it continues, in Book 2, with 'A Table richly spred, in regal mode' (*PR*, II:340) appearing to Jesus, in a scene reminiscent of the Bower of Bliss in Book 2 of Edmund Spenser's *Faerie Queene* or the vanishing banquet in Shakespeare's *The Tempest*.[20] The third temptation, that of the pinnacle of the temple, creates a memorable and dramatic climax to the poem, but is dealt with fairly quickly.

The temptation that Milton elaborates most fully is the second temptation, in which Satan promises to give Jesus the kingdoms of the world on condition that Jesus worships him. This temptation is expanded to fill Book 3 and most of Book 4 of the poem. Whilst the narrative in Luke's gospel says that 'the devil, taking him up into an high mountain, shewed unto him all the kingdoms of the world in a moment of time' (Luke 4:5), in Milton's version Satan gives Jesus a survey of the nations around him, followed by a closer look at three kingdoms one after the other, those of Parthia, Rome and Athens, each of which comes with an accompanying temptation. It is the temptation of Athens that has posed most difficulty for Miltonists, and that is most pertinent to a consideration of the ambivalent role of rhetoric in Milton's understanding of how redemption is accomplished.

In the cases of both Scythia and Rome, the temptation is for Jesus to attain his prophesied throne as Messiah through the use of military power, and with Rome the temptation to pursue wealth is also present. The temptation of Athens differs markedly from those of Scythia and Rome, inasmuch as it is not so much political power over Athens with which Satan tempts Jesus as the cultural resources of Athens. This is a temptation not found in the biblical source text, and which perhaps reflects an anxiety of Milton's own about how to reconcile his love of the pagan classics with his Protestant Christian convictions.

After Jesus has turned down the offer to become Roman Emperor, Satan switches tack, noting that:

> thy self seem'st otherwise inclin'd
> Then to a worldly Crown, addicted more
> To contemplation and profound dispute.

(PR, IV:212–14)

Satan then appeals to this contemplative disposition (in which one suspects Milton may be moulding the Son of God into his own image) by urging Jesus to

> Be famous then
> By wisdom; as thy Empire must extend,
> So let extend thy mind o're all the world.

(PR, IV.221–3)

It is noteworthy that Satan here describes the quest for wisdom as an imperial one, the gaining of knowledge as a mode of mastering the world.

Seemingly sensibly enough, Satan observes that 'All knowledge is not couch't in *Moses* Law' (*PR*, IV:225), that there is also knowledge among the Gentiles that will be of use to Jesus if he wishes to rule the Gentile nations 'by perswasion as thou mean'st' (*PR*, IV.230), knowledge that is particularly to be found in the tradition of classical rhetoric. Satan here plausibly aligns himself with the mission of the rhetorical redemption of the world that Milton's God takes on in *Paradise Lost*. It is at this point that Satan brings before Jesus the sight of '*Athens* the eye of *Greece*, Mother of Arts / And Eloquence' (*PR*, IV:240–1). Satan offers to Jesus the cultural riches of classical Greece in the forms of philosophy, poetry, music, and rhetoric.

While it is the full panoply of the classical arts that Satan proposes to enhance and enforce the Son's kingship over the nations, it is Satan and the Son's respective

218 *The Rhetoric of Conversion in English Puritan Writing*

attitudes towards rhetoric that most exemplify the ambivalence towards rhetoric in the Puritan tradition traced throughout this study. One of the things that is suspicious about classical Athens in *Paradise Regained* is its reputation as the original democracy, since democracy makes the state subject to the power of oratory to manipulate the malleability of the mob. Satan speaks admiringly of

> the famous Orators [...]
> Those antient, whose resistless eloquence
> Wielded at will that fierce Democratie.
>
> (PR, IV:267–9)

The phrase 'resistless eloquence' suggests both that the nature of the orators' rhetoric is coercive and that the people are malleable, unable to resist cunning speech. Since these are Satan's words, it is not clear that we should accept at face value that the rhetoric of the classical orators is absolutely 'resistless', but whether this is so or not, it seems clear that the very notion of 'resistless eloquence' is a sinister one. The 'fierce Democratie' is wielded by various speakers to ulterior ends: the violent speech of coercive rhetoric results in violent action. Jesus here echoes the critiques of sophistry put forward by Plato, but applies these to the Greek rhetorical tradition as a whole: classical rhetoric is morally dubious because it can persuade to error as easily as to truth and to bad action as easily as to good.

Jesus', or rather Milton's, suspicion of democracy can be inferred earlier when Jesus disdains the idea of winning the acclaim of the crowds:

> For what is glory but the blaze of fame,
> The peoples praise, if always praise unmixt?
> And what the people but a herd confus'd,
> A miscellaneous rabble, who extol
> Things vulgar, & well weigh'd, scarce worth the praise.
>
> (PR, III:47–51)

Milton's rejection of democracy, however distasteful to today's readers, is not particularly shocking in an early modern context in which 'democracy' is frequently conflated with mob rule. Jesus notes that being disapproved of by the crowd is 'His lot who dares be singularly good' since 'Th' intelligent among them and the wise / Are few' (*PR*, IV:55–7).

Milton's Jesus here does not sound very much like the Jesus of Luke's Gospel, who says elsewhere in the gospel, 'I thank thee, O Father, Lord of heaven and earth, that thou hast hid these things from the wise and prudent, and hast revealed them unto babes: even so, Father; for so it seemed good in thy sight'

Resistible Rhetoric of Redemption in John Milton   219

(Luke 10:21). He does, however, sound suspiciously like Milton in some of his prose works, such as his 1644 pamphlet *Of Education*, which links virtue, knowledge gained through education, and the saving knowledge of God:

> The end then of learning is to repair the ruins of our first parents by regaining to know God aright, and out of that knowledge to love him, to imitate him, to be like him, as we may the neerest by possessing our souls of true vertue, which being united to the heavenly grace of faith makes up the highest perfection.[21]

This passage exemplifies the fact that, despite Milton's Arminian viewpoint (at least in his later life) that denies a Calvinist understanding of a group of elect individuals whose salvation is predetermined, Milton maintains his own idiosyncratic version of the elect few who are open to his message throughout his career. This is most famously the case in his assertion in *Paradise Lost* that he seeks 'fit audience [...] though few' (*PL*, VII:31). Gordon Campbell and Thomas Corns suggest that this is a habit of Milton's mind evident from his student days onwards, noting of one of his college disputation exercises, seeking to persuade his fellow students that day is better than night, that 'One sentiment anticipates a familiar assertion of Milton's late poems, namely, that he values the opinion of the few over that of the multitude'.[22]

In contrast to the assertion of many Puritans (especially separatists such as Bunyan, his pastor John Burton, and the Baptist cobbler Samuel How) that divine election tends to favour the poor and unlearned,[23] Milton seems to conflate the elect with an educational or intellectual elite having the privileges of education to inform their right thinking. Milton's fit audience is thus characterized by an odd blend of Puritan particularism, humanist/classical ideals of the virtuous and learned man, and claims to prophetic divine inspiration more characteristic of religious radicals.[24]

The Miltonic 'Elect' surfaces in *Paradise Lost* in a passage that puzzles scholarly readers aware of Milton's Arminian theology. This is in God the Father's account of how his grace will offer redemption to humans after their Fall:

> Some I have chosen of peculiar grace
> Elect above the rest; so is my will:
> The rest shall hear me call, and oft be warnd
> Thir sinful state, and to appease betimes
> Th' incensed Deitie, while offerd Grace
> Invites; for I will cleer thir senses dark,
> What may suffice, and soft'n stonie hearts

To pray, repent, and bring obedience due. [...]
This my long sufferance and my day of Grace
They who neglect and scorn, shall never taste;
But hard be hard'nd, blind be blinded more,
That they may stumble on, and deeper fall;
And none but such from mercy I exclude.

(PL, III:183–90, 198–202)

The notion of those 'Elect above the rest' has confused critics, given Milton's Arminian theology that denies the elect as a group of individuals irresistibly predestined to salvation, and has given rise to a number of competing explanations. Stephen Fallon calls it 'an apparent residue of Calvinist teaching on election' that 'disturbs the otherwise Arminian and libertarian doctrine of the mature Milton', but soon goes on to qualify this.[25] Fallon points out that 'The division of souls here is trifold: those elect by special grace, those who with the aid of general grace accept God's call to salvation, and those who reject this general grace and who are thus damned'.[26] By contrast, more typical versions of both Calvinism and Arminianism posit only a twofold division – those who are saved (for Calvinists through irresistible election and for Arminians through human free will accepting divine grace) and those who are damned (for Calvinists through their reprobation or non-election and for Arminians through their rejection of offered grace). Fallon suggests that the Father's speech begins with an apparently Calvinist outlook that collapses into an Arminian framework as the speech continues.

One possible way of resolving this is to recognize, as Dennis Danielson notes, that the language of election (divine choice) need not necessarily mean individual election to salvation from eternity, but can refer to what Milton in De Doctrina calls 'the election by which [God] chooses an individual for some employment, [...] whence they are sometimes called elect who are superior to the rest for any reason'.[27] This understanding of election to an earthly vocation rather than to ultimate salvation is particularly present in the theological discourse of Arminians and of the modified Calvinism of French Reformed theologian Moïse Amyraut, as Myers ably surveys.[28] Fallon gestures towards this understanding by linking 'Elect above the rest' to Milton's 'characteristic self-understanding as elect prophet' but sees this as 'a self-understanding acquired at the expense of his otherwise consistent soteriology'.[29] This need not be an inconsistency (as Fallon perceives), however, if Milton sees his election as election to the vocation of a prophet to the nation rather than election to personal salvation. Milton could thus be among those 'Elect above the rest' not in the sense that he is irresistibly and irreversibly chosen for salvation, but rather in the sense that he has been specially chosen for the purpose of transmitting the divine 'call' to the 'rest', seeking to persuade them to repent and to receive the grace made available to them. Milton's election to a prophetic vocation is thus a divine bestowal of rhetorical *ethos* similar to that which William Perkins attributes to the godly minister as 'prophet' or the more direct claim to being a divine mouthpiece made by radical prophetic figures such as Abiezer Coppe.[30]

In seeking to understand Milton's apparently elitist but non-deterministic elect, we can find a key in the biblical exegesis that Milton offers in *De Doctrina*. Milton explains away an apparent biblical assertion of individuals being predestined to salvation that is problematic for his Arminian theology of free will in terms of the virtuous predispositions of certain people to receive the divine message. Addressing Acts 13:48, which says that, upon the Gentiles of Pisidian Antioch hearing the gospel from Paul and Barnabas, 'as many as were ordained to eternal life believed', Milton acknowledges the difficulty that the apparent sense of the text poses for his non-deterministic understanding of salvation. However, Milton takes refuge here in an alternative interpretation of the Greek word translated 'ordained' by the King James Version:

> the more discerning interpreters (in my judgement at least) suppose that some ambiguity lurks in the Greek word *tetagmenoi*, which is translated 'Ordained', and that *tetagmenoi* has the same force as *eu ētoi metriōs diatetheimenoi*, 'well, or else tolerably, ordered or conditioned', 'with a settled, attentive, alert, and not irregular mind'. [...] For in man there are certain remnants of the divine image – as we shall show below – out of whose combination this person becomes more fit and, as it were, more ordered for the kingdom of God than that one. [...] By what means could anyone have been worthy before the gospel was heard, unless by the fact that he had been ordained, that is, well-spirited and ordered for eternal life?[31]

Milton is enough of a Protestant to affirm defensively that 'we did not argue that [God] looked at righteousness' in conferring salvation (thus aligning himself with the Reformation's rejection of salvation on the basis of human good works). However, there seems to be a creeping back in of the works righteousness rejected by the Reformers in Milton's conclusion that some individuals are worthier of grace than others on the basis of their prior predisposition, a predisposition that appears to be a combination of moral and intellectual preparedness to receive the truth of the gospel.[32]

222 *The Rhetoric of Conversion in English Puritan Writing*

The idea of an elite and elect few who are morally and intellectually predisposed to receive Milton's prophetic call to repentance is also present in the striking conclusion to Milton's 1660 pamphlet *The Readie and Easie Way to Establish a Free Commonwealth* that presents Milton's fit audience as an elect group that is fluid in its composition, perhaps few but not fixed in number. *The Readie and Easie Way* is a political tract in defence of a republican form of government published in the midst of events moving dangerously swiftly towards the restoration of the monarchy.

While Milton's persuasive goals are those of political deliberative rhetoric, seeking to persuade his follow citizens of the desirability of a particular political outcome, his conclusion is framed in strongly biblical and religious terms that invoke the motifs of religious conversion:

> What I have spoken, is the language of the good old cause: if it seem strange to any, it will not seem more strange, I hope, then convincing to backsliders. Thus much I should perhaps have said, though I were sure I should have spoken only to trees and stones, and had none to cry to, but with the Prophet, *O earth, earth, earth:* to tell the verie soil it self what God hath determined of *Coniah* and his seed for ever. But I trust, I shall have spoken perswasion to abundance of sensible and ingenuous men: to som perhaps, whom God may raise of these stones, to become children of libertie; and may enable and unite in thir noble resolutions to give a stay to these our ruinous proceedings and to this general defection of the misguided and abus'd multitude.[33]

Milton's stirring conclusion, akin to the passionate peroration that the classical rhetoricians recommended to conclude a speech, uses biblical archetypes to portray Milton as a lonely prophet. He is, like John the Baptist, a voice crying in the wilderness, and he appropriates for himself the words of the prophet Jeremiah '*O earth, earth, earth*'[34] to emphasize that he feels a compulsion to speak even if there are not many or even any humans receptive to his message.

Nevertheless, despite taking on the rhetorical *ethos* of the lonely prophet, Milton has not given up hope of an audience receptive to his divine persuasion: 'I trust, I shall have spoken perswasion to abundance of sensible and ingenuous men', despite the apparent absence of such men at present. The 'language of the good old cause' that may appear 'strange', as with the 'language of Canaan' considered in Chapter 4 of this book, is intended to be 'convincing to backsliders'. Both 'convincing' and 'backsliders' are words freighted with meaning in Puritan religion, with 'convincing' carrying the sense of conviction of sin and guilt as well as rational persuasion, and 'backsliders' being those of the professing godly who have fallen away from the path of true faith and righteous action.

Resistible Rhetoric of Redemption in John Milton 223

Angela Esterhammer observes that

> In Jeremiah's original utterance, 'O earth, earth, earth, hear the word of the LORD', the prophet is not addressing a planet but a human audience; 'earth' refers metonymically to 'inhabitants of the earth.' Milton undoes the trope in his allusion to the biblical verse[.] [...] Milton's literalization of the call to the earth is a reproach to his readers, implying that they are less responsive than soil, stones, and trees.[35]

Yet while Esterhammer may be correct that Milton reduces Jeremiah's populated earth to lifeless stones, she misses the fact that Milton goes on to repopulate that earth with stones brought to life. In expressing the hope that 'God may raise [some] of these stones, to become children of libertie', the speaker alludes to the words of John the Baptist to the Jewish religious authorities: 'Bring forth therefore fruits worthy of repentance, and begin not to say within yourselves, We have Abraham to our father: for I say unto you, That God is able of these stones to raise up children unto Abraham' (Luke 3:8; cf. Matthew 3:8-9). The biblical prophet in the wilderness, while castigating the outwardly godly as religious hypocrites, suggests that God can gather his own from people whose appearance is as seemingly unpromising as inanimate stones. For Milton, too, those who seem to be hard-hearted stones may not be irretrievably beyond redemption.

Milton's elect audience is thus select but fluid and not fixed – in Boyd Berry's words, 'God extends election to all men' but '[s]ome [...] are more elect than others'.[36] This appears to be the case for Milton in the theological context of access to eternal salvation as well as in the political context of those who favour temporal liberty. Both of these aspects of the Miltonic elect few are in view in Milton's *Paradise Regained*. In Book 1 of *Paradise Regained*, Milton's Jesus recalls his studiously contemplative childhood and adolescence (somewhat in the mould of Milton's own), and recalls how through his contemplations he came gradually to discern his vocation 'To rescue *Israel* from the *Roman* yoke' (*PR*, I:217) and then to quell injustice across the earth. However, the Son comes to learn that the political vanquishing of Israel's enemies is not to be accomplished just yet, as this final messianic victory awaits the future final judgement, and in the meantime the Messiah will use the gentler means of a non-coercive rhetoric to extend his reign:

> By winning words to conquer willing hearts,
> And make perswasion do the work of fear;
> At least to try, and teach the erring Soul.

> (*PR*, I:222–4)

The word 'try' could have its early modern sense here of 'to test' or 'to distinguish' and need not convey the tentativeness of its sense in modern English of 'to attempt' to do something, but yet there is the possibility of humans resisting divine persuasion in this age. It is the task of the prophet (including Christ in his prophetic office) and perhaps of the prophetic poet to teach individuals and nations to turn from their erring ways to the ways of God, but to teach is not to compel.

Readers have often (though not universally) found it hard to get along with the explicitly divine discourse of the council of heaven in Book 3 of *Paradise Lost*, in which God the Father explains his lack of culpability for the Fall and the Son volunteers himself for the mission of redemption. Many readers find the exposition of doctrine in Book 3 to be dry, God's theological self-justifications unappealing, and the divine personae of Father and Son to be lacking in the human interest of Adam and Eve or even the more humanlike Satan with whom readers can more readily feel sympathy.

William Pallister partially accounts for this with the observation that the 'revelatory divine speech' of Book 3 'takes most of its rhetorical content from the office of teaching, *docere*, as God foretells the future, explains the aetiology of the Fall – that responsibility for it rests squarely on man – and illuminates the conditions of the doctrine of free will'.[37] Teaching (*docere*), is one of the three offices of the Ciceronian orator alongside moving (*movere*) and delighting (*delectare*), and classical recommendations for *docere* tend to entail a plain style that is less emotionally engaging, as Stanley Fish notes in his account of the Father's expository plain style rhetoric in opposition to Satan's seductively appealing but deceptive 'grand style'.[38] This may well help to account for the relative emotional flatness of the divine rhetoric of Book 3 of *Paradise Lost* as experienced by many readers.

I disagree with Pallister, however, in his assertion that 'God and the Son do not – cannot – persuade one another' since they already know what is going to happen and the parts that they have both already decided to play in the drama of redemption.[39] For Pallister, the Father's request for someone to sacrifice themselves as humanity's intermediary and the Son's volunteering of himself to fulfil this role are not real actions but an act put on for the immediate audience of the angels and the indirect audience of Milton's readers. I differ from Pallister on two points – firstly, I am not persuaded that the Son of *Paradise Lost* is necessarily omniscient. Pallister notes that Milton denies the Son's omniscience in *De Doctrina* but claims that this does not apply to the character of the Son in *Paradise Lost* as 'the Son of God in *Paradise Lost* is "Equal to God, and equally enjoying / God-like fruition" (III. 306–7) and affirms himself "Image of [the

Father] in all things" (VI. 736)' and 'demonstrates that he possesses foreknowledge by outlining the future consequences of his willingness to become the agent of Atonement'.[40] However, the biblical language of Christ being equal to God and the image of the Father was read by Arians and Socinians whose Christology resembles Milton's as a functional equality in which the Son fully represents the Father rather than an absolute equality in which the Son possesses the exact attributes of the Father, and so need not imply absolute omniscience when used by Milton. Foreknowledge of how certain events will follow from other events need not entail absolute knowledge of all possible events, and so there is still room left for uncertainty in the Son's knowledge.

Secondly, and more importantly, I disagree with Pallister that uncertainty is necessary for persuasion to take place. One aspect of the orthodox Reformed understanding of the work of salvation to which Milton conforms despite theological heterodoxy elsewhere is that God is persuaded to accept believers by means of the Son pleading the merits of his obedience and sacrifice for their forgiveness.[41] Within this theological framework, the Father is indeed truly persuaded by the Son's actions and pleas to redeem the elect portion of humankind even though this means of persuasion had been agreed between them in advance (from all eternity in more orthodox Reformed understandings of the 'covenant of redemption' but perhaps within heavenly time in Milton's version).

However, I would argue that the divine rhetoric of *Paradise Lost* is not found only in the words explicitly put in the mouths of the Father and the Son. Rather, the entire poem is a piece of divine rhetoric, seeking to entice the reader through imaginative means towards conversion and godly belief and behaviour. In the words that Stanley Fish borrows from Milton's prose, Milton and Milton's God teach by entangling, not only by the propositional unfolding of correct doctrine.[42] The divine rhetoric of *Paradise Lost* is thus present throughout, making instrumental use even of the diabolical rhetoric of Satan and the fallen angels to accomplish the divine purpose.

The serpentine slipperiness of paradiastolic persuasion

As well as the presence of divine rhetoric in Milton akin to that propounded by the Puritan divines considered earlier in this book, Milton also masterfully explores the dynamics of diabolical rhetoric, not least through his creation of one of the most influential literary portrayals of Satan. Milton's Satan in *Paradise*

Lost is routinely recognized by readers as an eloquent orator and a persuasive tempter. This is most notably so in the 'council of Hell' of Books 1 and 2 of *Paradise Lost*, in which not only Satan but other fallen angels deliver set piece speeches displaying eloquence reminiscent of the classical Ciceronian tradition, and in Book 9, in which Satan in the form of the serpent seduces Eve through more insidiously deceptive speech.

However, I will focus in this chapter on an understudied dynamic in the rhetoric of Milton's Satan, that of paradiastole, the rhetorical figure by which vice is represented as virtue and vice is represented as virtue that I have identified as characterizing satanic rhetoric in the work of other Puritan writers. The paradiastolic dynamic provides a fruitful key to understanding Satan's insidiously persuasive deceptions in *Paradise Lost*, and is also present elsewhere in Milton's writing to characterize not only Satan himself but also other figures who are aligned with the powers of darkness. As a key to understanding Milton's Satan, paradiastole has only recently attracted critical discussion, with the helpful beginnings of such a discussion in a 2017 study by Paul Hammond: Hammond notes that 'Satan is a master of *paradiastole*'.[43]

It is a perennial question in Milton criticism since William Blake whether Milton is 'of the Devils party without knowing it.'[44] I find Stanley Fish's proposed resolution helpful. Fish acknowledges that Satan is an attractive character, but argues that this is a sign of the fallen nature of the reader, allowing Milton to enact and thus expose temptation through the experience of the reader.[45] Fish's reading of the poem allows us as readers to feel the force of Satan's persuasive powers while still evaluating Satan as evil.

Introducing his survey of the debate on Milton's Satan, John Leonard recognizes that whether one considers the character of Satan admirable depends in part on the reader's ethical valuation of ambiguous qualities: 'Critics on both sides of the argument agree that Satan's most conspicuous characteristic is pride. The contentious point is whether his pride is a vice or a virtue. Satan's vices often resemble virtues.'[46] This slippery boundary between virtue and vice is one that this book has identified as crucial to the operation of satanic rhetoric, via the rhetorical figure of paradiastole that excuses vice by identifying it with a similar-looking virtue and attacks virtue by making it appear to be vice. Relating Leonard's observation to this discussion, it appears that the operation of the paradiastolic dynamic on the reader is one of the fault lines underlying three centuries of critical debate on Milton's Satan.

The word 'virtue' is a loaded word in *Paradise Lost*, carrying with it the ambiguities of its varied historic meanings going back to the word's Latin root *virtus* from *vir* meaning 'man': its classical roots denote manly courage, and it can have the senses of strength or skill (both of which can be deployed for nefarious ends), as well as the sense of moral goodness. In *Paradise Lost* these senses of the word jostle against one another and cannot always be easily disambiguated. These coexisting senses of 'virtue' inform the problematic dynamic whereby Satan and the fallen angels are at times described as possessing virtues. For instance, when Satan volunteers to undertake the perilous journey to the newly created world in which the race of Man dwells, the fallen angels praise his apparently altruistic courage:

> Nor faild they to express how much they prais'd,
> That for the general safety he despis'd
> His own: for neither do the Spirits damnd
> Loose all thir vertue; least bad men should boast
> Thir specious deeds on earth, which glory excites,
> Or close ambition varnisht ore with zeal.

> (*PL*, II:480–5)

Alastair Fowler's justly celebrated annotated edition of the poem offers a way out of the discomfort we might feel here, drawing on an article by Barbara Riebling to gloss 'virtue' as 'classical *virtus* and Machiavellian *vertù*, not Christian virtue', but I think Fowler and Riebling take too easy a way out here.[47] While the word 'virtue' is indeed an ambiguous one in *Paradise Lost*, which carries with it the classical associations of strength and power that need not be put to moral ends, here it appears that it is specifically the quality of self-sacrifice that is praised as virtue, and the narrator compares Satan's motivation favourably in moral terms to the self-centred motivations of 'glory' and 'ambition' (a more Machiavellian motivation) that inspire 'bad men [...] on earth'. Perhaps Satan's virtue is a 'splendid vice', a phrase often used to summarize St Augustine's attitude to the classical virtue of pagans that is not rightly directed towards the Christian God and is thus sinful despite its virtuous appearance.[48]

The paradiastolic dynamic of the slippery boundary between virtue and vice is endemic to the rhetoric of the fallen angels in *Paradise Lost*, including but not limited to Satan – John Leonard notes that 'The lesser devils are also sublime. They are orators in the classical tradition and their speeches in the debate in Hell are tours de force worthy of Demosthenes or Cicero'.[49] It is through the rhetorical skill of his 'perswasive accent' (*PL*, II:118) that Belial, for instance, 'could make the worse appear / The better reason' (*PL*, II:113–14).

228   *The Rhetoric of Conversion in English Puritan Writing*

Hammond's observation that 'Satan is a master of *paradiastole*' is made in the context of his temptation of humankind: 'So the desire for knowledge which Satan seeks to instil or to evoke is a form of ambitious rebellion which entails redescribing God (for Satan is a master of *paradiastole*) as an envious tyrant.'[50] In his temptation of Eve, Satan relies on paradiastolic redescription that makes God's loving rule appear to be tyranny and Eve's disobedient eating of the fruit appear to be praiseworthy courage. Satan's temptation of Eve is in some ways a negative mirror of conversion rhetoric – the goal at which he aims is an anti-conversion, or a perversion of her faculties of thinking, feeling and willing. Indeed, conversion is the remedy to the fallen state into which Satan seduces humankind. Satan's sophistry is a 'perversion of rhetoric',[51] just as his goal of seduction away from God is a perversion of the process of conversion.

John Leonard has recently offered a lively and entertaining reading of Satan's temptation of Eve as a confidence trick that follows the six stages outlined by Edward H. Smith's *Confessions of a Confidence Man: A Handbook for Suckers* (1922): 'Smith identifies six stages that a successful con must go through: (1) "Foundation Work"; (2) "The Approach"; (3) "The Build-Up"; (4) "The Convincer" or "Payoff"; (5) "The Hurrah"; (6) "The In-and-In". Satan goes through all six in the correct order.'[52] Leonard notes that the foundation is laid for Satan by God's prohibition, as 'Prohibition is always good for gangsters', before proceeding to talk about Satan's 'Approach' to his mark:

> Wonder not, sovran Mistress, if perhaps
> Thou canst, who art sole Wonder, much less arm
> Thy looks, the Heav'n of mildness, with disdain,
> Displeas'd that I approach thee thus[.]
>
> (*PL*, IX:532–5)

Leonard notes Satan's flattery: 'Satan knows that his first word will excite wonder, so he makes "Wonder" his first word. But he does not immediately talk about his talking. A successful con is centred on the sucker.'[53] The flattery of one's audience is a rhetorical strategy adopted not only by 1920s conmen but also by classical rhetoricians such as Cicero who state that the exordium, the opening portion of an oration, should feature a *captatio benevolentiae*, a winning or capturing of the audience's goodwill.

Satan, in the guise of the talking serpent, does so by his flattering address to Eve, praising her as 'sole wonder' and insinuating that her beauty is wasted in an environment where there is only one rational creature (Adam) to appreciate it: 'Who sees thee? (and what is one?) who shouldst be seen / A Goddess among

Gods' (*PL*, IX:546–7). Satan's exordium is already beginning its deceptive work – the narrator follows his flattering comments with 'So gloz'd the Tempter, and his Proem tun'd; / Into the Heart of *Eve* his words made way' (*PL*, IX:549–50). Even before the serpent makes any substantive claims, he is already glozing (lying). Satan here begins with an appeal to *pathos*, targeting the weaker link of Eve, seen by Satan as less rational and more susceptible to being swayed through the passions than Adam, 'Whose higher intellectual more I [Satan] shun' (*PL*, IX:483).

It is midway through the temptation, once the serpent has enticed Eve to come to the tree, that he is described explicitly in comparison with a classical orator:

> As when of old som Orator renound
> In *Athens* or free *Rome*, where Eloquence
> Flourishd, since mute, to som great cause addrest,
> Stood in himself collected, while each part,
> Motion, each act won audience ere the tongue,
> Somtimes in highth began, as no delay
> Of Preface brooking through his Zeal of Right:
> So standing, moving, or to highth upgrown
> The Tempter all impassiond thus began.
>
> (*PL*, IX:670–8)

Satan, as a master orator in the classical tradition, makes use of the persuasive powers of two aspects of Ciceronian *actio* (performance) to win over his audience: physical appearance (the upright serpent) and gesture ('each part, / Motion, each act').

While starting with *pathos* in recognition of Eve's susceptibility to corruption via the affections, the serpent moves on to perverse and lying forms of appeal to *ethos* (his perceived authority as a speaker) and *logos* (appeal to rational argument). With regard to *ethos*, the very fact that the serpent speaks in human language gives him credibility in Eve's eyes, and the serpent links his humanlike reason and speech to his eating of the fruit. He speaks of his 'hunger and thirst' as 'Powerful perswaders' that appealed to his bestial appetites (*PL*, IX:586 –87), but led him to higher reasoning and linguistic powers conferred on him through eating the fruit. However, this is a lying *ethos* both in that the serpent's story of how he acquired speech is false and in that this is not truly a brute serpent elevated to reason but rather a fallen angel imbruted into the form of a serpent. With regard to *logos*, the serpent adopts deceptive sophistical forms of reasoning that seek to show that God's warnings are untrue or unjust.

230 *The Rhetoric of Conversion in English Puritan Writing*

One of these arguments involves a paradiastolic redescription of the defiant disobedience to which he is seeking to persuade Eve as the 'vertue' of courage:

> will God incense his ire
> For such a petty Trespass, and not praise
> Rather your dauntless vertue, whom the pain
> Of Death denounc't, whatever thing Death be,
> Deterrd not from atchieving what might leade
> To happier life, knowledge of Good and Evil.
>
> (PL, IX:692–7)

The serpent mischaracterizes the foolhardy act of eating the fruit in the face of the divine prohibition as the 'dauntless vertue' of seeking truth and happiness in the face of the threat of death (though that threat itself is weakened by exploiting Eve's experiential ignorance of 'whatever thing Death be').

While the serpent's exordium creeps into Eve's heart via perverse *pathos*, his peroration (the climax to a classical oration) wins her heart via corrupt *logos*:

> He ended, and his words replete with guile
> Into her heart too easie entrance won:
> Fixt on the Fruit she gaz'd, which to behold
> Might tempt alone, and in her ears the sound
> Yet rung of his perswasive words, impregnd
> With Reason, to her seeming, and with Truth.
>
> (PL, IX:733–8)

As often in *Paradise Lost*, the syntax delays the resolution of meaning in a way that invites the reader momentarily to consider and adopt a false perspective – we read that the serpent's 'perswasive words' are 'impregn'd / With Reason', before this is undercut by the qualifying phrase 'to her seeming'.

As I noted in the previous chapter on Bunyan, conversion in a Puritan context manifests itself in part by the reinscription of the convert's language, who learns to speak in the 'language of Canaan'. Similarly, Eve's speech is reinscribed in the terms of satanic rhetoric, as Hammond notes of her speech in praise of the Tree of Knowledge of Good and Evil: 'The same speech exhibits a loss of reverence towards God, now thought of – in Satanic *paradiastole* – as "Our great Forbidder", and a loss too of openness towards Adam, as she calculates how to manage their relationship to her best advantage. This is a Fall into falsehood.'[54] Of thirteen instances of the word 'vertue' in Book 9 of *Paradise Lost*, Eve herself applies the word to the powers of the forbidden fruit five times. Yet by believing in the virtues of the fruit and in Satan's mischaracterizing of her eating of it as virtue, Eve instigates a chain of events that leaves both Adam and Eve 'destitute and bare / Of all thir vertue' (*PL*, IX:1062–3) by the book's end.

In his analysis of Milton's Arminianism, Myers stresses that 'For all his might, Satan is not capable of overpowering the human will [...] Satan can only try to talk Adam and Eve into misusing their own freedom; he cannot interfere with their contingent ability to choose.' If *Paradise Lost* is read through the lens of Milton's *De Doctrina*, Myers is probably correct in his theological analysis of Adam and Eve's ability to resist. However, his account perhaps underestimates the dramatic power of Satan's temptation. Myers writes that 'Satan's role is reduced to a matter of mere rhetoric', but 'mere rhetoric' is itself a rather reductive phrase.[55] While Satan's rhetoric is not strictly irresistible, it is in practice extremely hard to resist.

The dynamics of diabolic persuasion, like those of divine persuasion, are found throughout Milton's writing career and not only in the famous biblical epics of his late career. For example, the paradiastolic dynamic of satanic temptation is apparent in one of the works of Milton's early career through a character who is not explicitly identified with the devil, but that critics have often identified as a prototype for Satan in *Paradise Lost*.[56]

This is the figure of Comus, the evil magician of *A Maske Presented at Ludlow Castle, 1634* – though the villain of the piece, his prominence is such that his name has often been taken as the title of the work. Milton's *Comus* falls within the earlier period of his life where his Puritan credentials are most under debate in current scholarship – while Maryann Cale McGuire in the 1980s designated it as 'Milton's Puritan Masque', critiquing courtly excess and Laudian ceremonialism in the person of the sorcerer Comus, Gordon Campbell and Thomas Corns's 2008 biography of Milton states conversely that '*A Masque* constitutes the most complex and thorough expression of Laudian Arminianism and Laudian style within the Milton oeuvre'.[57] Both of these readings arguably over-read the symbolic details of the text through theological categories not explicitly present within it, but for the purposes of our discussion we can sidestep this debate. I would like to note simply that some of the concerns present within Puritan practical divinity regarding how to resist the slipperiness of satanic temptation to sin find parallels within Milton's *Maske*, regardless of the precise political and theological convictions of the young Milton at the moment of writing.

Milton's *Maske* was written for the occasion of the ceremonial progress marking the installation of John Egerton, earl of Bridgewater, as Lord President of Wales and the Marches. The masque depicts Egerton's three children getting lost in the woods on the way to Ludlow Castle where their father will be installed.

232   *The Rhetoric of Conversion in English Puritan Writing*

Along the way, 'the Lady' (played by the fifteen-year-old Alice Egerton) becomes separated from her two younger brothers, and is deceived into following the sorcerer Comus in the guise of a shepherd, who captures and seeks to seduce the Lady into surrendering her chastity to him. While Comus immobilizes the Lady in an '*inchanted Chair*' through his magical powers, he seeks to seduce her through verbal means.[58]

Comus revels in the devious persuasiveness of his pernicious verbal rhetoric:

> I under fair pretence of friendly ends,
> And well plac't words of glozing courtesie
> Baited with reasons not unplausible
> Wind me into the easie-hearted man,
> And hugg him into snares.

(Mask, 160–4)

What is at stake in the debate between Comus and the Lady is not only sexual abstinence narrowly conceived, but the broader concept of temperance, the moderate enjoyment of goods at their right time and in the right proportion.

Comus disparages the Lady's abstemiousness by a paradiastolic characterization of it as an ungrateful refusal of the gifts of Nature and of God, which is an offence against their giver:

> if all the world
> Should in a pet of temperance feed on Pulse,
> Drink the clear stream, and nothing wear but Freize,
> Th'all-giver would be unthank't, would be unprais'd,
> Not half his riches known, and yet despis'd,
> And we should serve him as a grudging master,
> As a penurious niggard of his wealth,
> And live like Natures bastards, not her sons,
> Who would be quite surcharg'd with her own weight,
> And strangl'd with her waste fertility[.]

(Mask, 721–30)

Comus characterizes the virtue of 'temperance' as a vice, paradiastolically eliding temperance with extreme asceticism of a kind that early modern Protestants, with their rejection of monasticism, would repudiate. Comus sees this as an offence against the feminine 'Nature' and the masculine 'all-giver', who is implicitly identified as the Christian God. If the good things of the world are not enjoyed to the full, Comus argues, Nature will be suffocated by unconsumed goods, and the Creator God will not receive his due praise. By his verbal slight of hand, Comus thus characterizes temperate restraint as a form of impiety. It is this perverse paradiastolic rhetoric that provokes the Lady into responding:

> I had not thought to have unlockt my lips
> In this unhallow'd air, but that this Jugler
> Would think to charm my judgement, as mine eyes
> Obtruding false rules pranckt in reasons garb.
>
> (*Mask*, 757–60)

The Lady resists Comus's quasi-satanic sophistry as a deceptive simulation of right reason akin to the disguise of the humble shepherd with which Comus has enticed her into danger.

The Lady's refutation of Comus's characterization of temperance as an impious refusal of the gifts of nature and of God accords with Aristotle's understanding of temperance, taken up by medieval and early modern moral theology, as the moderate enjoyment of the gifts of creation in their due place, time and proportion:

> Impostor do not charge most innocent nature,
> As if she would her children should be riotous
> With her abundance, she good cateress
> Means her provision onely to the good
> That live according to her sober laws,
> And holy dictate of spare Temperance:
> If every just man that now pines with want
> Had but a moderate and beseeming share
> Of that which lewdly-pamper'd Luxury
> Now heaps upon som few with vast excess,
> Natures full blessings would be well dispenc't
> In unsuperfluous eeven proportion,
> And she no whit encomber'd with her store,
> And then the giver would be better thank't[.]
>
> (*Mask*, 763–76)

The Lady's verbal resistance to seduction is through the unpicking of the rhetoric of paradiastole. Yet she does not think Comus himself worthy of her persuasion:

> Thou hast nor Eare, nor Soul to apprehend
> The sublime notion, and high mystery

234 *The Rhetoric of Conversion in English Puritan Writing*

That must be utter'd to unfold the sage
And serious doctrine of Virginity,
And thou art worthy that thou shouldst not know
More happines then this thy present lot.
Enjoy your deer Wit, and gay Rhetorick
That hath so well been taught her dazling fence,
Thou art not fit to hear thy self convinc't[.]

(*Mask*, 785–93)

The word 'convinc't' here may carry the modern meaning of 'persuaded', but it also has overtones of the older sense of 'convicted', found guilty of a crime or sin. Puritan understandings of conversion necessitate both of these happening to a prospective convert, who must be persuaded both of the truth of the gospel and of his or her own sinfulness before being able to lay hold of saving grace. Comus is deemed by the Lady to be unworthy of either. On one level, the Lady is saying simply that Comus's arguments are so contemptible as not to be worth refuting; on another, she is arguably saying that he himself is so contemptible that he is not worthy of being persuaded to repentance. It appears that, at least to the Lady, Comus is irretrievably reprobate. He has 'nor Eare nor Soul to apprehend' the saving 'mystery' of the 'sage / And serious doctrine of Virginity'. Thomas Luxon's notes at the online Milton Reading Room link this to Jesus' admonition in the gospels, 'He that hath ears to hear, let him hear'.[59] Comus lacks the hearing ears of the elect that can receive saving 'doctrine' with understanding and is abandoned to the damnable worldly pleasure of his skilful but self-deceiving 'gay Rhetorick'.

Yet, if the Lady is not addressing Comus here, this raises the question of whom she is addressing instead. Luxon's online notes suggest that she is addressing the audience of the masque. I find this a very plausible suggestion but would like to suggest that it is also possible that she is addressing herself (whether instead of or as well as the audience), engaging in verbal self-defence against her own possible fall from virtue. The Lady's refutation may thus be a form of soliloquy of the kind recommended by Puritan divines such as Paul Baynes, Richard Sibbes and Richard Baxter.[60]

Milton's political prose of the 1640s and 1650s also addresses the paradiastolic characterization of virtue as vice and vice versa. For instance, in the opening to *The Tenure of Kings and Magistrates*, seeking to establish that rulers who usurp their power and become tyrants can be lawfully deposed, Milton writes that 'indeed none can love freedom heartilie, but good men; the rest love not freedom, but licence; which never hath more scope or more indulgence then under Tyrants'.[61] The 'rest' here are not advocates of true freedom, but rather excuse the vice of 'licence' by characterizing it as the virtue of freedom that it superficially resembles. Similarly, 'neither doe bad men hate Tyrants, but have been alwayes readiest with the falsifi'd names of *Loyalty,* and *Obedience,* to colour over thir base compliances.'[62] Thus the 'bad men' excuse the lack of true liberty exhibited in the vice of 'base compliances' by renaming their servility 'with the falsifi'd names of *Loyalty,* and *Obedience*'.

Paradiastolic redescription is at the heart of much of the political polemic reflected in pamphleteering of mid-seventeenth-century revolutionary England. The opposing sides of the multiple conflicts of these turbulent decades often lay claim to identical virtues and accuse the other side of identical vices. Indulging in the perverse rhetoric of paradiastole is itself an accusation that can be flung across the ideological divides on particular issues. This is apparent in the controversy around Milton's tracts in favour of easier divorce.

In *Tetrachordon,* Milton reports that some of his opponents make the same accusation as Socrates' opponents made towards him – that he is skilful in making the worse argument appear to be the better:

> Others, which is their courtesie, confesse that wit and parts may do much to make that seem true which is not (as was objected to Socrates by them who could not resist his efficacy, that he ever made the worse cause seem the better) and thus thinking themselves discharg'd of the difficulty, love not to wade furder into the fear of a convincement.[63]

By dismissing the persuasiveness of Milton's words as the product of 'wit' and verbal skill rather than truth, his opponents guard themselves against the danger of 'convincement', that is, persuasion both of the truth of Milton's view of divorce as a right interpretation of Scripture, and of their own guilt as hard-hearted legalists. Milton in turn accuses his opponents of '*rejecting the force of truth, as the meer cunning of eloquence, and Sophistry*'.[64] Forceful truth can be rhetorically dismissed, Milton warns, by its mischaracterization as deceptive sophistry. Thus, in the maze of polemical pamphlet war, to accuse one's ideological opponent of making error appear to be truth can itself be a rhetorical move to defend error against truth. While Milton seeks to pre-empt his opponents here, anticipating and denying the charge of paradiastolic sophistry that may be levelled against him, the tangle of claim and counter-claim might reduce a neutral reader's confidence in his or her ability to discern who is the bold proponent of truth here and who is the eloquent purveyor of error.

This is apparent in Milton's Sonnet 12, dealing with the fallout from his divorce tracts, in which Milton navigates the thorny thickets of paradiastolic redescription surrounding the distinction between 'licence' and 'liberty'. Milton protests that 'I

236   *The Rhetoric of Conversion in English Puritan Writing*

did but prompt the age to quit their clogs / By the known rules of antient libertie,' (lines 1–2), before being surrounded by the opposition of braying beasts who make the noise 'Of Owles and Cuckoes, Asses, Apes and Doggs' (line 4).[65] Yet Milton says of his opponents that they call for 'freedom' while refusing it when offered:

> That bawle for freedom in their senceless mood,
> And still revolt when truth would set them free.
> Licence they mean when they cry libertie;
> For who loves that, must first be wise and good[.]

> (lines 9–12)

Those who reject the 'libertie' offered by Milton's interpretation of scriptural teaching on marriage and divorce have their own version of 'libertie' that Milton dismisses as 'licence' (licentiousness). There has been some divergence in the critical reading of this sonnet as to who 'they' are. The majority of critics, such as Barbara Lewalski, argue that it is the censorious Presbyterians who condemn Milton's views on divorce that Milton condemns as themselves licentious, 'echo[ing] Livy's somewhat comparable charge against aristocratic youth corrupted by wealth who sought their own license (freedom and privileges) rather than the liberty of all'.[66] Nathaniel H. Henry, by contrast, thinks that it is the antinomian 'lunatic fringe of the Independents' that Milton has in view here, such as the notorious Mrs Attaway of Coleman Street who reportedly deserted her husband upon reading Milton's *The Doctrine and Discipline of Divorce*.[67] Christopher Donato writes of 'Milton's Sonnet XII against the Ranters', without elaborating on why he thinks this is the case.[68]

Henry's reading seems prompted by the incongruity of the Presbyterians, more conservative than Milton in ecclesiastical and ethical matters, being characterized as licentious: ' "Licence" is not a word usually associated with Presbyterians and Scots'.[69] However, perhaps that very incongruity is the point. Both Milton and his Presbyterian critics see the other as putting forward a false version of 'liberty' that is in fact 'licence' – Milton has a reason to associate Presbyterians with licence even if such an association is not usual. Both accuse the other of paradiastolic deception.

'Evil be thou my Good': Satan's rhetorical self-deception

The slipperiness of the paradiastolic dynamic and the challenges in using it to discern truth from error illuminate some of the paradoxes encapsulated in a key moment of *Paradise Lost* in which Satan's slippery rhetoric is directed towards himself. While Milton's Satan is widely recognized to be an eloquent rhetorician in his rallying of the fallen angels and in his temptation of Eve,[70] I would like here to focus on Satan's rhetoric in a scene where he is ostensibly alone, that is, in his soliloquy on Mount Niphates that opens Book 4 of *Paradise Lost*. Here Satan pauses, having landed on Earth and being within sight of the Garden of Eden where God has placed Adam and Eve, to survey the landscape and to reflect on his rebellious enterprise.

This is an episode that Miltonists identify as crucial to the whole poem, particularly with regard to the characterization of Satan. John Carey calls this 'The one part of the poem where access is provided to the "true" Satan', and observes that Satan's 'inner debate and self-criticism reveal him as a creature of dynamic tensions' as he 'vacillates between remorse and defiance'.[71] During this lengthy speech, Satan appears to be deliberating with himself, and to hint at some regret (and perhaps remorse) over his choices and their consequences – the sight of the sun reminds him of the heaven that he has lost by his rebellion, and Satan appears to recognize that God 'deservd no such return / From mee' (*PL*, IV:42–3). Satan's regret at the punishment he has incurred culminates in the self-directed exclamation 'O then at last relent: is there no place / Left for Repentance, none for Pardon left?' (*PL*, IV:79–80), before turning back towards defiance with the recognition that repentance would require a 'submission' (*PL*, IV:81) that his pride forbids.[72]

It is somewhat ironic that while the proto-Satanic figure of Milton's Comus seems to be irretrievably reprobate and beyond persuasion to repentance, Milton's depiction of Satan himself raises at least the dramatic possibility of his repentance here. Critical opinion is divided on whether Milton's Satan is genuinely capable of repentance here; similarly, while the majority of theologians in Christian history have rejected the Church Father Origen's assertion that even the devil would finally be saved, whether he could in theory repent and be saved is a trickier question.[73]

Puritan divines distinguish between remorse and repentance, and it can be argued that Satan displays the former but not the latter. It could also be argued that Satan displays the kind of inadequate temporary repentance followed by falling away that proponents of practical divinity including William Perkins and John Bunyan believed could be displayed by the reprobate. Alternatively, Satan's soliloquy can be read as beginning the process of repentance along the lines of the soliloquies recommended in the practical divinity of Richard Sibbes and Richard Baxter, but then wilfully abandoning it.

The key passage in this speech for our purposes is its conclusion, in which Satan resolves his conflicted thoughts by recommitting himself to obstinate rebellion against God:

So farwel Hope, and with Hope farwel Fear,
Farwel Remorse: all Good to me is lost;
Evil be thou my Good; by thee at least
Divided Empire with Heav'ns King I hold,
By thee, and more then half perhaps will reigne;
As Man ere long, and this new World shall know.

(*PL*, IV:108–13)

Satan's imperative exclamation 'Evil be thou my Good' is a defiant refusal of repentance and conversion, whether or not such repentance is theoretically possible for Satan. It is also an utterance that has occasioned much scholarly debate. The main point at issue is whether Satan in fact believes evil to be in some sense truly good, or whether he is simply taking evil to be his 'good' in the Aristotelian sense of his *telos*, that is, the desired end to which he aspires, while knowing that *telos* to be objectively evil.

This second sense of 'good' as *telos* is presented in Mammon's speech in the council of hell in Book 2 of *Paradise Lost*, in which Mammon calls on his fellow rebel angels not to return to

our state
Of splendid vassalage, but rather seek
Our own good from our selves, and from our own
Live to our selves, though in this vast recess,
Free, and to none accountable[.]

(*PL*, II:251–5)

In exhorting his comrades to 'seek / Our own good from our selves', Mammon rejects the true moral good that is defined in relation to God and advocates its replacement with an alternative 'good' emanating 'from our selves'. The fallen angels need a *telos*, a purpose, which is designated their 'good', even though that 'good' is in fact evil.

Stephen Fallon has argued that Satan's 'Evil be thou my Good' is an instance of the philosophical nominalism advocated by Thomas Hobbes, in which, Hobbes asserts, 'these words of Good, Evill, and Contemptible, are ever used with relation to the person that useth them: There being nothing simply and absolutely so; nor any common Rule of Good and Evill, to be taken from the nature of the objects themselves.'[74] In other words, for Hobbes, there is no such thing as intrinsic good or evil – rather, good and evil are defined by the perspective of the speaker who defines them as such.

This nominalism has theological roots in some strands of medieval scholasticism, notably in the work of thinkers such as William of Ockham, who defined God's divine freedom and sovereignty over the universe so radically as to affirm that everything is as it is only because God declares it to be so. In this 'voluntarist' tradition, God's will is so radically determinative that even good actions are so not because they have an intrinsic goodness in themselves, but only because God has chosen to define these actions as good when he could have done otherwise. In the medieval voluntarist tradition, however, unlike the Hobbesian tradition highlighted by Fallon, it is only God who has the power to define good and evil. Thus, Milton's representation of Satan's perverse moral reasoning could be read as a critique of Hobbesian nominalism: when he declaims 'Evil be thou my good', Satan is a voluntarist attempting to usurp the divine prerogative of voluntarism. Because he is not qualified to define the moral order, the moral universe fails to comply.

Neil Forsyth has argued that only on Mount Niphates does Satan recognize his rebellion as 'evil', noting that Satan refuses Michael's naming of the angelic revolt as 'evil' earlier on in the narrative sequence of *Paradise Lost* (though the reader encounters this exchange later on given the work's epic use of narrative flashbacks).[75] Forsyth notes that 'Only later, when Satan has arrived on Earth and seen the newly created physical world [...] does his initial choice become the famous and paradoxical cry, "Evil be thou my good" (4.110).'[76] Paul Stevens recognizes Satan's inversion of values as implicitly already condemned by a scriptural text that it echoes:

> On Niphates, his challenge is immediately confounded by the Word: when he insists 'Evil be thou my good' (110), Scripture echoes his words and interprets his defiance as the solipsism of unaided reason: 'Woe unto them that call evil good, and good evil. ... Woe unto them that are wise in their own eyes, and prudent in their own sight!' (Isaiah 5:20)[77]

The verse from Isaiah that Stevens cites arguably functions as a divine denunciation of paradiastole, opposing the redefining of moral values by moral agents in ways that suit their own ends.

Besides the debate over this passage by literary scholars, Elizabeth Anscombe, a noted twentieth-century Catholic philosopher and pupil of Ludwig Wittgenstein, has sparked much significant discussion of Satan's words 'Evil be thou my good'

240 *The Rhetoric of Conversion in English Puritan Writing*

in the literature of ethics and moral philosophy (although Anscombe herself does not explicitly note that these are the words of Milton's Satan). After some probing analysis, Anscombe concludes on balance that this is an intelligible (if perhaps misguided) maxim for a moral agent:

> If then the answer to this question at some stage is 'The good of it is that it's bad', this need not be unintelligible; one can go on to say 'And what's the good of its being bad?' to which the answer might be condemnation of good as impotent, slavish, and inglorious. Then the good of making evil my good is my intact liberty in the unsubmissiveness of my will. *Bonum est multiplex*: good is multiform, and all that is required for our concept of 'wanting' is that a man should see what he wants under the aspect of some good.[78]

Attributing this action to 'a man' suggests that this may not be an interpretation of Milton's Satan, but rather a borrowing of Satan's words as a pithy summary of an ethical attitude held by some human agents. Anscombe here displays a debt to classical philosophical ethics and to the medieval scholastic tradition when she deploys the notion that evil can be embraced under the aspect of good (*sub specie boni*). 'Bonum est multiplex' is a quotation from Thomas Aquinas's *Summa Theologiae*: 'The will can tend to nothing except under the aspect of good. But because good is of many kinds [*bonum est multiplex*], for this reason the will is not of necessity determined to one.'[79] Aquinas expresses the idea more simply elsewhere: 'whatever man desires, he desires it under the aspect of good [*sub specie boni*]' even if this is a disordered desire that in fact leads to evil.[80]

Milton's Satan has thus, via Anscombe and others, become a proxy in a discussion among modern moral philosophers, who seek to distinguish 'perverse' motivations for evil, in which moral agents pursue ends perceived to be good but in a distorted manner that leads to evil, and 'pure' evil, in which a moral agent pursues that which is evil because it is evil.[81] For example, David McNaughton posits a provisional distinction between the 'bad person' who is willing to do morally wrong things in pursuit of given objectives, and the 'wicked person' who 'would be attracted to a course of action because it was cruel, unjust, sordid, or obscene. He is the mirror image of the virtuous person – like Milton's Satan his motto is: "Evil, be thou my good." '[82] However, McNaughton goes on to conclude that Milton's Satan 'embraces evil, not for its own sake, but because it is the only way to satisfy his ambition and preserve his pride'.[83]

One recent philosophical critic of Anscombe's reading of Milton is Robert Dunn, who sees Milton's Satan as an example of 'perverse agency', exemplifying how moral agents such as ourselves are not always 'lovers of the good' (as an Aristotelian model might suggest) but sometimes 'mere lovers of success in action' (even if the goals achieved might be morally objectionable).[84] Dunn objects that Anscombe is turning Satan into 'a closet lover of the good', and argues instead that

> When Satan resolves, 'Evil be thou my Good', he of course is not revising his theory of moral good and evil. What makes him satanic is that, while holding his moral theory constant, he substitutes evil for good as his goal in action, seeing the pursuit of evil as a means to several ends.[85]

Dunn thus takes Satan's 'good' to be something closer to the Aristotelian *telos* – Dunn agrees with Anscombe that Milton's Satan sees evil as the means to ends he desires, but disagrees with her contention that Satan (mistakenly) sees those ends as truly good. Paul Hammond likewise sees Satan as adopting evil as his *telos* knowing it to be evil: ' "Evil be thou my Good": this apparent paradox recalls and perverts the Platonic idea that no one does evil willingly, knowing it to be evil, but always represents it to themselves as a form of the good.'[86] Hammond thus interprets Milton's Satan as a figure of perverse evil who knowingly subverts the classical tradition that offers some mitigation for evildoers.

I would argue that Satan's words in his soliloquy on Mount Niphates can be plausibly interpreted in both directions. Perhaps the paradiastolic dynamic offers a middle way that allows Milton's Satan to be read as an exemplar both of perverse and of pure evil. Commenting on Satan's claim to be able to 'make a Heav'n of Hell, a Hell of Heav'n' (*PL*, I:255), Paul Hammond notes that 'Satan, the master of rhetoric, has allowed rhetoric to deceive him',[87] echoing in relation to rhetoric an insight into Milton's Satan offered decades earlier by C. S. Lewis: 'I do not know whether we can distinguish his constant lies from the blindness which he has almost willingly imposed on himself'. By 'persuad[ing] himself' of the truth of 'his own propaganda', Lewis observes, 'he has become more a Lie than a Liar, a personified self-contradiction.'[88] 'Evil be thou my Good' is thus paradiastole pushed to its extreme. Satan is a master of deception, so masterful that he succeeds in deceiving himself – he is self-tempted and thus self-deceived.

It thus appears that, while 'resistless eloquence' (*PR*, IV:268) that forces the will to submit is a satanic fantasy in relation to persuading humans, the resistless character of satanic rhetoric is a reality for Satan himself. While divine rhetoric may teach and implore and satanic rhetoric may seduce, no rhetoric is irresistible in the Miltonic cosmos when faced with the inviolable freedom of the human will to choose and to resist. When it comes to Satan, however, his powers of persuasion are greater than those possessed by humans, but his nature is also more deeply corrupted than that of humans, who in Milton's theology

242   *The Rhetoric of Conversion in English Puritan Writing*

are assisted by divine grace to enable them (but not compel them) to choose the good. Satan's fuller corruption, denied the aid of divine grace, means that Satan is himself the victim of his own resistless eloquence.

A plain and rhetorical God

Having given the devil his due, it is fitting to conclude this book by returning to the divine persuasion celebrated by the authors considered in this book. While Milton's Arminian theology gives a more emphatic place to the role of the human will in conversion, all the writers considered in this book believe that human and divine wills concur in the process of conversion. They thus believe that the divine rhetoric of conversion works by appealing persuasively to the human mind and emotions, and that God accomplishes this work of conversion through the human persuasion of preachers and writers, just as the devil seeks to pervert humans through a counter-rhetoric that parodies and subverts divine rhetoric. In seeking to further the divine rhetoric of conversion, God's human agents imitate the varied rhetorical strategies found in the divinely authored text of Scripture.

This is a dynamic well expressed in a prayer from John Donne, a celebrated preacher and poet of the early modern period whom few would label a Puritan either stylistically or theologically, but whose prayer summarizes well many of the dynamics that this book has located in Puritan writers.[89] Donne is often placed in opposition to Puritan preachers due to his florid 'metaphysical' style in both his preaching and his poetry that seems at odds with Puritan plain style. Nevertheless, I trust that the present study has established that the ideal of plainness in communication did not preclude rhetorical eloquence on the part of Puritans, and that Puritan writers recognized both perspicuous plainness and rhetorical performance in Scripture, as does Donne in this highly rhetorical prayer:

> My *God*, my *God*, Thou art a *direct God*, may I not say, a *literall God*, a *God* that wouldest bee understood *literally*, and according to the *plaine sense* of all that thou saiest? But thou art also (*Lord* I intend it to thy *glory*, and let no *prophane mis-interpreter* abuse it to thy *diminution*) thou art a *figurative*, a *metaphoricall God* too: A *God* in whose words there is such a height of *figures*, such *voyages*, such *peregrinations* to fetch remote and precious *metaphors*, such *extentions*, such *spreadings*, such *Curtaines* of *Allegories*, such *third Heavens* of *Hyperboles*, so *harmonious eloquutions*, so *retired* and so *reserved expressions*, so *commanding*

perswasions, so *perswading commandements*, such *sinewes* euen in thy *milke*,
and such *things* in thy *words*, as all *prophane Authors*, seeme of the seed of the
Serpent, that *creepes*; thou art the *doue*, that flies.[90]

Over the course of the period covered by this book, the people known as
Puritans also discovered their God to be both a direct and a metaphorical God,
both a plain and a rhetorical God; a God, who, in the words of Richard Sibbes,
'*effectually perswadeth by a divine kinde of rhetoricke*'.[91]

Notes

1   N. H. Keeble, 'Milton and Puritanism', in *A Companion to Milton*, ed. Thomas N.
    Corns (Oxford: Blackwell, 2001), p. 126.

2   Catherine Gimelli Martin, *Milton among the Puritans: The Case for Historical
    Revisionism* (Farnham: Ashgate, 2010), p. 21.

3   Compare especially Barbara K. Lewalski, *The Life of John Milton: A Critical
    Biography* (rev. edn. Oxford: Wiley-Blackwell, 2003), whose approach mirrors
    that of most twentieth-century biographies of Milton, and Gordon Campbell and
    Thomas N. Corns, *John Milton: Life, Work, and Thought* (Oxford: Oxford University
    Press, 2008). A mediating position with which I am inclined to agree is taken
    by Nicholas McDowell, who argues in his recent biography that 'The aspects of
    Milton's upbringing and education that have long been regarded as evidence of the
    intellectual formation of an oppositional Puritan need to be understood within
    the context of a less polarized society in which being "Puritan" did not necessarily
    entail religious non-conformism or heterodox belief', and so the young Milton
    prior to the 1640s should not be assigned to either side of a binary opposition
    between Laudian conformist and oppositional Puritan radical (Nicholas McDowell,
    Poet of Revolution: The Making of John Milton (Princeton: Princeton University
    Press, 2020), p. 12).

4   On Milton's formal education and self-education, including exposure to classical
    rhetorical texts by Cicero and Quintilian, see, for instance, Harris Francis Fletcher,
    The Intellectual Development of John Milton, 2 vols. (Urbana: University of Illinois
    Press, 1956–61), McDowell, *Poet of Revolution*, esp. Chapters 1–7, and Quentin
    Skinner, *From Humanism to Hobbes: Studies in Rhetoric and Politics* (Cambridge:
    Cambridge University Press, 2018), Chapter 6, 'The Generation of John Milton at
    Cambridge', pp. 118–38.

5   John Milton, *De Doctrina Christiana*, ed. John K. Hale and J. Donald Cullington,
    in *The Complete Works of John Milton* [henceforth *CWJM*], 11 vols. projected, gen.
    eds. Thomas N. Corns and Gordon Campbell (Oxford: Oxford University Press,
    2008–) VIII:653.

6 Stephen M. Fallon, *Milton's Peculiar Grace: Self-Representation and Authority* (Ithaca, NY: Cornell University Press, 2007), esp. Chapter 2, 'The Least of Sinners: Milton in Context', pp. 21–44; Martin, *Milton among the Puritans*, esp. Chapter 3, 'Vocation, Prophecy, and Secular Reform in the Early Poems and Prose', pp. 105–40.

7 Richard Baxter, *Reliquiæ Baxterianæ: Or, Mr Richard Baxter's Narrative of the Most Memorable Passages of His Life and Times*, ed. N. H. Keeble, John Coffey, Tim Cooper, and Tom Charlton, 5 vols. (Oxford: Oxford University Press, 2020), I:221. Fallon is right, however, to note that Baxter retains a sense of his own sinfulness at odds with Milton's self-assured accounts of his youthful virtue (*Milton's Peculiar Grace*, pp. 22–23, 28, 35–36).

8 Benjamin Myers, *Milton's Theology of Freedom* (Berlin: de Gruyter, 2006), p. 144.

9 John Milton, *Paradise Lost* [henceforth *PL*], ed. Helen Darbishire (Oxford: Oxford University Press, 1963). Further citations of *Paradise Lost* are in the body of the text by book and line number.

10 Richard Baxter, *The Vain Religion of the Formal Hypocrite, and the Mischief of an Unbridled Tongue (as against Religion, Rulers, or Dissenters) Described* (London, 1660), p. 16.

11 Myers, *Milton's Theology of Freedom*, p. 158.

12 Richard Sibbes, *A Description of Christ*, in *Beames of Divine Light Breaking Forth from Severall Places of Holy Scripture, as They Were Learnedly Opened, in XXI. Sermons* (London, 1639), pp. 39–40.

13 Myers, *Milton's Theology of Freedom*, p. 152, citing Jacobus Arminius, *The Works of James Arminius*, 3 vols., trans. James Nichols and William Nichols (Grand Rapids: Baker, 1986), II:722. Myers also cites the English Arminian John Goodwin, who 'similarly writes that the grace of God enables human beings to decide "whether they will or no," giving them a possibility of willing salvation, but also "a possibility … of nilling" ' (ibid., citing John Goodwin, *The Remedie of Unreasonableness* (London, 1650), p. 8).

14 Myers, *Milton's Theology of Freedom*, pp. 147–8.

15 Milton, *De Doctrina Christiana*, in *CWJM*, VIII:9.

16 See John Coffey, *Persecution and Toleration in Protestant England, 1588–1689* (Harlow: Longman, 2000), esp. Chapter 3, 'The Protestant Theory of Toleration' (pp. 47–77).

17 William Dell, *The Stumbling-Stone* (London, 1653), p. 22.

18 Dell, *The Stumbling-Stone*, p. 22.

19 Dell, *The Stumbling-Stone*, p. 22.

20 John Milton, *Paradise Regain'd* [henceforth *PR*], ed. Laura Lunger Knoppers, in *CWJM*, II:29. Further references in text by book and line number.

21 John Milton, *Of Education* [1644], ed. Donald C. Dorian (1959), in *Complete Prose Works of John Milton* [henceforth *CPW*], gen. ed. Don M. Wolfe, 8 vols (New Haven: Yale University Press, 1953–82), II:366–7.

22 Campbell and Corns, *John Milton*, p. 37.

23 See, for instance, John Burton, 'To the Reader', in John Bunyan, *Some Gospel-Truths Opened According to the Scriptures*, ed. T. L. Underwood, in *The Miscellaneous Works of John Bunyan*, 13 vols., gen. ed. Roger Sharrock (Oxford: Clarendon, 1976–94), I:11; and Samuel How, *The Sufficiencie of the Spirits Teaching, without Humane-Learning* ([Amsterdam], 1640), sig. C3v: '[God] *chooseth* not onely for *salvation* but for *ministration* the *foolish* in Mans account'.

24 On the elitism of Milton's conception of education and proposed curriculum, see Timothy Raylor, 'Milton, the Hartlib Circle, and the Education of the Aristocracy', in *The Oxford Handbook of Milton*, ed. Nicholas McDowell and Nigel Smith (Oxford: Oxford University Press, 2011), pp. 382–406. Nicholas McDowell's recent biography sees Milton's formative decades prior to the crises of the 1640s as more profoundly shaped by the ideals of humanist education than those of Puritanism: 'The moments in Milton's life and writing prior to the later 1630s that have been claimed both for non-conformist Puritanism and ultra-conformist Laudianism have in fact less to do with ideology than with Milton's intense engagement with humanist ideals of learning and poetic eloquence' (McDowell, *Poet of Revolution*, p. 12; see also pp. 35–44, 66–78, and *passim*).

25 Fallon, *Milton's Peculiar Grace*, p. 184.

26 Fallon, *Milton's Peculiar Grace*, p. 185.

27 Dennis R. Danielson, *Milton's Good God: A Study in Literary Theodicy* (Cambridge: Cambridge University Press, 1982), p. 83, citing John Milton, *Christian Doctrine*, ed. Maurice Kelley, trans. John Carey (1973), in *CPW*, VI:172.

28 Myers, *Milton's Theology of Freedom*, pp. 75–9. Myers also finds in Arminian and Amyraldian theology an alternative understanding that, although all people are given sufficient grace to be able to choose salvation, some are given a greater chance than others (pp. 79–80), and in the Catholic theologian Ambrosius Catharinus the notion that 'certain specially elected individuals, such as Mary and the Apostles, are saved by the operation of irresistible grace, while the rest of humanity is offered a sufficient grace that can be either accepted or rejected' (p. 80). I find the latter suggestion implausible as a guide to Milton's meaning, since I have found no suggestion elsewhere in Milton of anyone at all being saved by irresistible grace.

29 Fallon, *Milton's Peculiar Grace*, p. 186.

30 For a classic study of Milton's claims to prophetic inspiration and their relation to the varied early modern understandings of 'prophecy', see William Kerrigan, *The Prophetic Milton* (Charlottesville: University Press of Virginia, 1974).

31 Milton, *De Doctrina*, pp. 91, 93.

32 Milton, *De Doctrina*, p. 93.

33 John Milton, *The Readie and Easie Way to Establish a Free Commonwealth*, ed. N. H. Keeble and Nicholas McDowell, in *CWJM*, VI:520–2. Keeble and McDowell present

the text of the first edition of February 1660 in parallel with that of the second edition of around April 1660 – I cite here the text of the first edition.

34 'O earth, earth, earth, hear the word of the LORD' (Jeremiah 22:29).

35 Angela Esterhammer, *Creating States: Studies in the Performative Language of John Milton and William Blake* (Toronto: University of Toronto Press, 1994), p. 141.

36 Boyd M. Berry, *Process of Speech: Puritan Religious Writing and Paradise Lost* (Baltimore: John Hopkins University Press, 1976), p. 255.

37 William Pallister, *Between Worlds: The Rhetorical Universe of Paradise Lost* (Toronto: University of Toronto Press, 2008), p. 126.

38 Stanley Fish, *Surprised by Sin: The Reader in Paradise Lost* (1967; 2nd edn. Cambridge, MA: Harvard University Press, 1998), Chapter 2, 'The Milk of the Pure Word', pp. 12–91.

39 Pallister, *Between Worlds*, p. 129.

40 Pallister, *Between Worlds*, p. 126.

41 See, for instance, John Bunyan, *The Advocateship of Jesus Christ*, ed. Richard L. Greaves, in *The Miscellaneous Works of John Bunyan* (13 vols.), gen. ed. Roger Sharrock (Oxford: Clarendon Press, 1976–94), XI:93–216.

42 Fish, *Surprised by Sin*, esp. Chapter 1, 'Not so much a Teaching as an Intangling', pp. 1–11.

43 Paul Hammond, *Milton's Complex Words: Essays on the Conceptual Structure of Paradise Lost* (Oxford: Oxford University Press, 2017), p. 67.

44 William Blake, 'The Marriage of Heaven and Hell', in David V. Erdman (ed.), *The Complete Poetry and Prose of William Blake*, 2nd edn. (New York: Anchor, 1988), p. 35.

45 Fish, *Surprised by Sin, passim.*

46 John Leonard, *Faithful Labourers: A Reception History of Paradise Lost, 1667–1970*, 2 vols. (Oxford: Oxford University Press, 2013), II:394.

47 John Milton, *Paradise Lost*, ed. Alastair Fowler (2nd ed. Harlow: Longman, 1998), II:483n (p. 132), citing Barbara Riebling, 'Milton on Machiavelli: Representations of the State in *Paradise Lost*', *Renaissance Quarterly*, 49.3 (Autumn 1996), pp. 573–97 (p. 589).

48 See, for instance, Jennifer A. Herdt, *Putting On Virtue: The Legacy of the Splendid Vices* (Chicago: University of Chicago Press, 2008), esp. Chapter 2, 'Augustine: Disordered Loves and the Problem of Pride', pp. 45–71.

49 John Leonard, *The Value of Milton* (Cambridge: Cambridge University Press, 2016), p. 75.

50 Hammond, *Milton's Complex Words*, p. 67.

51 Hammond, *Milton's Complex Words*, p. 123.

52 Leonard, *The Value of Milton*, p. 98.

53 Leonard, *The Value of Milton*, p. 99.

54 Hammond, *Milton's Complex Words*, p. 123.

55 Myers, *Milton's Theology of Freedom*, p. 116.

56 For instance, John Leonard writes, 'Comus is the first great tempter in Milton's English poetry, a clear precursor of Satan' (*The Value of Milton*, p. 33).

57 Maryann Cale McGuire, *Milton's Puritan Masque* (Athens, GA: University of Georgia Press, 1983); Campbell and Corns, *John Milton*, p. 84.

58 John Milton, *A Mask Presented at Ludlow-Castle, 1634*, in *The Shorter Poems*, ed. Barbara Kiefer Lewalski and Estelle Haan, *CWJM*, III:89. Further references in text by line number.

59 Matthew 11:15, Mark 4:9, Luke 8:8, Luke 14:35.

60 See, for instance, Paul Baynes, *Holy Soliloquies: or, a Holy Helper in Gods Building* (London, 1618); Richard Sibbes, *The Soules Conflict with It Selfe, and Victory over It Self by Faith* (London, 1635), pp. 220 and 251; and Richard Baxter, *The Saints Everlasting Rest* (London, 1650), p. 750.

61 John Milton, *The Tenure of Kings and Magistrates* [1650], ed. Merritt Y. Hughes (1962), in *CPW*, III:190.

62 Milton, *Tenure of Kings and Magistrates*, in *CPW*, III:190–1.

63 John Milton, *Tetrachordon* [1645], ed. Arnold Williams (1959), in *CPW*, II:583. The accusation that Socrates makes the weaker argument appear the stronger is reported by Plato in *Apology* 18b.

64 Milton, *Tetrachordon*, in *CPW*, II:583–4.

65 John Milton, Sonnet XII 'On the Same', in *The Shorter Poems*, ed. Lewalski and Haan, *CWJM*, III:241.

66 Lewalski, *The Life of John Milton*, p. 204.

67 Nathaniel H. Henry, 'Who Meant Licence When They Cried Liberty?', *Modern Language Notes*, 66.8 (December 1951), p. 511.

68 Christopher John Donato, 'Against the Law: Milton's (Anti?)nomianism in *De Doctrina Christiana*', *Harvard Theological Review*, 104.1 (January 2011), p. 75.

69 Henry, 'Who Meant Licence When They Cried Liberty?', p. 511.

70 See, for instance, Pallister, *Between Worlds*, pp. 151–96.

71 John Carey, 'Milton's Satan', in Dennis Danielson (ed.), *The Cambridge Companion to Milton*, 2nd edn. (Cambridge: Cambridge University Press, 1999), p. 163.

72 There is a similar moment in Book 9 that could be read as suggesting the possibility of repentance, when Satan's admiration of Eve's beauty distracts him temporarily from his malicious intent (IX:457–72).

73 Among those suggesting that Milton's Satan can repent at this point is Paul Hammond: 'Milton does demonstrate that Satan's embrace of evil is his own free choice, and is not predetermined. He could have chosen the good' (*Milton's Complex Words*, p. 118).

74 Thomas Hobbes, *Leviathan*, ed. Noel Malcolm, 3 vols (Oxford: Oxford University Press, 2012), II:80–2, cited and discussed in Stephen M. Fallon, *Milton among the Philosophers* (Ithaca, NY: Cornell University Press, 1991), p. 219.

75 When Michael calls Satan 'Author of evil', Satan fights back with a paradiastolic redescription of his rebellion as a quest for glory: 'The strife which thou callst evil, but wee stile/The strife of Glorie' (*PL*, VI:262, 289–90).

76 Neil Forsyth, 'Satan', in Louis Schwartz (ed.), *The Cambridge Companion to Paradise Lost* (Cambridge: Cambridge University Press, 2014), p. 25.

77 Paul Stevens, 'The Pre-Secular Politics of *Paradise Lost*', in *Cambridge Companion to Paradise Lost*, ed. Schwartz, p. 105.

78 G. E. M. Anscombe, *Intention*, 2nd edn. (Oxford: Basil Blackwell, 1963), p. 75.

79 Thomas Aquinas, *Summa Theologiae*, trans. Fathers of the English Dominican Province (2nd ed. 1920; online New Advent edition, 2017): I.82.a2. Accessed at https://www.newadvent.org/summa/1082.htm#article2

80 Aquinas, *Summa Theologiae*, I-II.1.a6. Accessed at https://www.newadvent.org/summa/2001.htm.

81 For instance, see survey in Mark Smith Ferguson, 'A Prolegomenon on Evil: "What Does It Mean to Be Evil?"' (MA thesis, University of Central Oklahoma, 2009), pp. 17–26.

82 David McNaughton, *Moral Vision: An Introduction to Ethics* (Oxford: Basil Blackwell, 1988), 135.

83 McNaughton, *Moral Vision*, p. 142.

84 Robert Dunn, *Values and the Reflective Point of View: On Expressivism, Self-Knowledge and Agency* (Aldershot: Ashgate, 2006), p. 61.

85 Dunn, *Values*, p. 64.

86 Hammond, *Milton's Complex Words*, p. 113.

87 Hammond, *Milton's Complex Words*, p. 28.

88 C. S. Lewis, *A Preface to Paradise Lost* (London: Oxford University Press, 1942), p. 95.

89 Though see Daniel W. Doerksen, '"Saint Paul's Puritan": John Donne's "Puritan" Imagination in the Sermons', in Raymond-Jean Frontain and Frances M. Malpezzi (eds.), *John Donne's Religious Imagination: Essays in Honor of John T. Shawcross* (Conway, AR: UCA Press, 1995), pp. 350–65, and Catherine Gimelli Martin's claim of continuities between Donne and William Perkins in 'Experimental Predestination in Donne's Holy Sonnets: Self-Ministry and the Early Seventeenth-Century "Via Media"', *Studies in Philology*, 110.2 (Spring 2013), 350–81.

90 John Donne, *Devotions upon Emergent Occasions* [1624], ed. Anthony Raspa (1975, repr. Oxford and New York: Oxford University Press, 1987), p. 99.

91 Richard Sibbes, *The Bruised Reede, and Smoaking Flax* (London, 1630), sig. a7v.

Bibliography

Primary sources

Aquinas, Thomas. *Summa Theologiae*, trans. Fathers of the English Dominican Province (2nd ed. 1920; online New Advent edition, 2017). Available at https://www.newadvent.org/summa/.

Aristotle. *The 'Art' of Rhetoric*, trans. John Henry Freese, Loeb Classical Library (Cambridge, MA: Harvard University Press/London: Heinemann, 1926).

Aristotle. *The Nicomachean Ethics*, trans. H. Rackham, Loeb Classical Library (rev. ed.; Cambridge, MA: Harvard University Press, 1934).

Arminius, Jacobus. *The Works of James Arminius*, 3 vols., trans. James Nichols and William Nichols (Grand Rapids: Baker, 1986).

Augustine. *De Doctrina Christiana*, trans. and ed. R. P. H. Green (Oxford: Clarendon, 1995).

Austin, Samuel. *The Character of a Quaker in His True and Proper Colours, or, The Clownish Hypocrite Anatomized* (London, 1672).

Austin, Samuel. *Plus Ultra, or The Second Part of the Character of a Quaker* (London, 1672).

Barclay, Robert. *An Apology for the True Christian Divinity, as the Same Is Held Forth, and Preached by the People, Called, in Scorn, Quakers* (London, 1678).

Baynes, Paul. *Holy Soliloquies: or, a Holy Helper in Gods Building* (London, 1618).

Baxter, Richard. *A Call to the Unconverted* (London, 1658).

Baxter, Richard. *A Christian Directory* (London, 1673).

Baxter, Richard. *Church-History of the Government of Bishops and Their Councils Abbreviated* (London, 1680).

Baxter, Richard. *Directions and Perswasions to a Sound Conversion* (London, 1658).

Baxter, Richard. *Gildas Salvianus; The Reformed Pastor* (London, 1656).

Baxter, Richard. *The Last Work of a Believer His Passing Prayer Recommending His Departing Spirit to Christ to be Received by Him* (London, 1682).

Baxter, Richard. *The Life of Faith in Three Parts* (London, 1671).

Baxter, Richard. *Methodus Theologiae Christianæ* (London, 1681).

Baxter, Richard. *Of Saving Faith* (London, 1658).

Baxter, Richard. *Poetical Fragments* (London, 1681).

Baxter, Richard. *The Poor Man's Family Book* (London, 1674).

Baxter, Richard. *The Reasons of the Christian Religion* (London, 1667).

Baxter, Richard. *Reliquiæ Baxterianæ: Or, Mr Richard Baxter's Narrative of the Most Memorable Passages of His Life and Times*, 5 vols., ed. N. H. Keeble, John Coffey, Tim Cooper and Tom Charlton (Oxford: Oxford University Press, 2020).

Baxter, Richard. *The Saints Everlasting Rest* (London, 1650).

250 *Bibliography*

Baxter, Richard. *A Treatise of Conversion Preached, and Now Published for the Use of Those That Are Strangers to a True Conversion, Especially the Grosly Ignorant and Ungodly* (London, 1657).

Baxter, Richard. *The Vain Religion of the Formal Hypocrite, and the Mischief of an Unbridled Tongue (as against Religion, Rulers, or Dissenters) Described* (London, 1660).

Bayly, Lewis. *The Practise of Pietie Directing a Christian How to Walke That He May Please God* (3rd ed.; London, 1613).

Baynes, Paul. *Holy Soliloquies: or, a Holy Helper in Gods Building* (London, 1618).

Bernard, Richard. *The Isle of Man: Or, the Legall Proceeding in Man-shire against Sinne* (4th ed.; London, 1627).

Blake, William. 'The Marriage of Heaven and Hell', in David V. Erdman (ed.), *The Complete Poetry and Prose of William Blake* (2nd ed.; New York: Anchor, 1988), pp. 33–44.

Brooks, Thomas. *The Unsearchable Riches of Christ* (London, 1655).

Broughton, Hugh. *A Comment vpon Coheleth or Ecclesiastes* (London, 1605).

Bunyan, John. *Grace Abounding to the Chief of Sinners*, ed. Roger Sharrock (Oxford: Clarendon, 1963).

Bunyan, John. *The Holy War*, ed. Roger Sharrock and James F. Forrest (Oxford: Oxford University Press, 1980).

Bunyan, John. *The Miscellaneous Works of John Bunyan*, 13 vols., gen. ed. Roger Sharrock (Oxford: Clarendon, 1976–94).

Bunyan, John. *The Pilgrim's Progress from This World to That Which Is to Come* (London, 1678).

Bunyan, John. *The Pilgrim's Progress from This World to That Which Is to Come*, ed. James Blanton Wharey; rev. ed., ed. Roger Sharrock (Oxford: Clarendon, 1960).

Bunyan, John. *The Pilgrim's Progress*, ed. N. H. Keeble (Oxford: Oxford University Press, 1984).

Burton, John. 'To the Reader', in John Bunyan, *Some Gospel-Truths Opened According to the Scriptures*, ed. T. L. Underwood, in *The Miscellaneous Works of John Bunyan*, 13 vols. (Oxford: Clarendon, 1976–94), I:7–12.

Calamy, Edmund. *An Historical Account of My Own Life: With Some Reflections on the Times I Have Lived in (1671–1731)*, 2 vols. (2nd ed.; London: Henry Colburn and Richard Bentley, 1830).

Calvin, John. *Institutes of the Christian Religion*, 2 vols., ed. John T. McNeill, trans. Ford Lewis Battles (London: SCM/Philadelphia: Westminster, 1961).

'Certaine Questions and Answeres Touching the Doctrine of Predestination', in *The Bible and Holy Scriptures Conteyned in the Olde and Newe Testament* (London, 1579).

Cicero. *De Oratore*, trans. E.W. Sutton and H. Rackham, Loeb Classical Library (London: Heinemann/ Cambridge, MA: Harvard University Press, 1942).

Clarkson, Lawrence. *A Single Eye All Light, No Darkness* (London, 1650).

Crisp, Stephen. *Scripture-Truths Demonstrated* (London, 1707).

Day, Angel. *A Declaration of All Such Tropes, Figures or Schemes, as for Excellencie and Ornament in Writing, Are Speciallye Used in This Methode*, in *The English Secretary, or Methode of Writing of Epistles and Letters* (London, 1599), pp. 75–100 (second pagination).

Deacon, John. *The Grand Impostor Examined: or, The Life, Tryal and Examination of James Nayler, the Seduced and Seducing Quaker* (London, 1656).

Dell, William. *A Plain and Necessary Confutation of Divers Gross and Antichristian Errors, Delivered to the University Congregation, the Last Commencement, Anno 1653, by Mr. Sydrach Simpson, Master of Pembroke Hall in Cambridge* (London, 1654).

Dell, William. *The Stumbling-Stone* (London, 1653).

Dell, William. *The Tryal of Spirits Both in Teachers & Hearers* (London, 1653).

Dent, Arthur. *The Plain Mans Path-way to Heaven Wherein Every Man May Clearly See Whether He Shall Be Saved or Damned* (London, 1601).

Doe, Charles. *A Collection of Experience of the Work of Grace* (London, 1700).

Doe, Charles. 'The Struggler (for the preceding Preservation of Mr. *John Bunyans* Labours in *Folio*) Thinks It May Answer the Desires of Many to Give the Following Relation', ed. W. R. Owens, in *The Miscellaneous Works of John Bunyan*, 13 vols., gen. ed. Roger Sharrock (Oxford: Clarendon, 1976–94), XII:453–60.

Donne, John. *Devotions upon Emergent Occasion*, ed. Anthony Raspa (1975; repr. Oxford: Oxford University Press, 1987).

Erbery, William. *Nor Truth, Nor Error, Nor Day, Nor Night, but in the Evening There Shall Be Light, Zach. 14. 6, 7* (London, 1647).

Farnworth, Richard. *The Pure Language of the Spirit of Truth* (London, 1655).

Featley, Daniel. *Katabaptistai kataptüstoi: The Dippers Dipt* (London, 1645).

Fisher, Samuel. *Baby-baptism Meer Babism* (London, 1653).

Fisher, Samuel. *Rusticus ad Academicos in Exercitationibus Expostulariis, Apologeticiis Quatuor: The Rustick's Alarm to the Rabbies* (London, 1660).

Ford, Emanuel. *Parismenos: The Second Part of the Most Famous, Delectable, and Pleasant Historie of Parismus, the Renowned Prince of Bohemia* (London, 1599).

Fox, George. *A Journal or Historical Account of the Life, Travels, Sufferings, Christian Experiences and Labour of Love in the Work of the Ministry of That Ancient, Eminent and Faithful Servant of Jesus Christ, George Fox, Who Departed This Life in Great Peace with the Lord, the 13th of the 11th Month, 1690* (London, 1694).

Fox, George. *Selections from the Epistles of George Fox*, ed. Samuel Tuke (Cambridge, MA: Riverside Press, 1879).

Fox, George, and Ellis Hookes. *Instructions for Right Spelling, and Plain Directions for Reading and Writing True English* (London?, 1673).

Fox, George, John Stubs, and Benjamin Farley. *A Battle-door for Teachers & Professors to Learn Singular & Plural* (London, 1660).

Fuller, Thomas. *The Church-History of Britain: From the Birth of Jesus Christ, Untill the Year M.DC.XLVIII* (London, 1655).

Gale, Thomas (ed.). *Rerum Anglicarum Scriptorum Veterum*, 2 vols. (Oxford, 1684).

Gataker, Thomas. *Certaine Sermons* (London, 1637).

Goodwin, John. *The Remedie of Unreasonableness* (London, 1650).

Gouge, William. *Of Domesticall Duties* (London, 1622).

Greenham, Richard. *The Workes of the Reuerend and Faithfull Seruant of Iesus Christ M. Richard Greenham, Minister and Preacher of the Word of God* (London, 1605).

Gurnall, William. *The Christian in Compleat Armour* (London, 1655).

Hemminge, Nicholas [Niels Hemmingsen]. *The Preacher, or Methode of Preaching*, trans. John Horsfall (London, 1574).

How, Samuel. *The Sufficiencie of the Spirits Teaching, without Humane-Learning* (Amsterdam, 1640).

Illyricus, Matthias Flacius. *Clavis Scripturae Sacrae, seu de sermone sacrarum literarum, in duas partes divisae* [1652] (Leipzig, 1695).

Lawson, Thomas. *A Mite into the Treasury, Being a Word to Artists, Especially to Heptatechnists, the Professors of the Seven Liberal Arts, So Called, Grammer, Logick, Rhetorick, Musick, Arithmetick, Geometry, Astronomy* (London, 1680).

Luther, Martin. *A Commentarie of M. Doctor Martin Luther upon the Epistle of S. Paul to the Galathians* (London, 1575).

Luther, Martin. *Luther's Works*, gen. eds. Jaroslav Pelikan, Helmut T. Lehmann and Christopher Brown, 75 vols. projected (St Louis: Concordia/Philadelphia: Muehlenberg and Fortress, 1955–).

Luther, Martin. *A Treatise, Touching the Libertie of a Christian*, trans. James Bell (London, 1579).

Mather, Increase. *The Life and Death of That Reverend Man of God, Mr. Richard Mather, Teacher of the Church in Dorchester in New-England* (Cambridge, MA, 1670).

Milton, John. *Areopagitica: A speech of Mr. John Milton for the Liberty of Unlicens'd Printing, to the Parlament of England* (London, 1644).

Milton, John. *Complete Prose Works of John Milton*, 8 vols, gen. ed. Don M. Wolfe (New Haven: Yale University Press, 1953–82).

Milton, John. *The Complete Works of John Milton*, 11 vols. projected, gen. eds. Thomas N. Corns and Gordon Campbell (Oxford: Oxford University Press, 2008–).

Milton, John. *Paradise Lost*, ed. Helen Darbishire (Oxford: Oxford University Press, 1963).

Milton, John. *Paradise Lost*, ed. Alastair Fowler (2nd ed.; Harlow: Longman, 1998).

Milward, Matthias. *The Souldiers Triumph and the Preachers Glory* (London, 1641).

Peacham, Henry. *The Garden of Eloquence* (London, 1577).

Penn, William. 'The Preface, Being a Summary Account of the Divers *Dispensations of God* to Men, from the Beginning of the World to That of Our Present Age, by the Ministry and Testimony of His Faithful Servant *George Fox*, as an Introduction to the Ensuing *Iournal*', in George Fox, *Journal* (London, 1694), sig. A1r–M2v.

Perkins, William. *A Godly and Learned Exposition or Commentarie upon the Three First Chapters of the Revelation* (London, 1606).

Perkins, William. *How to liue, and That Well in All estates and Times, Specially When Helps and Comforts Faile* (Cambridge, 1601).

Perkins, William. *M. Perkins, His Exhortation to Repentance, Out of Zephaniah: Preached in 2. Sermons in Sturbridge Faire. Together with Two Treatises of the Duties and Dignitie of the Ministrie: Deliuered Publiquely in the Vniuersitie of Cambridge* (London, 1605).

Bibliography

Perkins, William. *A Warning against the Idolatrie of the Last Times* (Cambridge, 1601).

Perkins, William. *Workes of That Famous and Worthie Minister of Christ in the Vniversitie of Cambridge, M. W. Perkins*, 3 vols. (Cambridge, 1608–9).

Plato, *Gorgias*. In *Lysis, Symposium, Gorgias*, trans. W. R. M. Lamb, Loeb Classical Library (Cambridge, MA: Harvard University Press, 1925), pp. 247–533.

Puttenham, George. *The Arte of English Poesie* (London, 1589).

Quintilian. *The Orator's Education [Institutio Oratoria]*, 5 vols, ed. and trans. Donald A. Russell, Loeb Classical Library (Cambridge, MA: Harvard University Press, 2001).

Rous, John et al. 'The Testimony of Some of the *Author's Relations*', in George Fox, *Journal* (London, 1694), pp. x–xi.

Schaff, Philip, and Henry Wace (eds.). *A Select Library of Nicene and Post-Nicene Fathers of the Christian Church*, 28 vols in 2 series (New York: Christian Literature Co./ Edinburgh: T & T Clark, 1886–1900).

Sibbes, Richard. *Beames of Divine Light Breaking Forth from Severall Places of Holy Scripture, as They Were Learnedly Opened, in XXI. Sermons* (London, 1639).

Sibbes, Richard. *Bowels Opened, or, A Discovery of the Neere and Deere Love, Union and Communion betwixt Christ and the Church, and Consequently betwixt Him and Every Beleeving Soule* (London, 1639).

Sibbes, Richard. *The Bruised Reede, and Smoaking Flax* (London, 1630).

Sibbes, Richard. *Evangelicall Sacrifices* (London, 1640).

Sibbes, Richard. *A Fountain Sealed: or, The duty of the Sealed to the Spirit, and the Worke of the Spirit in Sealing* (London, 1637).

Sibbes, Richard. *A Learned Commentary or, Exposition, upon the Fourth Chapter of the Second Epistle of Saint Paul to the Corrinthians* (London, 1656).

Sibbes, Richard. *The Soules Conflict with It Selfe, and Victory over It Self by Faith* (London, 1635).

Smith, Nigel (ed.). *A Collection of Ranter Writings from the Seventeenth Century* (London: Junction Books, 1983).

Smith, Thomas. *The Quaker Disarm'd* (London, 1659).

Sturm, Johannes. *De universa ratione elocutionis rhetoricae, libri IV* (Strasbourg, 1575, 1576).

Susenbrotus, Johannes. *Epitome troporum ac schematum et Grammaticorum & Rhetorume arte rhetorica libri tres* (Zurich, 1540).

Sylvester, Matthew. *Elisha's Cry after Elijah's God Consider'd and Apply'd, with Reference to the Decease of the Late Reverend Mr. Richard Baxter* (London, 1696).

A True Narrative of the Examination, Tryall and Sufferings of James Nayler (London, 1657).

Watson, Thomas. *The Beatitudes: or A Discourse upon Part of Christs Famous Sermon on the Mount* (London, 1660).

Watson, Thomas. *The Saints Delight* (London, 1657).

Wilson, Thomas. *The Arte of Rhetorique* (London, 1553).

Wyatt, Sir Thomas. *Collected Poems of Sir Thomas Wyatt*, ed. Kenneth Muir and Patricia Thomson (Leicester: Leicester University Press, 1969).

Secondary sources

Alpaugh, David J. 'Emblem and Interpretation in *The Pilgrim's Progress*', *ELH*, 33.3 (September 1966), pp. 299–314.

Anscombe, G. E. M. *Intention* (2nd ed.; Oxford: Basil Blackwell, 1963).

Auksi, Peter. *Christian Plain Style: The Evolution of a Spiritual Ideal* (Montreal and Kingston: McGill-Queen's University Press, 1995).

Barfield, Robin. 'John Bunyan's Solomonic Pedagogy', *Christian Education Journal*, forthcoming.

Batson, E. Beatrice. *John Bunyan: Allegory and Imagination* (London: Croom Helm, 1984).

Bauman, Richard. 'Aspects of Seventeenth Century Quaker Rhetoric', *Quarterly Journal of Speech*, 56.1 (1970), pp. 67–74.

Beeke, Joel R., and Paul M. Smalley. *Prepared by Grace, for Grace: The Puritans on God's Ordinary Way of Leading Sinners to Christ* (Grand Rapids, MI: Reformation Heritage Books, 2013).

Berger, Peter L. *A Rumour of Angels: Modern Society and the Rediscovery of the Supernatural* (1969; repr. London: Allen Lane, 1970).

Berger, Peter L. *The Sacred Canopy: Elements of a Sociological Theory of Religion* (1967; repr. New York: Anchor, 1969).

Berry, Boyd M. *Process of Speech: Puritan Religious Writing and Paradise Lost* (Baltimore: John Hopkins University Press, 1976).

Breen, Margaret Sönser. 'Race, Dissent, and Literary Imagination in John Bunyan and James Baldwin', *Bunyan Studies*, 21 (2017), pp. 8–31.

Breward, Ian. 'Introduction', in Ian Breward (ed.), *The Work of William Perkins* (Abingdon: Sutton Courtenay Press, 1970), pp. 1–13.

Brooke, Christopher. 'Learning and Doctrine 1550–1660', in Victor Morgan with Christopher Brooke, *A History of the University of Cambridge*, Vol II. *1546–1750* (Cambridge: Cambridge University Press, 2004), pp. 437–63.

Bruhn, Karen. '"Sinne Unfoulded": Time, Election, and Disbelief among the Godly in Late Sixteenth- and Early Seventeenth-Century England', *Church History*, 77.3 (September 2008), pp. 574–95.

Burke, Peter. 'William Dell, the Universities and the Radical Tradition', in Geoff Eley and William Hunt (eds.), *Reviving the English Revolution: Reflections and Elaborations on the Work of Christopher Hill* (London: Verso, 1988), pp. 181–9.

Burton, Simon J. G. *The Hallowing of Logic: The Trinitarian Method of Richard Baxter's Methodus Theologiae* (Leiden: Brill, 2012).

Camden, Vera J. 'John Bunyan and the Goodwives of Bedford: A Psychoanalytic Approach', in Anne Dunan-Page (ed.), *The Cambridge Companion to Bunyan* (Cambridge: Cambridge University Press, 2010), pp. 51–64.

Camden, Vera J. '"That of Esau": The Place of Hebrews xii. 16, 17 in *Grace Abounding*', in N. H. Keeble (ed.), *John Bunyan: Reading Dissenting Writing* (Bern: Peter Lang, 2002), pp. 133–64.

Bibliography

Campbell, Gordon, and Thomas N. Corns. *John Milton: Life, Work, and Thought* (Oxford: Oxford University Press, 2008).

Carey, John. 'Milton's Satan', in Dennis Danielson (ed.), *The Cambridge Companion to Milton* (2nd ed.; Cambridge: Cambridge University Press, 1999), pp. 160–74.

Carroll, Kenneth L. 'Early Quakers and "Going Naked as a Sign"', *Quaker History*, 67.2 (Autumn 1978), pp. 69–87.

Clarke, Elizabeth. *Politics, Religion and the Song of Songs in Seventeenth-Century England* (Houndmills, Basingstoke: Palgrave Macmillan, 2011).

Clement, Jennifer. 'Bowels, Emotion, and Metaphor in Early Modern English Sermons', *The Seventeenth Century*, 35.4 (2020), pp. 435–51.

Coffey, John. *Persecution and Toleration in Protestant England, 1558–1689* (Harlow: Longman, 2000).

Coffey, John, and Paul C. H. Lim. 'Introduction', in John Coffey and Paul C. H. Lim (eds.), *The Cambridge Companion to Puritanism* (Cambridge: Cambridge University Press, 2008), pp. 1–16.

Coleridge, Samuel Taylor. *Coleridge on the Seventeenth-Century*, ed. Roberta Florence Brinkley (Durham, NC: Duke University Press, 1955).

Coleridge, Samuel Taylor. *The Collected Works of Samuel Taylor Coleridge*, vol. 5: *Lectures 1808–1819: On Literature*, Part 2, ed. R. A. Foakes (London: Routledge & Kegan Paul, 1987).

Coleridge, Samuel Taylor. *The Literary Remains of Samuel Taylor Coleridge*, 4 vols., ed. Henry Nelson Coleridge (London, 1836–39).

Collinson, Patrick. *The Elizabethan Puritan Movement* (1967; repr. Oxford: Oxford University Press, 1990).

Condie, Keith. '"Light Accompanied with Vital Heat": Affection and Intellect in the Thought of Richard Baxter', in Alec Ryrie and Tom Schwanda (eds.), *Puritanism and Emotion in the Early Modern World* (Houndmills, Basingstoke: Palgrave Macmillan, 2016), pp. 13–45.

Condie, Keith. 'The Theory, Practice, and Reception of Meditation in the Thought of Richard Baxter' (PhD diss., University of Sydney, 2010).

Conley, Thomas M. *Rhetoric in the European Tradition* (Chicago: University of Chicago Press, 1994).

Cope, Jackson I. 'Seventeenth-Century Quaker Style', *PMLA*, 71.4 (September 1956), pp. 725–54.

Costello, William T. *The Scholastic Curriculum at Early Seventeenth-Century Cambridge* (Cambridge, MA: Harvard University Press, 1958).

Crawford, Jason. *Allegory and Enchantment: An Early Modern Poetics* (Oxford: Oxford University Press, 2017).

Croll, Morris W. *Style, Rhetoric, and Rhythm: Essays by Morris W. Croll*, ed. J. Max Patrick and Robert O. Evans (Princeton, NJ: Princeton University Press, 1966).

Cummings, Brian. *The Literary Culture of the Reformation: Grammar and Grace* (Oxford: Oxford University Press, 2002).

Damrosch, Leo. *The Sorrows of the Quaker Jesus: James Nayler and the Puritan Crackdown on the Free Spirit* (Cambridge, MA: Harvard University Press, 1996).

Danielson, Dennis R. *Milton's Good God: A Study in Literary Theodicy* (Cambridge: Cambridge University Press, 1982).

Davies, Horton. *Like Angels from a Cloud: The English Metaphysical Preachers, 1588–1645* (San Marino, CA: Huntington Library, 1986).

Davies, Michael. *Graceful Reading: Theology and Narrative in the Works of John Bunyan* (Oxford: Oxford University Press, 2002).

Davies, Michael, and W. R. Owens (eds.), *The Oxford Handbook of John Bunyan* (Oxford: Oxford University Press, 2018).

Davis, Nick. 'Bunyan and Romance', in Michael Davies and W. R. Owens (eds.), *The Oxford Handbook of John Bunyan* (Oxford: Oxford University Press, 2018), pp. 379–95.

Dever, Mark. *Richard Sibbes: Puritanism and Calvinism in Late Elizabethan and Early Stuart England* (Macon, GA: Mercer University Press, 2000).

Dixon, Leif. *Practical Predestinarians in England, c. 1590–1640* (Farnham: Ashgate, 2014).

Doerksen, Daniel W. '"Saint Paul's Puritan": John Donne's "Puritan" Imagination in the Sermons', in Raymond-Jean Frontain and Frances M. Malpezzi (eds.), *John Donne's Religious Imagination: Essays in Honor of John T. Shawcross* (Conway, AR: UCA Press, 1995), pp. 350–65.

Donato, Christopher John. 'Against the Law: Milton's (Anti?)nomianism in *De Doctrina Christiana*', *Harvard Theological Review* 104.1 (January 2011), pp. 69–92.

Duffy, Eamon. 'The Long Reformation: Catholicism, Protestantism and the Multitude', in Nicholas Tyacke (ed.), *England's Long Reformation, 1500-1800* (London: UCL Press, 1998), pp. 33–70.

Dunan-Page, Anne (ed.). *The Cambridge Companion to Bunyan* (Cambridge: Cambridge University Press, 2010).

Dunn, Robert. *Values and the Reflective Point of View: On Expressivism, Self-Knowledge and Agency* (Aldershot: Ashgate, 2006).

Dyrness, William A. *Reformed Theology and Visual Culture: The Protestant Imagination from Calvin to Edwards* (Cambridge: Cambridge University Press, 2004).

Esterhammer, Angela. *Creating States: Studies in the Performative Language of John Milton and William Blake* (Toronto: University of Toronto Press, 1994).

Fabiny, Tibor. 'The "Strange Acts of God:" The Hermeneutics of Concealment and Revelation in Luther and Shakespeare', *Dialog: A Journal of Theology* 45.1 (Spring 2006), pp. 44–54.

Fallon, Stephen M. *Milton among the Philosophers* (Ithaca, NY: Cornell University Press, 1991).

Fallon, Stephen M. *Milton's Peculiar Grace: Self-Representation and Authority* (Ithaca, NY: Cornell University Press, 2007).

Feingold, Mordechai. *The Mathematician's Apprenticeship* (Cambridge: Cambridge University Press, 1984).

Ferguson, Mark Smith. 'A Prolegomenon on Evil: "What Does It Mean to Be Evil?"' (MA thesis, University of Central Oklahoma, 2009).

Ferrell, Lori Anne, and Peter McCullough (eds.). *The English Sermon Revised: Religion, Literature and History 1600–1750* (Manchester: Manchester University Press, 2000).

Fish, Stanley. *Self-Consuming Artifacts: The Experience of Seventeenth-Century Literature* (Berkeley and Los Angeles: University of California Press, 1972).

Fish, Stanley. *Surprised by Sin: The Reader in Paradise Lost* (1967; 2nd ed. Cambridge, MA: Harvard University Press, 1998).

Fletcher, Harris Francis. *The Intellectual Development of John Milton*, 2 vols. (Urbana: University of Illinois Press, 1956–61).

Flinker, Noam. 'The Poetics of Biblical Prophecy: Abiezer Coppe's Late Converted Midrash', in Ariel Hessayon and David Finnegan (eds.), *Varieties of Seventeenth- and Early Eighteenth-Century English Radicalism in Context* (Farnham: Ashgate, 2011), pp. 113–27.

Flinker, Noam. *The Song of Songs in English Renaissance Literature: Kisses of Their Mouths* (Cambridge: D. S. Brewer, 2000).

Forrest, James F. 'Allegory as Sacred Sport: Manipulation of the Reader in Spenser and Bunyan', in Robert G. Collmer (ed.), *Bunyan in Our Time* (Kent, OH: Kent State University Press, 1989), pp. 93–112.

Forster, E. M. *Aspects of the Novel* (San Diego, CA: Harcourt, 1955).

Forsyth, Neil. 'Satan', in Louis Schwartz (ed.), *The Cambridge Companion to Paradise Lost* (Cambridge: Cambridge University Press, 2014), pp. 17–28.

Frost, R. N. *Richard Sibbes: God's Spreading Goodness* (Vancouver, WA: Cor Deo, 2012).

Golder, Harold. 'Bunyan's Giant Despair', *Journal of English and Germanic Philology*, 30.3 (July 1931), pp. 361–78.

Graves, Michael P. *Preaching the Inward Light: Early Quaker Rhetoric* (Waco, TX: Baylor University Press, 2009).

Greaves, Richard. *Glimpses of Glory: John Bunyan and English Dissent* (Stanford, CA: Stanford University Press, 2002).

Greaves, Richard L. 'Lawson, Thomas (bap. 1630, d. 1691)', *ODNB*.

Gunderson, Erik. 'Introduction', in Erik Gunderson (ed.), *The Cambridge Companion to Ancient Rhetoric* (Cambridge: Cambridge University Press, 2009), pp. 1–24.

Hall, Basil. 'Puritanism: the Problem of Definition', in G. J. Cuming (ed.), *Studies in Church History*, vol. II (London: Nelson for Ecclesiastical History Society, 1965), pp. 283–96.

Haller, William. *The Rise of Puritanism; or, The Way to the New Jerusalem as Set Forth in Pulpit and Press from Thomas Cartwright to John Lilburne and John Milton, 1570–1643* (New York: Columbia University Press, 1938), pp. 25–35.

Hallett, Raphael. 'Pictures of Print: Pierre Ramus, William Perkins and the Reformed Imagination', in Tara Hamling and Richard L. Williams (eds.), *Art Re-formed: Re-assessing the Impact of the Reformation on the Visual Arts* (Newcastle: Cambridge Scholars, 2007), pp. 201–14.

Hammond, Paul. *Milton's Complex Words: Essays on the Conceptual Structure of Paradise Lost* (Oxford: Oxford University Press, 2017).

Hammond, Paul. 'Smith, Thomas (1624–1661)', *ODNB*.

Hancock, Maxine. *The Key in the Window: Marginal Notes in Bunyan's Narratives* (Vancouver: Regent College Publishing, 2000).

Harding, Susan Friend. *The Book of Jerry Falwell: Fundamentalist Language and Politics* (Princeton: Princeton University Press, 2000).

Harline, Craig. *Conversions: Two Family Stories from the Reformation and Modern America* (New Haven: Yale University Press, 2011).

Hawkins, Anne. 'The Double-Conversion in Bunyan's *Grace Abounding*', *Philological Quarterly*, 61.3 (Summer 1982), pp. 259–76.

Hays, Richard B. *The Conversion of the Imagination: Paul as Interpreter of Israel's Scripture* (Grand Rapids, MI: Eerdmans, 2005).

Henderson, Judith Rice. 'Must a Good Orator Be a Good Man? Ramus in the Ciceronian Controversy', in Peter L. Oesterreich and Thomas O. Sloane (eds.), *Rhetorica Movet: Studies in Historical and Modern Rhetoric in Honor of Heinrich F. Plett* (Leiden: Brill, 1999), pp. 43–56.

Henry, Nathaniel H. 'Who Meant Licence When They Cried Liberty?', *Modern Language Notes*, 66.8 (December 1951), pp. 509–13.

Herdt, Jennifer A. *Putting On Virtue: The Legacy of the Splendid Vices* (Chicago: University of Chicago Press, 2008).

Hessayon, Ariel. 'Abiezer Coppe and the Ranters', in Laura Lunger Knoppers (ed.), *The Oxford Handbook of Literature and the English Revolution* (Oxford: Oxford University Press, 2012), pp. 346–74.

Hessayon, Ariel. 'Coppe, Abiezer (1619–1672?)', *ODNB*.

Hill, Christopher. 'Puritans and "the Dark Corners of the Land"', in *Change and Continuity in Seventeenth-Century England* (1974; rev. ed.; New Haven: Yale University Press, 1991), pp. 3–47.

Hill, Christopher. *A Turbulent, Seditious, and Factious People: John Bunyan and His Church 1628-1688* (Oxford: Clarendon Press, 1988).

Hill, Christopher. *The World Turned Upside Down: Radical Ideas during the English Revolution* (London: Temple Smith, 1972).

Hindmarsh, D. Bruce. *The Evangelical Conversion Narrative: Spiritual Autobiography in Early Modern England* (Oxford: Oxford University Press, 2005).

Hinds, Hilary. *George Fox and Early Quaker Culture* (Manchester: Manchester University Press, 2011).

Hudson, Hoyt H. 'Rhetoric and Poetry', *Quarterly Journal of Speech*, 10.2 (1924), pp. 143–54.

Hunt, Arnold. *The Art of Hearing: English Preachers and Their Audiences, 1590–1640* (Cambridge: Cambridge University Press, 2010).

Iser, Wolfgang. *The Implied Reader: Patterns of Communication in Prose Fiction from Bunyan to Beckett* (Baltimore: Johns Hopkins University Press, 1974).

Jardine, Lisa. 'Humanism and the Sixteenth Century Cambridge Arts Course', *History of Education*, 4 (1975), pp. 16–31.

Johnson, George Arthur. 'From Seeker to Finder: A Study in Seventeenth-Century English Spiritualism before the Quakers', *Church History*, 17.4 (December 1948), pp. 299–315.

Kaufmann, U. Milo. *The Pilgrim's Progress and Traditions in Puritan Meditation* (New Haven: Yale University Press, 1966).

Keeble, N. H. 'Baxter, Richard (1615–1691)', *ODNB*.

Keeble, N. H. 'John Bunyan's Literary Life', in Anne Dunan-Page (ed.), *The Cambridge Companion to Bunyan* (Cambridge: Cambridge University Press, 2010), pp. 13–25.

Keeble, N. H. *The Literary Culture of Nonconformity* (Leicester: Leicester University Press, 1987).

Keeble, N. H. 'Milton and Puritanism', in Thomas N. Corns (ed.), *A Companion to Milton* (Oxford: Blackwell, 2001), pp. 124–40.

Keeble, N. H. *Richard Baxter: Puritan Man of Letters* (Oxford: Clarendon Press, 1982).

Keeble, N. H. 'Richard Baxter's Preaching Ministry: Its History and Texts', *Journal of Ecclesiastical History*, 35.4 (October 1984), pp. 539–59.

Kendall, R. T. *Calvin and English Calvinism to 1649* (Oxford: Oxford University Press, 1979).

Kendall, R. T. 'The Preaching of the Word and Spirit', in Paul Cain and R. T. Kendall (eds.), *The Word and the Spirit* (Eastbourne: Kingsway, 1996), pp. 59–72.

Kenny, Robert. '"In These Last Dayes": The Strange Work of Abiezer Coppe', *The Seventeenth Century*, 13.2 (1998), pp. 156–84.

Kerrigan, William. *The Prophetic Milton* (Charlottesville: University Press of Virginia, 1974).

Kinneavy, James L. 'Kairos: A Neglected Concept in Classical Rhetoric', in Jean Dietz Moss (ed.), *Rhetoric and Praxis: The Contribution of Classical Rhetoric to Practical Reasoning* (Washington, DC: Catholic University Press, 1986), pp. 79–105.

Knight, Janice. *Orthodoxies in Massachusetts: Rereading American Puritanism* (Cambridge, MA: Harvard University Press, 1994).

Knott, John R., Jr. *The Sword of the Spirit: Puritan Responses to the Bible* (Chicago: University of Chicago Press, 1980).

Kuhn, Thomas S. *The Structure of Scientific Revolutions* (4th ed.; Chicago: University of Chicago, 2012).

Lake, Peter. 'Defining Puritanism: Again?' in Francis J. Bremer (ed.), *Puritanism: Transatlantic Perspectives on a Seventeenth-Century Anglo-American Faith* (Boston, MA: Massachusetts Historical Society/Northeastern University Press, 1993), pp. 3–29.

Lake, Peter. *Moderate Puritans and the Elizabethan Church* (Cambridge: Cambridge University Press, 1982).

Lane, Belden C. *Ravished by Beauty: The Surprising Legacy of Reformed Spirituality* (Oxford: Oxford University Press, 2011).

Leonard, John. *Faithful Labourers: A Reception History of Paradise Lost, 1667–1970*, 2 vols. (Oxford: Oxford University Press, 2013).

Leonard, John. *The Value of Milton* (Cambridge: Cambridge University Press, 2016).

Lewalski, Barbara K. *The Life of John Milton: A Critical Biography* (rev. ed.; Oxford: Wiley-Blackwell, 2003).

Lewalski, Barbara K. 'Milton on Learning and the Learned-Ministry Controversy', *Huntington Library Quarterly*, 24.4 (August 1961), pp. 267–81.

Lewalski, Barbara K. *Protestant Poetics and the Seventeenth-Century Religious Lyric* (Princeton, NJ: Princeton University Press, 1979).

Lewis, C. S. *The Allegory of Love* (rev. ed.; London: Oxford University Press, 1938).

Lewis, C. S. *A Preface to Paradise Lost* (London: Oxford University Press, 1942).

Longfellow, Erica. *Women and Religious Writing in Early Modern England* (Cambridge: Cambridge University Press, 2009).

Lowance, Mason I., Jr. *The Language of Canaan: Metaphor and Symbol in New England from the Puritans to the Transcendentalists* (Cambridge, MA: Harvard University Press, 1980).

Luxon, Thomas H. 'Calvin and Bunyan on Word and Image: Is There a Text in Interpreter's House?', *English Literary Renaissance*, 18.3 (Autumn 1988), pp. 438–59.

Luxon, Thomas H. '"Other Mens Words" and "New Birth": Bunyan's Antihermeneutics of Experience', *Texas Studies in Literature and Language*, 36.3 (Fall 1994), pp. 276–83.

Luxon, Thomas H. 'The Pilgrim's Passive Progress: Luther and Bunyan on Talking and Doing, Word and Way', *ELH*, 53.1 (Spring 1986), pp. 73–98.

Lynch, Beth. *John Bunyan and the Language of Conviction* (Cambridge: D. S. Brewer, 2004).

Lynch, Kathleen. *Protestant Autobiography in the Seventeenth-Century Anglophone World* (Oxford: Oxford University Press, 2012).

Mack, Peter. *Elizabethan Rhetoric: Theory and Practice* (Cambridge: Cambridge University Press, 2002).

Mack, Peter. *A History of Renaissance Rhetoric, 1380–1620* (Oxford: Oxford University Press, 2011).

Martin, Catherine Gimelli. 'Experimental Predestination in Donne's Holy Sonnets: Self-Ministry and the Early Seventeenth-Century "Via Media" ', *Studies in Philology*, 110.2 (Spring 2013), pp. 350–81.

Martin, Catherine Gimelli. *Milton among the Puritans: The Case for Historical Revisionism* (Farnham: Ashgate, 2010).

Martz, Louis L. *The Poetry of Meditation: A Study in English Religious Literature of the Seventeenth Century* (1956; rev. ed.; New Haven: Yale University Press, 1962).

McCullough, Peter E. *Sermons at Court: Politics and Religion in Elizabethan and Jacobean Preaching* (Cambridge: Cambridge University Press, 1998).

McCullough, Peter, Hugh Adlington, and Emma Rhatigan (eds.). *The Oxford Handbook of the Early Modern Sermon* (Oxford: Oxford University Press, 2011).

McDowell, Nicholas. *The English Radical Imagination: Culture, Religion, and Revolution, 1630–1660* (Oxford: Clarendon, 2003).

McDowell, Nicholas. *Poet of Revolution: The Making of John Milton* (Princeton: Princeton University Press, 2020).

Bibliography 261

McGregor, J. F. 'Seekers and Ranters', in J. F. McGregor and Barry Reay (eds.), *Radical Religion in the English Revolution* (Oxford: Oxford University Press, 1984), pp. 121–40.

McGregor, J. F., and Barry Reay (eds.), *Radical Religion in the English Revolution* (Oxford: Oxford University Press, 1984).

McGuire, Maryann Cale. *Milton's Puritan Masque* (Athens, GA: University of Georgia Press, 1983).

McKelvey, Robert J. '"That Error and Pillar of Antinomianism": Eternal Justification', in Michael A. G. Haykin and Mark Jones (eds.), *Drawn into Controversie: Reformed Theological Diversity and Debates within Seventeenth-Century British Puritanism* (Göttingen: Vandenhoeck & Ruprecht, 2011), pp. 223–62.

McKim, Donald K. *Ramism in William Perkins' Theology* (New York: Peter Lang, 1987).

McNaughton, David. *Moral Vision: An Introduction to Ethics* (Oxford: Basil Blackwell, 1988).

Mitchell, W. Fraser. *English Pulpit Oratory from Andrewes to Tillotson* (London: SPCK/ New York and Toronto: Macmillan, 1932).

Morgan, John. *Godly Learning: Puritan Attitudes Towards Reason, Learning, and Education, 1560–1640* (Cambridge: Cambridge University Press, 1986).

Morgan, Victor, with Christopher Brooke. *A History of the University of Cambridge*, Vol II. *1546–1750* (Cambridge University Press, 2004).

Morrissey, Mary. *Politics and the Paul's Cross Sermons, 1558–1642* (Oxford: Oxford University Press, 2011).

Morrissey, Mary. 'Scripture, Style and Persuasion in Seventeenth-Century English Theories of Preaching', *Journal of Ecclesiastical History*, 53.4 (October 2002), pp. 686–706.

Muller, Richard A. *Christ and the Decree: Christology and Predestination in Reformed Theology from Calvin to Perkins* (Durham, NC: Labyrinth Press, 1986).

Muller, Richard A. *Grace and Freedom: William Perkins and the Early Modern Reformed Understanding of Free Choice and Divine Grace* (Oxford: Oxford University Press, 2020).

Muller, Richard A. 'Perkins' *A Golden Chaine*: Predestinarian System or Schematized *Ordo salutis?*', *The Sixteenth Century Journal*, 9.1 (April 1978), pp. 68–81.

Mullett, Michael A. 'Bunyan's Life, Bunyan's Lives', in Michael Davies and W. R. Owens (eds.), *The Oxford Handbook of John Bunyan* (Oxford: Oxford University Press, 2018), pp. 21–35.

Murray, Molly. *The Poetics of Conversion in Early Modern English Literature: Verse and Change from Donne to Dryden* (Cambridge: Cambridge University Press, 2009).

Myers, Benjamin. *Milton's Theology of Freedom* (Berlin: de Gruyter, 2006).

Nuttall, Geoffrey F. *The Holy Spirit in Puritan Faith and Experience* (1946; repr. with introduction by Peter Lake, Chicago: University of Chicago Press, 1992).

Nuttall, Geoffrey F. *Richard Baxter* (London: Thomas Nelson, 1965).

Orme, William. *The Life and Times of Richard Baxter*, vol 1. of *The Practical Works of the Rev. Richard Baxter: With a Life of the Author, and a Critical Examination of His Writings*, 23 vols, ed. William Orme (London: James Duncan, 1830).

Pallister, William. *Between Worlds: The Rhetorical Universe of Paradise Lost* (Toronto: University of Toronto Press, 2008).

Parry, David. 'As an Angel of Light: Satanic Rhetoric in Early Modern Literature and Theology', in Gregor Thuswalder and Daniel Russ (eds.), *The Hermeneutics of Hell: Devilish Visions and Visions of the Devil* (Cham, Switzerland: Palgrave Macmillan, 2017), pp. 47–71.

Parry, David. '"God breaketh not all men's hearts alike": Early Modern Conversion Narratives in Contemporary Perspective', *The Glass*, 25 (Spring 2013), pp. 3–17.

Parry, David. '"Lutherus non vidit Omnia": The Ambivalent Reception of Luther in English Puritanism', in Herman J. Selderhuis (ed.), *Luther and Calvinism: Image and Reception of Martin Luther in the History and Theology of Calvinism* (Göttingen: Vandenhoeck & Ruprecht, 2017), pp. 379–407.

Patterson, W. B. *William Perkins and the Making of a Protestant England* (Oxford: Oxford University Press, 2014).

Pettit, Norman. *The Heart Prepared: Grace and Conversion in Puritan Spiritual Life* (1966; 2nd ed.; Middletown, Conn., Wesleyan University Press, 1989).

Pigman, G. W., III. 'Versions of Imitation in the Renaissance', *Renaissance Quarterly*, 33.1 (Spring 1980), pp. 1–30.

Pooley, Roger. 'Bunyan's Reading', in Michael Davies and W. R. Owens (eds.), *The Oxford Handbook of John Bunyan* (Oxford: Oxford University Press, 2018), pp. 101–16.

Pooley, Roger. 'Dell, William, d. 1669', *ODNB*.

Pooley, Roger. 'Language and Loyalty: Plain Style at the Restoration', *Literature & History*, 6.1 (Spring 1980), pp. 2–18.

Pooley, Roger. '*The Pilgrim's Progress* and the Line of Allegory', in Anne Dunan-Page (ed.), *The Cambridge Companion to Bunyan* (Cambridge: Cambridge University Press, 2010), pp. 80–94.

Pooley, Roger. 'Plain and Simple: Bunyan and Style', in N. H. Keeble (ed.), *John Bunyan: Conventicle and Parnassus: Tercentenary Essays* (Oxford: Clarendon, 1988), pp. 91–110.

Porter, H. C. *Reformation and Reaction in Tudor Cambridge* (Cambridge: Cambridge University Press, 1958).

Powicke, Frederick J. *A Life of the Reverend Richard Baxter 1615–1691* (London: Jonathan Cape, 1924).

Powicke, Frederick J. *The Reverend Richard Baxter under the Cross (1662–1691)* (London: Jonathan Cape, 1927).

Raylor, Timothy. 'Milton, the Hartlib Circle, and the Education of the Aristocracy', in Nicholas McDowell and Nigel Smith (eds.), *The Oxford Handbook of Milton* (Oxford: Oxford University Press, 2011), pp. 382–406.

Read, Sophie. *Eucharist and the Poetic Imagination in Early Modern England* (Cambridge: Cambridge University Press, 2013).

Read, Sophie. 'Puns: Serious Wordplay', in Sylvia Adamson, Gavin Alexander and Katrin Ettenhuber (eds.), *Renaissance Figures of Speech* (Cambridge: Cambridge University Press, 2007), pp. 79–94.

Reid, Steven J., and Emma Annette Wilson (eds.), *Ramus, Pedagogy and the Liberal Arts: Ramism in Britain and the Wider World* (Farnham: Ashgate, 2011).

Reisner, Noam. *Milton and the Ineffable* (Oxford: Oxford University Press, 2009).

Rempel, Brett A. 'The Trinitarian Pattern of Redemption in Richard Sibbes (1577–1635)', *Journal of Reformed Theology*, 13.1 (June 2019), pp. 3–25.

Riebling, Barbara. 'Milton on Machiavelli: Representations of the State in *Paradise Lost*', *Renaissance Quarterly*, 49.3 (Autumn 1996), pp. 573–97.

Rivers, Isabel. *Reason, Grace and Sentiment: A Study of the Language of Religion and Ethics in England, 1660–1780*, 2 vols. (Cambridge: Cambridge University Press, 1991–2000).

Roads, Judith. 'Quaker Convincement Language: Using Pathos and Logos in the Seventeenth Century', *Quaker Studies*, 25.2 (2020), pp. 189–205.

Rosenfeld, Nancy. *John Bunyan's Imaginary Writings in Context* (New York: Routledge, 2018).

Ryrie, Alec. *Being Protestant in Reformation Britain* (Oxford: Oxford University Press, 2013).

Schaefer, Paul R. 'Protestant "Scholasticism" at Elizabethan Cambridge: William Perkins and a Reformed Theology of the Heart', in Carl R. Trueman and R. S. Clark (eds.), *Protestant Scholasticism: Essays in Reassessment* (Carlisle: Paternoster, 1999), pp. 147–64.

Schultz, Howard. *Milton and Forbidden Knowledge* (New York: Modern Language Association of America, 1955).

Screech, M. A. *Laughter at the Foot of the Cross* (Harmondsworth: Penguin/Allen Lane, 1997).

Searle, Alison. 'Performance, Incarnation, Conversion: Theology and the Future of Imagination', in Trevor Cairney and David Starling (eds.), *Theology and the Future: Evangelical Assertions and Explorations* (London: Bloomsbury T & T Clark, 2014), pp. 197–212.

Sharpe, Kevin. *The Personal Rule of Charles I* (New Haven: Yale University Press, 1992).

Sharrock, Roger. 'Bunyan and the English Emblem Writers', *Review of English Studies*, 21.82 (April 1945), pp. 105–16.

Sherwood, Yvonne. 'Prophetic Performance Art', *The Bible and Critical Theory*, 2.1 (2006). pp. 1.1–1.4.

Shuger, Debora K. *Sacred Rhetoric: The Christian Grand Style in the English Renaissance* (Princeton, NJ: Princeton University Press, 1988).

Sipiora, Phillip, and James S. Baumlin (eds.), *Rhetoric and Kairos: Essays in History, Theory, and Praxis* (Albany, NY: State University of New York Press, 2002).

Sisson, Rosemary. 'William Perkins, Apologist for the Elizabethan Church of England', *Modern Language Review*, 47.4 (October 1952), pp. 495–502.

Skinner, Quentin. *From Humanism to Hobbes: Studies in Rhetoric and Politics* (Cambridge: Cambridge University Press, 2018).

Skinner, Quentin. 'Paradiastole: Redescribing the Vices as Virtues', in Sylvia Adamson, Gavin Alexander and Katrin Ettenhuber (eds.), *Renaissance Figures of Speech* (Cambridge: Cambridge University Press, 2007), pp. 149–64.

Skinner, Quentin. *Reason and Rhetoric in the Philosophy of Hobbes* (Cambridge: Cambridge University Press, 1996).

Smith, Nigel. *Perfection Proclaimed: Language and Literature in English Radical Religion, 1640-1660* (Oxford: Clarendon, 1989).

Spargo, Tamsin. *John Bunyan* (Tavistock: Northcote House, 2016).

Spencer, Carole Dale. 'The Man Who "Set Himself as a Sign": James Nayler's Incarnational Theology', in Stephen W. Angell and Pink Dandelion (eds.), *Early Quakers and Their Theological Thought:1647–1723* (Cambridge: Cambridge University Press, 2015), pp. 64–82.

Spurgeon, C. H. *The New Park Street Pulpit*, 6 vols. (London: Passmore & Alabaster, 1855–60).

Spurr, John. *English Puritanism, 1603–1689* (Basingstoke: Macmillan, 1988).

Steiner, Mark Allan. *The Rhetoric of Operation Rescue: Projecting the Christian Pro-life Message* (New York/London: Continuum, 2006).

Stevens, Paul. 'The Pre-Secular Politics of *Paradise Lost*', in Louis Schwartz (ed.), *The Cambridge Companion to Paradise Lost* (Cambridge: Cambridge University Press, 2014), pp. 94–108.

Stout, Harry S. *The New England Soul: Preaching and Religious Culture in Colonial New England* (Oxford: Oxford University Press, 1986, rep. 2012).

Sullivan, Erin. *Beyond Melancholy: Sadness and Selfhood in Renaissance England* (Oxford: Oxford University Press, 2016).

Talon, Henri. *John Bunyan: The Man and His Works*, trans. Barbara Wall (London: Rockliff, 1951).

Taylor, Charles. *A Secular Age* (Cambridge, MA: Belknap/Harvard University Press, 2007).

Vickers, Brian. *In Defence of Rhetoric* (Oxford: Clarendon, 1988).

Virtanen, Tuija, and Helena Halmari. 'Persuasion across Genres: Emerging Perspectives', in Helena Halmari and Tuija Virtanen (eds.), *Persuasion across Genres: A Linguistic Approach* (Amsterdam/Philadelphia: John Benjamins, 2005), pp. 3–24.

Walker, Eric C. *William Dell: Master Puritan* (Cambridge: W. Heffer and Sons, 1970).

Wallace, Dewey D., Jr. 'Bunyan's Theology and Religious Context', in Michael Davies and W. R. Owens (eds.), *The Oxford Handbook of John Bunyan* (Oxford: Oxford University Press, 2018), pp. 69–85.

Ward, Graham. 'To Be a Reader: John Bunyan's Struggle with the Language of Scripture in *Grace Abounding to the Chief of Sinners*', *Literature and Theology*, 4.1 (March 1990), pp. 29–49.

Warren, Martin L. 'The Quakers as Parrhesiasts: Frank Speech and Plain Speaking as the Fruits of Silence', *Quaker History*, 98.2 (Fall 2009), pp. 1–25.

Webb, Stephen H. *Blessed Excess: Religion and the Hyperbolic Imagination* (Albany, NY: SUNY Press, 1993).

Webster, Charles. 'William Dell and the Idea of University', in Mikuláš Teich and Robert Young (eds.), *Changing Perspectives in the History of Science: Essays in Honour of Joseph Needham* (London: Heinemann, 1970), pp. 110–26.

White, Eric Charles. *Kaironomia: On the Will to Invent* (Ithaca: Cornell University Press, 1987).

White, Helen C. *English Devotional Literature (Prose), 1600–1640* (Madison: University of Wisconsin, 1931).

Williamson, George. *The Senecan Amble: A Study in Prose Form from Bacon to Collier* (Chicago: University of Chicago Press, 1966).

Worden, Blair. 'Toleration and the Cromwellian Protectorate', in W. J. Sheils (ed.), *Persecution and Toleration* (Oxford: Blackwells for Ecclesiastical History Society, 1984) (*Studies in Church History* 21), pp. 199–233.

Index

accommodation, doctrine of 125, 131, 141
actio/pronuntiatio (delivery/performance) 31, 32, 63–4 n.42, 74–6, 91, 105–7, 119, 126, 146, 229
allegory, *allegoria* 2, 7–8, 15–17, 27, 38–9, 42, 45, 49, 144–5, 162–3, 181–93, 196, 199–200, 201 n.10, 242
Alpaugh, David 190
Ames, William 33
amplificatio 134–5, 141, 147
Amyraut, Moïse, and Amyraldianism 220, 245 n.28
Anabaptists. *See* Baptists
anaphora 52, 104, 119, 138
Andrewes, Lancelot 120–1
Anscombe, Elizabeth 239–41
anthropopathia 26
antinomianism 25, 91, 109 n.35, 236
apodeixis (demonstration) 32, 83, 96
Apostles' Creed 28, 35–6
Aquinas, Thomas 240
Arians 225
Aristotle and Aristotelian thought
 ethics 53, 55, 233, 238, 240–1
 logic 79–80
 rhetoric 11–14, 25, 32, 33, 63 n.35, 63 n.39, 74, 76, 83, 95, 115 n.131, 120, 126, 133, 140, 167, 191. (*See also ethos, logos* and *pathos*)
Arminius, Jacobus, and Arminianism 9, 16, 202 n.29, 209–11, 214–15, 219–21, 231, 242, 244 n.13, 245 n.28
assurance of salvation 4, 8, 11, 16, 25–6, 50, 54–6, 60, 61 n.4, 134, 162, 169, 195, 210–11, 213
Attaway, Mrs 236
Augustine of Hippo, St 13, 49, 64 n.42, 122, 142, 153–4 n.31, 227
Austin, Samuel 103
Averroes (Ibn Rushd) 79–80

Bacon, Francis 121
Baptists, Anabaptists, 1, 3, 84, 99–101, 135, 163
Barclay, Robert 95–6
Bauman, Richard 105
Bayly, Lewis 196
Baxter, Richard 3, 10–11, 15–16, 75, 92, 117–60, 170, 198, 211, 234, 244 n.7
 Aphorismes of Justification 145
 A Call to the Unconverted 136–42
 A Christian Directory 124, 126, 130
 Gildas Salvianus: The Reformed Pastor 122, 127–30
 The Life of Faith 141
 Methodus Theologiae Christianae 123–4, 145, 150–1
 The Poor Man's Family Book 144–5, 158 n.160
 Reliquiae Baxterianae 128–9, 244 n.7
 The Saints Everlasting Rest 124–5, 145–50, 159 n.169, 159 n.175
 A Treatise on Conversion 120
Baynes, Paul 146, 234
Berger, Peter 6, 163, 186
Bernard, Richard 12, 196, 201 n.10
Berry, Boyd 223
Bevis of Southampton 37, 205 n.104
Bible, books of
 Acts of the Apostles 34–5, 88, 111 n.65, 180, 221
 Amos 39
 1 Chronicles 110 n.54
 Colossians 62. n.20
 1 Corinthians 32, 83, 96, 102–3, 166–7, 171
 2 Corinthians 53, 132, 189, 197–9
 Daniel 149
 Deuteronomy 111 n.65
 Ecclesiastes 44–5, 189, 206 n.126
 Ephesians 167
 Exodus 87

Index

Ezekiel 69 n.145, 90–1, 139–41
Galatians 29, 59, 114 n.119, 128, 198
Genesis 7, 27, 58–9, 115 n.134
Hebrews 89, 111 n.74, 115 n.137, 140, 147, 167
Hosea 91, 183
Isaiah 27, 28, 30–1, 68 n.133, 69 n.154, 71 n.178, 81–2, 88, 97, 106, 115 n.134, 165–6, 172, 239
James 115 n.134
Jeremiah 222–3
John 69 n.144, 111 n.65
1 John 38, 62 n.20
Joshua 29
1 Kings 65 n.68, 207 n.144
2 Kings 65 n.68, 78
Lamentations 47–8
Luke 172, 180, 216–9, 223, 247 n.59
Matthew 115 n.134, 185, 223, 247 n.59
Mark 115 n.134, 247 n.59
Numbers 70 n.169, 164–5
Proverbs 189, 206 n.127
Psalms 115 n.134
Revelation 23, 90, 149
Romans 10, 115 n.134, 198–9
2 Samuel 110 n.54
Song of Songs (Song of Solomon) 27, 102
Zephaniah 46–50
Bible, versions of
Geneva Bible 9, 45
King James/Authorized Version 45, 62. n.20, 221
Blake, William 226
Bolton, Robert 118
Brooks, Thomas 67 n.114
Broughton, Hugh 67 n.114
Bruhn, Karen, 10, 18 n.11.
Bunyan, John 2–3, 7–8, 12, 15–16, 23, 39, 42, 45, 49, 66 n.82, 75, 77, 82, 85, 89, 104, 135, 142, 145, 150, 161–208, 209, 211, 219, 237
The Barren Fig-tree 194–5
A Book for Boys and Girls 163, 190
Come and Welcome to Jesus Christ
The Doctrine of the Law and Grace Unfolded 163, 168
A Few Sighs from Hell 205 n.104

Good News for the Vilest of Men 168–9, 179–81, 195
Grace Abounding to the Chief of Sinners 104, 164–5, 169–71, 173, 175, 178, 204 n.77, 195, 197
The Holy War 196–8
Instruction for the Ignorant 163
The Pilgrim's Progress (first and second parts) 2, 49, 145, 161–9, 179, 182–8, 190–3, 197–200
Profitable Meditations 187, 195
Some Gospel-Truths Opened 171–2, 206 n.111
The Strait Gate 2, 164, 173–80, 196
Burrough, Edward 198
Burton, John 85, 171–2, 219
Burton, Simon 153 n.19, 156 n.93
Button, Ralph 111 n.75

Calamy, Edmund 150
Calvin, John 3, 10, 62 n.29, 75
Calvinism 4, 9, 13, 81–2, 95, 103, 153 n.22, 168, 177, 194, 210, 214–6, 219–21. *See also* election, predestination *and* reprobation
Campbell, Gordon 210, 219, 231, 243 n.3
captatio benevolentiae 47, 228
Carey, John 237
Catharinus, Ambrosius 245 n.28
Catholicism and anti-Catholicism 3–4, 34–6, 65 n.70, 74, 133–4, 143, 239, 245 n.28
Charles I 77
Charles II 101, 162
Charlton, Mary 133
chiasmus, chiastic form 105, 133, 213–14
Church of England 5, 12–14, 20 n.44, 24, 60 n.4, 77, 83, 92, 99, 143, 163, 198, 210
Cicero, Ciceronian rhetoric, 11, 31, 32, 47, 63 n.35, 63 n.39, 74–5, 79–80, 83, 91, 95–6, 98, 103, 113 n.97, 121–2, 126, 129, 150, 184, 224, 226–9
Clarkson, Lawrence 110–11 n.61
Clement, Jennifer 62 n.20, 66 n.95
cognitive minorities 6, 162–3
Coleridge, Samuel Taylor 182–3, 193
Collinson, Patrick 3
Comenius, Jan Amos 109 n.35

Condie, Keith 127
confirmatio 176
Congregationalists 135. *See also*
　　Independents
Constantine, Constantinianism 79, 81, 215
conviction (of sin) 1–2, 17 n.5, 37–8, 55,
　　134, 164–8, 176–8, 195, 201 n.12,
　　222, 234
Cope, Jackson I. 103
Coppe, Abiezer 74, 83–92, 95, 97, 99,
　　106–7, 110 n.51, 111 n.75, 221
　　A Fiery Flying Roll 87, 91
　　Some Sweet Sips, of Spirituall Wine
　　　88–90
Corns, Thomas 210, 219, 231, 243 n.3
cosmic imaginary 6–8, 162–3, 186
Crawford, Jason 17 n.5, 201 n.12
Crisp, Stephen 97
Croll, Morris 121
Cromwell, Bridget 77
Cromwell, Oliver 73–4, 77

Damrosch, Leo 103, 105
Danielson, Dennis 220
Davies, Horton 153 n.22
Davies, Michael 168
Davis, Nick 184
Day, Angel 12, 53
Deacon, John 73, 107 n.1
decorum 31, 46, 57, 85, 97, 123, 125, 130,
　　131, 141–2, 173, 179–80
deliberative rhetoric 130, 139, 174, 179,
　　222
Dell, William 15, 77–84, 88–9, 96–7, 99,
　　109 n.35, 111 n.73, 215–16
　　A Plain and Necessary Confutation
　　of divers Gross and Antichristian
　　Errors 78–80
　　The Stumbling-Stone 77–8, 215–16
　　The Tryal of Spirits both in Teachers
　　and Hearers 78–9, 81
Demosthenes 227
Dent, Arthur 37–8, 172, 196, 201 n.10
Derrida, Jacques 11
despair 8, 52, 55, 57, 70 n.161, 132, 134,
　　173, 177–8, 192–3, 195
delectare (delighting) 142, 145, 150, 159
　　n.171, 184, 187, 224
Dever, Mark 45
devil. *See* Satan

dialectic. *See* logic
dialogues, didactic 14, 36–40, 45, 54–5,
　　144–5, 201 n.10
Diggers 75
dispositio (arrangement) 31, 63–4 n.42
Dixon, Leif 9
docere (teaching) 130, 142, 173, 184, 187,
　　199, 224
doctrine and use preaching 46, 103, 146,
　　173–4, 181
Dod, John 172
Doe, Charles 170, 173
Donato, Christopher 236
Donne, John 242–3
Duffy, Eamon 4
Dunn, Robert 240–1
Dyrness, William 7, 43, 64 n.47

Edwards, Thomas 76
Egerton, Alice 232
Egerton, John, earl of Bridgewater 231
election, elect 8–10, 34, 54, 81, 104–5,
　　165, 168–9, 176, 194, 204 n.77, 207
　　n.142, 213, 216, 219–23, 225, 234.
　　See also Calvinism, predestination
　　and reprobation
Eliot, John 136
Elizabeth I 48
elocutio (style) 31, 33, 63–4 n.42, 98, 119,
　　129
enargia 135, 142–3, 145, 148–50
epideictic rhetoric 176
episcopalians 74, 100
epistrophe 48
epizeuxis 90–1
Erasmus, Desiderius 189
Erbery, Dorcas 92–3
Erbery, Mary 92–3
Erbery, William 92
established Church. *See* Church of
　　England
Esterhammer, Angela 223
eternal justification 19 n.34
ethos (appeal to speaker's authority) 12–15,
　　28, 30–2, 41, 46–7, 59, 74, 76, 81–3,
　　85, 87, 90, 93, 95, 98, 105–7, 120,
　　123, 128–9, 133, 136–8, 140–1,
　　146–7, 150, 168–72, 221–2, 229
evidentia (vividness) 147
exordium (opening) 47, 228–30

Index 269

faculties, mental, and faculty psychology 5–6, 34, 42–3, 126–7, 146, 182, 184–6, 228
Fairfax, Sir Thomas 77
Fallon, Stephen 211, 220–1, 238–9, 244 n.7
fancy. *See* imagination
Farnworth, Richard 106
Featley, Daniel 100
Fish, Stanley 47, 224–6
Fisher, Samuel 99–101, 105–6, 114 n.113, 114 n.116, 114 n.119
Flinker, Noam 90
Ford, Emanuel 192–3
forensic rhetoric 139, 147
Forster, E. M. 39
Forsyth, Neil 239
Fowler, Alastair 227
Fox, George 74, 93, 95–7, 103–6
Friends. *See* Quakers
Frost, R. N. 33–4
Fuller, Thomas 109 n.33

Gataker, Thomas 10–11, 118
Gifford, John 162
Golder, Harold 192
Goodwin, John 244 n.13
Goodwin, Thomas 25
Gouge, William 28, 62 n.24
grammar 12, 30, 79–80, 89, 97–8, 100, 113 n.109, 123
grammar schools 11, 30–1, 89
grand style 224
Graves, Michael 94
Greaves, Richard 202 n.29
Green, R. P. H. 153–4 n.31
Greenham, Richard 4, 9
Gregory the Great 130
Gurnall, William 11

Hall, Joseph 120–1
Haller, William 37
Hallett, Raphael 35
Halmari, Helena 19 n.27
Hammond, Paul 226–7, 230, 241, 247 n.73
Hancock, Maxine 192
Hanmer, Mary 133
Harding, Susan Friend 1–2, 5
Hawkins, Anne 201 n.14
Hays, Richard 16
Hemmingsen, Niels 48

Henry VIII 89
Henry, Nathaniel H. 236
Henshaw, Joseph 120–1
Hill, Christopher 74, 196–7
Hinds, Hilary 94–5, 105
Hobbes, Thomas 238–9
Holy Spirit, Holy Ghost 12–15, 20 n.44, 23–35, 41–2, 49, 51, 54, 56, 75–6, 82–3, 94, 96, 100, 123, 131, 137, 141, 147, 150, 168–70, 172, 186, 194–5, 203 n.56, 210–15
homoioteleuton 119
Hooker, Thomas 118
Hookes, Ellis 98
Hooper, John 40
How, Samuel 85, 172, 203 n.56, 219, 245 n.23
Hudson, Hoyt 182
Hunt, Arnold 10–11, 118
hypocrisy, hypocrites 55, 122–3, 128, 173, 178, 180, 189–91, 194–6, 207 n.142, 223

Ibn Rushd. *See* Averroes
iconoclasm 7, 14, 35–6, 65 n.70, 143
idolatry 14, 35–6, 49, 53–4, 65 n.70, 78–9, 143
Ignatius of Loyola, St 35–6
illustratio 134
Illyricus, Matthias Flacius 159
imagination 5–8, 14–17, 18 n.22, 23–4, 33–46, 48–52, 55–60, 104, 115 n.134, 135, 142–50, 162–3, 167–8, 173, 180–93, 199–200, 209, 225
Independents 3, 77–8, 84, 99, 162, 236
inventio 31, 63–4 n.42
inward light (Quaker concept) 74, 94, 98–9, 104–5, 198
Ireton, Bridget. *See* Cromwell, Bridget
Ireton, Henry 77

Jesuits 35
Jonson, Ben 201 n.22

kairos 49, 68 n.134
Kaufmann, U. Milo 42, 142, 146, 160 n.194, 186, 191–2
Keeble, N. H. 118–19, 121, 141–4, 151–2 n.1, 152 n.3, 160 n.194, 166, 209, 245–6 n.33

270 *Index*

Kendall, R. T. 12–13, 55
Kenny, Robert 110 n.51
Knight, Janice 33–4
Knott, John R., Jr. 117, 149, 159 n.169
Kuhn, Thomas 7, 18 n.21

Lake, Peter 4
language of Canaan 150, 160 n.198, 163–8, 193, 222, 230
latitudinarians 143, 163, 198
Laud, William, and Laudianism 210, 231
Law and Gospel 31, 46, 48–9, 52, 54, 169–70, 173, 180, 190, 197–8
Lawson, Thomas 101–3, 109 n.33, 113 n.109
Leonard, John 226–8, 247 n.56
Lewalski, Barbara 236, 243 n.3
Lewis, C. S. 241
liberal arts 12, 30, 32, 63 n.39, 79–80, 97–8, 100–1
Lily, William, *Grammar* 89
Livy 236
Locke, John 215
logic, dialectic 12, 23, 30, 50, 58, 63–4 n.42, 79–80, 98, 100, 123, 125, 131, 161, 170. *See also* trivium
logos (appeal to reason) 12–14, 25, 30, 33–8, 41, 46–7, 76, 89, 103–5, 115 n.131, 120, 126–31, 133, 140–1, 145–7, 173–5, 180, 182, 191–3, 199, 229–30
Luther, Martin 7, 33, 48, 59, 69 n.145, 70 n.174, 71 n.178, 125, 169
Galatians commentary 59, 71 n.178
Lectures on Genesis 7, 59
Luxon, Thomas 234

McDowell, Nicholas 76, 87–9, 114 n.113, 243 n.3, 245 n.24, 245–6 n.33
McGuire, Maryann Cale 231
McKim, Donald 35
McNaughton, David 240
magnitudo 135–6, 141, 145, 147
Martin, Catherine Gimelli 209–11
Martz, Louis 36
Mather, Increase 64 n.47
Mather, Richard 64 n.47
Mede, Joseph 63 n.35
meditation 15, 35–6, 136, 145–50, 159 n.169, 160 n.194

Ignatian meditation 35–6
meditation upon the creatures 43–4, 142, 160 n.194
Melanchthon, Philip 33
memoria (memory) 31
metaphysical preaching 12, 120–1, 153 n.22, 242
Midgley, Graham 175
Milton, John 16, 23, 101, 109 n.35, 135, 150, 170, 206 n.114, 209–48
Areopagitica 206 n.114
De Doctrina Christiana 210–11, 214–5, 220–1, 224, 231
The Doctrine and Discipline of Divorce 236
Of Education 219
A Maske Presented at Ludlow Castle, 1634 (Comus) 231–4, 237, 247 n.56
Paradise Lost 16, 209, 211–17, 219–21, 224–31, 236–42, 247 n.56, 247 n.72, 247 n.73, 248 n.75
Paradise Regained 216–9, 223–4
The Readie and Easie Way to Establish a Free Commonwealth 222–3, 245–6 n.33
Sonnet 12 'On the Same' 235–6
The Tenure of Kings and Magistrates 234–5
Tetrachordon 235
Milward, Matthias 28, 62 n.24
Mitchell, W. Fraser 153 n.22
Morrissey, Mary 12, 20 n.42, 20 n.44, 31–2
movere (moving) 130, 142, 173, 184, 187, 199, 224
Muggletonians 75
Muller, Richard 60–1 n.4
Mullett, Michael 168
munus triplex (threefold office of Christ) 29, 62 n.29, 87
Murray, Molly 5, 93
Myers, Benjamin 211, 213–15, 220, 231, 244 n.13, 245 n.28
mythos 191–3

Nayler, James 73–6, 91, 93, 106–7, 107 n.1, 108 n.13
New Model Army 77
Nicene Creed 29

novels 39, 163, 182, 199–200
Nuttall, Geoffrey 76

Ockham, William of. *See* William of
 Ockham
officia oratoris (tasks of the orator)
 142, 145, 150, 184, 224. *See also*
 delectare, *docere* and *movere*
Origen 237
Orme, William 117, 135
Ovid 64 n.47
Owen, John 172

Pallister, William 224–5
parables 34, 44–5, 49, 181, 194
 parable of the barren fig tree 194–5
 parable of the lost coin (groat) 181
 parable of the lost sheep 181
 parable of the prodigal son 181
 parable of the sower 34
 parable of the wheat and the tares 49
paradiastole 26, 52–60, 83, 91, 132–4,
 194–200, 209, 225–42, 248 n.75
pathos (appeal to emotion/affections)
 12–15, 25, 30, 33–8, 41, 46, 66 n.95,
 76, 103–5, 115 n.131, 120, 126–31,
 133, 138, 140, 145–7, 170–1, 173–6,
 180–1, 191, 199, 229–30
Patterson, W. B. 38, 60 n.4, 64 n.47
Paulet, Elizabeth, Countess of Bolingbroke
 82–3
Peacham, Henry 11, 53–4, 133, 197
Penington, Isaac 96
Penn, William 95–7
Perkins, William 7, 14–15, 23–40, 42,
 45–50, 52–5, 60, 60–1 n.4, 63 n.35,
 63 n.39, 63–4 n.42, 64 n.47, 65 n.70,
 66 n.82, 70 n.161, 74, 76–8, 81–2,
 85, 87, 90, 95–7, 101, 103, 113 n.97,
 118, 126, 128–30, 135, 141, 143–4,
 146, 168–70, 172, 183, 188, 195, 202
 n.32, 210–11, 221, 237
 The Arte of Prophecying 14, 23, 26–7,
  31–3, 46–7, 87, 113 n.97, 129–30,
  183, 188, 195
 Commentarie [...] *upon* [...] *Galatians*
  128
 *A Dialogue of the State of a Christian
  Man* 54–5

An Exhortation to Repentance 46–50
 'The First Epistle of Iohn, in the Forme
  of a Dialogue' 38
 The Foundation of Christian Religion
  36–7
 *A Fruitfull Dialogue concerning the
  Ende of the World* 39–40
 A Golden Chaine 25, 54
 *A Treatise on the Duties and Dignity of
  the Ministry* 30
 *A Warning against the Idolatrie of the
  Last Times* 35
peroration 49–50, 222, 230
Peter of Blois 79, 109 n.33
plain style 12, 16, 120–3, 138, 143, 153
 n.22, 171, 188, 224, 242
Plato, Platonic thought 11, 58, 161, 199,
 218, 241, 247 n.63
plausibility structures 6–8, 106–7, 163, 186
pleonasm 27
Pooley, Roger 143, 185
popery. *See* Catholicism
Poppins, Mary 187
Porphyry 79–80
Porter, H. C. 9
practical divinity 2–5, 8, 11, 14–15, 23, 31,
 48, 95, 118, 130, 173, 176, 179, 186,
 196, 209–11, 213, 231, 237
practical syllogism 168–9, 202 n.32
praesentia 135–6, 148
predestination 4, 8–10, 51, 81, 168–9, 194,
 210, 216, 219–21. *See also* election
 and reprobation
preparationism 51, 181–2
Presbyterians 3, 76, 84, 99, 236
presumption 15, 31, 50, 54–7, 132–4, 169,
 173, 195–6
prevenient grace 211–15
pronuntiatio. See actio
prophecy, prophets 15, 28–30, 39–40,
 47, 74, 76, 78, 82, 83–96, 99–100,
 106–7, 165, 195, 217, 219–24
prose romances 37, 167–8, 184, 192–3,
 205 n.104
prosopopoeia 58, 133, 176, 198
puns 48, 50, 89, 107 n.1, 175
Purefoy, George 84
Puritanism, definition of 2–4, 60–1 n.4
Puttenham, George 11, 53

Index

quadrivium (arithmetic, geometry, music and astronomy) 80, 98

Quakers (Friends) 15, 73–6, 92–107, 107 n.1, 109 n.33, 114 n.113, 115 n.131, 133–4, 163, 171–2, 186, 198, 206 n.111

Quarles, Francis 189

Quintilian 7, 11, 124, 144

radicals 15, 73–115, 133–4, 172, 215, 219, 221

Ramus, Peter, and Ramism 63 n.39, 63–4 n.42, 119, 153 n 19

Ranters 15, 75, 110–11 n.61, 186, 206 n.111, 236

refutatio 176

Reisner, Noam 160 n.198

reprobation, reprobate, 10, 34, 51, 54–5, 104–5, 168, 194, 220, 234, 237. *See also* election *and* predestination

Restoration 15, 20 n.44, 77, 95, 111 n.75, 117–18, 143, 162, 170, 180–1, 198, 222

Riebling, Barbara 227

Rivers, Isabel 143, 169

Roads, Judith 96, 115 n.131

Rogers, John 118

Romanticism 43, 142

Rosenfeld, Nancy 39

Ryrie, Alec 58, 70 n.174

St Paul's School, London 210

Satan, satanic rhetoric, 16, 26, 52–60, 80, 117, 126, 129, 132–4, 161–2, 194–200, 204 n.77, 209, 215–8, 224–31, 233, 236–42, 247 n.56, 247 n.72, 247 n.73, 248 n.75

Schaefer, Paul 34

scholasticism, medieval, 79–80, 143, 239–40

Scoggin's Jests 37

Searle, Alison 108 n.13

sectarians. *See* radicals

Seekers 75, 92–3

Seneca, Senecanism 119–21, 125

Shakespeare, William 216

Sharpe, Kevin 9

Sharrock, Roger 190

Sherwood, Yvonne 74, 91

Shuger, Debora 32, 113 n.97, 134–5, 159 n.171

Sibbes, Richard 11, 14–16, 23–8, 30–1, 33–5, 40–6, 50–60, 61 n.6, 62 n.20, 66 n.95, 67 n.114, 69 n.145, 70 n.174, 71 n.178, 74, 76–7, 82, 85, 102, 118, 126, 146, 159 n.175, 170–1, 188–9, 211, 213–4, 234, 237, 243

Bowels Opened 27, 45–6, 50–2, 66 n.95, 69 n.145

The Bruised Reede, and Smoaking Flax 23, 58–9, 71 n.178, 118

The Soules Conflict 14, 33, 42–5, 56–7, 60, 146

Simpson, Sidrach 78–9

Sisson, Rosemary 66 n.82

Skinner, Quentin 53–4

Smith, Edward H. 228

Smith, Nigel 40, 76–7

Smith, Thomas 170

social imaginary 6, 38

Socinians 225

Socrates 235, 247 n.63

soliloquy 146, 234, 236–42

sophistry 54, 57–8, 79–80, 102, 161–2, 218, 228–9, 233, 235

Spenser, Edmund 8, 216

Spirit. *See* Holy Spirit

Spurgeon, Charles Haddon 135

Steiner, Mark Allen 8

Stevens, Paul 69 n.154, 239

Stout, Harry S. 63 n.40

Strange, Hannah 73

Strange, John 73

Sturm, Johannes 134–5, 147

Sullivan, Erin 70 n.161

Susenbrotus, Johannes 52–3, 132, 198

Sylvester, Matthew 128–9

Taylor, Charles 6–7, 162–3, 186

Tillyard, E. M. W. 211

tricolon 120, 171

trivium (grammar, logic and rhetoric) 12, 30, 79–80, 98, 100, 123

Trotsky, Leon 74

Index

universities 4, 11–12, 15, 28–31, 76–80, 85, 88–9, 95, 99–100, 109 n.35, 111 n.75, 114 n.113, 118, 170–2, 210
    Cambridge 4, 15, 30, 63 n.35, 77–80, 95, 99, 101, 109 n.33, 170, 210
        Christ's College 63 n.35, 101, 170, 210
        Emmanuel College 77
        Gonville and Caius College 77
        Pembroke College 78
    Oxford 78, 84, 88–9, 95, 97, 99, 111 n.75
        All Souls College 84
        Christ Church 88–9, 111 n.75
        Merton College 84
        Trinity College 99
Ussher, James 130

Vespasian 106
Virtanen, Tuija 19 n.27

Wallace, Dewey D., Jr. 202 n.29
Watson, Thomas 28, 62 n.24, 166
White, Eric Charles 131
White, Helen 145
Wiburn, Percival 3
Wickstead, Richard 118
Wilkins, John 124
William of Ockham 239
Williams, Roger 215
Williamson, George 121
Wilson, Thomas 53–4, 142
Witherley, George 73, 107 n.1
Withers, George 189
Wittgenstein, Ludwig 239
Wyatt, Sir Thomas 53

Zeno of Citium 50

Printed in the USA
CPSIA information can be obtained
at www.ICGtesting.com
LVHW011645091223
766046LV00004B/86